Black Matrilineage, Photography, and Representation:
Another Way of Knowing

I0419923

Black Matrilineage, Photography, and Representation

Another Way of Knowing

EDITED BY
LESLY DESCHLER CANOSSI AND ZORAIDA LOPEZ-DIAGO

LEUVEN UNIVERSITY PRESS

CONTENTS

PART FOUR

"IN SEARCH OF MY MOTHER'S GARDEN, I FOUND MY OWN": BLACK FEMALE PHOTOGRAPHERS AND THE MATRILINEAL SPACE 231

PART FIVE

"THE ASSERTION OF THE LIFEFORCE": A SELECTION OF WORKS CURATED BY WOMEN PICTURING REVOLUTION 273

Thank you to my family, my sons Marcel and little Naeem. You are my heart. To my dear and loving husband Mike. During the course of this book, we brought our little baby Naeem into the world. And through motherhood and Black motherhood in this particular moment, you have held my hand, held me as I've cried, and comforted me when I needed it most. You encouraged me to push through and inspire me more than you could ever know. Words cannot express how thankful I am for you.

I am so thankful for the community of women who raised me and continue to provide guidance and love. For my rock, my mother Marcia Zoraida Bonitto. Thank you for loving me, believing in me and from an early age, showing me that Black girls and Black women could accomplish anything and everything. I am forever indebted to my grandmother, Rosetta Bonitto, who like so many grandmothers, took care of me so my mother could work. Thank you grandma, for ensuring your girls would always get an education.

I dedicate this book to the women in my family, the root of my Black matrilineage, those who always beckon me home.

—Zoraida Lopez-Diago

To my family Andrew, Noa, and Mateo for quietly supporting the late nights and early mornings dedicated to this project, I thank you. Together we create love and light in the everyday and I am endlessly in love with the home we've made. To my mama community, thank you for your deep and lasting commitment to mutual care. There is power where women co-create and I am indebted to the women artists in my life for your camaraderie and dedication to one another. To my students, time spent with you is a pleasure and privilege, I am grateful for your willingness to stay curious and move deeper into your images. To my stepfather, my dad Larry Schultz, thank you for being there (for everything) and especially when the chips were down in Baltimore. I will never forget. To my siblings and especially my sister Teresa Gallaway for your unwavering big sister encouragement, which kept me going more times than you know, I thank you. And to our mother Jacqueline Anne Canossi Schultz who centered our lives in laughter and kindness, you are missed. Twenty-four years without you is absurd.

To the women lost to history or violence, unnamed, or renamed—this book is dedicated to you.

—Lesly Deschler Canossi

ACKNOWLEDGEMENTS

This book would not be possible without the support of many, whom we'd like to acknowledge and thank. Thank you Leuven University Press for believing in this project. We deeply appreciate KU Leuven Fund for Fair Open Access and Knowledge Unlatched for making this work accessible, independent of one's financial means. Thank you to our editor Mirjam Truwant for her extraordinary guidance, and just the right amount of impatience to bring what could have been an endless labor of love, to a beautiful end. Our gratitude extends to Columbia University's Institute for Research in African-American Studies, the International Center of Photography, and Fast Forward: Women in Photography, for their belief in the Women Picturing Revolution. In the early formation of Women Picturing Revolution, Suzanne Nicholas, Dr. Samuel K. Roberts, Lacy Austin, and Dr. Deborah Willis encouraged us to dream big. We extend a heartfelt thank you to the many contributors to this project, without your scholarship and artistic brilliance this would not be possible. It is in the shared spaces of conversation and collaboration that ideas such as this book, *Black Matrilineage, Photography, and Representation: Another Way of Knowing* are born.

We as co-editors of this volume we capitalize Black when we or essayists in this volume are referring to groups in racial, ethnic, or cultural terms. Through this effort, we hope to demonstrate how Black reflects a shared sense of community and identity for Black mothers throughout the African Diaspora.

OUR MOTHER, MY MUSE

SALAMISHAH TILLET AND SCHEHERAZADE TILLET ⸺⸺⸺⸺

Growing up in Boston, in the late 1970s, we saw Black motherhood as insepa-
rable from Black Glamour. Our mother, Volora, a young R&B and jazz singer,
and model had two types of photographs in our apartment, professional
photographs of herself stored in a black leather portfolio with riveted han-
dles and color polaroid images taken by our father, which lived in our family
albums. As the older sister, I adored a color photograph of our mother and our
aunt, our father's sister, Annette, modeling together, side by side. I'd return
to the image over and over again, sometimes sharing with Scheherazade, and

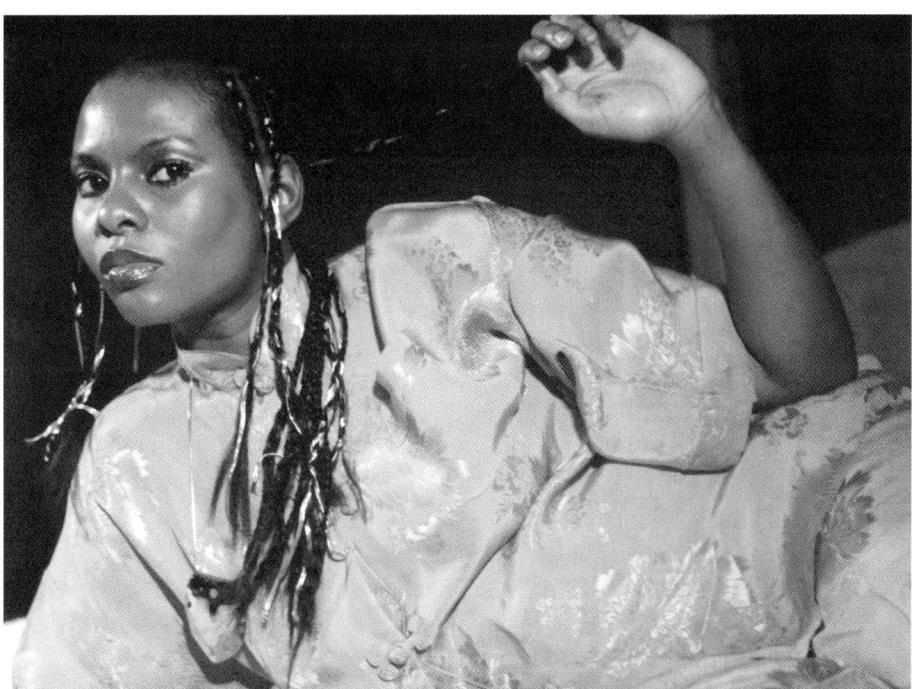

Wes Williams, Mother modeling photograph at Wes Williams Studio in Boston, seven months pregnant with Scheherazade. 1978.
Chromogenic print.

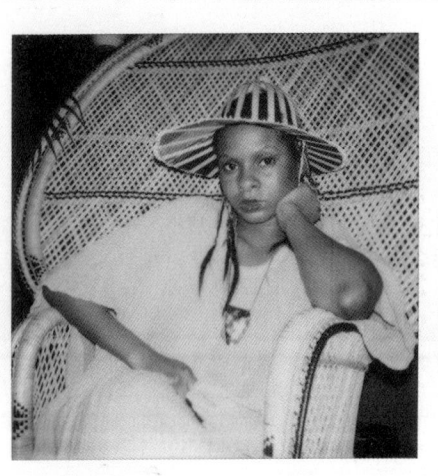

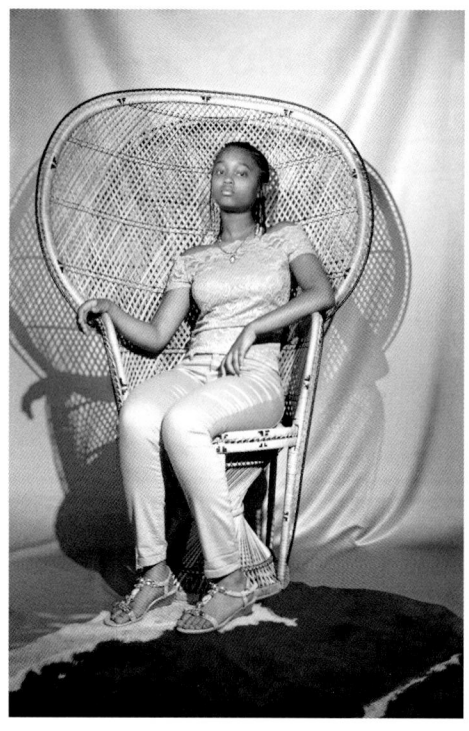

Lennox Tillet, *Volora in the Wicker Chair* (Our mother, age 19). 1975. Polaroid.

Scheherazade Tillet, *Asha, Age 12, Dancer*, from series *My Family Chair,* 2018. Inkjet archival print.

together we'd stare at their slightly smiling faces to understand the magical process of Black women defining their own beauty.

As the younger sister, my favorite image was a photograph of our mother seven months pregnant with me as she gazed directly into the camera playfully twirling one of the golden woven ribbon braids in her hair. As early as four years old, I would whisper to Salamishah about this image right before we went to bed, and created my own fairytale in which we imagined our mother nesting and eagerly awaiting my birth. I immediately recognized the power of being able to tell the story of who we are, *and* who we could become, in pictures.

We were lucky that we had those family albums, and had the opportunity to press our tiny fingers against the padded album covers or delicately loosen those stuck together pages that sounded like sparklers going off when you tried to turn them. Image after image, we found slightly faded but beautiful portraits of our mother sitting stylishly in the iconic wicker chair with her hair beautifully braided. Through her gaze, we were able to see her strong sense of self as she navigated the harsh realities that lay beyond the frame of the picture and outside of our family home. When I (Scheherazade) began to document African-American girl leaders in Chicago, with whom we work within our organization A Long Walk Home, I immediately witnessed those same traits of self-possession and self-definition that my mother exuded when she was a young woman. They, like her, continue to inspire me and help shape my own representations of Black girls coming of age on their own terms.

Like many Black mothers, ours had to navigate the public demands of racism and sexism, and the gendered inequities of home life. For example, in the 1980s, as we were in the full throes of our Black girlhood, President Ronald Reagan demonized Black women as "Welfare Queens," and canonized the stereotype that all Black mothers were destitute, bearing countless children, and taking advantage of the social safety net and social services. It was a lie.

But, despite the fact that most welfare recipients are white families, the image of the Welfare Queen was so successfully pernicious, that President Bill Clinton was able to rely on it to push through his massive "Welfare Reform" Bill, a decade later. That racist and sexist image—as well as that of "crack babies"—put Black mothers further under attack.

Against such a vicious backdrop, our mother, and Black mothers across the country, resisted these attacks by turning to each other, sharing the latest beauty and hair trends, staging family photoshoots, and teaching their children the value of self-presentation *and* self-representation. Such acts were deeply political and profoundly loving, and we both learned that Black motherhood is an embattled status, a place in which Black women fight for themselves, and their children. Glamour was not an anathema in such spaces, but one more strategy for these women to be their fullest selves.

But, even such gestures were limited by the respectability politics of their time. Now that I, Salamishah, am a mother of two young children, I also think about all that is missing from these photo albums. The police report of her sexual assault by a stranger late one night. Evidence of her body bruised by our step-father's fists. Her quest to find the real identity of her biological father. Her sexual desires and intermittent romantic relationships. Her ambition to be a renowned jazz singer. And her most devastating tragedy of all, the loss of her mother, and her only son, our brother, Shaka at the young age of twenty-six due to a year-long battle with cancer, both within the same year.

These days, the image of the grieving Black mother has replaced the dominance of photographs from the 1960s of Black widows in mourning. Then, we saw Myrlie Evers, Betty Shabazz, and Coretta Scott King. Now, it is Sabrina Fulton (Trayvon), Lezley McSpadden (Michael), Geneva Reed-Veal (Sandra),

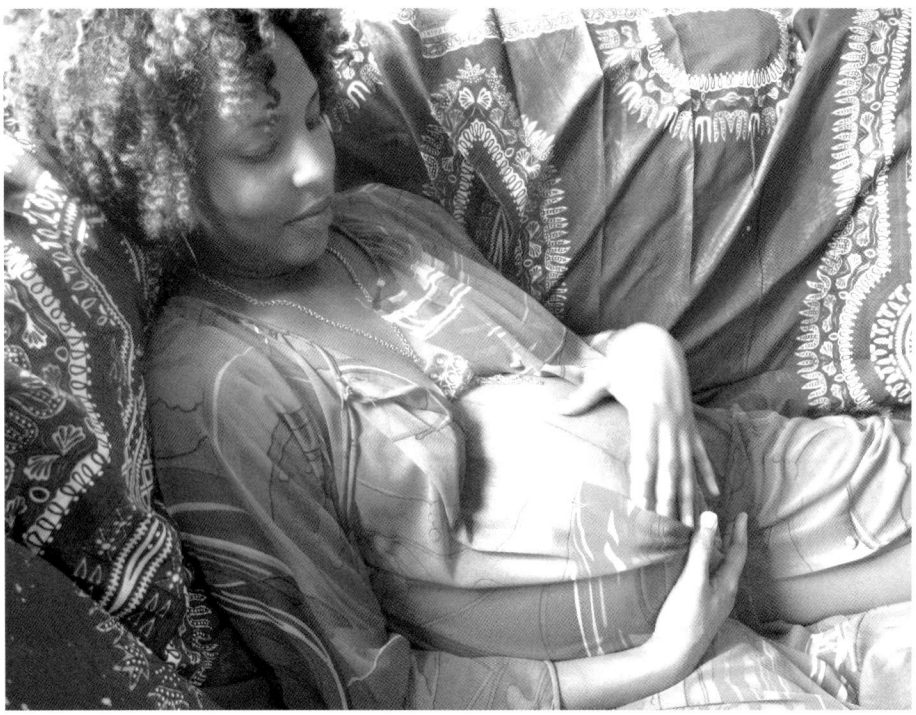

Scheherazade Tillet, *At the Beginning* (Salamishah, age 36, while pregnant with her first child). 2012. Inkjet archival print.

Gwen Carr (Eric), Lucia McBath (Jordan), and Tamika Palmer (Breonna). Their public mourning is in service of the movement for Black Lives Matter, but what is beyond the camera's eye is the complexity of their rage, depression, and hope.

We must pay attention to these documents of their grief without overusing these images. We must refuse the impulse to freeze these women in the moment of their most insurmountable loss, and approach this moment and movement with the urgency that it requires, and the recognition of Black life that it demands.

In the final days of Salamishah's pregnancy in May 2012, I photographed her wearing a blue sheer robe that we picked up at a vintage store. Reminiscent of our friend Mickalene Thomas's paintings of Black women in repose, reclined on a chair or couch, I wanted to pay homage to the complexity of Salamishah's identity and body as she understood it as she lay waiting and on the cusp of motherhood. The image is both intentionally nostalgic and undeniably modern—a symbol that we created together to make this moment in time as brand new.

Black Matrilineage, Photography, and Representation: Another Way of Knowing brilliantly achieves this by challenging the norm and by recognizing that visual representations of Black motherhood and Black mothering are multidimensional, layered, and complicated. In this book, we find a retelling of history through carefully selecting and sharing images by Black women that reveal the myriad of emotions in our lives while elevating analysis that thoughtfully considers their past, present, and future experiences; it humanizes Black women, Black mothers, and all of their humanity.

BLACK MATRILINEAGE, PHOTOGRAPHY, AND REPRESENTATION

Another Way of Knowing

Lesly Deschler Canossi and Zoraida Lopez-Diago ⎯⎯⎯⎯⎯⎯⎯

Black women are called, in the folklore that so aptly identifies one's status in society, "the mule of the world," because we have been handed the burdens that everyone else-everyone else-refused to carry. We have also been called "Matriarchs," "Superwomen," and "Mean and Evil Bitches." Not to mention "Castraters" and "Sapphire's Mama." When we have pleaded for understanding, our character has been distorted; when we have asked for simple caring, we have been handed empty inspirational appellations, then stuck in the farthest comer. When we have asked for love, we have been given children. In short, even our plainer gifts, our labors of fidelity and love, have been knocked down our throats. To be an artist and a black woman, even today, lowers our status in many respects, rather than raises it and yet, artists we will be. Therefore, we must fearlessly pull out of ourselves and look at and identify with our lives the living creativity some of our great-grandmothers were not allowed to know. I stress some of them because it is well known that the majority of our great-grandmothers knew, even without "knowing" it, the reality of their spirituality, even if they didn't recognize it beyond what happened in the singing at church-and they never had any intention of giving it up.[1]
— Alice Walker

A young Black female photographer sits in class at the Philadelphia College of Art in the mid-1970s. During class and in front of a room full of students, her male professor tells her that she is "out of place and out of order as a woman." He continues by telling her that all she could and would do is "have a baby when a good man could have had her seat." The woman is "shocked into silence"[2] but remains undeterred and continues to make photographs.

Roughly twenty years later, a Jamaican-born, Black female photographer participates in the Whitney Museum of American Art's Independent Study

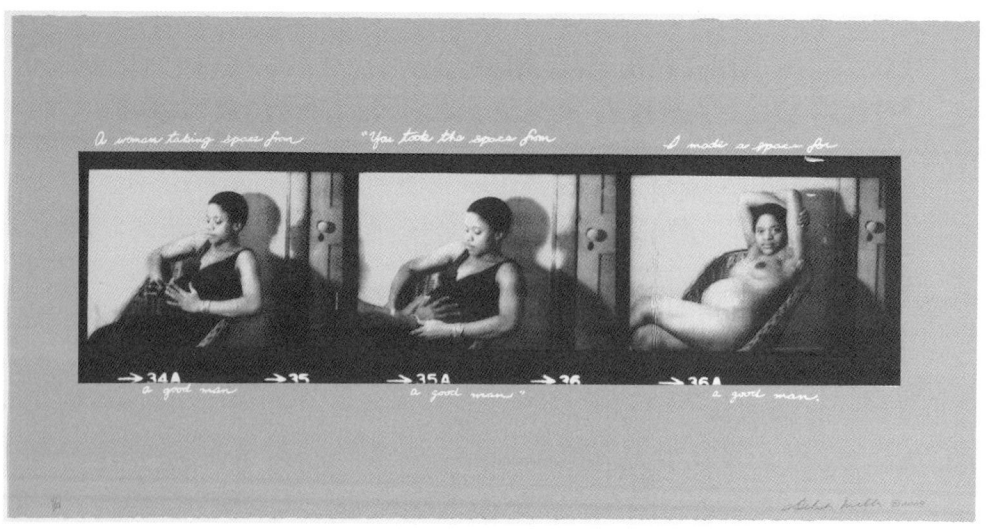

Deborah Willis, *I Made Space for a Good Man*, 2009. Courtesy of the RISD Museum, Providence, RI

Program. She is the first pregnant artist to do so. She tells people in her program that she is pregnant and was met with a response of "Oh my God, are you sure? What are you going to do?" She is outraged and knows that motherhood would not end her career.[3]

Less than ten years ago, a mother, a Black female photographer whose work includes documenting her family, enrolled in an M.F.A. program at a prestigious New York photography institution. A younger white woman who is also enrolled in the program, shares that her (the photographer's) presence is "devaluing the degree."[4]

Proclamations of Black Motherhood

The stories described above happened to Dr. Deborah Willis, artist Renee Cox, and photographer Nona Faustine, respectively. In 2009, Dr. Deborah Willis revisited images she made of her pregnant body in the 1970s and created the triptych *I Made Space for a Good Man*, 2009. The text left to right reads "A woman taking space from a good man" / "You took space from a good man." / "I made space for a good man."[5] In this work, she gazes squarely at the camera in a manner that forces the viewer to reckon with her body and presence in a manner that cannot be ignored.

For over thirty-five years, Dr. Willis has been a leading photography historian, authoring dozens of books focused on the intersection of history, race,

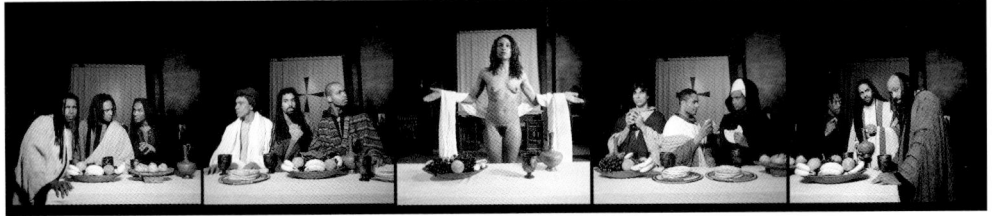

Renee Cox, *Yo Mama's Last Supper*, 1996. Five-color coupler prints. Courtesy of Renee Cox © artist Renee Cox estate

and gender photography. Her many awards include a MacArthur Fellowship, a John Simon Guggenheim Fellow, and a Richard D. Cohen Fellow in African and African American Art at Harvard University's Hutchins Center. Her legacy of mentoring and uplifting Black women photographers has been monumental in shaping and shifting the historical, present, and future visual landscape.

Through visual representations of people from the African Diaspora, particularly Black women and mothers, artist Renee Cox reveals a new way of seeing our past, present, and potential future by positioning Black women as Afro-centric superheroes rich with sexual agency and power. From 1993-1996, Cox created *Yo Mama*, a series in which she embodied a Black Mother Goddess while challenging the whiteness of western religious iconography.[6] Inspired by Queen Nanny, an 18th-century iconic female figure in Jamaican history who helped free nearly 1,000 enslaved people on the island, Cox created *Queen Nanny of the Maroons*, a series of images exhibited at the Jamaican Biennial in 2006. By portraying 21st-century women and men of color in place of the Founding Fathers in *The Signing*, —Cox's recent project, an ambitious 12-foot-long photograph— she serves a sharp response to Howard Chandler Christy's painting, *Scene at The Signing of the Constitution of the United States.*[7]

Nona Faustine graduated from her program and in a few short years

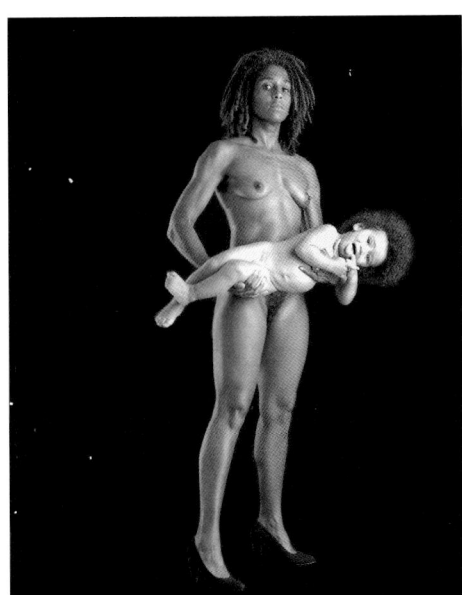

Renee Cox, *Yo Mama*, 1993. Gelatin silver photograph, Brooklyn Museum, Gift of the Carol and Arthur Goldberg Collection. © artist Renee Cox

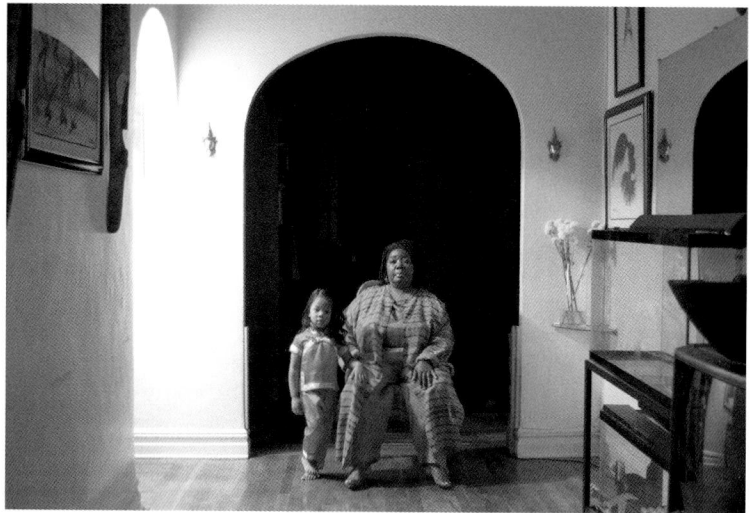

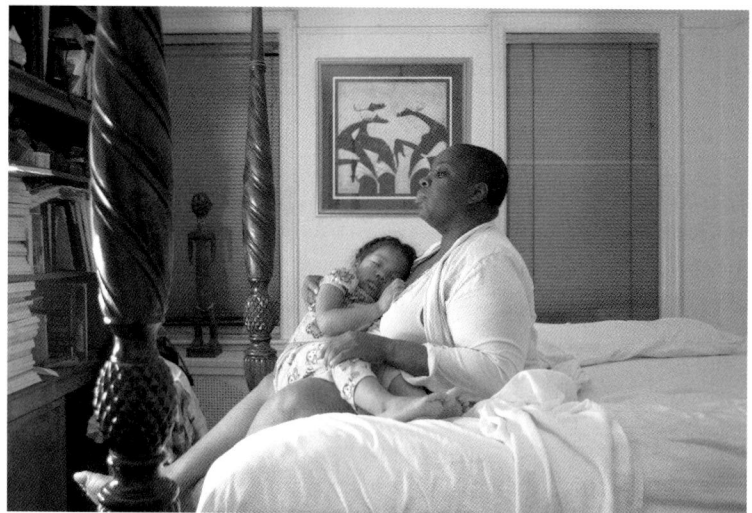

her work had been shown at institutions including the Ford Foundation, the Smithsonian and acquired by leading art organizations including Brooklyn Museum and the Carnegie Museum.

In her series Mitochondria[8], Faustine offers representations of Black motherhood in photographs she has taken of herself, her mother, her sister, and her daughter in their shared home in Brooklyn, New York. In this work, Faustine creates images calling on the viewer to think about "how we (Black mothers) have mothered and sustained our families with love and richness," and "the beauty of how we carry ourselves in our everyday lives. Or how we make and create out of nothing."[9]

How do Black women subjected to the double oppression of racism and sexism use the camera to portray themselves truthfully? How do they, as photographer Ayana V. Jackson describes, fight "photography with photography?"[10] In *Black Matrilineage, Photography, and Representation: Another Way of Knowing*, we ask how the Black female body, specifically the Black maternal body, navigates the interlocking Western socio-political structures that place a false narrative on her body and that of her mother, her grandmother and so on. We buck these falsities by elevating analysis and visual representations that highlight the joy, depth, dynamism and intrinsic brilliance that are a part of Black motherhood. We are interested in filling the gaps that exist in photographic representation and disrupting the destructive, racist, and limiting image of Black motherhood.

The link between photography, representation and Black activism can be traced back to the early days of the medium when prominent abolitionists and orators Sojourner Truth and Frederick Douglass understood how images could mold narratives. Both Truth and Douglass knew that through photography, they could engage in what scholar Leigh Raiford calls critical Black memory, or how photography could serve as "an important resource for framing and mobilizing African American social and political identities and movements."[11] Douglass frequently wrote about photography and deeply understood how it could serve as a necessary tool for Black people across the globe to be seen and represented as fully human. With this in mind, he demonstrated what Black freedom and dignity looked like—confident, in control and unafraid—when he posed throughout his lifetime and became the most-photographed person of the 19th century. Fellow abolitionist, women's rights activist and orator, Sojourner Truth sold carte de visites, or small-sized photographs often mounted on cardboard, which included the phrase "I Sell the Shadow to Support the Substance. Sojourner Truth," at her lectures and via the postal service to earn a living. As she became increasingly popular, Truth shrewdly registered her cartes de visite as engravings and in turn, legally owned the copyright of her image in her etchings. Upon this, Truth reflected that she "used to be sold for other people's benefit, but now she sold herself for her own."[12]

This double oppression of racism and sexism bound to the social stigmas of motherhood situates the overwhelming visual representation of Black motherhood as a site of grief and disempowerment, layered with mythologies tied to what Patricia Collins called controlling images.[13] In this, Black mothers are offered a limited script of mammy, matriarch, welfare queen or jezebel as they are not afforded the full range of emotional expression. In her 1993 essay *Racism and Patriarchy in the Meaning of Motherhood*, Dorothy E. Roberts examines the interaction between racism and patriarchy in the social construction of motherhood. She argues that the "patriarchy denied to Black mothers the authority and joy of mothering which it allowed white mothers."[14] These beliefs, rooted in slavery, falsely portray Black mothers as less deserving of motherhood and have been prevalent throughout history. As early as the first photographs, the Black mother in pictures existed as a "faithful" wet nurse posing with her (white) charge in colonial family albums[15]. She is invisible and dehumanized while her own experience as a mother is denied. At the turn of the 20th century when Black mothers were represented with their children, social workers and sociologists took photographs of young mothers and misleadingly positioned them and their families as poor and dependent on welfare; in exchange, the mothers received what was rightly theirs, access to health services, food and assistance obtaining employment.[16] A deep and expansive exploration into the topic of Black women in photographic history can be found in *The Black Female Body: A Photographic History* by Deborah Willis and Carla Williams. Through their research, we see examples of European 19th century photography that used Black female bodies to support colonialism, scientific evolution via medical apartheid[17] and the sexualizing and fetishizing of Black women and girls. In Post-Emancipation

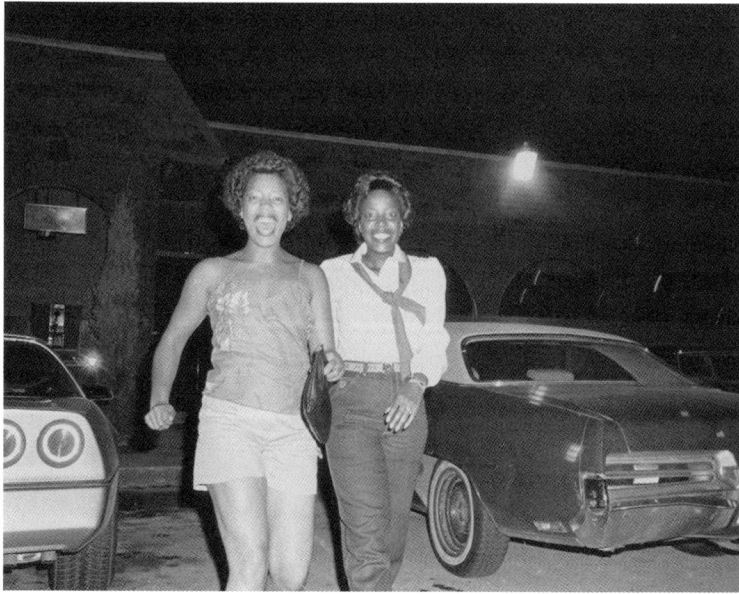

Carrie Mae Weems,
Welcome Home, 1978-1984.
Vintage gelatin silver print
with text, 8 1/2 x 13 inches.
Courtesy of the artist and Jack
Shainman Gallery, New York.
© Carrie Mae Weems

and Post-Reconstruction America, "the desire to act rather than be acted upon, to be a subject rather than an object, took hold with regard to representation."[18] In contemporary image making, not unlike Truth's radical understanding of the medium, Black women photographers "have used their own likeness and those of other black women to create an autobiography of the body and to develop themes of home, family gender, representation and identity in contemporary society."[19]

Family Pictures

In the early 1980s, while in graduate school, artist Carrie Mae Weems was documenting her own multigenerational family story as seen in her body of work titled "Family Pictures and Stories." In this series, Weems photographs her family to provide an intimate and truthful look at African-American family life. Nearly forty years later, photographer Nona Faustine began the ongoing

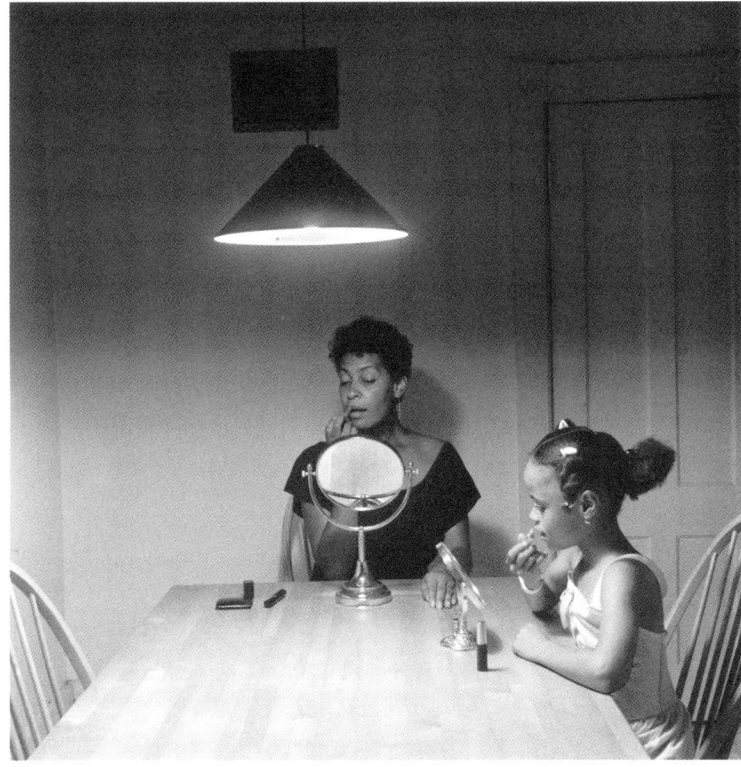

Carie Mae Weems, *Untitled (Woman and Daughter with Make Up)*, 1990, gelatin silver print, 27 1/4 x 27 1/4 inches. Courtesy of the artist and Jack Shainman Gallery, New York. © Carrie Mae Weems

photographic series *Mitochondria* (2008–) working consciously to give her daughter a visual diary as evidence of how much she was loved.

Although Weems' *Family Pictures and Stories* and Faustine's *Mitochondria* are separated by time, both bodies of work serve as counterpunches to the 1965 report, "The Negro Family: A Case Study for National Action," also known as the Moynihan Report. The report, which became one of the most controversial documents of the twentieth century, continues to reinforce racist stereotypes and paint a false and denigrating depiction of the Black family. Weems and Faustine not only rebuke false claims made in the report but expose a deeper and more complicated understanding of power dynamics, society, and history while also sharing sensitive and nuanced expressions of Black love.

In 1990 Weems created The Kitchen Table Series (1990), a twenty image and fourteen text panel series of staged narrative scenes centered around a kitchen table lit by a single light. She performs the role of the women, of which the characters of her relationships appear and disappear—friends, a lover, and children. The series became a seminal body of work and opened the way for future women artists, and Black women in particular. Speaking specifically about the image *Untitled (Woman and Daughter with Makeup)*, scholar Salamishah Tillet writes that the women and daughter pictured "see each other, their black woman and black girl selves, in spite of the gendered and racial invisibility into which they both were born." Reflecting upon the image, she shares a memory of seeing her own daughter looking in the mirror and writes "reflected back is a child who hasn't been taught to un-love herself."[20]

This act of re-envisioning how we see and make images is one in which Black female artists are tethered to their matrilineal precursors. And the connection is not rooted in a legacy filled with guilt and burden, but rather, is full of devotion and love; Black women and artists bind themselves together in this manner to continue the quest for Black freedom, ensure their histories are not forgotten, and bring forward the spirit of their ancestors, both familial and artistic. This can be seen when Alice Walker designates her precursor an author of Black legend and Black female liberation (Zora Neale Hurston), a woman who facilitates what Adrienne Rich calls "re-vision" and who enables female possibility; her dedication, that is, her inscription and devotion to Hurston acknowledges that, without predecessors, a writer cannot write, since texts enable other texts.[21]

While *Black Matrilineage, Photography, and Representation: Another Way of Knowing* supports and centers the discussion surrounding motherhood in marginalized communities, we acknowledge there is much work left to be done and recognize that motherhood can be defined in many ways. Research on LGBTQA+

Black motherhood pioneered by scholar Mignon Moore as well as images taken by H. Lenn Keller, founder of California's Bay Area Lesbian Archives, provide a more holistic view of how race, class, and gender identity intersect with family formation and societal acceptance. In "Mama's Baby, Papa's Maybe: A New American Grammar Book" literary critic and Black feminist scholar Hortense Spillers reminds us that "motherHOOD is a status granted by patriarchy to white middle-class women, those women whose legal rights to their children are never questioned, regardless of who does the labor (the how) of keeping them alive," and continues, "MotherING is another matter, a possible action, the name for that nurturing work, that survival dance, worked by enslaved women who were forced to breastfeed the children of the status mothers while having no control over whether their birth or chosen children were sold away."[22] Motherhood encompasses care in its many iterations and mothering is not limited to gender identity as can be seen in the "house mothers in ball culture who provide spaces of self-love and expression for/as queer youth of color in the street."[23]

Othermothering, which is rooted in principles of African collectivism, is defined as the practice by which female neighbors, sisters, aunts, grandmothers, or other women step in to care for children they have not biologically birthed. Where we find othermothering, we often find extended communities concerned with mutual care, public health and social activism. This can be seen when Black women artists Kay Brown, Dindga McCannon, and Faith Ringgold, formed a childcare collective to help ensure fellow Black mother artists had time and space to create.[24] Most recently, we have seen how Black women continue to organize and manage critical mutual aide networks in response to COVID-19; for example, Tanya Fields, owner and founder of the Black Feminist Project, created a South Bronx-based food pantry program that ensured families in need received farm-fresh local produce, with no questions asked, while offering a pay-what-you-can model. Black motherhood and othermothering continue to exist in these ways and as "mothering of the mind,"[25] a means to share knowledge and build confidence through the sisterhood that binds Black women together.

How do Black women and Black mothers in particular, care for themselves and continue to claim spaces that rightfully belong to them with power and joy?

For nearly twenty years, photographer Sheila Pree Bright has documented the complexities of Black life. With her extensive body of work *#1960Now*, she

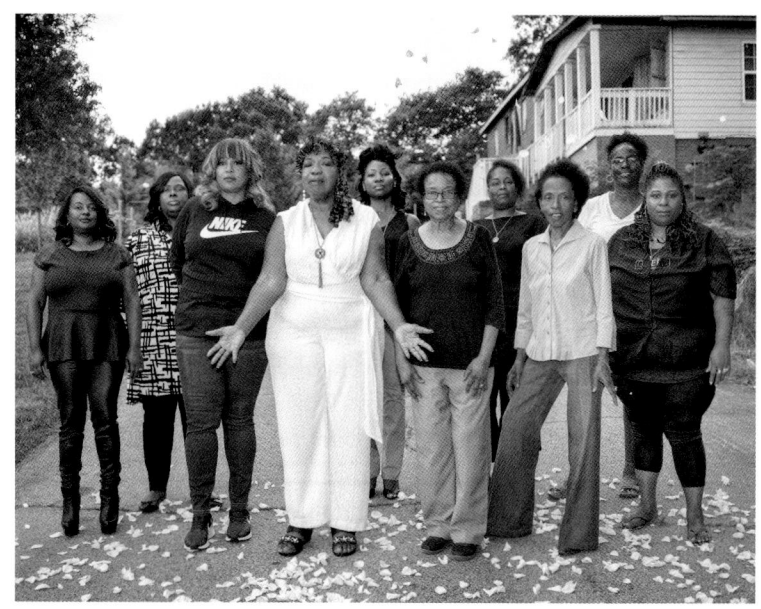

Sheila Pree Bright, Mothers, 2019. Tynesha Tilson (Atlanta); Wanda Johnson (Oakland, CA.); Felicia Thomas (Atlanta); Gwen Carr (New York); Monteria Robinson (Atlanta); Dr. Roslyn Pope, author of "An Appeal for Human Rights" (Atlanta); Dalphine Robinson; (Atlanta); Patricia Scott (Atlanta); Montye Benjamin (Atlanta); and Samaria Rice (Cleveland). © Sheila Pree Bright, courtesy of the artist

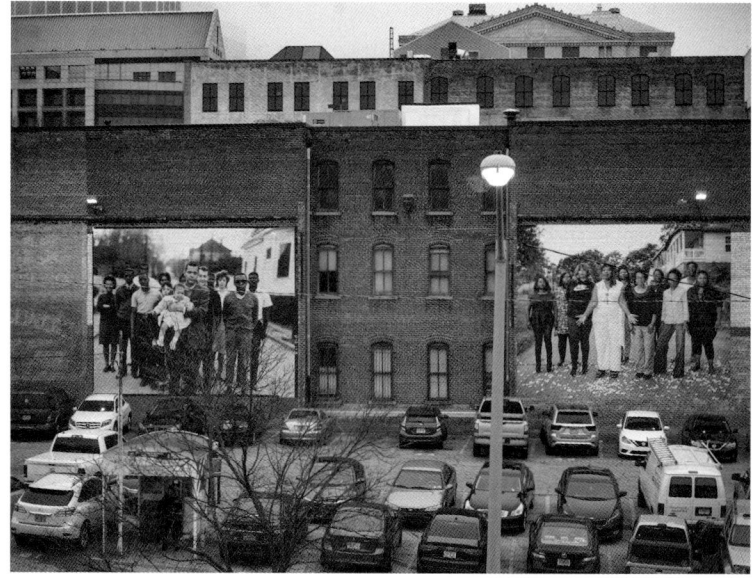

Sheila Pree Bright, Installation at 190 Pryor Street in Atlanta, 2019, © Sheila Pree Bright, courtesy of the artist

has photographed protests across the country, fulfilling the role of timeless visual bonds that tether the Black Lives Matter movement of today and the Civil Rights protests of the 1960s, together. More recently her lens has focused on the mothers who lost their children to police brutality and other acts of racial violence. When asked why she tirelessly documents the tensions and conflicts between police and the communities most affected by racial violence and police brutality, Pree Bright responds, "I was unwilling to sit on the sidelines."[26] "When a Black body is born, they're born into a movement whether they're conscious of it or not, and it's called the Black Liberation Struggle," "It's a perpetual revolution."[27]

When Bright was chosen to create a public art piece in Atlanta in celebration of the 2019 Super Bowl, she knew she wanted to produce a photo-mural recalling the activism of the 1960s. During her research Bright found an image taken in 1963 by acclaimed American photographer Richard Avedon. In the photo, there are several young activists standing with Julian Bond, co-founder of the Student Nonviolent Coordinating Committee (SNCC), holding his young daughter in his arms. When Bright saw the image, she thought of the mothers who lost their children to police brutality and other acts of racial violence and knew she wanted to photograph them.

In the summer of 2019, Bright and Felicia Thomas, mother of Nicholas Thomas, killed by the police in 2015, came together to create a safe space for mothers to openly share unimaginable experiences, lean on one another, and build community. They organized a retreat in Atlanta and invited mothers from across the country including Samaria Rice, the mother of Tamir Rice, who was killed by the police at the age of 12; Oscar Grant's mother, Wanda Johnson; and Eric Garner's mother, Gwen Carr. Bright found an Airbnb to host the women; in our conversations with her, she noted that the mothers were treated to massages, meals cooked by a local chef, and given plaques to acknowledge their activism. During this time, Bright created the photograph that would become the photo mural *Mothers, March On*, in the Vine City neighborhood, where women activists, women's labor advocates, and members of SNCC's Atlanta Vine City Project once lived.

"The retreat brought us together so the moms didn't feel like they were alone," Ms. Thomas said in a recent New York Times article. "It was such a spiritual moment when all of the moms were there at the photo shoot and you could feel the camaraderie, love, joy and what we stand for. We also needed a break from it all to just have fun and get to know each other. It's so important to take care of yourself. If you can't take care of yourself, you can't take care of your family and you can't think clearly and move forward in the world."[28]

*
* *

Black Matrilineage, Photography, and Representation: Another Way of Knowing begins with an analysis of Black mothers who create innovative counter-cultures and communal digital networks, in a manner similar to Truth and Douglass, while generating new visual representations demonstrating the complexities of Black life. These themes serve as the underlying thread in **"More Black and More Beautiful: Social Media & Digital Culture in Rewriting the Self,"** the first section of this volume. In "Regarding the Pain of Our Own: Jazmine Headley, Portraiture, and the Sorrow of Black Motherhood," scholar Brie McLemore explores writer and activist Susan Sontag's work *Regarding the Pain of Others*, by looking at what it means for the pain and violence inflicted upon Black mothers to "go viral." She discusses how photography can serve as a testimony to the history of trauma and a radical tool for Black mothers to see themselves. Jennifer L. Turner's essay investigates how memes can perpetuate false tropes of Black mothers and the impact they have on how Black mothers view their ability to care and mother.[29] In "Black Motherhood Online, A Reimagined Representation," historian Kellie Carter Jackson speaks with Tomi Akitunde, co-founder and editor-in-chief of *mater mea* a blog and podcast series dedicated to Black moms. In the essay, Carter Jackson describes how photography "was rooted in our pain. And even when you see these vintage photos of Black families, the pain is still there, the pain of their circumstances is still there." Carter Jackson and Akitunde continue by discussing how with technological advances, "We're telling our story and joy, finding joy in our stories…" Through sharing her personal journey into social media as a site to resist stale narratives, writer and mother Marly Pierre-Louis pens an essay that asks what happens when Black motherhood moves beyond being the act of protest. The answer is a celebration full of love and joy as well as an exploration and acknowledgement of the erotic lives of Black mothers.

The second section, titled **"'Turning the Face of History to Your Face': Seeing the Self Through Representations of Black Motherhood,"** considers the role of photographs, as both a family and community archive, in rerooting the Black experience to a place grounded in truth, depth, dignity and pride. How photographer Deana Lawson situated Black mothers as beings who conjure a cosmic and primordial relationship with themselves, their families and communities and the earth, is detailed in an interview between Lawson and Susan L. Thompson, independent writer and curator. Writer and activist Eslanda

Robeson's ability to use photography as a means to create and uplift connections between Africa and the Diaspora is discussed in Emily Brady's essay ""I Like to Make Pictures of Children": African American Women Photographers and Wielding the Weapon of 'Motherhood'. The critical role early 20th century Black female photographers and business owners Wilhelmina Pearl Selina Roberts, Elnora Teal, and Florestine Collins, played in combating racist stereotypes of Black families through making portraits is discussed in detail. In "Photographic Afterimages: Nationalism and Images of Motherhood in Canada," Rachel Lobo sheds light on how, through photography, Black women in Canada were able to "create representations that corresponded to the realities, hopes, and aspirations within their own lives." In Atalie Gerhard's "Losses Not to Be Passed On: Paula C. Johnson's and Sara Bennett's Portraits Rewriting (Ex-) Incarcerated Black Mothers," we see how photography can provide Black mothers in particular, with tools to critique structural systems of oppression, counter tropes and be memorialized with truth, dignity and respect. The section ends with a poem by historian Sasha Turner, which calls on the reader to reckon with imperialism, white supremacy, capitalism and patriarchy.

The third section entitled **"'You Are Your Best Thing': Self-Care as a Site of Resistance,"** proceeds with a timely discussion on the importance of self-care, self-preservation and how networks of Black women support one another to ensure this critical work happens. The history and legacy of visual representations of Black pregnant women, in addition to the ways in which visual media can be used to liberate the body and create more truthful narratives, are examined in Haile Eshe Cole's essay, "Worth a Thousand Words: Visualizing Black Motherhood and Health." In Nicole J. Caruth's interview with artist Andrea Chung & Public Health Administrator and Change Agent D'Yuanna Allen-Robb, she asks the crucial question: what is the role of photography in contemporary movements for maternal justice? Caruth looks to midwifery and art as a means of healing. In "Three Black Mothers in a Cleveland Cabaret," Rhaisa Williams examines how Black mothers prioritize bliss and self-love through photographs of Black social nightlife, privileging Black mothers showcasing what bell hooks calls "pictorial genealogies" of families, extended communities.[30]

Section four titled **"'In Search of My Mother's Garden, I Found My Own': Black Female Photographers and the Matrilineal Space,"** explores Black matrilineage and the ways in which it intersects with maternal legacies. Renée Mussai poignantly opens this section with "Letter IV: Where Are They – M/othering R/evolutions," a deeply personal piece to artist and friend Muholi, marked in time by the anniversary of the 1956 Women's March on Pretoria. Mussai's piece explores how Muholi demonstrates that "all r/evolutions also, existentially, fundamentally, begin with our mothers and acts of m/othering."[31] Artist Nona Faustine's intimate relationships with herself, her mother, her sister, and her daughter are traced back to the Eve Gene, the first shared ancestor of every living human on Earth in historian, and curator of Afro-Diasporic fashion and visual culture Jonathan Michael Square's essay "Every day is Mother's Day in My Book: Black Motherhood in the Work of Nona Faustine Simmons". In "The Impossibility of Breathing When the Sun Covers Your Face," artist Marcia Michael retrieves lost narratives and oral histories of her ancestors, revealing how these stories survived in her mother's body, and describes the process by which the narratives live within her. The section ends with "The Motherland Between Us," an essay by scholar Grace Ali. Using her familial ties to Guyana as an example, Ali taps into a deeper meaning unveiling the ways in which motherland, migration, death, and loss are inextricably linked.

Curated Plates: The Assertion of the Lifeforce

How do Black women artists hear the calls of their maternal bonds, both living and dead, the whispers from a motherland spoken in a mother tongue? What do their answers look like? A visual exploration of Black motherhood through pictures made by Black female identifying photographers serves as a response to the call, a reflection of the past and a portal to the future. While there is no one story told by these artists, there is a thread or cord of sorts that connects their images and brings a material reality of what cannot be seen, but rather felt.[32] In this, these artists begin to fill the gaps of representation of Black mothers and mothering with what Audre Lorde named the erotic or "the assertion of the lifeforce of women; of that creative energy empowered, the knowledge and use of which we are now reclaiming in our language, our history, our dancing, our loving, our work, our lives."[33] This act of knowing is often told in the secret language passed between mothers, daughters, kin and defies time as seen in the works of Lebohang Kganye, Adama Delphine Fawundu, Keisha Scarville, and Marcia Michael, who reminds us that "we search for our mothers in order to find ourselves."[34] Artist Nydia Blas reveals a visual meditation that is delicately spun into a mythical allegory with young Black women and girls fulfilling the roles of mothers, warriors, sirens and saints. Photographer, writer and curator Qiana Mestrich continues this repositioning of Black women and Black mothers in particular, by properly placing them as the original makers and their children as collaborators with both inseparably connected to nature, in the images included in this section. Andrea Chung's intricate and tactile collages elevate materials of the everyday and the natural world while examining history, slavery, medicine, connections to the mother(land), and how Black women continue to serve as the "protectors of mothers, women and babies."[35] Through the use of collage, found objects and magazine cuttings, artist Wangechi Mutu creates portraits that further explore colonialism, fetishization, and the impact of medical apartheid on Black women.

Notions of dignifying the ordinary are further explored by Deana Lawson and Mickalene Thomas, who reveal the divine matrilineal legacy of Black people and Black women in particular to locate "the magnificent and have it come through in the picture."[36] Placing Black women in control of their image and legacy by unraveling false histories connected to place is seen in the works by Nona Faustine and Samantha Box who describes how "in chaos of these slippery intersections, there is the chance to measure (my) knotty personal, ancestral, and historical narratives."[37] While partaking in "memory work," Ayana V. Jackson's elucidates history through unearthing links to the past, unveiling and questioning "have been taught to forget."[38] In their photographs and three-dimensional creations, Mary Sibande and vanessa german create a world that is self-affirming, exploratory, and fantastical. And this world, which incorporates elements of Afrofuturism, articulates a present as well as future experience that insists on the presence of Black women and girls made by Black women and girls. The artists in this special curated section serve as talismans conjuring maternal and matrilineal legacies while reclaiming the innate brilliance of Black women through personal stories, history, political acts, connections to place, moments of pleasure, and communal celebration.

As artists, mothers and photo educators with a curatorial practice, we as *Women Picturing Revolution* work to expand the framework for understanding history and visual representation through examining the work of woman lens-based artists who document crises, conflicts, revolution and joy in private realms and public spaces. We were most interested in themes of mother(ing), human rights, mutual care in areas of conflict which became central to our conversations on photography. We began to ask who the women documenting conflict in private realms and public spaces are. We gathered hundreds of examples of work being made by both well known and lesser known photographers. We were particularly interested in work that uses social media to bear witness, or connected people displaced by violence. We asked what the long term effects of trauma are. What does it look like when women tell these stories on their own terms?

The topic of this volume began with a one day seminar at Columbia University's Institute for Research in African-American Studies (IRAAS) entitled "Woman Picturing Revolution: Focus on Africa and the African Diaspora." We examined contemporary photography and the conditions under which women in and/or from Africa or the African Diaspora make images. These works included photography made as a personal response to the legacy and locales of slavery, political oppression, and the inability to act, to well-known photojournalists and emerging voices using social media platforms to document political and social upheavals.

With over forty contributors hailing from North America, Africa and Europe and work ranging from academic writing, interviews, poetry, documentary practice to fine art photography, *Black Matrilineage, Photography, and Representation: Another Way of Knowing* offers a cross section of analysis and art on the topic of Black motherhood, representation, and the participation of photography in the process. We offer this volume as a probe to uncover the intersection of representational justice,[39] Black motherhood and photography. By situating photographs and contemporary scholarship made by and/or about Black motherhood at a critical intersection that supports the heritage and legacies initiated by Black women and their female ancestors, we bear witness to and help bring forth a wider and richer expression of motherhood—in essence, another way of seeing and knowing.

Research for this volume began in 2018 and throughout its creation we were working together but in our separate households, less than one mile apart. Our separation was due to a global pandemic that left the world with no choice but to bear witness to the murders of Black men, women, and children. And we hear the voice of George Floyd crying out for his mother with his last breath. Black mothers have not only been summoned at the moment but have been answering this call as community anchors since time immemorial. Black mothers continue to be truth-bearers showing all of us "another way of knowing;" will we listen?

Notes

1   Walker, A. (1983) *In Search of Our Mothers' Gardens: Womanist Prose.* San Diego: Harcourt Brace Jovanovich. 237.

2   Willis, D. (2017) "Deb Willis and Hank Willis Thomas: A mother and son united by love and art." *TED: Ideas Worth Spreading*, Dec. 2017. https://ted2srt.org/talks/deborah_willis_and_hank_willis_thomas_a_mother_and_son_united_by_love_and_art.

3   Cox, R. (2016) "Renée Cox: A Taste of Power." Interview by Uri McMillian. *Aperture Issue 225, "On Feminism,"* Fall 2016. https://aperture.org/blog/renee-cox-taste-power/.

4   Faustine, N. Personal Interview. July 28, 2020.

5   Willis, D. (2017) "Deb Willis and Hank Willis Thomas: A mother and son united by love and art." *TED: Ideas Worth Spreading*, Dec. 2017.

6   In 2001, *Yo Mama's Last Supper*, 1996 was exhibited at the Brooklyn Museum exhibition *Committed to the Image: Contemporary Black Photographers*, a show of some 200 works by 98 African-American photographers. The then mayor of New York, Mayor Rudolph Giuliani deemed an image from Cox's Yo Mama series indecent and anti-Catholic and declared he would appoint a commission to set decency standards; his commission was never realized.

7   Aspire Design and Home (2021). *Artist Renee Cox Re-Imagines The Signing Of The U.S. Constitution.* [online] Available at: ‹https://aspiremetro.com/renee-cox-the-signing/.

8   The series' title *Mitochondria* refers to the mitochondrial DNA encoded in human genes, which is inherited solely from the mother.

9   Berger, M. (2017) "In Brooklyn, Three Generations in Family Photos." *New York Times.* July 11, 2017. https://lens.blogs.nytimes.com/2017/07/11/in-brooklyn-three-generations-in-family-photos-nona-faustine/?module=BlogPost-Title&version=Blog%20Main&contentCollection=Multimedia&action=Click&pgtype=Blogs&region=Body.

10 Estrin, J. (2016) "Honoring the Legacy of African-American Women." *New York Times.* May 26, 2016. https://lens.blogs.nytimes.com/2016/05/26/honoring-the-legacy-of-african-american-women/.

11 Raiford, L. (2009) "Photography and the Practices of Critical Black Memory." *History and Theory* 48, no. 4: 112–29. http://www.jstor.org/stable/25621443.

12 Creswell, M. (2020) "Sojourner Truth and the Power of Copyright Registration." Library of Congress-Copyright Blog. December 8, 2020. https://blogs.loc.gov/copyright/2020/12/sojourner-truth-and-the-power-of-copyright-registration/.

13 Collins, P. H. (2015) *Black Feminist Thought: Knowledge, Consciousness, and the Politics of Empowerment.* Routledge.

14 Roberts, D. E. (1993) "Racism and Patriarchy in the Meaning of Motherhood." *Faculty Scholarship at Penn Law.* 595. https://scholarship.law.upenn.edu/faculty_scholarship/595.

15 Mestrich, Q. (2018) "Envisioning A Black Maternal Authority." Mae Preta Exhibition Catalogue (Brazil).

16 Hartman, S. (2020) *Wayward Lives.* New York, NY: W.W. Norton & Company. 18–19.

17 Washington, H. A. (2006) *Medical apartheid: the dark history of medical experimentation on Black Americans from colonial times to the present.* New York: Doubleday books.

18 Willis, D., and C. Williams (2002) *The Black Female Body: A Photographic History.* Philadelphia: Temple University Press, 2.

19 Willis, D., and C. Williams (2002) *The Black Female Body: A Photographic History*, 5.

20 Tillet, S. (2021) "Vision & Justice: Around the Kitchen Table – Aperture Foundation." *Aperture*, May 4, 2021, https://aperture.org/editorial/vision-justice-around-kitchen-table/.

21 Sadoff, D. F. (1985) "Black Matrilineage: The Case of Alice Walker and Zora Neale Hurston." *Signs* 11, no. 1: 4–26. http://www.jstor.org/stable/3174284.

22 Spillers, H. J. (1987) "Mama's Baby, Papa's Maybe: An American Grammar Book." *Dia-critics* 17, no. 2: 65–81. https://doi.org/10.2307/464747.

23 Spillers, H. J. (1987) "Mama's Baby, Papa's Maybe: An American Grammar Book." *Dia-critics* 17, no. 2: 65–81. https://doi.org/10.2307/464747.

24 This arrangement resulted in the exhibition *"Where We At"—Black Women Artists, 1971,* as was described in the Brooklyn Museum's paramount exhibition, *We Wanted a Revolution: Black Radical Women, 1965–85.*

25 Story, K. A. and P. H. Collins (2014) *Reconceiving Motherhood.* Bradford (UK): Demeter Press.

26 Bright, S. P. interview with editors on November 5, 2016.

27 Smith, K. (2018) "Sheila Pree Bright connects movements of the past and present in #1960Now." ArtsAtl, October 11, 2018. https://www.artsatl.org/sheila-pree-bright-con-nects-movements-of-the-past-and-present-with-1960now/.

28 Shakur, F. (2019) "From the Civil Rights Movement to Black Lives Matter: Honoring Black Mothers Who Lost Their Sons." *New York Times.* January 29, 2019. https://www.nytimes.com/2019/01/29/lens/sheila-pree-bright-civil-rights-black-lives-matter-moth-ers-atlanta.html.

29 We (Women Picturing Revolution) and essayist Dr. Jennifer L. Turner, made the con-scious decision not to show the memes referenced in her essay in an effort to rebuke the perpetuation of these images.

30 hooks, bell (2005) *"In Our Glory," Family, History, Memory: Recording African-American Life.* Irvington: Hylas Publishing, 51.

31 Mussai, R. (2021) Letter to Muholi. "Letter IV: Where Are They – M/Othering R/Evolu-tions." London, England, August 9, 2021.

32 Lesleyheller.com (2021) Keisha Scarville: "Elegy: Selections from Mama's Clothes". [online] Available at: ‹http://www.lesleyheller.com/exhibitions/20180420-keisha-scar-ville-elegy-selections-from-mamas-clothes#:~:text=Her%20ongoing%20body%20 of%20work,that%20are%20triggered%20by%20absence%E2%80%A6&text=Keisha%20 Scarville%20(b› [Accessed 27 October 2021].

33 Lorde, A. (1978) *Uses of the Erotic: the Erotic as Power.* Freedom, Calif.: Crossing Press.

34 The Object of My Gaze. [online] Available at: ‹https://skindeepmag.com/articles/the-object-of-my-gaze› [Accessed 27 October 2021].

35 Rooklidge, E. "Andrea Chung with HereIn." *HereIn*, November 1, 2020), https://www.hereinjournal.org/conversations/andrea-chung-with-herein.

36 Lawson, D. and A. Jafa (2018) "A Match Made in Heaven: Deana Lawson and Arthur Jafa on Destiny, Intuition, and Influence." *Garage. Vice*, September 4, 2018. https://garage.vice.com/en_us/article/paww9m/deana-lawson-arthur-jafa-interview.

37 Box, S. "Artist Statement." Samantha Box. Accessed October 31, 2021. https://www.samanthabox.net/statement.

38 Jackson, A. V. "Ayana v. Jackson: 20 September – 26 October 2019 – Overview." Mariane Ibrahim Gallery. Accessed November 1, 2021. https://marianeibrahim.com/exhibi-tions/22-ayana-v.-jackson-take-me-to-the-water/overview/.

39 Lewis, S. "Aperture Magazine 223 'Vision & Justice': Sarah Lewis Guest Editor Note." *Aperture*, May 4, 2021, https://aperture.org/editorial/vision-justice/.

PART ONE

MORE BLACK AND MORE BEAUTIFUL: SOCIAL MEDIA & DIGITAL CULTURE IN THE REWRITING OF SELF

1   REGARDING THE PAIN OF OUR OWN

Jazmine Headley, Portraiture, and the Sorrow of
Black Motherhood

Brie McLemore _____

On December 7th, 2018, Jazmine Headley, a 23-year-old Black woman, and her
1-year-old son, sat down on the floor of a social service building in Brooklyn
due to a lack of available seating. She was asked to move and when she opted
not to, social service employees called the police, claiming that Jazmine was
obstructing the hallway. It is unclear how events unfolded after the officers
arrived. It is clear, however, that a video was uploaded to Facebook showing
police brutally ripping Jazmine's son from her arms after tackling her to the
floor. The video soon went viral, appearing on every social media platform, as
well as prominent news outlets.

I watched the video only once, but it stuck with me for days. Even after the
video had ended, I could hear Jazmine's frantic cries that her son was in pain
and the entire force of the State saying that it did not care. Her cries sounded
familiar. They have been yelled by Black women for centuries as their children are ripped from their arms. And now, Jazmine's cries have been replayed
more than 60,000 times on YouTube. What does it mean for Jazmine's pain
to go "viral"? How can we make sense of the "Black Lives Matter" hashtag
that accompanied this brutality and Jazmine's anguish as her story (and the
accompanying video) spread like wildfire? This occurrence should come as
no surprise, as this declaration has been resounded by activists across social
media, in the halls of Congress, and even in university classrooms. However,
the harsh and brutal treatment of Black subjects remains, which begs an inter-
rogation of philosopher Calvin L. Warren's provocative question of not only
do Black Lives Matter, but is there such a thing as a Black Life? As he states:

> The human *being* provides an anchor of declaration for the declaration,
> and since the *being* of the human is invaluable, then black life *must* also
> matter, if the black is a human…But we reach a point of terror with this

syllogistic reasoning. One must take a step backward and ask the fundamental question: is the black, in fact, a human *being*? (Warren 2018: 2, emphasis in original)

It is possible that the legacy of slavery, in which Blackness was rendered as commodity rather than human, has not been abandoned in this not so distant future. Warren's perturbing query can provide insight into the gravitas and the heinousness of Jazmine's encounter with law enforcement in which they saw her not as some*one* undesirable, but as some*thing* distinctly apart from them; some*thing* that affirms their humanity at the expense of hers; some*thing* that might not be human at all.

In order to fully understand the limitations of Black life, we must first have a reckoning with death. Philosopher Achille Mbembe asserts that the enslaved found themselves within a "state of injury"—a liminal space between life and death, in which their existence is justified through the value of their labor. The result is a form of cruelty in which the enslaved experienced death within life (Lawson 2018: 720).

The commodification of Black mothering during slavery has had implications for death itself. Interjecting a specifically gendered understanding of this liminal space, feminist scholar Erica S. Lawson contends with the particular implications for Black mothers who birth that which is so closely related to death. For Black women, whose value stemmed from their ability to reproduce slavery through childbearing, this has had particularly devastating consequences. Slavery situated Black women as the producers of "father-lacking" stock, commodities and property, as opposed to human beings (Spillers 1987: 80; emphasis in original). Their existence, which could only be quantified through currency, resulted in the complete disregard of Black mothers by their enslavers, who regarded them as "not mothers at all" (Roberts 1997: 24; Baptist 2014: 33–34). Black mothers were seen as producers of the "kinlessness," in which familial ties "can be invaded at any given and arbitrary moment by the property relations," as mothers can be separated and sold apart from their children (Spillers 1987: 74–80). This loss—of off-spring, freedom, autonomy, and a sense of belonging, which finds its origins in slavery—is an historical legacy that has shaped Black motherhood (Rodriguez 2016: 62).

As Lawson states, "death itself and the multidimensional meanings attributed to it shaped social relations in the plantation such that life and death were deeply intertwined with motherhood" (Lawson 2018: 721). This has had lasting implications in the modern day, in which Black women's bodies still serve as a contentious battle ground for the State (Lawson 2018: 721). Although Black motherhood has transformed post-slavery, it is still trapped within a "mortuary politics" as the racial state continues to "manage" Black mothers and their children in the contemporary (Lawson 2018: 721). Policing plays an integral role in this endeavor. Quoting Assata Shakur, Lawson asserts that the carceral state can be understand as a reconfiguration of chattel slavery in "ways that are remarkably similar" (Lawson 2018: 722).

Perhaps Lawson's assessment can provide insight into the historical legacies that conspired against Jazmine Headley on that fateful day, but in order to understand its "virality," we must first contend with photography. According to Susan Sontag, "photography has kept company with death" (Sontag 2004: 24). Photographs serve as an immediate and authoritative medium, an objective yet personal testimony, for "conveying the horror of mass-produced death" (Sontag 2003: 24–26). Despite their presumably factual existence, what exactly photographs are supposed to convey and what exactly they are supposed to bear witness to is highly contested.

While photographs can be used to showcase the terrors of war, this meaning can be disrupted, distorted, and misconstrued. What of the portrayal of pain? Sontag offers various possibilities, ranging from calls of peace to cries for revenge. However, there is another possibility: that of spectacle. Photography can give rise to "...simply the bemused awareness, continually restocked by photographic information, that terrible things happen." (Sontag 2003: 13)

The consequences detailed by Sontag must be contended with in the modern day, as videos and photographs of Black brutality and death spread rapidly. The viral imagery of Black death in recent years has led many critics to deem the sharing and liking of such images to be 'trauma porn,' which Chloé Meley defines as a "perverse fascination with other people's misfortune; a phenomenon which has become increasingly pervasive in a digital era where pain is commodified, and upsetting portrayals of it stripped of their emotional impact as they sink into the depths of content overload" (Meley 2019).

Meley echoes similar concerns as Sontag, such as the possible inability of these images to galvanize social change, instead rendering its viewers powerless, desensitized, or perhaps cynical, in which the images before us are open to debate. The virality of Black death can also have another, perhaps far-reaching consequence: that of dehumanization. As Sontag warns, "violence turns anybody subjected to it into a thing" (Sontag 2004: 12). This is due to the bifurcation of lived experiences, in which, for those most distant from the images they retweet and share, photography serves as necessary visual proof that the pain of Blackness exists. As Meley states, "the implicit idea is that marginalised communities' pain has to be portrayed, as if the telling of it wasn't enough, as if additional, visual proof was required" (Meley 2019). Within this testimony as evidence, the Black body in pain is relegated to that of evidence to be critiqued, substantiated, or dismissed.

This is a sentiment furthered by activist and writer Ashlee Marie Preston, when she states: "Sharing images of Black death on social media won't save Black lives. Instead of eradicating our murders, it normalizes them. Year after year, life after life, innocent Black blood is spilled, and yet the system responsible is left intact" (Preston 2020). Preston reminds us that the sharing of images depicting violence upon Black bodies is as traditionally American as apple pie (Preston 2020). The dissemination of images depicting brutality and death upon Black people was an essential component of lynching, in which photography allowed a White audience, both present and distant, to bear witness to the violence, turning both the lynching and its aftermath into a spectacle (Preston 2020).

But what about those who watched the video and saw a reflection of themselves or of those they love? What of the trauma inflicted upon those who understand Jazmine's pain because, as Black mothers or the children of Black mothers, it was all too familiar? What can we say to those who "don't need to see suffering to know that it exists and that it shouldn't?" (Meley 2019). Photographs and flyers of lynchings did not solely serve to satiate a White craving for Black destruction—it also served to terrorize and humiliate Black people (Preston 2020). Since murder at the hands of police is an extension of lynching (Niedermeier 2019), the sharing of such viral videos furthers White Supremacy's propagation of Black disposability (Preston 2020). The sharing of such images effectively produces a modern-day lynching and, even as White people participate in this endeavor under the façade of 'allyship,' the motivation remains the same. As Preston states: "The purpose of publicly torturing Black bodies, then and now, is to deter Black Americans from challenging white supremacy. And by re-sharing, liking, or posting videos of Black people being murdered, you're inadvertently helping to spread that message" (Preston 2020).

For these reasons, I have chosen not to reproduce the indelible images of Jazmine's brutalization that circulated on social media. Instead, I will engage with another image, a portrait of Jazmine crying, which appeared in the *New York Times* article "They Grabbed Her Baby and Arrested Her. Now Jazmine Headley is Speaking Out." However, before doing so, we must first grapple with the fact that the video of Jazmine's child being ripped from her arms did, in fact, go viral.

If she thought the baby was being injured as the mother she should have released him. And if she behaves like this in public I am fearful of her private behavior. Also. Anyone know if she has a history with social services.

2d   Like   Reply   13

It's New York...that kid is a future criminal anyway

2d   Like   Reply

Why didn't she let go of the baby? she used that baby as a tool.

2d   Like   Reply   1

Mother doesn't deserve a child. Good job officers. Big Paul

2d   Like   Reply   14

Screenshot Huffpost, "If she thought the baby was being injured as the mother she should have released him. And if she behaves like this in public I am fearful of her private behavior. Also. Anyone know if she has a history with social services." "It's New York…the kid is a future criminal anyway." "Why didn't she let go of the baby? she used that baby as a tool." "Mother doesn't deserve a child. Good job officers. Big Paul," Facebook, December 10, 2018, https://www.facebook.com/HuffPost/posts/10156719307186130

How can we make sense of the "virality" of the state-sanctioned brutality inflicted upon Jazmine? According to Imani Perry, the digital age has resulted in the expansion of the 'simulacra'—that territory which expands beyond the map, in which information, desires, and interpretive frameworks are communicated (Perry 2018: 129–130). Building off of the work of Baudrillard and Jameson in order to account for photography in the digital age, Perry's conception of the simulacra can expand Sontag's analysis, asserting that the implications for dehumanization are more pronounced than ever within the digital realm due to the possibility for the rapid reproduction of Black pain (Perry 2018: 143). As Perry warns, "we ought now to consider how ways of seeing and consuming people, in an ongoing fashion, through the simulacra continue to pervert our capacity for fellow feeling" (Perry 2018: 147). This disregard of the pain of Blackness is evident within the social media commentary espoused in response to the videos depicting Jazmine's brutality.

While many spoke in defense of Jazmine and condemned the State for subjecting her to such treatment, this was not an interpretation shared by all. Many who viewed the imagery did not see the pain of a mother attempting to protect her son as he was brutally ripped from her arms. Instead, they situated Jazmine as deviant, criminal, and fraudulent in order to establish her as a bad mother, justifying the brutality inflicted upon her. Within these moments, Jazmine was "haunted" by the historical perceptions of Black mothers, ranging from slavery to the 'welfare queen' and the supposed crack baby epidemic.

Avery Gordon describes a haunting as the process in which that which is not observed actually operates as a "seething presence" that impacts, shapes, and meddles with our realities (Gordon 2008: 8). This analysis situates ghosts as a social figure that unearths that which is perceived to not be present, thus exposing how history and subjectivity construct social life (Gordon 2008: 8). That Jazmine's brutal treatment occurred at a social welfare office is no coincidence but is instead emblematic of the historical violence and dehumanization of Black mothers, in which the "Welfare Queen" is always present, serving to shape, reconfigure, and distort perceptions of Black women today.

The digital simulacra provided a terrain in which these "ghosts" were able to capture Jazmine, freezing her in time, and subjecting her to the interpretations of those who never sought to understand. This is a testament to what Saidiya Hartman characterizes as the "precariousness of empathy," in which the role of spectator and voyeur can become increasingly blurred, perhaps collapsing in upon itself (Hartman 1997: 4). Of this occurrence, Hartman asks "Are we witnesses who confirm the truth of what happened in the face of the world-destroying capacities of pain, the distortions of torture, the sheer unrepresentability of terror, and the repression of the dominant accounts? Or are we voyeurs fascinated with and repelled by exhibitions of terror and sufferance?" (Hartman 1997: 3).

But we are not powerless in the consumption of digital images. And resistance is not impossible. As Perry states, "we are at once saturated by gender and racial narratives and stereotypes, yet we are constantly invited to refute them, as we have ready pathways to counter-hegemonic assertions about gender and race on digital platforms. This is a two-way street" (Perry 2018: 131). Perry's analysis opens up the possibility of using the very mechanism of dehumanization as a powerful tool to challenge persistent beliefs about Black motherhood and provide new possibilities for what Black mothering can entail. The discourse around the proliferation of Black death is profound. There has been a much needed, critical analysis of the spectacle of these images and the pain it inflicts. Missing from this conversation, however, is the possibility of opposition. Can the very medium of photography seek to rectify the harm that has been done? Is there a possibility for portraits to reshape the "civil imagination" of how Black motherhood is conceptualized?

The portrait of Jazmine Headley that appeared in the New York Times article cited above provides the possibility for reshaping how Black motherhood is theorized, situating photography as both a testimony to the history of trauma inflicted by the State upon Black mothers, but also a radical tool for Black mothers to convey their sorrow—an expression of humanity historically denied to them.

The portrait, which was photographed by Sara Naomi Lewkowicz, depicts Jazmine in anguish, her hand covering her face, possibly holding back tears. This photo stands in stark contrast to the viral images that catapulted Jazmine's name into notoriety just a few weeks before. A video of tangled bodies, blurred expressions, and haunting screams. Now Jazmine appeared in sharp clarity and with something to say.

Sarah Naomi Lewkowicz, the visual journalist who took the photo, is all too familiar with violence. She is most known for her multimedia project depicting intimate partner violence, situating her as a central photojournalist for depicting interpersonal violent encounters, but now at the hands of the State. While Lewkowicz might have experience photographing the victims of violence, she lacks an essential element necessary for photographing Jazmine Headley: the experience of being a Black mother. It begs the question of why Lewkowicz was chosen by the *New York Times* for this task, when other equally if not more qualified Black women photographers, such as Miranda Barnes, Carrie Mae Weems, Deana Lawson, Laylah Amatullah Barrayn, and Lorna Simpson (to name a few) were not? Barnes, for example, shot intimate portraits of Black mothers reeling from the aftermath of miscarriages that ran in the *New York Times* just two months prior to Jazmine's story (Silver-Greenberg and Kitroeff 2018). By capturing Jazmine through a white photographic gaze, the *New York Times* perpetuated the sentiment that whiteness can serve as an authoritative voice to tell the stories of Blackness in the mainstream, propagating racial erasure and historical amnesia (Valentine 2020).

White photographers consistently photograph Black subjects as a way to further the white gaze, in which photos of Blackness affords Whiteness the permission to stare (Weber 2019). These photographs also bestow Whiteness with accolades and awards, while providing Blackness with nothing in return. In 2016, 2017, and 2018 the winners of the Taylor Wessing Photographic Portrait Prize, who were gifted awards of $20,000 and dedicated gallery space at the UK's National Portrait Gallery, were awarded to four white photographers who utilized Black people as disposable subjects (Weber 2018; "Taylor Wessing Photographic Portrait Prize"). The now infamous photograph captured by white photographer Robert Cohen of Black activist Edward Crawford throwing a tear gas canister back at police during the uprising in St. Louis in 2015 garnered Cohen a Pulitzer Prize. Meanwhile Crawford was found dead under mysterious circumstances (Valentine 2020). There is a long history of white photographers devouring and regurgitating Black bodies when they see fit.

The image of a distraught Jazmine photographed by a White woman, which appears in a newspaper commonly associated with the White, liberal elite could easily be dismissed as "an aestheticization of suffering," (Azoulay 2015: 1) or a more palatable form of the 'trauma porn' discussed above. However, I assert that such quick judgments would do a disservice to the power of this image, essentially negating its ability to refute the "controlling images" so often placed upon Black mothers as deviant and criminal (Hill-Collins 2009: 84). Further, this image allows Jazmine to openly and unapologetically express grief and despair as a response to the tragedy she has endured, an emotion that Black mothers have historically been seen as incapable of. The portrait of Jazmine might simultaneously stand as both a testimony to the history of trauma inflicted by the State upon Black mothers, as well as a declaration that Black mothers do, in fact, weep. This portrait is part of a long legacy of photography being utilized to transform and challenge the limitations imposed upon Black mothers and their ability to "legitimately" grieve.

The constant threat of losing one's children, either through enslavement, infant mortality, or police and state sanctioned violence, places Black mothering in a constant state of sorrow (Davis 2016: 8). As anthropologist Dána-Ain Davis states "What is illegible but needs to be made legible is the trauma of Black motherhood and mothering; the trauma is wrapped tightly around our bodies but does nothing to keep us warm" (Davis 2016: 9). This trauma is intricately connected to grief and "like molasses, grief is thick, slow-moving, and sneaky, coating every surface it touches and affecting everything that lies within and beneath" (Williams 2016: 18).

However, the ability for Black women's pain to be perceived as justified or warranted is limited. Citing the work of Anne Cheng, performance studies theorist Rhaisa Kameela Williams highlights that not everyone has access to grief in the state imaginary, in that there are those who have historically been afforded the ability to grieve, due to their proximity to Whiteness, and those who have not (Williams 2016: 19). Williams interjects a specific analysis of the stakes for Black mothers, tracing the path of grief to the Atlantic Slave Trade. As described above, slavery ruptured the ability of Black mothers to parent, thus denying their "claims to dominant conceptions of motherhood" (Williams 2016: 20). If mothering was predicated on the ability to nurture and protect one's child, and that child was ripped from your arms and deemed a commodity rather than human, then, by definition, a "Black mother" is an oxymoron (Williams 2016: 20). And if slavery did not allow for a Black mother to exist, then how could it be possible for a Black mother to grieve?

And even as slavery formally ended, the inability to perceive Black mothers did not. As stereotypes such as "sapphire" and the "angry Black women" latched onto Black mothers in a supposedly emancipated world, so did perceptions of them as irrational, impulsive, and lacking decorum. It wasn't *necessarily* that Black mothers could not grieve, it was that their grief was immaterial and not worthy of redress since she is always unjustly dissatisfied (Williams 2016: 20).

This historical legacy makes Black maternal grief in the digital age complicated, to say the least. Erica Lawson recounts how Black mothers, particularly those who parent sons who have died by legal or extralegal forms of violence, can be vilified or lauded, complicating their ability to grieve. This often contradictory state of affairs is most evident by assessing the public treatment and depiction of the "Mothers of the Movement," seven Black mothers whose children were killed due to state-sanctioned violence. The Mothers of the Movement have received a national platform, have been featured on prominent news stations, and even spoke at the 2016 Democratic Convention. They have been able to evoke maternal sorrow in order to challenge the demonization of their children, as well as situate themselves as victims worthy of empathy.

The "Mothers of the Movement" have exhibited what Lawson refers to as 'public motherhood,' in which expressions of maternal grief are not relegated to the private sphere, but instead fuel a political community (Lawson 2018: 713). However, the ability of the Mothers of the Movement to be regarded as aggrieved is tenuous at best. While they have been celebrated in some circles, they have also been heavily demonized in others. In an article published by *USA Today*, Ron Hosko of the Law Enforcement Legal Defense Fund blamed the grieving mothers for the deaths of not only their own children, but for all Black lives. In the article, he quoted Dallas Police Chief David Brown, who, arguing that the police were tasked with way too much, stated: "70% of the African-American community is being raised by single women. Let's give it to the cops to solve that as well" (Hosko 2016).

This depiction of the "Mothers of the Movement" showcases the complicated implications of 'public mothering' for Black women due to the symbol of the 'matriarch,' which, according to Patricia Hill Collins, serves as a controlling image for Black women and their perceived failure at motherhood. Black women are portrayed as overly aggressive, emasculating, and incapable of supervising their children. As a result, Black communities are characterized as impoverished and criminal, and Black women as solely responsible (Hill-Collins 2009: 84). Expressing a similar observation as Hill-Collins, Elijah

Anderson states, "...the black woman with children in tow might be perceived as loud and boisterous, seemingly unfeminine yet sexualized more bestial than human" (Anderson 2012: 16).

However, this is not to say that the endeavor is all for naught. Black women have always challenged the stereotypical narratives imposed upon them. Crying images of Mamie Till grieving alongside the open casket of her brutally murdered teenage son Emmett elicited controversy but also galvanized the Civil Rights Movement (Lawson 2018: 724). The infamous photo of Mamie not only situated her as an "unsung" hero of the movement, but also provided the foundation for Black maternal mourning, in which anguish is articulated through grievance, and the body and voice are mobilized to travel between and among various platforms in the public sphere in search of justice. Mamie Till called upon Black newspapers and magazines to photograph her son's open casket so the world would be forced to see what she did: the brutalization of White Supremacy branded onto the body of her young son (Brown 2018). As Williams states, "Refusing to mourn silently and privately, she wrote against the powerful stillness that has historically dominated discursive constructions of Black mothers who, largely until that point, were expected by White judicial actors to accept their children's tragic fate as a disciplining project inherent to the social system" (Williams 2016: 21).

This sentiment is similar to that of Sheila Pree-Bright, a Black photographer who created a massive installation in Atlanta, the chosen location for the 2019 Super Bowl. Pree-Bright's black and white photo depicted ten Black mothers who had lost their sons. In the middle stood Gwen Carr, mother of Eric Garner, wearing white with her arms stretched out before her. Of the very public locale, Pree-Bright stated, "Most murals are usually in marginalized communities. I wanted to go to the voices of the unheard and take something I was in conflict with and make something of beauty" (Shakur 2019). Similar to Mamie Till's public displays of grief, Pree-Bright also utilized photography and a national platform to highlight the perils of White Supremacy and also situate Black mothers as worthy of empathy.

Bereaved Black motherhood seeks to identify and unearth structural, as well as intersecting, forms of violence, while simultaneously devising ways to challenge them (Lawson 2018: 725). Black mothers' bereavement situates their grief within a "longer temporality of violent racial practices" rooted within slavery (Lawson 2018: 716). This site of entry situates "maternal politics as a counternarrative to the view that political legitimacy is only possible by engaging practices that validate the prescribed performance of citizenship"

(Lawson 2018: 734). More specifically, "public mothering" allows Black women to embody the highly gendered emotion of grief, commonly associated with femininity and motherhood (Lawson 2018: 717).

This can have lasting implications for what Lawson refers to as the "democratic imagination," which can activate, shape, and inform political involvement (Lawson 2018: 734). Public expressions of grief, which are all too often relegated to the private, can shape a particular form of democratic imagination and serve as a response to injustice (Lawson 2018: 734). Perhaps it is possible to infuse Lawson's assertion with the theoretical framework provided by visual cultural theorist Ariella Azoulay in order to understand the specific role photographs can play in shaping understandings, but more importantly responses, to injustice.

Azoulay affords photography a role in shaping a "political imagination," which she defines as "the ability to imagine a political state of being that deviates significantly from the prevailing state of affairs" (Azoulay 2015: 3). This imagination transcends that of the individual and can, in fact, exist between and amongst others—a "shared experience of human beings" (Azoulay 2015: 5). While Azoulay asserts that political imagination can be activated through various mechanisms, one in particular seems apt for this analysis: the portraiture, or, to be more exact, "the public transmission of portraits of individuals disseminated through the world in a manner not dependent on the presence of these individuals themselves" (Azoulay 2015: 6).

For Azoulay, portraits provide an opportunity to disrupt the presumed "aesthetic vs. political" debate, in which images validated in one arena can be dismissed in the other. There are certain images, perhaps those generally relegated to the realm of political, that embody a special status and exist within the "citizenry of photography" (Azoulay 2015: 51). Judging these images based on aesthetics alone enacts a form of violence that expels them from their political or civil space "...within whose borders the photographed subjects fight for their rightful place by means of the photograph and the space of appearance that it opens before them" (Azoulay 2015: 51).

By Azoulay's logic, the role of the "spectator" is anything but. Those who view such images play a vital role in dictating its importance and the level of imagination it is afforded. While Azoulay's assessment focuses primarily on those who enact a 'professional gaze' of photography, I would assert that this analysis can be extrapolated to all who view such images, thus dictating who is allowed to exist within the "citizenry of photography," which hinges on the spectator who serves as addressee (Azoulay 2015: 44).

This entails a relationship between the image, the artist, and the spectator—as well as other spectators one encounters within "a space that is inexorably political" (Azoulay 2015: 61). Azoulay asserts that this mutually dependent relationship: "...can itself motivate the spectator to recognize the existence of a common domain and to ask questions regarding not only what is put on display within it, but also regarding the actors who are authorized to participate in it or who are banished from it" (Azoulay 2015: 61).

What does Sara Naomi Lewkowicz's portrait of Jazmine motivate us to reckon with? What domain can come into existence? Could the possible imaginative domain that Jazmine's portrait provides be one of a "public mothering" grounded in grief and bereavement? As Lawson describes, grieving is considered to be a maternal and feminine attribute—so what does this entail for Black mothers who have historically been constructed as unfeminine? I suggest that Jazmine's portrait serves as both a mechanism for expressing the sorrow of Black mothers, as well as a tool for shifting the civic imagination of Black motherhood in order to unearth historically foreclosed-upon possibilities. It is possible that this portrait provides an escape, albeit brief, from the trope of the "matriarch"—a stereotype that rests on the assertion of Black women as unfeminine, aggressive, castrating, and inept mothers, essentially failing to fulfill their traditional "womanly" duties (Hill-Collins 2009: 268).

A portrait of Jazmine Headley unabashedly expressing grief, anguish, and sorrow could effectively alter this perception. Photographs have the ability to "turn the world upside down (Gordon 2008: 102); and "fiddle with the scale of the world" (Sontag 2004: 4). Photographs can serve as a form of evidence—either solidifying what we already perceive to know, or to confirm that which is "doubted, but suspected," teetering on the line between familiarity and strangeness, hurting and healing (Gordon 2008: 102–103). Photographs are also rooted in hegemony, quickly at the disposal of those traditionally in power and those traditionally subordinated. Gordon states:

> We have seen that the photograph's very power to haunt—the animating force we do not want to reduce—can be used by the state to intimidate, to wage war against the imagination, to control the balance of certainty and doubt, reality and unreality that disappearance manipulates. The photograph, then, takes its place in this contest of haunting (Gordon 2008: 108).

Building off of the work of Roland Barthes, Gordon adopts the studium and punctum divide for exploring the potentially haunting role of photography. The studium is that which is recognizable and comprehensible, "the most obvious tableaux of the photograph" (Gordon 2008: 106). It is those photographs that participate in cultural, historical, and political transference of knowledge. It educates in a civil, polite, and even detached manner; "it may shout, but it does not wound" (Gordon 2008: 106).

The punctum, on the other hand, is that which breaks the studium, disrupts its existence and the assumptions attributed to it. It is the "off-center detail," the unexpected, that makes the photograph and its reference come alive (Gordon 2008: 107). The punctum is not bounded to the image itself, but can instead evoke a "blind field," in which one's perception of an image relies on what the photograph depicts, as well as the interpretations and expectations one adds to the photo, establishing a " life external to the photo" (Gordon 2008: 107). It might be said that the punctum exists within the realm of possibility. It is that which might be present yet cannot be named. It is longed for yet cannot be identified. It is already present, but never seen. If the punctum is that which haunts, then the blind field might be where ghosts thrive (Gordon 2008: 107–108).

Gordon provides numerous examples of the sort of images that constitute the studium and that have the potential to serve as a punctum. For the purposes of this analysis, the most important is that of the "dignified portrait." Both Gordon and Barthes quickly relegate the portrait to that of the studium because of its ability to signify that which is "recognizable" and "comprehensible" (Gordon 2008: 106). However, Gordon leaves potential for photographs to serve as counterimages that challenge organized systems of repression—a role often afforded to the studium. Gordon looks to the Mothers of the Plaza de Mayo, who pinned photographs of their missing children to their hearts as a direct challenge to military authority and economic repression in Argentina (Gordon 2008: 108). Photographs served as testimonies of absence, speaking to that which should be, but is not there. This act of defiance provided the opportunity for mothers to "repossess" their children and challenge the State apparatus that had rendered them disposable (Gordon 2008: 109).

Portraiture was a necessity for this project, which, in turn, altered the images themselves. As Gordon states, "the Mothers transformed the docile portrait or, in the case of the photocopies, the disembodied mechanical reproduction of a bodily organ into a public *punctum*" (Gordon 2008: 109; emphasis in original). This suggests a possibility for portraits to serve simultaneously as both punctum and studium, as both a testimony of and a provocation to the "status-quo" of state violence.

This analysis is essential for understanding the potential of Jazmine Headley's portrait. Her anguish reminds us of the apparatus of death the State commonly inflicts upon Black mothers. Her tears share a common lineage to Black women who have cried for their children for centuries. In this sense, her portrait exists within the realm of the studium, reminding all who look upon it that the ripping of Black children from their mothers exists within the purview of the State's charge—it has happened before and we would be foolish to assume that it will not happen again. As Jazmine herself stated: "It's the story of many other people, it's not just my story. My story is the only one that made it to the surface" (Southall and Stewart 2018).

But might I suggest that the "surface" Jazmine's portrait rests upon provides an opportunity for transformative potential. Maybe it marks the convergence of both the "blind field" of the punctum and the civil space of imagination—both serving as realms in which a new vision is possible. Jazmine's public display of pain and heartbreak in one of the most widely circulated newspapers in the nation forges a new understanding of Black women as those who hurt and long for their children, as any mother would. This, effectively, challenges the historical narratives of Black women—caught between the unfeeling matriarch and their complete dispossession of motherhood through slavery.

This portrait also punctures the state violence that so commonly goes unnoticed, such as in the time before social media, when police brutally attacked Black women hidden from the purview of hashtags and share buttons. As stated before, this portrait also transforms the civil imagination that limits the ability of Black women to express pain. In a sense, Jazmine's portrait refuses to remain silent, forcing a reckoning with State terror and its aftermath.

Upon looking at Jazmine's portrait, it might be easy to dismiss it as that which simply glorifies Black mother's trauma without providing radical tools for change. I will not deny this assessment. Lewkowicz's portrait of Jazmine Headley will not end police brutality against Black mothers and it will not end the State's annihilation of Black lives. However, I would like to suggest that Jazmine's portrait serves as an opening—a potential for transforming the socially constructed limitations of Black motherhood. With that, I conclude with Gordon's assessment that viewing portraits that exist as both studium and punctum requires a "second sight" in order to truly contend with their transformative potential. This is a glance that is forward looking, resting on the potentials of our imaginations. Gordon states, " This second sight, which transports longing between the somewhere in myself that is right here in the middle of all the terror and the utopian elsewhere that I imagine for my future, is what embracing the ghostly image can sometimes bestow" (Gordon 2008: 109). May we all take the time for a second look.

Works Cited

Anderson, E. (2012). "The Iconic Ghetto," *The ANNALS of the American Academy of Political and Social Science*, 642, 1: 8–24.

Azoulay, A. (2012). *Civil Imagination: A Political Ontology of Photography*. London: Verso Books.

Baptist, E. E. (2014). *The Half Has Never Been Told: Slavery and the Making of American Capitalism*. New York: Basic Books.

Brown, D. L. (2018). "Emmett Till's Mother Opened His Casket and Sparked the Civil Rights Movement," *The Washington Post*, July 12, 2018, https://www.washingtonpost.com/news/retropolis/wp/2018/07/12/emmett-tills-mother-opened-his-casket-and-sparked-the-civil-rights-movement/ (accessed July 15, 2021).

Davis, Dána-Ain (2016). "'The Bone Collectors' Comments for Sorrow as Artifact: Black Radical Mothering in Times of Terror," *Transforming Anthropology*, 24, 1: 8–16.

Gordon, A. (1997/2008). *Ghostly Matters: Haunting and the Sociological Imagination*. Minneapolis: University of Minnesota Press.

Hartman, S. (1997). *Scenes of Subjection: Terror, Slavery, and Self-Making in Nineteenth Century America*. Oxford: Oxford University Press.

Hill-Collins, P. (1990/2009). *Black feminist thought: Knowledge, consciousness, and the politics of Empowerment*. New York: Routledge, 1990/2009.

Hosko, R. (2016). "Mothers of the Movement Bear Responsibility for Black Lives Lost," *USA Today*, July 27, 2016, https://www.usatoday.com/story/opinion/2016/07/27/mothers-movement-michael-brown-black-lives-matter-justice-police-democrats-column/87581112/ (accessed July 15, 2021).

Lawson, E. S. (2018). "Bereaved Black Mothers and Maternal Activism in the Racial State," *Feminist Studies*, 44, 3: 713–735.

Meley, C. (2019). "The Pointless Consumption of Pain in the Era of Trauma Porn," *Incite Journal*, (March 2019).

Niedermeier, S. (2019). *The Color of the Third Degree: Racism, Police Torture, and Civil Rights in the American South, 1930-1955*, Translated by Paul Allen Cohen. Chapel Hill: The University of North Carolina Press.

Perry, I. (2018). *Vexy Thing: On Gender and Liberation*. Durham: Duke University Press.

Preston, A. M. (2020). "Sorry, Consuming Trauma Porn is not Allyship," *Marie Claire*, (June 2020).

Rodriguez, C. (2016). "Mothering While Black: Feminist Thought on Material Loss, Mourning, and Agency in the African Diaspora," *Transforming Anthropology*, 24, 1: 61–69.

Shakur, F. (2019). "From the Civil Rights Movement to Black Lives Matter: Honoring Black Mothers Who Lost Their Sons," *The New York Times*, January 29, 2019, https://www.nytimes.com/2019/01/29/lens/

sheila-pree-bright-civil-rights-black-lives-matter-mothers-atlanta.html (accessed July 15, 2021).

Silver-Greenberg, J. and N. Kitroeff (2018). Miscarrying at Work: The Physical Toll of Pregnancy Discrimination, *The New York Times*, October 21, 2018, https://www.nytimes.com/interactive/2018/10/21/business/pregnancy-discrimination-miscarriages.html (accessed July 15, 2021).

Sontag, S. (2004). *Regarding the Pain of Others*. London: Picador Press.

Southall, A. and N. Stewart, (2018). They Grabbed Her Baby and Arrested Her. Now Jazmine Headley Is Speaking Out. *New York Times*, December 16, 2018, https://www.nytimes.com/2018/12/16/nyregion/jazmine-headley-arrest.html (accessed July 15, 2021).

Spillers, H. J. (1987). "Mama's Baby, Papa's Maybe: An American Grammar Book," *Feminisms*, 17, 2: 384–405.

"Taylor Wessing Photographic Portrait Prize," *National Portrait Gallery*, https://www.npg.org.uk/whatson/twppp2021/exhibition/past-winners (accessed July 15, 2021).

Valentine, G. (2020). Non-Black Photographers Need to Step Aside and let Black People Tell Their Stories. It's the Most Helpful Thing They Can Do, *Insider*, June 12, 2020, https://www.insider.com/black-photographers-community-stories-george-floyd-white-media-2020-6 (accessed July 15, 2021).

Warren, C. L. (2018). *Ontological Terror: Blackness, Nihilism, and Emancipation* (Durham: Duke University Press Books.

Weber, J. (2018). Discerning Photography's White Gaze, *Hyperallergic*, November 19, 2018, https://hyperallergic.com/466560/discerning-photographys-white-gaze/ (accessed July 15, 2021).

Williams, R. K. (2016). "Toward a Theorization of Black Maternal Grief as Analytic," *Transforming Anthropology*, 24, 1: 17–30.

2 BEYOND "WELFARE QUEENS" AND "BABY MAMAS"

Low-Income Black Single Mothers' Resistance to Controlling Images

Jennifer L. Turner ⎯⎯⎯⎯⎯⎯⎯⎯⎯⎯⎯⎯⎯⎯⎯

Introduction

In her pioneering book, *Black Feminist Thought*, Patricia Hill Collins coined the term "controlling images" to refer to stereotypes about Black women used to justify and normalize their oppression. In addition to the mammy, jezebel, and bad Black-girl images, two other prominent controlling images have come to define Black womanhood in the U.S.: the welfare queen, a woman (presumably, a Black woman) who continues to have multiple children in order to collect a government check, and the baby mama, a woman (also presumably Black) whose central purpose in life is to milk her child(ren)'s father for as much money as she can get from him (Stephens and Few 2007: 52). These images have helped to portray Black mothers in the American imagination as unfit and Black motherhood as a social ill to be curtailed (Roberts 1997). As Adair (2000: xi) writes about master narratives of poor women,

> These narratives, often packaged as literature, film, photography, polit-ical sloganeering, journalism, social anecdote, and even social science, define the landscape of the national imaginary, providing a lens through which we read ourselves, the material world, and others who share that world with us. These popular and widely disseminated visions fix and juxtapose the "deserving"—white, middle class, married—against the "undeserving" poor American woman. In this way the very bodies of poor women and children are produced as sites of extreme pathology and danger, juxtaposed always against the innocence, order, and logic of the privileged.

In contemporary popular culture, internet users often reproduce controlling images (typically, through the vehicle of photography) in the form of memes, which are used to express ideas, transmit information, or as sources of comedy. Merriam-Webster (2020) defines a meme as "an amusing or interesting item (such as a captioned image or video) or genre of items that is spread widely online through social media" (n.p.). One does not have to search very hard to find memes depicting low-income Black single mothers as lazy government moochers who have multiple children simply to collect a welfare check, or memes portraying Black single mothers as "bitter baby mamas" who seek to drain their baby daddy's bank accounts by taking them to court to request child support payments. As these illustrations and memes are so widely circulated, they may have an impact on how low-income Black single mothers see themselves and their mothering.

In this essay, I place two memes in conversation with data I collected from in-depth interviews with twenty-one low-income Black single mothers in Virginia to illustrate the salience of controlling images of low-income Black single motherhood and how internet users use photography to reproduce such controlling images. I also demonstrate that while these images are powerful (and the mothers in my study recognized them as such), they also actively resisted them by evoking the Strong Black Woman schema (Watson and Hunter 2016; Watson-Singleton 2017). While this trope may have harmful implications, such as increased anxiety and depression (Belgrave and Adams 2016), it also presents a counter-narrative to the stereotypes of low-income Black single mothers, such as the welfare queen. When responding to such stereotypes, the women in this study affirm their right to be mothers and their capabilities as mothers who, despite their difficult circumstances, will do whatever it takes to take care of their children.

Background of the Study

The topic of low-income Black single motherhood is personal for me, as my mother spent a large portion of her life as a low-income Black single mother. I have witnessed her experiences with poverty and interpersonal violence, and I consider her one of the strongest and most resilient women I know. In many ways, she embodies the Strong Black Woman schema, although her experiences have shown me that strength does not necessitate a superhuman ability to always remain steadfast, even in the direst of circumstances. While studying the impacts of neoliberalism on low-income single mothers (particularly, those of color) in graduate school, I was compelled to amplify the voices of low-income Black single mothers in an effort to dismantle the racist, sexist, and classist stereotypes that have been propped up against this group in the media and in public policy for decades. Thus, I decided to interview low-income Black single mothers to understand how they see themselves as mothers and how the intersection of race, class, and gender shapes their motherhood identities and mothering activities. For my dissertation research, I interviewed twenty-one low-income Black single mothers in southwest and central Virginia. The interview excerpts presented in this paper are drawn from that study.

Between September and December 2017, I recruited participants by hanging flyers in Social Services agencies in central and southwest Virginia, reaching out to Directors of Social Services agencies and organizations that serve low-income Black single mothers and asking them to share my flyer with clients, and speaking at churches (one in southwest Virginia and one in central Virginia). After speaking at churches, I met several people who worked with the types of organizations described above who then agreed to share my recruitment flyer with their clients. In addition, the director of a food pantry located in a church in southwest Virginia agreed to allow me to recruit participants there. Each participant received a $25 gift card to a local grocery store for their time.

Photography and Controlling Images of Black Womanhood

Photographic images of Black womanhood in the West developed as oppositional to photographic images of White womanhood (Willis and Williams 2002). White women were seen as the ultimate feminine subjects, while Black women were portrayed as the antithesis of femininity. Sojourner Truth eloquently elucidates this phenomenon in her seminal "Ain't I a Woman?" speech given at the Ohio Women's Rights Convention in 1851. She proclaims:

> That man over there says that women need to be helped into carriages, and lifted over ditches, and to have the best place everywhere. Nobody ever helps me into carriages, or over mud-puddles, or gives me any best place! And ain't I a woman? Look at me! Look at my arm! I have ploughed and planted, and gathered into barns, and no man could head me! And

ain't I a woman? I could work as much and eat as much as any man—
when I could get it—and bear the lash as well! And ain't I a woman? I
have borne thirteen children, and seen most all sold off to slavery, and
when I cried out with my mother's grief, none but Jesus heard me! And
ain't I a woman? (Truth 1851, cited in Guy-Sheftall ed. 1995: 36)

Truth's words show that "the ideology of femininity did not apply to Black
women" during slavery (Davis 1971, cited in Guy-Sheftall 1995: 205).

In the U.S., the images of the asexual mammy, the jezebel, and the "bad
Black-girl" became the defining standards of Black womanhood. These images
have shaped how Black women's sexuality, reproduction, and mothering are
perceived in the American imaginary. Enslaved Black women's reproductive
bodies were only valued to the extent that they produced more slaves and
nurtured and cared for their white slave master's children, which the mammy
image illustrates (Collins 2000; Davis 1981; Roberts 1997). Black women were
not only forced to breed during slavery, they also faced a pervasive threat of
sexual and domestic violence, which caused many of them to migrate to the
Northwest (Hine 1995). Images such as the jezebel and "bad Black-girl" illustrate that Black women have been hypersexualized and thus deemed unrapea-
ble (Willis and Williams 2002; Collins 2000).

In her seminal text, *Black Feminist Thought*, Collins (2000) argues that controlling images developed as a way to maintain Black women's subordination
and the economic system of chattel slavery. As controlling Black women's
sexuality and reproduction has historically been essential to the preservation
of race, class, and gender inequality in the U.S., these images serve as a means
of depicting Black women's reproduction and motherhood as deviant and as
a social ill to be curtailed (Collins 2000; Roberts 1997). One controlling image
that does this powerfully is that of the "Black matriarch" or the Black female
head-of-household. As Collins explains:

While the mammy typifies the Black mother figure in White homes,
the matriarch symbolizes the mother figure in Black homes. Just as the
mammy represents the "good" Black mother, the matriarch symbolizes
the "bad" Black mother. Introduced and widely circulated via a government report titled The Negro Family: The Case for National Action,
the Black matriarchy thesis argued that African-American women who
failed to fulfill their traditional 'womanly' duties at home contributed
to social problems in Black civil society (Moynihan 1965: 83).

The matriarchy thesis and the resulting controlling image of the Black matri-archy thus contributed to the vilification of Black single mothers in the U.S.. During the time of Moynihan's report, women, in general, were expected to be "just dependent enough" (i.e., not too dependent, but certainly not too inde-pendent) (Fraser and Gordon 1994: 325). White women thus were characterized as too dependent, while Black women were characterized as too independent (Fraser and Gordon 1994). As welfare dependency became increasingly stig-matized in the latter half of the twentieth century and white women began transferring to "first-track" public assistance programs, such as unemploy-ment and old age insurance, single Black mothers became the face of welfare dependency (Fraser and Gordon 1994).

While the historically popular belief that families of color comprise the majority of welfare recipients is false, families of color have, for decades, been disproportionately represented on the welfare rolls. For instance, between 1985 and 1992, fifty percent of non-Hispanic Black women and thirty-six per-cent of Hispanic Black women received some form of welfare benefits (Moffitt and Gottschalk 2001). According to Fraser and Gordon (1994: 327), "The ground [for Black single mothers becoming the face of welfare dependency] was laid by a long, somewhat contradictory stream of discourse about 'the black fam-ily,' in which African-American gender and kinship relations were measured against white middle-class norms and deemed pathological". Black mothers' leadership in their families, which was largely a result of Black men's unem-ployment and under-employment due to racist discrimination in the labor market, was seen as deviant.

The "welfare queen" controlling image became popularized during the Reagan administration and appears to be linked to Black women in the United States gaining access to social welfare benefits, as prior to this, there was no need for such a stereotype (Collins 2000). As the social welfare state expanded in the U.S., African-Americans fought for and gained access to social welfare benefits that were previously denied to them (Collins 2000; Gordon 1995). In the wake of the major neoliberal economic shifts of the 1980s and 1990s, which exacerbated poverty among African-Americans in the U.S., the "welfare queen" controlling image blamed Black mothers for their own poverty, as opposed to examining the political and economic structures that perpetuated poverty in Black communities (Collins 2000). This controlling image denotes a "highly materialistic, domineering, and manless working-class Black woman" who was "content to take the hard-earned money of tax-paying Americans and remain married to the state" (Collins 2000: 88). Politicians and policymakers employed this controlling image to justify cuts to social welfare programs, including eventually reforming the social welfare system, which occurred during the Clinton administration with his signing of the 1994 Personal Responsibilities and Work Opportunity Reconciliation Act (PRWORA).

Several of my participants recognized the "welfare queen" controlling image and attempted to distance themselves from it by describing themselves as hard-working and emphasizing that they were only relying on Social Services benefits temporarily. Historically, welfare recipients have not been seen as citizens in the same way as those who do not rely on the state for social support. As Shklar (1998: 22) explains, "To be on welfare is to lose one's independence and to be treated as less than a full member of society. In effect, the people who belong to the under-class are not quite citizens." Simply put, people on welfare lack the social standing necessary to be recognized as full citizens (Shklar 1998). The rise of neoliberalism has amplified the significance of being an independent wage-earner, as being a good "neoliberal subject" is dependent upon one's ability to be self-sufficient and thus to not rely on the state for social support (Brown 2005; Weigt 2006). Given this historical context, it makes sense that my participants would try to distance themselves from the idea that they are lazy government moochers.

The "baby mama" controlling image that emerged during interviews denotes a Black mother of an "illegitimate child" "who purposely becomes pregnant so that she [can] maintain a relationship while making the biological father financially indebted to her..." (Stephens and Few 2007: 52). The notion that single Black mothers must have multiple "baby daddies" stems from controlling images that portray Black women as sexually lascivious and immoral, namely, the "jezebel, whore, or 'hoochie'" controlling images (Collins 2000: 89). The jezebel controlling image is rooted in slavery and was used to portray Black women as sexually aggressive, "thus providing a powerful rationale for the widespread sexual assaults by White men typically reported by Black slave women," as well as justifying the exploitation of Black women's bodies to produce more slaves (Collins 2000: 89). Stemming from the jezebel controlling image, the whore or hoochie controlling images also signify Black women who enjoy sex. Unlike the "good girl," the hoochie is a "bad girl" that is good in bed and that men feel content with using only for sex (Collins 2000). Like the hoochie controlling image, Black women with strong sexual appetites are often labeled "freaks." As Stephens and Few (2007: 52) note, "The Freak is a 'bad girl' who gains male attention through an overt sexual persona. She appears sexually liberated, empowered, and seeks sex solely for physical satisfaction, not for a relationship". In many ways, the baby mama controlling image is a combination of the jezebel, whore, or hoochie controlling images and the "sapphire" or "angry Black woman" controlling image. Stigma attached to being a baby mama is part of the reason why single mothers who take their children's fathers to court seeking child support payments are often berated for doing so. As my participant, Tamara, put it, they are seen as "bitter baby mamas." Internet users reproduce both the welfare queen and baby mama controlling images through memes that often circulate on social media platforms. I now turn the discussion to two such memes.

The Reproduction of Controlling Images of Low-Income Black Single Motherhood through Memes

The first meme that I focus on in this paper depicts a low-income Black single mother sitting on a bed in what appears to be a hotel room with eleven of her children and it reads: "$200 per kid? Yea, I'll have some more!" (Pinterest. com). This meme alludes to the welfare queen controlling image, as it suggests that this mother's main goal in having many children was to collect a welfare check. Angel Adams, the woman pictured in the photograph made news headlines in 2012 after police officers used a Taser on her when she was eight months pregnant, upon coming to her home to talk to one of her sons. A *Daily Mail* headline reads: "Police use stun gun on pregnant mother expecting her SIXTEENTH child after scuffle inside her own home" (Daily Mail Reporter 2012). Another headline reads, "Mom expecting 16th child tazed by police" (Wise 2012). Both of these news sources seemed to be fixated on the fact that Adams was expecting her sixteenth child. The Daily Mail article also detailed previous incidents in which Adams made news headlines explaining:

> Two years ago, the mother of 15 first made headlines when she was evicted from her apartment and had to move into a tiny motel room with 12 of her 15 children. Blaming the system for her problems, she angered people when she demanded that, 'Somebody needs to pay for all this.' After having to legally prove her fitness as a mother, Adams received the support of the Department of Children and Families and moved into a six bedroom-home big enough for her family (Daily Mail reporter 2012: n.p.).

The fact that the author focused on Adams expecting her sixteenth child and having to prove her fitness as a mother after being evicted from her apartment a couple of years earlier, rather than keeping the focus of the article on Adams being tazed by a police officer while pregnant illustrates the shame that low-income Black single mothers (especially those receiving public assistance) often endure in the public eye (Hancock 2004). Adams' past housing troubles were not relevant to the central topic of the article, so one has to wonder why those facts were even discussed in the article.

The second meme that I focus on depicts Gabrielle Union's character, Mary Jane Paul, from Black Entertainment Television's (BET) drama series, *Being Mary Jane*. In the meme, Mary Jane is pictured sitting across from her niece, Niecy, explaining to her that "Being a Baby Momma is Not a Career" (Memebaby2019.blogspot.com 2019). Similar to the welfare queen controlling image, the implication here is that some women have children by men purely to secure their own financial gain. In the show, Mary Jane plays a successful television reporter who co-hosts a morning show on a major television network. In many ways, her character represents the "Black lady" ideal, which is a respectable middle-class Black woman who uplifts the race (e.g., Michelle Obama or Oprah Winfrey) (Reid-Brinkley 2008). The baby mama controlling image contrasts with the "Black queen," who is "characterized by sexual purity, motherhood, spirituality, commitment to the uplifting of the race, and in particular the uplifting of black men" (Reid-Brinkley 2008: 247). As Reid-Brinkley (2008) notes, "The stereotypical representations of poor and working-class black women 'become texts of what not to be' for middle- and upper-class black women" (246; citing Collins 2004). Thus, Black women may aspire to fit the ideal of the "Black lady" in an attempt to achieve ideals of femininity set forth by the "cult of true womanhood" and to achieve a certain level of respectability (Reid-Brinkley 2008).

For Black women, achieving the ideals of respectability politics has historically been a form of resistance to stereotypes about their sexual deviance and a means of protecting themselves against state-sanctioned sexual abuse, particularly at the hands of white men in the South (Gaines 1996; Reid-Brinkley 2008). Whites justified abuse against Black women by portraying them as immoral and sexually lascivious, thus suggesting that it was impossible to rape Black women, as their bodies were always available to men (both white and Black) whether they consented to sex or not (Reid-Brinkley 2008). Therefore, staking a claim to the virtues of femininity that traditionally were only reserved for white, middle-class women was Black women's way of attempting to "gain patriarchal protection" (245). To this day, ideals of white, middle-class femininity are the standards by which Black people judge Black women's behavior (Reid-Brinkley 2008).

Beyond Welfare Queens and Baby Mamas

As the memes discussed above illustrate, the welfare queen and baby mama controlling images have become symbols of pathology. Memes such as these are simultaneously meant to shame those who fit into those categories and draw a distinction between good citizens and bad ones. During interviews with participants, it became evident that such controlling images of low-income Black single motherhood largely shaped how they think of themselves as mothers, or their motherhood identity. Throughout the interviews, participants often referenced stereotypes about Black single mothers, especially those who receive public assistance. The "welfare queen" stereotype was especially prevalent. While they recognized racist and sexist stereotypes about Black single mothers, they also actively resisted them. When asked what it means to her to be a Black mother, Kenya, a 29 year-old mother of two explained:

> Stereotype a little bit, 'cause they think...I don't know...It's just some things you read, or you hear people say, they think Black moms just sit around and wait for the government to take care of them, and that is not the case...I mean, I've had my share of sitting down, but it's because I was always, you know...him and my middle son, they're behind each other, he's six and he's five. He was still crawling and I was pregnant with him, and then when he came, they were still both in diapers...I couldn't work, you know, so of course I've had to wait on food stamps and Medicaid and TANF, but once I was able, I got up...got out and worked, but...they just think that Black people are just lazy and that's far from the case, I'm far from lazy. I work so much overtime and I will work.

When asked who "they" were, she added:

> Government, the rich people, people like Donald Trump...I mean, white people. They're always saying, "we paying our taxes for them to just sit on their tail" while I work my tail off, and you know, just crazy stuff. And they don't know the people's situations. And in some cases, it is

true, some people are lazy and don't want to work. But other people, they have kids with disabilities, or they're disabled, or it's different...50 million situations...why a person may not be able to work, you know. But I feel if you're able to work, get up and work.

Kayla, a 29-year-old mother of three, began our interview with a statement about stereotypes of low-income Black single mothers receiving public assistance:

There's a great misconception about people who receive benefits, especially us, in that a lot of us are just uneducated people who just lay around having babies and just sitting on our butt being lazy. And that's the furthest from the truth. That's why I wanted to sign up for this [interview], just to speak on that because I work so hard, and to be defined by a stereotype, it can be very, I guess you could say hurtful. Some people are not sensitive. They see a lot of what's on social media or the Internet, but not the real thing. Not everybody should be categorized in that way. As I said, I did graduate from college with honors. And it took a lot for me to just push through it and do that. I did have help with childcare through Social Services. My main goal in life is to not have to be dependent on government or any programs. But we're using it as a stepping stone right now because it is needed. Not using the system, or taking advantage, or anything.

Both Kenya and Kayla attempt to dismantle the "welfare queen" stereotype. Like Kenya, Kayla immediately distances herself from the stereotype that low-income Black single mothers are lazy and uneducated by emphasizing that she works very hard and that she graduated from college with honors. Explaining that she is simply using Social Services benefits as a stepping stone reinforces the narrative that public assistance benefits should only serve as a temporary fix for recipients, rather than a source of long-term support. It is also indicative of the fact that, in the U.S., being a good citizen-subject is largely determined by one's employment status. Working is a means by which individuals demonstrate their self-sufficiency; therefore, if one does not work, they are not independent, and are thus met with disdain.

The "welfare queen" controlling image is pervasive in U.S. culture, as the memes discussed earlier illustrate. Politicians and policymakers also employ this controlling image to justify cuts to public assistance benefits and programs. Some of my participants discussed being blatantly stereotyped while they were out in public. Kayla described an experience of micro-level racism and classism in which people in the grocery store were making disparaging remarks about her because she was using her Electronic Benefits Transfer (EBT) card:

> If I'm in the grocery store using my food stamp card, and it's happened before. I would hear people or see people looking, saying little comments about how they can't get it. But I don't say anything, because it's bigger than just me. People don't see the real picture, that you have to be humble to even go and ask for this type of help. And there was a time, that was me. I would judge and say, oh, they got money to get their hair and nails done, and stuff like that, but here I am working hard, and whatever's coming out my check for taxes, whatever, is paying for their stuff. I was very judgmental, until I had to end up doing it myself. And now I see, okay, not everybody is abusing the system like that...and it is hurtful. But like I said, I don't hold it in my heart. Because people, if they don't know, and they're just being ignorant based off of what's on the Internet or what they see...

The above passage from Kayla illustrates the power of the welfare queen stereotype. It is so powerful that even she believed it until she started receiving Social Services benefits herself. Part of the power of the welfare queen stereotype stems from the fact that it stands in stark contrast to the cultural and political mandate to be a hard-working, tax-paying American citizen. It also runs counter to the American myth of meritocracy or the bootstrap myth, which suggests that if one works hard, they will be able to succeed. These myths systematically mask structural racism and classism, blaming victims of racism and classism (e.g., low-income Black single mothers) for their own predicament.

Similar to Kenya and Kayla, Leslie, a 27-year-old mother of four, also alludes to the welfare queen stereotype, specifically, the idea that because she is a single Black mother with multiple children, she cannot possibly be making ends meet without receiving public assistance:

> I feel like the way I'm viewed is the main thing that has to do with my race though, more than anything. I feel like a lot of times when I go somewhere, because all my kids are small, I get looked at. I've had

people make comments like they wonder how many baby daddies I have. That's one thing. I hate that word...like, "Do they all have the same dad?" I mean people are just very blunt about things they may ask. They may assume that I have multiple, that each one of mine is a different father, or assume that I have section 8. I've had that comment made about me to my son's father, some of his friends would make comments to him like, "Oh," there was rumors going around that I was on Section 8 and all this stuff, and I make $40,000 a year, you know, they just assume because I'm a young Black woman with a bunch of kids that that just must be how I'm surviving...or I've had...when I go to the grocery store and I have a cart full of food, it's automatically assumed you have EBT. I've been asked that before.

The assumption that Leslie must be on public assistance is rooted in the notion that single Black mothers with multiple children are lazy and enjoy "mooching" off the government. Another stereotype that Leslie alludes to is that of the "baby mama."

Tamara, a 26-year-old mother of one, discussed how Black mothers are often portrayed as "bitter baby mamas" on social media. When asked what it means to her to be a Black mother, she responded:

That the world's already against us, like I—read posts where like black women is this, black mothers is bitter baby mamas, and all [that] stuff, but honestly...you'd be bitter too, like not saying that all chicks is bitter, but it's like the perception they put out of us like we're bitter...You see it everywhere, like even when I was talking to my friend and he was like, 'Oh, because you put your ex-husband on child support, you bitter.' It was like, just because I put him on child support--and me and him broke up last year in May, and I had to put him on child support this May for him to actually give me money, that's not being bitter. I gave you a whole year to take care of your son and you didn't, so now I'm gonna make the government make you take care of your son...

Tamara's discussion of the posts she has seen calling Black mothers "bitter baby mamas" and her friend's comment accusing her of being bitter because she took her ex-husband to court to make him pay child support are symptomatic of the baby mama controlling image, as the idea behind such statements and accusations is that Black mothers take their children's fathers to court to pay child support out of spite, rather than so that they will own up to their responsibility of taking care of their children. The notion that baby mamas get pregnant in part to get money from their children's fathers suggests that they are "Gold Diggers," or women who trade sex for economic and material gain (Stephens and Few 2007). It is also important to note the accusatory phrasing of "putting" one's child's father on child support, which effectively demonizes the mother and disregards the father's responsibility to take care of his children. Obviously, if a father is already taking care of his children, a mother need not take him to court; however, in Tamara's case and that of most of my participants, their children's fathers are unfortunately not taking responsibility for helping to care for their children.

The Strong Black Woman Schema as Resistance

During interviews with my participants, the Strong Black Woman (SBW) Schema emerged as a potential means of resistance to controlling images of low-income Black single mothers. According to Watson-Singleton (2017), the Strong Black Woman Schema refers to "the culturally specific and multidimensional construct internalized by African American women to overcome oppression (e.g., racism, sexism). SBW encompasses both cognitive characteristics and stress-coping behaviors, like emotional suppression, self-reliance, and caregiving" (Watson-Singleton 2017: 779). While SBW appears to have positive connotations, it may have negative consequences for Black women's mental and physical health, as it perpetuates the idea that Black women are superhuman and thus it encourages them to suppress their emotions and to forego self-care practices (Belgrave and Abrams 2016).

When referencing what it meant to them to be a Black mother and/or how their race impacts the way they think of themselves as mothers, participants often referenced this schema by suggesting that Black women (particularly Black mothers) have a special ability to overcome even the grimmest of circumstances and to succeed despite facing many obstacles/barriers. Thus, for them, the Strong Black Woman Schema may serve as a means to affirm themselves as Black mothers. For instance, when asked what it means to her to be a Black mother, Jenise, a 28-year-old mother of three, replied, "Strong... there's many times where you know, I struggled...I was stressed and...one thing I can say for sure, even with the women in my family, my mother...we know how to make a way out of no way..." The notion that Black women have the ability to "make a way out of no way" is a common sentiment in the Black community, stemming from dominant narratives of Black women's "superhuman strength," which emerged during slavery and were used to justify Black women's enslavement (Watson-Singleton 2017).

Similar to Jenise, when asked how she feels her race impacts how she thinks of herself as a mother, Tamara replied:

> They put us down, but somehow, we succeed every day...So, [to] me being a Black mother in America is very hard, but somehow, we make it...Our kids still succeed...we're still able to get the education, and still able to strive without [the] other parent in the house...Black mothers is very...like, through everything, Black mothers survive...They always make a way for their kids...most of them...

Tamara makes reference to the structural inequalities that exist for Black single mothers in the U.S., which create barriers to getting an education and simply making ends meet, especially without a partner. She also mentions the unfortunate realities of racism, which Black single mothers in the U.S. must navigate. Despite all of this, she explains, Black mothers "survive" and "always make a way for their kids."

For Pamela, a 38-year-old mother of two, witnessing her own mother survive tough circumstances taught her how to do the same. When asked what it means to her to be a Black mother, she explained:

> ...Sometimes, it's a challenge. I don't let it get me discouraged because... like I said, I always keep pushing for it 'cause I gotta survive, and my mom was a single parent until she got married, so, me looking at that kind of gave me a better feel of how to survive...She had to work. She always had to work. And I was the oldest, so I always had to take care of my brothers.

Survival is key to the historical legacy of Black mothers in the U.S., as they have had to endure many hardships, including racism, sexism, and caregiving. Thus, embracing SBW may help Black women develop strategies to endure these hardships (Watson and Hunter 2016).

SBW perpetuates the notion that it is not okay for Black women to show any weakness. When asked what it means to her to be a mother to Black children, Pamela explained:

I guess it shows...[strength]. You don't want to let them see too much weakness, but then sometimes you have to because they gotta understand everything is not going to be [inaudible]...when my son got older, I could explain that to him because he was mature enough to understand what I was talking about.

Pamela's statement that "you don't want to let them see too much weakness" reveals some of the potential harmful effects of SBW as it creates a culture of silence around the emotional and mental health issues that Black women (particularly Black single mothers) may be facing (Belgrave and Abrams 2016).

Some participants mentioned being raised or largely influenced by the strong Black women in their lives. For instance, Briana, a 36-year-old mother of two was raised by her grandmother, who she identified as a "strong Black woman":

What I had was a strong Black woman and that she was a grandmother...I know my grandmother never...let us see her sweat and never let us see that she maybe didn't have [enough] for a bill. We never seen none of those problems...never seen her [say], 'Oh my goodness. How am I going to pay these light bills and still get food?' 'cause she raised five of us without my mother or my brothers' and sisters' father. Now, I know she had assistance, never knew that she had assistance, just knew that my grandmother got up every day, cook and clean, would see us off to school, and if she's not in the house when we coming home from school, she's meeting us and always had food, like I said, always cleaned, always made a way. To me, that's a strong Black woman because you don't see them sweat...So, it's like she knew how to stand up. She knew how to hold her head up high, didn't know what this world had to offer, but she still did it and that's what, like I said, the type of person that I am now. So through all of it, that was a strong Black woman, you know, made it to, like I said, it was four or five of us in the house. My brother played basketball, I danced, my sister always stayed in trouble, but she was always at the basketball games, always at a dance recital, always there for when my sister got in trouble. It wasn't 'Oh, because you acting up, I'm not going to be there.' Or, 'I'm just too tired 'cause I just did a double and my back hurt and I didn't get my back brace 'cause Medicaid didn't send it or I didn't have the money.' She was there. You seen her. So, that's what I mean by a strong Black woman. That was like my superwoman.

Like Pamela, Briana's idea of a strong Black woman is one who never lets anyone see them "sweat," which most likely means being silent about the burdens they are carrying and the pain they may be experiencing. Briana may never have heard her grandmother complain about bills or medical issues, but that does not necessarily mean that her grandmother did not have trouble with those things. Black women, in particular, often feel pressured to fit the mold of "superwoman," or the woman who somehow has a superhuman ability to effortlessly juggle many responsibilities, including working, raising children, and in the case of Briana's grandmother, raising grandchildren (Belgrave and Abrams 2016; Watson-Singleton 2017; Watson and Hunter 2016). It is clear that for Briana, Pamela, and others, their ideas of what it means to be a good Black mother are shaped largely by the mothering experiences of their own mothers and grandmothers. Although Briana suffers from a chronic illness, she still feels the pressure to be a "superhero" for her children:

> I always told myself that I am my kids superhero 'cause they see me every day, so I have to...I'm not gonna be able to [not do] that, but I have to be strong, I have to be that person that can do, like Superman or Spider-Man, that can do everything at once, even though I'm not built for it, but I have to do it.

Societal pressure to be a Strong Black Woman was so robust for Briana that she felt she had to "do everything at once," despite being chronically ill.

Conclusion

Controlling images of low-income Black single motherhood have permeated U.S. popular culture throughout history. Some of the most salient include the welfare queen and the baby mama. Photography is a prominent medium through which these images have been perpetuated. These images are so omnipresent that they are frequently reproduced in the form of internet memes, often using lens-based mediums. In this essay, I used a meme portraying the welfare queen controlling image and another portraying the baby mama controlling image to illustrate the prominence of these images and elucidate how internet users employ photography to perpetuate stereotypes about low-income Black single mothers. It is difficult to determine the identities of the individuals who create such memes (let alone their racial/ethnic identities);

however, it is clear that the purpose of such memes is to draw a distinction between whiteness/white people as inherently good, worthy, hard-working, and deserving, and blackness as bad, criminal, lazy, and undeserving. Beech (2017: 133) argues that the "circulators" of such memes "participate in varying degrees of explicit to implicit rhetorics of whiteness". Whites do this by employing "a rhetoric of innocence (be it with respect to discussions of affirmative action or other situations in which they perceive they are being taken advantage of)" while also evoking "a sense of black abstraction and an implied sense of blacks as the defilers of white innocence" (134).

In addition to memes, I drew on interviews with low-income Black single mothers to demonstrate that although they recognize these controlling images, they also actively resist them, which sometimes manifests itself in the form of them employing the Strong Black Woman schema as a means of affirming their identities as mothers. The women in this study alluded to stereotypes of low-income Black single mothers as welfare queens or "bitter baby mamas," but distanced themselves from these images by emphasizing how hard they work to provide and care for their children and asserting their right to receive state support and/or support from their children's fathers. Despite the often negative portrayals of low-income Black single mothers on social media, these mothers largely associated Black motherhood with strength, resilience, and tenacity.

Positive Counter-narratives
Artists have also used photography to provide a counter-narrative to the images mentioned above. For instance, photographers such as Beuford Smith, Renee Cox, Nona Faustine, and Carrie Mae Weems have used photographic mediums to provide a multidimensional portrayal of Black mothers and Black families[1]. In addition, Black women have begun embracing a movement towards radical self-care through podcasts and online and social media platforms such as *Girl Trek*, *Therapy for Black Girls*, and *Mater Mea*. Radical self-care helps Black women process the mental and emotional impacts of racism, sexism, heterosexism, and classism. Black feminist theorist Audre Lorde famously wrote that self-care is an "act of political warfare" (Lorde 1988). For Black women, "Self-care is 'an act of political warfare' not only because the personal is indeed political, but because when Black women take care of themselves, they challenge the myth of the superwoman (Michele Wallace) and simultaneously challenge structures of oppression that praise Black women for being the perpetual 'mules of the world' (Zora Neale Hurston)" (Brooks-Tatum 2012: n.p.).

Notes

1 See Beuford Smith's famous "Woman Bathing/Madonna" photograph, Renee Cox's "Yo Mama" series, Nona Faustine's "Mitochondria" series, and Carrie Mae Weems' "Family Pictures and Stories" series.

Works cited

Adair, V. (2000). *From Good Ma to Welfare Queen: A Genealogy of the Poor Woman in American Literature, Photography, and Culture.* New York: Garland.

Beech, J. (2017). "Facebook and Absent-Present Rhetorics of Whiteness." In *Rhetorics of Whiteness: Postracial Hauntings in Popular Culture, Social Media, and Education,* edited by Lilia D. Monzó and Peter McLaren, 132–144. Carbondale, IL: Southern Illinois University Press.

Belgrave, F. Z. and J. A. Abrams. (2016). "Reducing Disparities and Achieving Equity in African American Women's Health." *American Psychologist* 71(8): 723–33.

Brooks, T. (2012). "Subversive Self-Care: Centering Black Women's Wellness." *Feminist Wire,* Retrieved June 29, 2020 (https://thefeministwire.com/2012/11/subversive-self-care-centering-black-womens-wellness/).

Brown, W. (2005). "Neoliberalism and the End of Liberal Democracy." In *Edgework: Critical Essays in Knowledge and Politics,* 37–59. Princeton, NJ: Princeton University Press.

Collins, P. H. (2000). *Black Feminist Thought: Knowledge, Consciousness, and the Politics of Empowerment.* New York: Routledge.

Daily Mail Reporter (2012). "Police use stun gun on pregnant mother expecting her SIXTEENTH child after scuffle inside her home." *DailyMail.com,* Retrieved January 27, 2020 (https://www.dailymail.co.uk/news/article-2141464/Police-use-stun-gun-pregnant-mother-expecting-SIXTEENTH-child-scuffle-inside-home.html).

Davis, A. (1971). "Reflections on the Black Woman's Role in the Community of Slaves." In *Words of Fire: An Anthology of African American Feminist Thought,* edited by Beverly Guy-Sheftall, 200–18. New York, NY: New Press.

Davis, A. (1981). *Women, Race, and Class.* New York, NY: Vintage Books.

Fraser, N. and L. Gordon. (1994). "A Genealogy of Dependency: Tracing a Keyword of the U.S. Welfare State." *Signs* 19(2): 309–336.

Gaines, K. K. (1996). *Uplifting the Race: Black Leadership, Politics, and Culture in the Twentieth Century.* Chapel Hill: University of North Carolina Press.

Gordon, L. (1995). *Pitied but Not Entitled: Single Mothers and the History of Welfare; 1890-1935.* Cambridge, MA: Harvard Univ. Press.

Hancock, A-M. (2004). *The Politics of Disgust: the Public Identity of the Welfare Queen.* New York, NY: New York University Press.

Hine, D. C. (1995). "Rape and the Inner-Lives of Black Women in the Middle West: Preliminary Thoughts on the Culture of Dissemblance." In *Words of Fire: An Anthology of African American Feminist Thought,* edited by Beverly Guy-Sheftall, 380–395. New York, NY: New Press.

Lorde, A. (1988). *A Burst of Light: and Other Essays.* Mineola, NY: Ixia Press.

Memebaby2019.blogspot.com. 2019. "Baby Momma Memes." Retrieved January 4, 2019 (https://memebaby2019.blogspot.com/2018/01/baby-momma-memes.html).

Merriam-Webster. (2020). "meme." Retrieved January 27, 2020 (https://www.merriam-webster.com/dictionary/meme).

Moffitt, R. A. and P. T. Gottschalk. (2001). "Racial and Ethnic Differences in Welfare Receipt in the United States." In *America Becoming: Racial Trends and Their Consequences: Volume II*, edited by Neil J. Smelser, William Julius Wilson, and Faith Mitchell, 152–173. Washington, D.C.: The National Research Council.

Moynihan, D. P. (1965). *The Negro Family: The Case for National Action*. Washington, D.C.: Government Printing Office.

Pinterest.com. (2020). Retrieved January 27, 2020 (https://www.pinterest.com.mx/pin/426786502165925070/).

Reid-Brinkley, S. R. (2008). "The Essence of Res(ex)pectability: Black Women's Negotiation of Black Femininity in Rap Music and Music Video." *Meridians* 8(1): 236–260.

Roberts, D. (1997). *Killing the Black Body: Race, Reproduction, and the Meaning of Liberty*. New York, NY: Pantheon.

Shklar, J. (1998). *American Citizenship: The Quest for Inclusion*. Cambridge: Harvard University Press.

Stephens, D. P. and A. L. Few. (2007). "Hip Hop Honey or Video Ho: African American Preadolescents' Understanding of Female Sexual Scripts in Hip Hop Culture." *Sexuality & Culture* 11(4): 48–69.

Truth, S. (1851). "Woman's Rights." In *Words of Fire: An Anthology of African American Feminist Thought*, edited by B. Guy-Sheftall, 36. New York, NY: The New Press.

Tyree, T. (2009). "Lovin' Momma and Hatin' on Baby Mama: A Comparison of Misogynistic and Stereotypical Representations in Songs About Rappers' Mothers and Baby Mamas." *Women and Language* 32(2): 50–58.

Watson, N. N. and C. D. Hunter. (2016). "'I Had to Be Strong': Tensions in the Strong Black Woman Schema." *Journal of Black Psychology* 42(5): 424-52.

Watson-Singleton, N. N. (2017). "Strong Black Woman Schema and Psychological Distress: The Mediating Role of Perceived Emotional Support." *Journal of Black Psychology* 43(8): 778–88.

Weigt, J. (2006). "Compromises to Carework: The Social Organization of Mothers' Experiences in the Low-Wage Labor Market after Welfare Reform." *Social Problems* 53(3): 332–351.

Willis, D. and C. Williams. (2002). *The Black Female Body: A Photographic History*. Philadelphia, PA: Temple University Press.

Wise, S. (2012). "Mom expecting 16th child tazed by police." *6 News Richmond*, Retrieved January 27, 2020 (https://wtvr.com/2012/05/08/mom-expecting-16th-child-tazed-by-police/).

3 BLACK MOTHERHOOD ONLINE: A REIMAGINED REPRESENTATION

A Conversation with Tomi Akitunde

KELLIE CARTER JACKSON ⎯⎯⎯⎯⎯⎯⎯⎯⎯⎯⎯⎯⎯⎯⎯⎯

In January 2020 Kellie Carter Jackson, historian, author, educator sat in conversation with Tomi Akitunde, co-founder and editor-in-chief of *mater mea* a blog and podcast series dedicated to helping Black moms get answers to their motherhood, life, and career questions.

KELLIE CARTER JACKSON: I thought we could start with the first question, which is, the idea of how you use imagery on your blog. It's so rich and vibrant and it really shows all aspects of motherhood, like Black mothers just doing really benign things such as kissing their kids, hugging their kids, playing with them, just mothering, which is something that seems so natural, but yet it's also something that's never really captured. We don't often see mothers, Black mothers in particular, just kissing their kids or tickling their kids. Can you talk about your decision to use photography to capture Black motherhood that way and how you curated these images?

TOMI AKITUNDE: Having imagery was really important because this site started in 2012 and this was before the rise of personal brands and digital cameras being super ubiquitous as they are now. To your point, there wasn't a place you could go to see Black women existing outside of celebrity, or stereotype. So seeing that gap, knowing that, Black women and motherhood isn't synonymous with whiteness, it was really important to back it up with imagery because words can only do so much. The imagery around Black motherhood is often left to the imagination and the imagination is often informed by stereotypes and biases. There's the welfare mom, the welfare queen, the strong Black mom who has to work so much because of absentee fathers, and their kids are left to run the streets amuck and they're a drain on taxpayers and they become super predators. The imagery around Black motherhood was steeped in toxic stereotypes that were reinforced through imagery. So it was important to use that same kind of technology, to present a more holistic image of what it is to be a Black mother.

CARTER JACKSON: Can you talk about how the platform started and has evolved over time. Is it still what you envisioned it to be or have you had to change it or edit it to meet the needs or the desires of your subscribers?

AKITUNDE: That's a great question. I'm from a print background. I love magazines. I devoured them when I was a kid. So I was just super into the idea of having an online magazine with big glossy images and my writing telling the stories of successful Black women. I just wanted a magazine kind of feel. And then I started hearing that readers were not identifying with the women I was writing about. And I was annoyed. What do you mean you don't identify with these women? They're amazing! They're us! I was sensitive about that. Were people just saying that because the photography was beautiful or was it that these women were inaccessible because of the choice of images or representation? Did my readers feel different from them? Somehow my approach created a distance that wasn't intentional. Then I started realizing that I was doing the same thing as a mainstream publication such as *Cosmo* or, a *Vogue*. They choose to only highlight the success when they choose who to profile. In *mater mea*, the moms featured are very upfront about the difficulties they had to go through to get to the position that they're in. When they've come on my radar, I want it to be true. But the whole package was, this is a successful Black woman. And if you're someone who doesn't feel like you're there yet, it can feel isolating or it can feel [like] another thing that you're not living up to. So with that in mind, I didn't think of it as a Black motherhood website. I thought of it as a Black professional website focused on the work-life balance of women because that was a big conversation at the time—everyone was talking about leaning in and asking if women could have it all. The conversation asked how career and motherhood were positioned as counter to each other. So I definitely wanted to include photos of Black women doing both. But if you were to ask me, is this a parenting website, I would have said, no, it's a Black professional women website and the women are mothers.

On the evolution of *mater mea*, around 2014, people started asking me questions about unmedicated home births, but I didn't see Black women doing that. As in—is this something that we're doing? And if it's not, how do I go about finding a midwife? I'm a journalist by trade and passion and training.

I've never had a water birth at home, but I know I can find the people who have—specifically Black people. I wanted to speak to Black experts about these things. To answer that question for my readers. Or how do I talk to my child about race without creating a chip on their shoulder? There was one letter that I got from someone who was a single mom. I think she was 24 at the time. She was in LA renting a bedroom and bathroom from an "All Lives Matter" person with her two-year-old, constantly crying, her motherhood constantly being judged, making too much to qualify for government assistance, but not enough to survive and thrive. I've never been in that position. But again, I trust my ability to do research for my readers because I don't have that pressure of, you know, having to live your life and mother and go to work the way that she does. So while I would hear—these profiles were cute—I have real questions I need help with. I transitioned the website in 2014 to be more of a traditional blog and that at first, looked like more lifestyle type content.

But my interests tend to go to the more serious, [such as] how can I have a home birth or why is maternal mortality the way it is for Black women or a myriad of issues. So my hope now is that *mater mea* is one of the first things that pops up if you, if you're a Black mom Googling about a particular question that you have. I want modern *mater mea* to be a physical and online community space. So there's an opportunity for mommy groups plus it's not just let's all be cute with their kids, but, let's fortify ourselves through community while our kids meet and have friendships. I was really wishing I had a space to have conversations like this with women in my community. Or for those who felt they did not have a community of Black moms but wished there was an opportunity to have these conversations. So I was really hesitant because doing events is very, very hard, especially in New York, to try to find spaces. It was very important for me to have my events be child friendly too.

CARTER JACKSON: Which do you think has been the most effective tool of bringing women and mothers together? The in-person events? The blog itself? Is it the podcast interviews? What do you think women have responded to most positively?

AKITUNDE: The in-person events have been very stirring and moving. I decided in 2019 to create an event series called *mother work* and it was inspired by an academic reading of Toni Morrison's thoughts about Black motherhood and how it's political. It was how the work that you do as a mother spans beyond vanity, I'm raising my child to be a good human being. It's like I'm raising my child to be a part of a movement, to uplift the Black experience. It's a political endeavor being a Black mother.

I really wanted the programming to be actionable, educational and inspirational. And I wanted to make sure that you left knowing that there were Black women who you could reach out to for support as a community member, but then also as experts. For example, the first event was in February, so I was like, "Oh, Valentine's Day. Oh, sex and intimacy." Let's have a conversation about motherhood and sex because mothers aren't allowed to be sexual beings themselves. They're not allowed to desire themselves. It's always in response to a very heteronormative viewpoint. We're always in relation to how the man views you and how desirable you are to a man. So even a MILF is a male construct. I curated a panel with a Black woman sex therapist whose work was rooted in trauma because for a lot of people, sex is traumatic. We also had a Black woman who is a pleasure strategist, which I didn't even know was a job title. And so I met her and yes, it was amazing! Pleasure isn't just sexual pleasure, it's enjoyment of your body and the things that bring you joy. That's a type of pleasure that should be tapped into more. So, the structure of a mother work event is—a traditional Q&A panel, Q&A conversation.

And then we break out into workshops where each of the panelists does a deeper dive into a topic that's related to the broader topic that they're an expert in. Following this, there is a sister circle where we all talk about how we're feeling and what we want to share and ask of the community that's built here. With childcare included, the kids hang out with everybody until they kick us out of the space.

I was contacted by a woman who wanted to know if these events were only for mothers. She described herself as a mother to an angel baby which meant she had lost her baby to miscarriage. She's lost a child, but she is still a mother to that child and so the language made her feel like she might not be welcome. I responded that she is completely welcome, free to come. She said she felt like she could really get something out of it.

CARTER JACKSON: I appreciate you discussing this in your work. There's never really a space to talk about infertility or to talk about miscarriage or to talk about these issues that are intensely private and personal. You use so much imagery but there is no imagery to encapsulate a woman having a miscarriage or a woman going through infertility or a woman going through fertility treatments or things of that nature. It's not glamorous like a mother nursing her child, right? It's not the kind of photo optics that the public really wants to see, but at the same time, being able to see those things or at least talk about those things are so empowering, especially for people who need to be able to air that out and find strength within the community.

AKITUNDE: I do realize the power of images can also make people feel bad. I can feel that way just scrolling through my Instagram account, seeing influencers who are traveling nonstop or people who look like they have more money than me. I didn't make that connection until there were things that popped up in my journey to become a mom.

I wasn't thinking about becoming a mom the way I am now and so when the doctor told me that I wouldn't be able to have a vaginal delivery, I thought, okay, I don't want a vaginal delivery anyway because that's painful. But the more research I did about C-sections, the more I started identifying with the desire to have an unmedicated home birth. At that time, I noticed I was really upset by a lot of the imagery—people sharing their delivery stories with a picture of them with a baby fresh out of the womb. All of it—even baby announcements and sonograms and if you're dealing with infertility, those images hurt. But at the same time, I have only seen imagery around infertility and pictures of the needles, HCG strips, the oscillation sticks of the pregnancy—the multiple pregnancy tasks—it's rooted in the pain. There's a well known photograph of an infant surrounded by needles in a heart shape—is that the image of this story? There isn't a visual language around it yet.

CARTER JACKSON: We have not seen many images of Black women in their infertility. What we do see are stereotypes in plenty—Black women having a lot of children or Black women having too many children but rarely Black women struggling with fertility. I should say the most public example has probably been Gabrielle Union and her openness and vulnerability to talk about her miscarriages and her struggle and even her surrogacy on the path to becoming a mother.

That is a gap. What other gaps did you want to fill?

AKITUNDE: I was and still am interested in the question—do we believe we women can have it all? Since Black women weren't being asked about that question in the Atlantic or the New York Times or, these big mainstream publications, I wanted to hear what Black women had to say about that. I was trying to make something happen that was never meant for us. I just stopped asking the can women have it all question and I stopped calling it work-life balance, it just doesn't exist.

Those concerns are real for us, but not the way that, you know, the mainstream media I was considering was trying to frame it for all of us. I'm trying, I make it very, very clear that *mater mea* is for Black women. I've been trying to reach out to Black publications, to have a space on their platform to tell motherhood stories and they're like the gatekeepers of those publications and those outlets won't let me in.

CARTER JACKSON: Can you tell me about an image or a story that has really inspired you the most about Black motherhood?

AKITUNDE: All the images that I've seen around Black motherhood are so moving and so stirring to me.

CARTER JACKSON: I always say that Black people are America's foremost historians on race and racism. The stories about Black people have been informed through imagery. They've been informed by caricatures, the big lips, kinky hair and watermelon. And then when photography was invented, minstrelsy and, those kinds of images, right up to lynching. Photography, like everything, was rooted in our pain. And even when you see these vintage photos of Black families, the pain is still there, the pain of their circumstances is still there. Then you have the poverty porn epidemic in the eighties and nineties, and this period where we don't need ABC news or CNN to tell us our story. We're telling our story and joy, finding joy in our stories and in the photos that we're creating and sharing it just as it is, it's really beautiful to see.

I read an interview with Beyonce where she was talking transparently about her motherhood and what she wants her legacy to be for her kids. Beyonce is talking to Black women and Black moms in particular at this point in her career. She discussed how careful she is around crafting images around Black motherhood and how intentional she was about positioning herself in a Madonna type figure. That's an image that has been excluded to Black women. When you think of a Madonna figure, she's a white woman.

One of my favorite pictures is just me and my mom and I think I was probably two years old and I'm eating corn on the cob. We were at a park, with my mom's side of the family, her family reunion. We were laying on a blanket and my mom's sitting on the blanket and I'm laying in her lap eating corn on the cob. There's nothing special about that picture. You know, my mom's not wearing some glamorous dress, just a typical sundress. I've got corn all over my face, but it's the quintessential summer park with your family chilling, barbecuing, you know? I just remember or I can imagine how safe I would have felt being on that blanket laying there in between my mother's legs eating corn on the cob. It's not anything, it's so benign, almost forgettable.

Are there images that you have of you and your mom that inspire that same kind of simple joy where it's not necessarily like your graduation or birthday or wedding, rather a basic everyday encounter?

AKITUNDE: I love that question because I, I don't. I have a recent picture that I took of my mom when she was visiting me and my husband in New York. And there are pictures I love because we look like each other and it was something that she didn't see—the resemblance. And it's someone who felt very ugly and thought their mom was beautiful, it felt like a denial of any beauty in me when I was growing up. But I see in a picture that we do look alike, that we have the same cheeks and the same smile and we're really happy to be with each other. And we're friends. After years of, "I'm not one of your little friends," I am your parent. This feels good.

CARTER JACKSON: Every Black mom says that it's like a right of passage. "I'm not your friend."

AKITUNDE: Second is a picture that I recently found, where she's very young looking, in her thirties, and she's wearing a very pretty dress and I'm sitting in her lap. I feel like I've always worn glasses as if I came out of the womb with glasses. But I did not and it was a picture of me without glasses.

So that's a strange thing to see and I'm in her lap. You could tell that I'm happy. She's engaging in conversation probably with somebody else off to the side. But I just look very, very happy to be there.

CARTER JACKSON: You mentioned earlier how we see these very glossy like *Cosmo* magazine images of celebrities and parents mothering, and what it means for people like Beyonce and Serena Williams, and Alison Felix to talk about the fact that, "[Felix] was the fastest runner in the world and got dropped from my contract" or Williams to disclose, "I am the greatest tennis player ever, and my doctor almost killed me." I'm being flippant, but essentially these incredible women still faced incredible hardship despite their success and as a result of their motherhood. The paradox or the dichotomy between the beautiful Black mother with the fan blowing her hair versus how they're actually experiencing their motherhood gets underplayed.

AKITUNDE: And if it's happening to Serena Williams then it's definitely happening to others. As for representation, I want to figure out how to find some kind of balance. Black motherhood isn't drudgery. I think trends are negative because that's what people expect. But there's a lot of joy.

CARTER JACKSON: I feel like the dominant image that I have seen in the media via Black Lives Matter is the mourning Black mother, right? The mother who has had her son or daughter gunned down by the police and then that mother becomes the poster child for all things Black Lives Matter. But we never get to see those moms, unfortunately as just moms. Right? They're always grieving, We never get to see them parent, or be with their child in a very regular way. And so it takes away this ability to see Black motherhood outside of a space that's not grief, loss or even to see motherhood outside of a movement.

I think that's so troubling to me that I can't see Black motherhood untethered from white supremacy. I appreciate that on *mater mea* the first image that pops up on the screen is a mother playing with her toddler. And another of a kid resting on their mother's lap. It's just very simple—playing on the floor with your kid is something that needs to be seen. This is powerful and we just don't have enough of it to be honest.

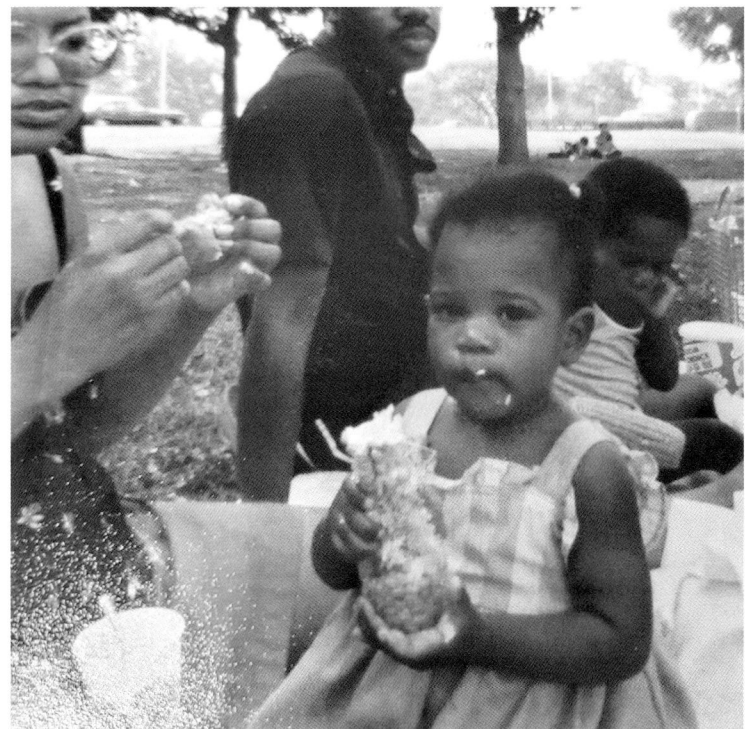

From the personal collection of Kellie Carter Jackson, Kellie, age 14 months with her mother, July 1983 at the Price Family Reunion, just outside of Detroit, Michigan

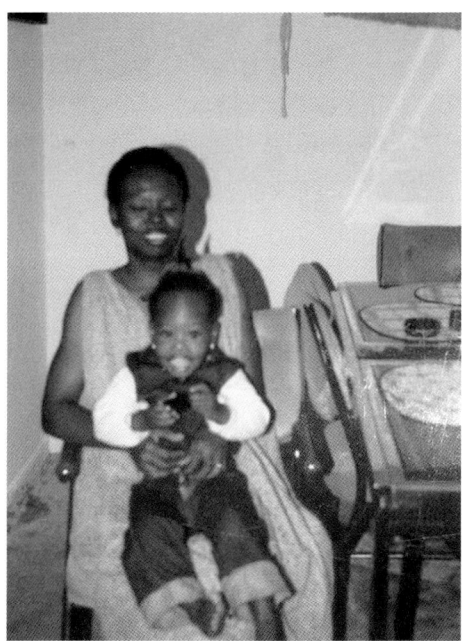

From the personal collection of Tomi Akitunde, Tomi Akitunde with her mother Emilia, circa 1985/1986

4 THOTTY MOMMIES

The Erotic Potential of Black Mothers Online

Marly Pierre-Louis _____

> *For those of us*
> *who were imprinted with fear*
> *like a faint line in the center of our foreheads*
> *learning to be afraid with our mother's milk*
> *for by this weapon*
> *this illusion of some safety to be found*
> *the heavy-footed hoped to silence us*
> *For all of us*
> *this instant and this triumph*
> *We were never meant to survive.*
> —Audre Lorde, *A Litany for Survival*[1]

In the last decade, digital technology has, in part, democratized photography, giving lay people powerful tools to share their stories and experiences. The Instagram photostream with its scrolling, gridded view provides a canvas for the fluid, visual self-expression and articulation of complex identities. Creators can add, delete, filter and edit their timelines as they see fit, building archives of activities, moments and experiences that expand how we are looked at (and how we look back). This "humanizing power" (Caldeira et al. 2018: 31), recasts users as active subjects with agency through the act of image making. In *In Our Glory: Photography in Black Life*, author, professor and Black feminist icon bell hooks writes, "More than any other image-making tool, the camera offered African-Americans, disempowered in white culture, a way to empower ourselves through representation" (hooks 1998: 60). In the early 1900s for example, activists such as Fannie Lou Hammer and W.E.B Du Bois used photographs to generate support for their work (Winter 2018) and in the 1950s–1970s the use of imagery in Black power and liberation movements was a critical tool in rejecting notions of respectability in favor of a self-defined vision of Blackness (Winter 2018).

"Underpants up, dresses down and legs closed"

Growing up, I was what my mother's generation might've called "fast" and what millennials might call a THOT. A THOT (That Hoe Over There) is used to describe an unapologetic and shamelessly sexual woman. Throughout my adolescence, I was a boy crazy, kissy hoe—making out with any willing cutie on the block. In high school, I was the first of my friends to buy a vibrator, using it with gusto after cruising chat rooms on Excite and Yahoo. I wore half shirts with scandalous sayings and skorts in the summer, lycra bell bottoms and tied-up button down shirts in the fall, and (once I discovered it) I became obsessed with dry humping and rubbed up against any and everything. I loved my body and was excited to explore what it could do and how it could feel. In college, I brazenly flirted with and pursued whomever appealed to me—I had an active sex life fueled by my own desires and curiosity.

College was also when I began to deepen my analysis of the world around me and where I became politicized. I read books by Assata Shakur, Angela Davis and bell hooks. I joined the Black Student Union and signed up for Black literature classes. Learning about racialized stereotypes like the Jezebel or reading about Sara Baartman being paraded as a sideshow "freak" across Europe because of how her body looked, I couldn't help but reflect on my own love of nudity and casual sex. Baartman was treated like an animal, her body deemed evidence of the inherent hypersexuality of African women. An ugly narrative began to materialize inside of me; to be an exposed Black body was to be vulnerable, to be lustful was to be vulgar. I had never felt a way about my extracurricular activities with boys before but around this point, shame crept in.

A few years after graduation I met the man I would marry. Together we joined a Black nationalist organization in Brooklyn. As a budding feminist and activist invested in liberation, dating a Black man invested in liberation, I felt like I had to look, sound and act the part. I started to conceptualize sex and desire as something reserved for white women. To engage in that behavior was to fulfill the ugly tropes white supremacy had constructed for me, that Black women were hypersexual and amoral. To be sexually free was to prove them right. Black feminist Cheryl Clark writes:

> We have expended much energy trying to debunk the racist mythology which says our sexuality is depraved. Unfortunately, many of us have overcompensated and assimilated the Puritan value that sex is for

procreation, occurs only between men and women, and is only valid within the confines of heterosexual marriage [...] Like everyone else in America who is ambivalent in these respects, Black folk have to live with the contradictions of this limited sexual system by repressing or closeting any other sexual/erotic urges, feelings, or desires. (Lomax 2018a: 191)

As I fell in love with my new man, shame pushed me to fashion myself after a more respectable kind of woman. She looked kind of like Erykah Badu, circa 1997. She wrapped her natural hair in African fabrics, wore long skirts and bangles and responded to every greeting with 'Peace and Blessings'. She was a Queen and chasing men for sport was beneath her. I put away my pum-pum shorts, half shirts and juicy lip glosses, in exchange for headwraps, incense and wooden earrings. I didn't wear makeup, didn't pluck my brows, didn't shave my legs.

I married that man and a year later became a mother. I had achieved a normative, Black family unit, something "quintessentially representative of Black racial progress and Black freedom" (Lomax 2018b: 191). But I wasn't happy. Around that time, if I met someone new and my son wasn't with me, I wouldn't disclose that I was a mother. I felt more and more that motherhood was a rejection of my true self, but at the same time I felt that expressing my thotty parts made me a bad mother. I struggled to reconcile who I was with who I had become.

Black feminist scholar, Patricia Hill Collins coined the termed "controlling images" (Collins 2015) to describe stereotypes birthed from slavery that reflected the ways in which the dominant society sought to subordinate Black women. If you've ever watched TV or been to a grocery store, you're familiar with them. The mammy is asexual, jolly and content in her role as caregiver to white families. She neglects her own children in favor of caring for white ones. Sapphire, the matriarch is aggressive and evil. Her children fear her and so does her man. The welfare queen had babies in order to scam taxpayers and often chose addiction over parenting. The thread that unites these images in our imagination is the enduring idea that Black mothers are inherently "bad" and incapable of having loving bonds with their children. Through these images, the sexual possibilities for Black women are policed, contained and managed. In an effort to distance myself from mammy, sapphire and them, I had unwittingly compartmentalized my chopped and screwed up identity into someone palatable but unrecognizable.

The first time I read Audre Lorde's *Uses of the Erotic*, it felt like a dirty secret had been whispered from Lorde's mouth to my ears. Even the word *erotic* from the mouth of a Black woman (a Black feminist no less) seemed scandalous and yet, Lorde incisively confronts this, boldly claiming the power available to all of us in the erotic. For Lorde, the denial of access to the erotic as a result of the shame inculcated through culture is an act of dominance, a way to "corrupt or distort those various sources of power within the culture of the oppressed that can provide energy" (Lorde 1984a: 87). The erotic offers deep knowledge, power and information to those who dare to claim it (Lorde 1984b: 88).

In a speech delivered at Harvard University in 1982, Lorde reflected on the movement space of the 1960s and her personal journey:

> As a Black lesbian mother in an interracial marriage, there was usually some part of me guaranteed to offend everybody's comfortable prejudices of who I should be. That is how I learned that if I didn't define myself for myself, I would be crunched into other people's fantasies for me and eaten alive. My poetry, my life, my work, my energies for struggle were not acceptable unless I pretended to match somebody else's norm.

Like Lorde, in trying to build an identity that felt "suitable" to my life and my politics, I had buried the freest parts of myself. I read the world in search of a vision of womanhood that integrated all of who I was and aspired to be.

Look back at it

Truth be told, I was never really a Beyonce fan. Give me Destiny's Child over pre-2013 Bey all day. So when her self-titled album dropped secretly in 2013 I wasn't pressed. My homegirl was like, "have you seen Beyonce's visual album? Girl. Bey's telling bitches to bow down and talking about giving head in the backseat of a taxi." I promptly paid iTunes and took a seat.

Here was a Black mother openly reveling in the beauty of her own image, shamelessly turned on by herself, absolutely dripping in eroticism. I was floored. Beyonce's visual album weaved together a body of work that illustrated the fullness of who she was as a woman; a wife, a mother, an artist, a businesswoman, a bad bitch and so much more. It was a revelation, an intervention.

In a video documenting the production of this album, Beyonce Giselle Knowles echoes Audre Lorde in reflecting on the explicit nature of her album's visuals:

I was very aware of the fact that I was showing my body. I know finding my sensuality, getting back into my body [...] I know that there's so many women that feel the same thing after they give birth. You can have your child and you can still have fun and still be sexy and still have dreams and still live for yourself. I don't at all have any shame about being sexual and I'm not embarrassed about it and I don't feel like I have to protect that side of me. Because I do believe that *sexuality is a power that we all have.* (YouTube.com)

The album stayed on repeat. I could not take my eyes off it. At the same time, resentment was running wild through me and my relationships. The effort of compartmentalizing had left me unfulfilled and straight up exhausted. Standards and expectations of beauty, womanhood, motherhood and Blackness created a soup of political consciousness I felt beholden to. My pursuit of pleasure, spontaneity and joy weren't motherly, they were a cause for guilt and shame. I had been worshipping at an altar of womanhood that wasn't my own. Beyonce gave me the mirror image I was longing for. I didn't want to be domestic and homely, I wanted booty shorts, crop tops and late nights out. I wanted to center the erotic and teach my son to spell. I wanted to enjoy my body, the gaze of others on it, and change diapers, make meals and patch up scraped knees. I wanted to be sexual and a good mother. I wanted a motherhood an erotic, "yes and" kind of motherhood; a thotty motherhood where all my parts could coexist. Beyonce opened a window to the possibility of a Black motherhood that was whole, nuanced and affirming and I crawled in in search of more. I found it on Instagram.

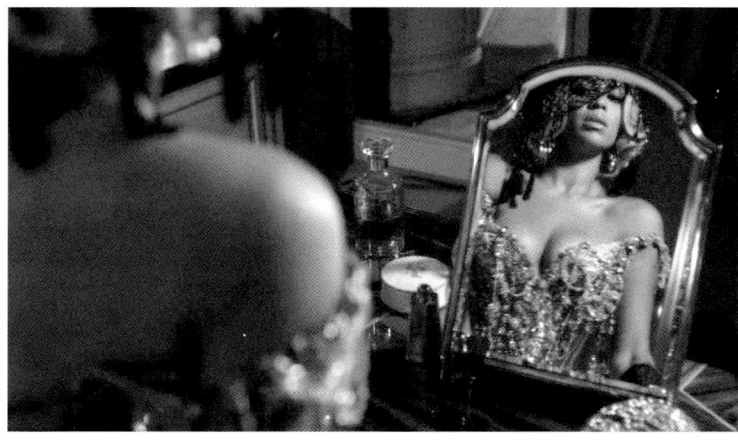

Beyonce_Partition—Medium, Beyonce, Partition video, screenshot from *Hollywood Reporter*

"While I share this body with my kids through breastfeeding, it's mine"

My son was born about a year after Instagram was launched and two years before the word "selfie" was added to the Oxford Dictionary. As a new mother, I happily posted pictures of his sweet face on Instagram for friends and families to coo over. But as I began to shed the layers of respectability I had been cloaked in, I stopped posting. Being a wife and mother didn't feel particularly sexy, it felt like these roles were stripping away all that was beguiling, alluring and sensuous about me.

Singer, songwriter, dancer, choreographer, director, model, mother and wife Teyana Taylor's photostream (@teyanataylor) turns any externally placed boundaries on her identity into dust: she poses seductively with her husband, she's grinding in Black leather and fishnets atop an audience participant, she's hand-in-hand with her daughter in gray sweats on the first day of school, she's face down, ass up in sheer panty hose on stage, she's in a sweatsuit and baseball cap behind the camera on set. In a post from May, we get to see Taylor with her two daughters singing the praises of her breast pump and how it's enabled her to be an "active mom, but also a dancer, singer, actress, director…", and in June she shares photos from her 'Sexiest Woman Alive' photoshoot with Maxim.

In her dissertation on identity and meaning making, Jessica de Aguiar Pereira quotes research by Yvonne Jewkes and Kay Sharp: "Within postmodern analysis, identity is neither inherent nor fixed, but is rather an ephemeral, fluid entity which is open to constant negotiation, change and manipulation" (Pereira 2016b: 17). In the triads of squared images and videos on her feed, Taylor is serving multitudes, and eroticism is the steady beat pulsing through. Being a mother only negates our sexuality in the gaze of those who wish to further subjugate us. By centering her own gaze and obliging what resonates from within, Taylor is fully herself no matter which photo she's posing for.

"A woman's place is wherever she desires"

Eryn Khristine (@erynamelism) is an entrepreneur and mother. Her timeline can be read as a celebration of her body and a resistance to the disassembling of sexuality, motherhood and home. In one photo shot from above she's lying on her back on a beach towel in a red bikini, her full breasts loll to one side, one hand touches her stomach, the other arm stretches above her head, her eyes closed, her skin aglow. In another she's at home holding a bright, yellow mug in a simple bra and underwear set, beaming down into her son's face. In another, she's perched on her kitchen counter, smoldering in a lace catsuit, her phone expertly angled to capture all her goodies.

Juicy with rolls and stretch marks, Khristine's provocative and sensual photos tell a story about self love and beauty standards. Posting almost only selfies, she centers her own gaze and what feels sexy and attractive to her, thus claiming her body (and the lens) as her own. By "appropriating the lens" (Pereira 2016a: 21), Khristine makes public the private erotics of her life and creates an "oppositional gaze" (hooks 1992) that looks back at the violence of dominant narratives.

"My body built my family"

Through the IG stream of model, producer, and mother Marz Lovejoy (@marzyjane) we see how mothering (i.e. breastfeeding, laboring, caretaking) and pleasure practices (i.e. fashion, beauty, dancing) can inform, facilitate and stimulate each other. In 2018, Lovejoy modeled in Rihanna's Savage x Fenty lingerie campaign in a bra set and baby bump, quickly becoming a vocal and visible champion of pregnant and postpartum bodies. Her stream reveals the possibility of sexual prowess and beauty *because* of motherhood, not despite it. In one photo Lovejoy is leaning back on a sofa pregnant, topless, two sparkly dots covering her nipples. In another, she's squatting (or perhaps caught mid-twerk) while her pregnant belly rests between her legs. Sometimes she's natural, sometimes she's dolled up, often she's nearly naked staring directly into the camera.

In May of 2020, Marz Lovejoy live streamed the delivery of her second baby on Instagram as a way to raise money for childbirth services for BIPOC and LGBTQI+ people. In the video, we see Lovejoy naked in a bathtub with her freshly born baby boy on her right breast and her left breast exposed. Lovejoy uses her body, her mothering as a way to do what might've been called "race work" fifty years ago but what looks radically different in the age of postmodern social media. This was not at all what the revolutionaries of the 60s imagined when they linked Black motherhood with the revolution. Lovejoy is not "uplifting the race" through maternity, she is delivering power through it and she is baring it all for us to witness.

"A longed for bed"

This is risky business.

All the women discussed here are privileged, conventionally attractive, CIS, able-bodied women. Trans mothers, queer mothers, poor mothers, differently-bodied mothers might all face material consequences to exposing their bodies and sexual selves on social media. In *Revisiting the Jezebel Stereotype: The Impact of Target Race on Sexual Objectification*, the authors write "the more removed from the ideal, the greater the objectification (or dehumanization) of Black women" (Anderson et al. 2108: 472). The more open and public about who we are, the more exposed we are to misogynoir.

But this has always been the case. And Black mothers are expert negotiators. Every day for us is a negotiation between safety and identity, safety and opportunity, safety and privacy, safety and power, safety and freedom. Working with Lorde's erotic, we learn that by suppressing our identities we become complicit in our oppression and that by owning our deepest desires our resistance becomes integrated and empowered from within (Lorde 1984). Self love is only possible when we reclaim our gaze. For how can we love the self if we don't know it? If the image of self always comes from elsewhere? (Nanda 2019)

Representation is resistance. By owning all parts of who they are, Beyonce, Taylor, Khristine and Lovejoy liberate themselves, and by projecting their truths onto the world they give us permission to do the same. Their images are a reminder of the radical nature of a Black woman fully embodying who she is despite the boxes she's been crunched into. Thinking of Eryn Khristine makes me want to lock my bedroom door and take sexy selfies by myself, for myself and rejoice in my baby-given stretch marks, saggy titties and loose tummy skin. Loving up on and flaunting our bodies for the sake of our own enjoyment is a radical act. Their images push back in moments when I find myself editing how I show up in space, and with a wink they whisper, 'we cannot be contained'.

In *Uses of the Erotic*, Lorde writes:

The aim of each thing which we do is to make our lives and the lives of our children richer and more possible. Within the celebration of the erotic in all our endeavors, my work becomes a conscious decision—a longed for bed which I enter gratefully and from which I rise up empowered. (Lorde 1984: 88)

This work, the work of owning who I am and how I show up; the work of looking shame and fear in the face, the work of nurturing my erotic self, is joyfully difficult work. My most fulfilling moments are when my intersections sing in harmony. When I twerk with my son to trap music while cooking dinner. When he helps me pick out my hoe outfit and makeup for a night out. When he combs out my wig while I read him a bedtime story. When we paint each other's nails.

The pain of Sarah Baartman and all our ancestors lives in our bones. We carry them on our shoulders and into our bedrooms. With each generation, we pass on their trauma. But what would it mean to pass on something else?

I often walk around my home naked. Mostly because I enjoy it but also because my body was the first body my 9-year-old son knew that wasn't his own. I want it to be a reference point for a Black, femme body free of trauma and shame and a Black mama safe in her skin. I like to imagine generations of children whose default understanding is that Black women are erotic, safe and whole. Children of thotty mommies everywhere finding only power, pleasure and possibility in their bodies. And that this wide open space looks like freedom.

Notes

1   Audre Lorde, A Litany for Survival, from The Collected Poems of Audre Lorde by Audre Lorde, 1978.

Works Cited

Anderson, J. R. et al. (2018). "Revisiting the Jezebel Stereotype." *Psychology of Women Quarterly*, 42, 4 (August 2018): 461–476.

Beyonce (2013). "'Self-Titled' Part 4. Liberation." YouTube, uploaded by Beyonce 30 December 2013, https://www.youtube.com/watch?v=1b1loWJfxaA.

Caldiera, S. P. et al. (2018). "Exploring the Politics of Gender Representation on Instagram: Self-Representations of Femininity," *Journal of Diversity and Gender Studies (DiGeSt)*, 5, 1: 23–42.

Collins, P. H. (2015). *Black Feminist Thought: Knowledge, Consciousness, and the Politics of Empowerment*. New York: Routledge, 2015.

De Aguiar Pereira, J. (2016). "Believe in yourself(ie): a study of young, ordinary, South African women who share selfies on Instagram." *A dissertation in fulfilment for Master of Arts in Media Studies*.

hooks, bell (1998). "In Our Glory: Photography and Black Life." In *Art on My Mind: Visual Politics*. New York: New Press. 54-64.

hooks, bell (1992). "The Oppositional Gaze: Black Female Spectators." In *Black Looks: Race and Representation*, Boston: South End Press. 115–131.

Lomax, T. (2018). "Black Bodies in Ecstasy: Black Women, the Black Church, and the Politics of Pleasure: An Introduction." *Black Theology*, 16, 3 (July 2018): 189–194.

Lorde, A. (1982). "Learning from the 60s." *Malcolm X Weekend Address, Harvard University*: Cambridge, MA, February 1982.

———(1984) "Uses of the Erotic." In *Sister Outsider*, edited by Audre Lorde, 53–59. Berkeley: Crossing Press.

Nanda, S. (2019). "Re-Framing Hottentot: Liberating Black Female Sexuality from the Mammy/Hottentot Bind." *Humanities*, 8, 4: 161.

Winter, J. (2018). "The Politics of Beyoncé's Pregnancy: Re-Articulating Lemonade's Narrative Agency through the Public Construction of Black Motherhood, MAI: Feminism and Visual Culture," 20 (November 2018), maifeminism.com/the-politics-of-beyonces-pregnancy-re-articulating-lemonades-narrative-agency-through-the-public-construction-of-Black-motherhood/ (accessed February 1, 2020).

PART TWO

"TURNING THE FACE OF HISTORY TO YOUR FACE"*: SEEING THE REAL SELF THROUGH REPRESENTATIONS OF BLACK MOTHERHOOD

* Jordan, June, and Archive Of Recorded Poetry And Literature. (1973) Poem: Getting Down to Get Over (dedicated to my mother) [excerpts] (min. 45:58). June Jordan reading her poems with comment in the Recording Laboratory. Audio. Retrieved from the Library of Congress, ‹www.loc.gov/item/94838932/›.

5 MOTHERHOOD IN THE WORK OF DEANA LAWSON

A conversation with the Artist

Susan Thompson

In her photographs, Deana Lawson pictures compelling individuals from across the African diaspora often posed within unique domestic interiors. Her subjects are mostly strangers recruited during chance encounters, and the preponderance of these sitters are women. Since many women have children, it is perhaps unsurprising that motherhood has arisen as a recurrent thematic within Lawson's work. In these photographs, the artist simultaneously highlights the subject's role as a mother—often through the inclusion of her children or their belongings in the image—while also conveying that this role is but one part of her identity within the greater whole of her being. This conversation focuses in particular on four works that capture women at different stages in early motherhood: the profound experience of pregnancy as seen in *Mama Goma, Gemena, DR Congo* (2014), the triumph of delivery and joy of new life in *The Beginning* (2008), the postpartum reclamation of physical autonomy and sexual identity in *Baby Sleep* (2009), and, finally, mothering young children through difficult circumstances in *Mohawk Correctional Facility: Jazmin & Family* (2013). Collectively, these works offer a portrait of the spiritual, physical, sexual, and social dimensions of the Black maternal experience.

Susan Thompson: References to mothers and children abound in your work. Perhaps we could start by discussing motherhood more broadly and how you choose to represent it in your photographs. I wonder if any part of your interest in portraying mothers grows out of your own experiences as a mother or of having been mothered.

Deana Lawson: My family community in my hometown of Rochester, NY, almost always involved children. Familial spaces of home, church, and family get-togethers were mostly intergenerational, so it was natural for children to be a lively presence within adult spaces. It feels normal to me to hear a crying child at church, and if a crying child isn't heard, somehow there's an unnatural absence. The women in my mother's generation and in my generation also had children when they were quite young, often between the ages of 16 and 20 years old. A lot of my cousins had children starting as early as 15, so when I was pregnant at the age of 22 it was like I got pregnant late. Being pregnant at 22 for me felt like a later stage, but in the culture at large it would appear to be at a young stage in life. I had just graduated college when I was carrying Judah Gilbert, who is now 18 years old.

In the making of my pictures there is often a child present, whether the child is in the final picture, or around the periphery of the photograph. In *Living Room, Brownsville, Brooklyn* (2015), we put a movie on for the young woman's son while taking the photograph. When photographing *Uncle Mack* (2016) I will never forget the image of my best friend Dana Brown holding my daughter Grace in one arm, and her niece Layla in the other. It was pure chaos, but I got the job done. Somehow the presence of children blesses the picture in its own way. You would think it would collapse it, but it's the opposite. I also think having a powerful community of women around who had always had children, especially at younger ages, really had an influence on my "get it done" positionality as a working artist and mother.

THOMPSON: *Mama Goma* was taken in the Democratic Republic of the Congo, where you traveled on a Guggenheim Fellowship in 2014. On this same trip, you also created *The Garden, Gemena, DR Congo* (2015), an iconic image that feels so much like a portrait of Adam and Eve. You've spoken previously of an ethnographic impulse in your work and of how you envisioned this trip to Africa as almost a way of going back in time to seek out something originary—even Edenic—within that setting.

LAWSON: Yes, *The Garden* is my vision of paradise in the heart of the continent of Africa: D.R. Congo. The story of Eden is envisioned through the Black body, the ultimate ancestors of all humanity. It is a story of primordial love and innocence, before the fall of mankind. The Fall is a stand-in for European invasion and colonialism. The male subject in *The Garden* has his hand on the woman's stomach, which many people have interpreted as a coming child.

THOMPSON: The Biblical figure of Eve is the mother of all humankind, the ur-mother. Even pictured in her nakedness before the Fall—before the birth of Cain and Abel and everyone who would come after—she is always somehow coded as pre-maternal. As the first mother, her motherhood is inscribed in her body as inevitable. Many have used the term "prelapsarian" to describe your work and the way it captures scenes of paradise before the Fall of humanity, before the advent of sin.

LAWSON: Yes, it's prelapsarian. The story of Eden is one of paradise, pleasure, and natural bounty. This paradise was also one of utmost isolation or quarantine. Adam and Eve were the only human beings of their kind to inhabit the earth. They were completely alone. The coming child represents the third member of the formation of a family/community/humanity. And Eve in particular, is the mother who begins the cycle of human evolution. Her body is a vehicle for the future. She has a look of concern on her face, but also of strength, displaying the conflicting notions of care and burden that comes with being a mother, and the tribulations of humanity at large. I wanted that to be embodied in her expression and her pose, which was taken from Hieronymus Bosch's *The Garden of Earthly Delights* (1490–1500).

THOMPSON: And if the woman in *The Garden* is Eve, the woman in *Mama Goma* is Madonna, Mother Mary. The image calls back to Renaissance representations of Mary: the expectant mother dressed in blue vestments as she gestates a holy being within her.

LAWSON: Her hands are open and upturned to "receive." The symbol of blue, or light blue in particular, I associate with the celestial. *The Book of Symbols* speaks of blue eloquently: "It is not quite of earth, this blue, which apart from sea and sky is the rarest color in nature. Given the unearthliness of blue and living as we do below the vast blue heavens, we have colored our gods blue—Kneph, Jupiter, Krishna, Vishnu, Odin—and our goddesses too…" So yes, Mary is cloaked in blue, and *Mama Goma* in my photograph is a Goddess in the flesh, draped in blue silk fabric. The same seafoam blue is seen on the dress of the baby girl in *Sons of Cush* (2016).

THOMPSON: For *Sons of Cush*, that particular dress was so important for the work; you brought it with you to the shoot. The dress in *Mama Goma* is very specific in its cut and it has a very handmade quality to it. Was it something the subject owned or did you bring it with you?

LAWSON: We made that. I bought the fabric in Kinshasa and as soon as I got to the smaller town there was a seamstress waiting for me. On the first day I arrived, we measured out the fabric and the subject and she made the dress within days.

THOMPSON: Did you have a specific vision for the design, with the cut-out for the belly and off-the-shoulder sleeves flowing like wings?

LAWSON: The dress was inspired by a photograph I'd seen of a young woman who went to prom, and her prom dress had a cutout for her pregnant belly. The young mother-to-be chose to celebrate the prom and her pregnancy by showing her beautiful body. She literally crowned her belly with this dress. Back in the day, mothers who got pregnant in high school had to leave the school because it was a mark of shame. But the way that this young woman wore her dress definitely was not with shame. It was with pride. And that just sat with me. I thought it was an odd dress, but also really beautiful and striking.

THOMPSON: You mentioned that *Mama Goma*'s palms are turned upwards to "receive," perhaps to receive a blessing. There is certainly something deeply spiritual in this work. Between the unique dress and the woman's prayerful, almost supplicant, pose it seems as if she is performing a rite to honor her swelling belly. That her hands are raised in a yogic gesture of openness creates a link between gestation and meditation, and celebrates the profound experience that is pregnancy.

    Mama Goma is such a captivating ode to pregnancy it makes me wonder if you were pregnant when you were shooting it.

LAWSON: You know, I think I conjured up my own pregnancy. I wasn't pregnant then, but a year after I made that photo, I was with child. And I didn't know it. I was about to go to Ethiopia and the doctor had given me malaria pills. And I was like, "Wait, I shouldn't take this if I'm pregnant, right?" And I didn't even know then, but my subconscious knew. I never took the pills and it turned out I was pregnant with my daughter. It's interesting when the photo begets reality. I think that was the case with Grace.

THOMPSON: *The Beginning* is a powerful image of the immediate aftermath of labor and delivery, capturing the intensity and beauty of that moment when a new life enters the world. The baby, who occupies the foreground, is brand new: simultaneously glossy from amniotic fluid and waxy from vernix case-ola. It is a very active scene in contrast to many of your other works that are more fixed. For other images, the setting is carefully staged and the sitter is directed into a pose. Obviously that's not possible with a moments-old baby. How did this image come about?

LAWSON: I was really thinking about birth as this space of knowledge that can only be arrived at through the body. No one can ever describe to you what it feels like to give birth until you do it. Most importantly, I was curious about a female child who first enters the world and how she might appear in a pho-tograph. I imagined birth through the womb as an event horizon that we all traverse as babies to make our way into the world. What does she look like when she's crossed this horizon?

I met a family in New Haven who welcomed me to photograph their birth. I was at a residency in Syracuse when the mother went into labor and I received the phone call. She gave birth to baby Ebony twenty minutes after I arrived. It was incredible. One minute she was pushing and I was waiting with the cam-era. And the next minute, the baby was out. I just started clicking the shutter and I thought, "wow, I just missed it." But of course, when I got my negatives back, I was like, "wait, no, there is something here."

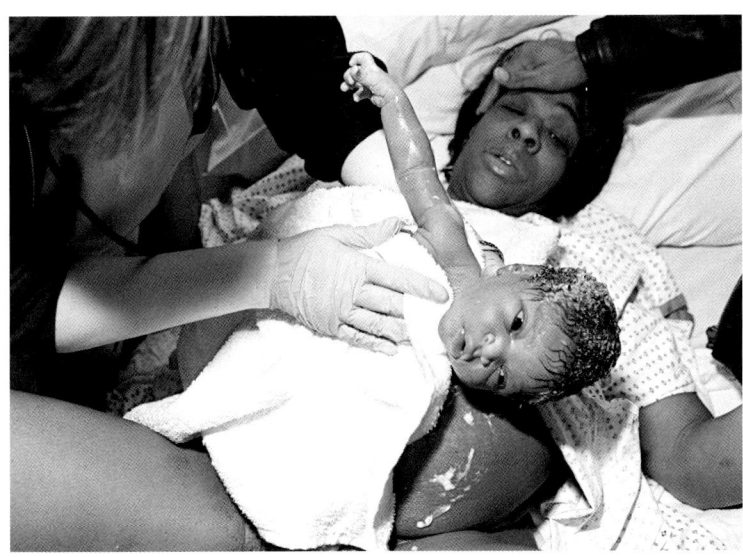

Deana Lawson, *The Beginning*, 2008. Artwork © Deana Lawson, courtesy of Sikkema Jenkins & Co., New York

THOMPSON: The image is so perfectly composed for having happened so suddenly in such an intense moment. The baby is positioned in the center with the mother's face looking on in the background.

LAWSON: And all the hands: the hands of the midwife, the hand of the husband on the mother's forehead, the baby's arm sticking out very straight in an almost-fist. There's a cacophony of hands.

THOMPSON: And the midwife's gloved hands are that same celestial blue. There is such an emotional heft in the work. It captures this climactic moment of birth, which is a moment of triumph for the mother and also the beginning of a new life. There are also social and political valences that this work brings to mind as well, specifically in regards to the staggering statistics around Black maternal mortality in the U.S. Due in part to added health risks like heart disease and hypertension connected to the physiological stress of racism and compounded by the biases of medical professionals in addressing Black patients' pain, Black mothers in the U.S. are three to four times more likely to die in childbirth and its aftermath than white mothers. In New York City, it's even higher than that. I guess that's part of why I describe this image as capturing a moment of triumph. Every birth is a triumph because of the work the mother has done to bring her baby into the world, but it feels like this image is also about survival because giving birth as a Black woman in the American medical system is a harrowing experience.

LAWSON: It is. And this subject was also at an older age having a child so there was added risk. She had eight kids, so it was a more difficult birth because she was past middle age. It is indeed a triumph.

THOMPSON: Let's turn to *Baby Sleep*, where we see a mother navigating family life with an infant at home. There's a baby asleep in a mechanized swing and a few toys strewn about on the floor: a soft book, a rattle, pieces from an alphabet play mat. On the left side of the image, a shirtless man sits on a wooden chair. A woman straddles him, completely naked except for a scarf in her hair. She is looking directly at the camera with confidence and self-assurance. She grips the back of the man's head and pulls his face into her neck for a kiss, a deeply sensual gesture. Referencing Audre Lorde's *Uses of the Erotic*, you've spoken previously of a notion of the erotic in your work that seems especially operative in *Baby Sleep*.

Lawson: What has always appealed to me about Lorde's framing of the erotic is that the sexual includes the spiritual, it includes family and community, which is markedly different from notions of "sexiness." And I wanted to use *Baby Sleep* as a way to make an image that was really beautifully sensual, but that also includes the presence of a child. What could that look like?

Thompson: I read this work as a mother who is navigating her postpartum identity to include her roles as a mother and as a lover. It asserts that the mother remains a sexual being; she hasn't been neutered by the transformation into motherhood. These different parts of her identity are not in conflict or mutually exclusive. Maternal love and adult desire can coexist within healthy family life. However, in a society that expects mothers to be fully devoted to their children, such an image reads as almost transgressive. There is a brazenness to the empowered, dominant woman as she rejects the social expectation that she can either be a doting, dedicated mother or a sexually desiring vixen, but not both.

Lawson: Right, I envisioned using Thais as a subject for this because she's such a queen. She embodies a philosophical and spiritual power. She is on top, in a dominant position of pleasure. This is a woman who is running a household, but who is also confident in her sexual relationship with her husband. There's another version of this image that I used on the cover of *Contact Sheet* at Light Work.

Thompson: One where her eyes are kind of rolling back in her head, right?

Lawson: Yes. And when you see the whites of someone's eyes like that it's often a sign that they've been mounted by spirits.

Thompson: It also strikes me that the man in the image has his back to the child. He doesn't need to negotiate the same dichotomy within himself in his roles as father and partner. He can really engage fully in that moment because he's not carrying the weight of societal expectation.

Lawson: And he's also a big man, but she still conquers him, you know? She's definitely not a victim in this picture at all. One of my other subjects saw the picture and said, "She looks like a succubus, like a woman who would eff the shit out of men and then leave them." And I actually wanted a little bit of that in the image. I was actually thinking about a praying mantis, about a woman who was a bit forceful in a way that maybe complicates ideas of womanhood, sexuality, and motherhood.

THOMPSON: *Mohawk Correctional Facility: Jazmin & Family* is a series of thirty images of your cousin Jazmin with her incarcerated partner, Erik, and their children taken in the visiting room of a penitentiary. These photographs document the family over the course of a few years, serving as commemorative markers of the limited moments of connection they shared during their prolonged separation. This piece is somewhat anomalous within your work as it features appropriated photographs rather than images you composed and shot. Do you see this work as operating differently within your practice? Did the process of making it feel more like a curatorial gesture than a photographic one?

Lawson: Not at all. The same instinctive attraction that draws me to photograph strangers was the same instinct that drew me to Jazmin's pictures, which she was posting on Facebook. As she posted the photos, I slowly learned the context as I started to see the same background. I knew she was pregnant and I knew her then-boyfriend (they're now married) was incarcerated, and I put two and two together that these were visitation pictures she was taking with her man and her son. In one, she's pregnant, but then she has the baby during his time in prison.

So much of my work is about picturing love in different dimensions and different manifestations, and this piece shows one way of love, of romance, of mothering. I wanted to show what it might possibly feel like in those shoes. Looking at those pictures and the quantity of them I actually began to understand what it must be

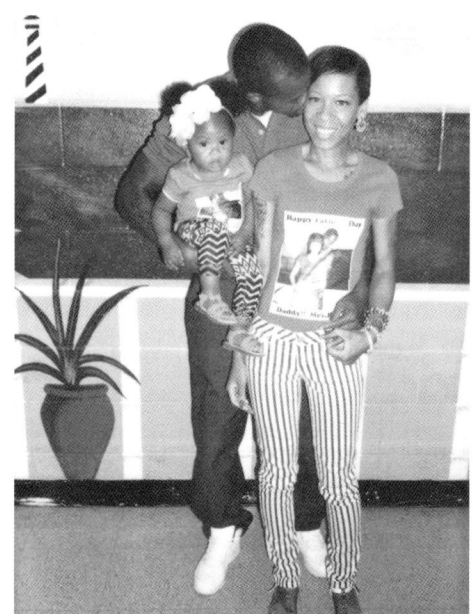

Deana Lawson, *Mohawk Correctional Facility: Jazmin & Family*, 2013, detail. Artwork © Deana Lawson, courtesy of Sikkema Jenkins & Co., New York

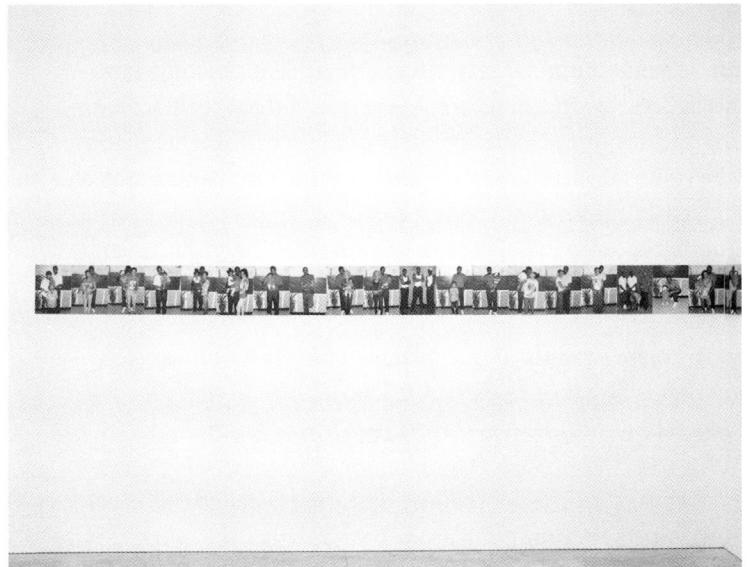

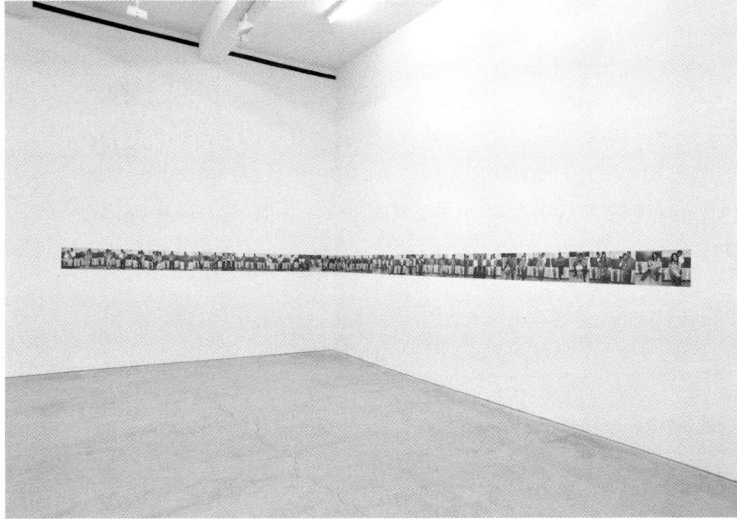

like for a woman to experience having the love of her life locked up. And having a child together. It seemed so lonely, but also there's something endearing about Jazmin and the discipline—and the longing—to go see her man, her child's father. To bring the kids, get dressed up, get her hair done, and then make sure a picture is taken every time. Not for anybody, not for an audience, just for her.

THOMPSON: There is something sweetly ritualistic and, ultimately, devotional about it as well. Creating the photographic record of these regular visits feels commemorative in a way that lends a gravity to the occasion, that marks its significance. The visits are clearly very important for her in maintaining a connection to her partner across distance and time, but it also seems to be a dedicated act of motherhood to make sure her children see their father and have a relationship with him. She is doing the work of creating a family.

LAWSON: Exactly. To create a family and to sustain a family within an architectural institution that is designed to destroy a Black family. In that way, this is really an act of refusal.

THOMPSON: It just speaks to the incredible, enduring strength of Black women as pillars within their communities, a testament to the work they do to hold everything together. And in naming the series after Jazmin in the work's title, you're honoring that work that she's doing as her family's matriarch and its champion.

LAWSON: Absolutely. And she didn't do this because she is an activist. She's not theorizing this in the way that we're talking about it. She's actually just doing this out of love. There is something so pure about those pictures that I felt needed to be seen. It's a visual testimony that says, "See, this is what we do." And Jazmin is one of many.

THOMPSON: The fact that you encountered these pictures on Facebook also shows how this was her way of sharing her life with her community.

LAWSON: Yeah, and with a sense of pride, posting for the world to see.

THOMPSON: There are of course many other works you've made featuring mothers that we haven't addressed here: *Barbara and Mother* (2017), *Wanda and Daughters* (2009), *Greased Scalp* (2008), *Woman with Child* (2017), and *Daughter* (2007), among others.

LAWSON: I'm glad you mentioned *Barbara and Mother* and *Greased Scalp* because they represent an older version of a mother and child. I think we tend to gravitate towards younger children. Of course, that phase requires the most work as a parent, but how do these relationships change over time? How do they manifest at a later stage in life? What does that look like? There are so many tumultuous relationships between mother and child in later stages of life. And that's a part of love, too. Some part of love is heartbreak. The two women in *Barbara and Mother* did not get along, but in the photograph, they put aside their differences and made a beautiful picture.

THOMPSON: In contrast to the works we've discussed, the piece *Sons of Cush* centers on fatherhood. When you were making this work, you said you'd felt like you had really focused on representations of women, and you now wanted to confront masculinity, and in particular Black masculinity and Black fatherhood.

LAWSON: I grew up with my father in the household. My parents are still together and my father is very much a part of his three daughters' lives. I've known Black men to be very caring, involved fathers, but representations in mass media always present Black men as absentee parents. I wanted to create an image of a beautiful man who is complicated and perhaps even intimidating, and to have this daughter be the epicenter of the photograph. I wanted to play off the contrast of fragility and strength, femininity and masculinity, through the relationship of father and daughter. It was important that the child be close to newborn, in that state where they're still a bit like little angels, still looking like they're from another world.

6   PHOTOGRAPHIC AFTERIMAGES

Nationalism, Care Work and Black Motherhood in Canada

RACHEL LOBO ⎯⎯⎯⎯⎯⎯⎯⎯⎯⎯⎯⎯⎯⎯⎯⎯⎯⎯⎯⎯⎯⎯

Photography affords the body a wealth of possibility. With it memory—frag-
mented, fluid, malleable, rigid and still—situates the black female body as
one photograph in a continually duplicating frame constantly looking back on
itself. And within that space is the possibility of freedom.
—Kimberly Juanita Brown, 2015:194

In the opening scene of the award winning documentary *Black Mother, Black Daughter* (1989), the film's writer and director Sylvia Hamilton remarks on the goal of the project: "I want you to meet Black women I've known, mothers and daughters, who have patiently fostered the survival of our Black culture and community." The film traces the history of Black settlement in the Maritimes region of Canada, beginning with histories of bondage and ending with women exchanging narratives, testimonies, and life histories about their mothers while weaving maple wood baskets. As Hamilton (1994: 54) explains elsewhere,

> some of the earliest sketches and photographs of the Halifax city mar-
> ket show Black women selling baskets overflowing with mayflowers...
> basket-weaving for them was not an activity used to fill in time; it was
> work that brought in money vital to the survival of the family.

One of the subjects discussed while the women weave is Rose Fortune, a 19th-century Black woman whose parents were enslaved in Pennsylvania and later fled to Annapolis Royal, Nova Scotia as Black Loyalists during the American Revolution. Fortune went on to start her own business in the area as a baggage carrier, and later established a "wake-up" service where she would alert local hotel patrons of departing ships. Among the women weaving is Daurene Lewis, Annapolis Royal's—and Canada's—first Black female mayor

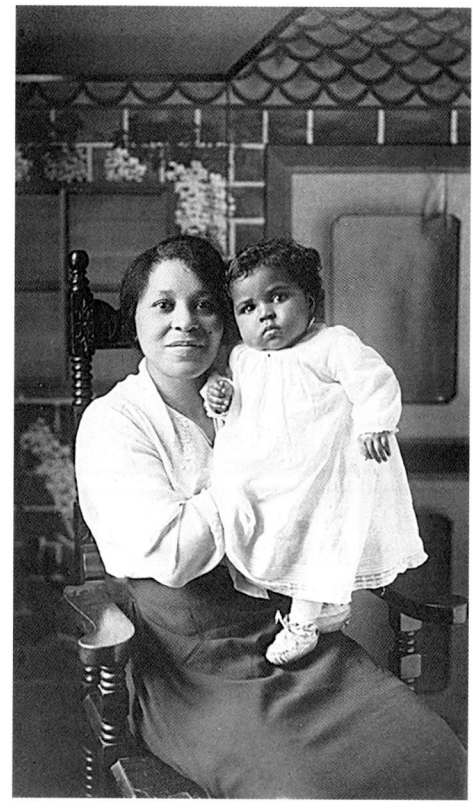

and Fortune's great granddaughter five times removed. In the film Lewis explains the importance of these historical memories of Fortune, describing the pride she feels in the fact that she is "not the first Black woman to try and do something in my family." A watercolor of Fortune [Figure 2] clad in an apron and boots is one of the first known representations of a Black woman in Canada and is featured in the film as Lewis speaks. In its documentary nature and use of print culture *Black Mother, Black Daughter* is one of very few visual mediums that explore the role of motherhood among African Canadian communities—a critical intervention in Canadian historiography. While perhaps not conceived as so-called "enduring objects" for historical study, I argue here that—like the maple wood baskets—vernacular photographs are socially salient objects that contribute to our understanding of public history and collective memory.

Against reigning ideologies that obscure the historical experience of racialized women, the aim of this paper is to highlight the potential of early 20th-century vernacular photography in situating Black motherhood within Canadian history, examining how the family photograph offered individuals a colloquial space in which to perform and subvert racialized, class-based, and gendered notions of national belonging. This paper explores how portraits of Black motherhood highlight the constructed status of signs mapped on the body and challenge the narrow conflation of Black women solely as workers *outside* of the home produced by the interlocking mechanics of capitalism, patriarchy and imperialism. These photographs highlight how the issue of motherhood and nation were bound up with racial discourses of the time. The materials for this investigation were drawn from the Alvin D. McCurdy fonds at the Archives of Ontario, a collection of nineteenth and early 20th-century

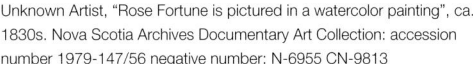
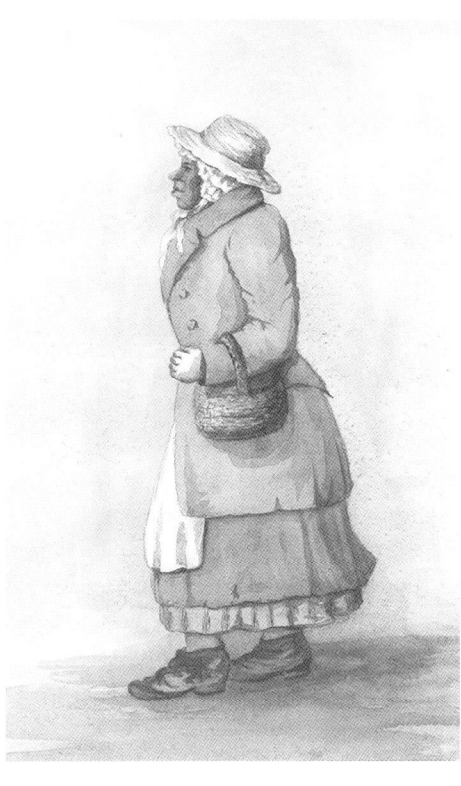

photographs of African Canadian communities in Amherstburg, Ontario—a major terminus of the Underground Railroad[1]. If, as Nikhil Singh (2013: 165) proposes, nations are "social creations engineered and lived primarily through techniques of narration and representation," this archive offers critical insight into how Black mothers reformulated and reinscribed national identity photographically.

This work relies on vernacular gelatin silver photographs as its primary source. Specifically, it studies deckle-edge amateur family photographs depicting domestic scenes of Black mothers with their children in Amherstburg, Ontario. These objects are read alongside more formal tintype portraits rendering whole family units in order to discern the representational practices unique to maternal photography. The readability of photographs as artifacts and as expressive texts depends upon understanding the socio-historical and cultural context of everyday image-making. As bell hooks (1994: 57) describes:

> Cameras gave to black folks, irrespective of our class, a means by which we could participate fully in the production of images. Hence it is essential that any theoretical discussion of the relationship of black life to the visual, to art making, make photography central.

My goal then is to put these ideas in conversation with Canadian histories of nation-building—examining how ideas about citizenship, race, gender, class, geographical belonging, and cultural memory have been visualized and promoted.

Foundational scholarship from the 1980s and 1990s (Brand 1991; Braithwaite and Benn-Ireland 1993; Bristow et al. 1994; Harris 1998) firmly situated Black women in Canada as agential and indispensable historical actors. Building on these studies, subsequent works incorporated gender analyses into the history of Black women's knowledge and cultural production, and resistance networks. However by nature of the fact that within prevailing hegemonic narratives many Black women have had their identity defined in terms of their labor (through both transatlantic slavery and domestic service programs), and because of unequal relations of archival power, within visual archives in Canada there is an over-representation of Black women as workers outside of their home. While these sources are undoubtedly invaluable to the study of both women's contribution to the labor market and the material conditions of their experiences, they offer a very limited view of their lives.

Though circulated mostly in the private sphere, the photographs of mothers within the McCurdy fonds have the profound ability to challenge the visual hegemony of white motherhood in Canada. They not only destabilize visual tropes of Black womanhood, but also assert the subjectivity of their sitters. In particular, these photographs showcase both familial life and the unpaid domestic labor of African Canadian women. The economic importance of women's domestic function to the capitalist economy has been well documented by social reproduction theory and movement-based knowledge generated from the transnational International Wages for Housework struggle. In her research on the history of the housewife, Catherine Hall (1992: 43) argues that, "If, as Marx suggested, wages represent only the reward for necessary labor time—that is, what is necessary for the worker to reproduce the conditions of his own labor-then in modern capitalism the housewife has become one of those hidden conditions, and thus the invisible support for the generation of surplus value." However, these discussions often centre around the white middle-class "housewife"; the child-rearing and housekeeping performed by racialized women are often further invisibilized. Angela Davis (2011: 132) asserts that Black women have seldom been "just housewives", they have carried the double burden of wage labor and housework which always demands that working women "possess the persevering powers of Sisyphus." Since the arrival of Black people in Canada in the 17th-century, Black women have been called upon to do domestic chores, as cleaners, laundresses, and general helpers. Up until World War II approximately 80% of Black women in Canadian cities worked in domestic service (Brand, 1994: 175). The intersecting race, class and gender based oppressions which dictated that the only suitable employment for Black women was as domestic servants in Canada, has meant that vast numbers of Black women have had to do their own housekeeping and other women's home chores as well.

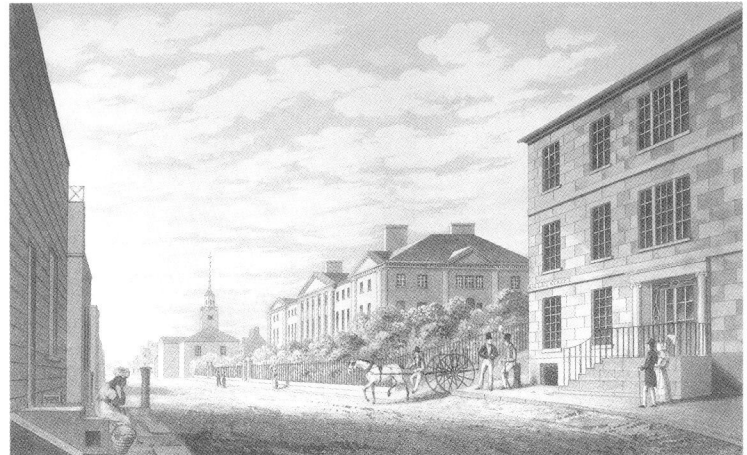

J. Clark, "Province House, Hollis Street, Halifax", ca. 1830s. In William Moorsom, *Letters From Nova Scotia: Comprising Sketches of a Young Country* (London: Colburn & Bentley, 1830), p. 10 opposite. Nova Scotia Archives, (F100 / M78) (microfilm 3870) negative number: N-492

Moving from the era of slavery and into the era of segregation or from racial dictatorship to so-called racial democracy, we see here the repeated trope of Black woman as an economic object to be exploited. Likely the same image alluded to by Hamilton, an engraving from 1830 within the Nova Scotia Archives depicting "Province House, Hollis Street, Halifax" [Figure 3] features in the left foreground a woman wearing a head wrap seated with her head in her hands with her basket placed at her feet. Positioned within the shadow of the building, across the street from this woman and soaked in the daylight are top-hatted men and a corseted woman carrying a parasol. While the white subjects in their pose and dress coupled with the warmth of the sunlight evoke a leisurely air, the woman seated on the street appears to be taking a short reprieve from her labor in the cool shade, head in hands, and wares by her side. In these examples, gendered notions of Blackness in stereotypical contexts were deployed as a way of depicting Black people in Canada as neither free (due to their continued reliance on forms of servitude as labor) nor citizens, since social and political equity were still very elusive (Crooks, 2019: 66).

This overrepresentation of Black women as unfree or wage workers within the visual archive is in part due to the fact that documents about working-class Black communities are often generated only when their lives intersect in some way with white people. This manifests most clearly in the holdings of Canadian archival institutions, where searches for visual records of Black motherhood during the nineteenth and early 20th-century produce scant historical evidence. As Ashley Farmer (2018) remarks: How should we address the paradox of simultaneously finding copious archival records on some Black women, while also accounting for the deafening archival silence on others?

Attending to epistemological issues that the visual archive presents, scholarly work that aims to recover the historical experience of Black women in Canada must adjust its methodology in order to better account for the power imbalances embedded in archival practice. This study positions vernacular, familial photography as a generative social practice for identifying new sites of historical inquiry. Taking up Gillian Rose's (2016: 1) argument we need then "to think about family photography not simply as a collection of images, or as a textual archive, or as an ideology... but rather as something that people do: that is, as a social practice." However much of the critical literature on family photographs marginalizes these objects based on their lack of visual innovation. The most critical response to family photographs comes from within the realm of feminist scholarship (Evans 2007; Chamber, 2001; Spence 1986; Walkerdine 1990; Kuhn 2002), where it is argued that family albums in "their erasure of domestic labor, and the restricted emotional tones they convey, are complicit with women's physical and emotional exploitation" (Rose 8). While these critiques cite the limited terrain of signifying possibility dictated by the tropes of the genre and the seemingly artificial representations of familial life, they overlook the fact that all photographic practices are a mediated form of communication rather than an objective truth. We must then reorient our ideas about family photography towards an understanding that though it is an ambivalent practice, nonetheless it may work as a powerful and complex resource in reconstructing historically marginalized subject positions and social relations.

For many, family photographs and their talismanic properties are critical to achieving the state of being at home (Gregson 2011: 24). In documenting family history, representing private sentiment and displaying pride in one's lineage, these objects are then important tools for placemaking and the production of domestic space. In her discussion of how the camera and photographs affect Black lives, bell hooks (1994: 59) situates the home as a powerful site for an oppositional Black aesthetic:

> The walls and walls of images in southern Black homes were sites of resistance. They constituted private, Black-owned and -operated, gallery space where images could be displayed, shown to friends and strangers. These walls were a space where, in the midst of segregation, the hardship of apartheid, dehumanization could be countered.

In the shadow of histories of terror, enclosure, and surveillance and the representational practices that they engendered, the family photograph and its placement within the private sphere becomes a practice of counter-archiving. Speaking to the comforting presence of a hand-painted photo of her great-grandmother Katie Jackson, contemporary photographer Ayana Jackson describes a similar experience upon entering her grandparents' living room in East Orange, New Jersey. For Jackson the photographs of relatives and their placement within the home had a clear message: "You have a history, you have a legacy and there's something to look up to and live up to as a part of this family" (Estrin 2016). Here the wall of the home becomes a palimpsest documenting intergenerational triumphs and struggles, offering its viewer a space to encounter the ways in which family members gave materiality to their achievements, and aspirations.

Tina Campt's (2012: 5) work on the African diaspora in Europe suggests that photography can also function as a site of diasporic, racial and gendered subject-formation, challenging negative stereotypes and assumptions and creating a counterimage of who these subjects are, as well as who they might be, or become. They therefore have the ability to visualize creative forms of family produced over and against the disparate geographies and temporalities that constitute diasporic migration, settlement, and dwelling (Ibid.). Linking national identity to objects, Campt (2012: 163) argues that within these portraits props created a tangible link to the photographic subject. For instance, the purse formed part of a Sunday best outfit, which, when photographed and sent "back home", placed relatives and friends in a visual context of people "keeping faith" oceans away (Ibid.). Or, in the case of the McCurdy fonds where the circulation of photographic portraits across the Detroit River borderlands is evidenced by photographic studios or postage stamps naming sites from both sides of the Detroit River, "rivers away". In this context, the feminized work of taking, curating and distributing photographs played an essential role in maintaining familial bonds and documenting family histories. The objects within the fonds then speak to the transnational character of life in the borderlands, where photographs map and sustain networks of kinship. Here style became more than just a superficial means of cultural engagement but also a visual affirmation of their cultural and social relevance in their new home (164).

Within Canada the dual processes of settler colonialism—which annexed territory, forced Indigenous peoples onto reserves, instituted patriarchal governance, and destroyed cultural practices—and European immigration, helped to secure the dominion of white settlers over stolen land and resources (Maynard 2017: 32). As Robyn Maynard (Ibid.) argues, "both white supremacy and the outer appearance of racial tolerance were integral to the nation-building process and the creation of Canadian national identity." Racial formation shifts from its dependency on placing bodies within a hierarchy defined by scientific racism to situating bodies in conflict with racialized notions of cultural and national character. Sunera Thobani (2007: 158) explains: racial hierarchies become organized through the discourse of cultural and national difference, not of biological inferiority. Specifically "The inscription of specific 'national' characteristics into these subjects as elements of their innate humanity elevates such traits from the realm of 'natural' human existence and writes them into the body politic, thereby catapulting them into the sociocultural realm of the national symbolic." (Tobani 2007: 8). Cultural and national belonging are then racialized, and if we believe photographs to be social objects that produce social positions and social relations then they provide a fruitful site for examining how women negotiate subjectivity.

Because "all nationalisms are gendered", the function of gender power is crucial in understanding the formation of the nation-state (McClintock 2015: 352). Specifically, McClintock (355) identifies five ways in which women have been implicated in nationalism: as biological reproducers of the members of national collectivities; as reproducers of the boundaries of national groups (through restrictions on sexual or marital relations); as active transmitters and producers of the national culture; as symbolic signifiers of national difference; and, as active participants in national struggles. Nationalism is thus constituted from the very beginning as a gendered discourse and thus cannot be understood without a theory of gender power. The centrality of race to the Canadian nation building project is clearly articulated in dominant ideologies of Motherhood of the era (Arat-Koç 1989; Anderson 2009). The concept of Motherhood gained increased importance in Canada at the turn of the century. Faced with a declining British-Canadian birth rate, an influx of immigration, and the loss of the nation's white men during the Great War, the Canadian state turned to women of British background to act as the saviors of the race through their position as mothers (Green 2017). However, while emphasizing domesticity and motherhood as ideal roles for white women, dominant ideologies and institutions within Canada located racialized women as workers first and foremost even when this worker status was achieved at the expense of separation from family and children.

While studies of how Black women laborers navigated marginalized forms of work are crucial to our understanding of Canadian history, in some ways the visual discourse of Black womanhood in Canada has fostered a way of seeing.

This power dynamic that the archive reproduces contributes to an imbalance in what can be understood via visual sources about the historical experiences of these women. Derived from Audre Lorde's poem "Afterimages" about the murder of Emmett Till and its famous photographic representation, Kimberly Juanita Brown (2015: 1) conceptualizes the term "photographic afterimage" as the force of the photographic in engendering a discourse in the service of violated Black bodies—both past and present. Specifically, she employs the "afterimage" as a tool for navigating the trace of slavery's memory in Black women's literary and visual representations. In her own words:

> If we think of the afterimage as a violation of the gaze, the 'force that remains within,' the repetition of this force creates a visual circle that can seem unyielding. The afterimage as temporal motif, then, is the organizing mechanism suturing black women to the cultural narratives that have been used to placate black Atlantic subjectivities in flux. (Brown 2015:11)

She positions repetition as an ocular residue, a visual duplication as well as an alteration—perpetuating the visuality of hegemony (Brown 2015:13). For Brown, the visual solidifies representation and directs the trajectory of discourse. Here the body is infused with layers of meaning, with representations of these "marked bodies" having a profound ability to linger throughout the diaspora. Exploring the relationship between violence, sexuality and maternity within the institution of slavery, Brown (2015: 72) argues that "the racial and gendered construction of the mythology of Black women's maternal capacities is a vestige of the past revisited on the present and repeated, surviving efforts to dismantle it." This manifested most innocuously in the figure of the mammy—a symbolic image of service and surrogate mothering. In all of these constructions or tropes, the body represents a conflation of temporality and space, or an "archive of time" that simultaneously prefigures future slaughter and conquest, and survives it (177). Here Brown takes up Paul Gilroy's (2007) argument that the ineffable terrors of slavery were kept alive in ritualized social forms—that its residual traces still contribute to historical memories at the core of Afro-Atlantic cultural creation.

However the vernacular photographs of Black motherhood within the McCurdy fonds challenge what Brown (2015: 7) describes as the "enactments of hypervisibility [that] black women cannot escape." These photographs, then, assert Black subjectivities that may potentially rupture the "controlling

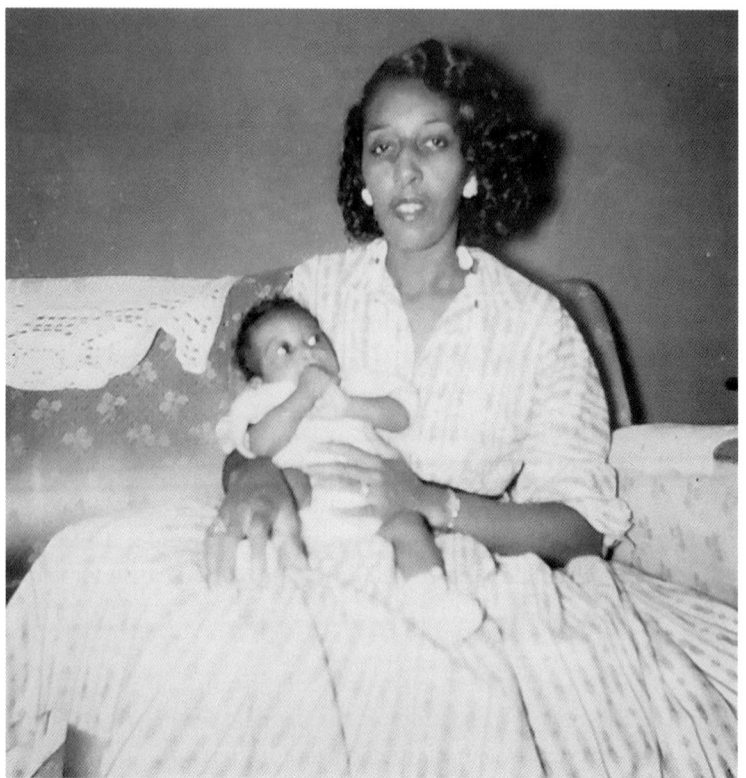

"Unknown Woman and Child", ca.1920s. Alvin D. McCurdy fonds, Archives of Ontario

images" of Blackness within Canadian visual culture. While careful not to name self-portraiture photography as a solution to the problem of racial legibility and slavery's afterlives, Brown (2015: 181) does concede that the medium and the pattern of "forced recognition" that it fosters allows for a greater measure of visual mobility. Here,

> the task of convincing a collective constituency of the subject's right to render the vicissitudes of her history a thing that is *seen* and therefore *known* falls to the image-maker herself, and the body she carries with her through the world (Brown 2015: 181).

Rather than the positivist renderings of the maternal that Brown describes throughout her text in which the sitter is framed as an object to be empirically "known", within the McCurdy fonds vernacular representations of motherhood assert the sitter's agency in directing the gaze, disclosing what she pleases. So while the previous examples illustrate how the Canadian visual archive conflates the Black body with servitude—bound to reproductive and productive processes— here, "mystery is freedom" (Ibid). Self-representation is then a site of struggle: the feminized work that stages the colloquial space and elicits the performance of poses required to produce the photographs under investigation here becomes crucial oppositional labor in countering the hierarchies of patriarchy, nation and state. These photographic practices offer us a richer picture of Black life in Amherstburg, Ontario.

Several of the photographs within the McCurdy fonds recuperate these invisibilized histories, documenting the family life of African Canadian women during the turn of the century. While tintype and cabinet card photographs were customarily the medium for documenting entire family units, the deckle-edge amateur photograph appears to be the common medium for picturing a mother and her children. One example from the McCurdy fonds features a mother seated on a floral sofa complete with a lace cover holding her child on her lap [Figure 4]. The skirt of her dress takes up more than half of the frame, the young infant nestled among the folds of her voluminous dress. Though not as neatly staged as a studio portrait, this photograph is clearly orchestrated to demonstrate the sitter's self-containment. This is most legible in the obvious coordination between her dress and that of her child's, as well as her freshly

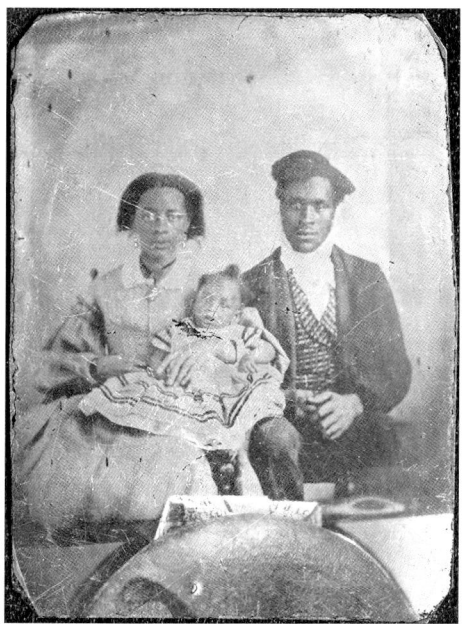

applied lipstick and her ring finger prominently displayed just below the centre of the image's frame. What this photograph represents then is mastery of the domestic space—an obedient child, and immaculately turned out mother, within the clean and well-appointed home—at once demonstrating and masking the immense labor and energy put into this performance. While we will never know who is taking the image, this trend speaks to the idea that vernacular photography was viewed as a more appropriate site for

"Tintype of unknown family, Amherstburg, Ontario", ca. 18--.
Alvin D. McCurdy fonds, Archives of Ontario

representing maternal relationships. Father figures are very rarely pictured in these amateur photographs, rather they make their appearance in the more formal family photographs taken outside of the domestic space [Figure 5]. This may be because of the low cost of the gelatin silver print compared to a formal portrait taken in a studio where certain modes of dress were enforced. The maternal photograph then existed most frequently in an informal or candid state—speaking perhaps to both the intimacy of the relationship and how it was regarded as somewhat secondary to the larger family dynamics.

These representational strategies speak to Frantz Fanon's observation that "there are close connections between the structure of the family and the structure of the nation" (McClintock 2015: 360). Fanon destabilizes the idea that this projection is normal or natural, and reads familial normality as a product of social power—of social violence. In particular, as McClintock (360) explains,

> Fanon is remarkable for recognizing, in this early text, how military violence and the authority of a centralized state borrow on and enlarge the domestication of gender power within the family: Militarization and the centralization of authority in a country automatically entail a resurgence of the authority of the father.

It can be said then that picturing the family patriarch required a more formal and therefore costly medium, more suitable to representing a cohesive structure as well as a rigid hierarchical structure. It follows then that the surplus excess of the handheld camera, with its affordability and reproducibility made it more suitable for the task of maternal photographs taken within the domestic space.

By nature of this fact, within the McCurdy fonds the house front becomes a popular setting for staging maternal photographs. This thematic was commented on by Hirsch (1981: 48): "Entire houses, house fronts, and stoops in varying scales and proportion, show us the family's territory, symbolic of its place in the world." Throughout the McCurdy fonds there are numerous photographs that feature women, with and without their children, standing proudly in front of their homes [Figure 6]. The home front functions within these amateur photographs as a declaration of property, a suggestion of spatial mastery. Similar to the photographs taken inside of the home, these house front stagings are organized like a more formal portrait taken within a studio. In one example a woman and her daughter stand outside their home on a sun drenched porch [Figure 7]. Both mother and child are fashionably dressed and

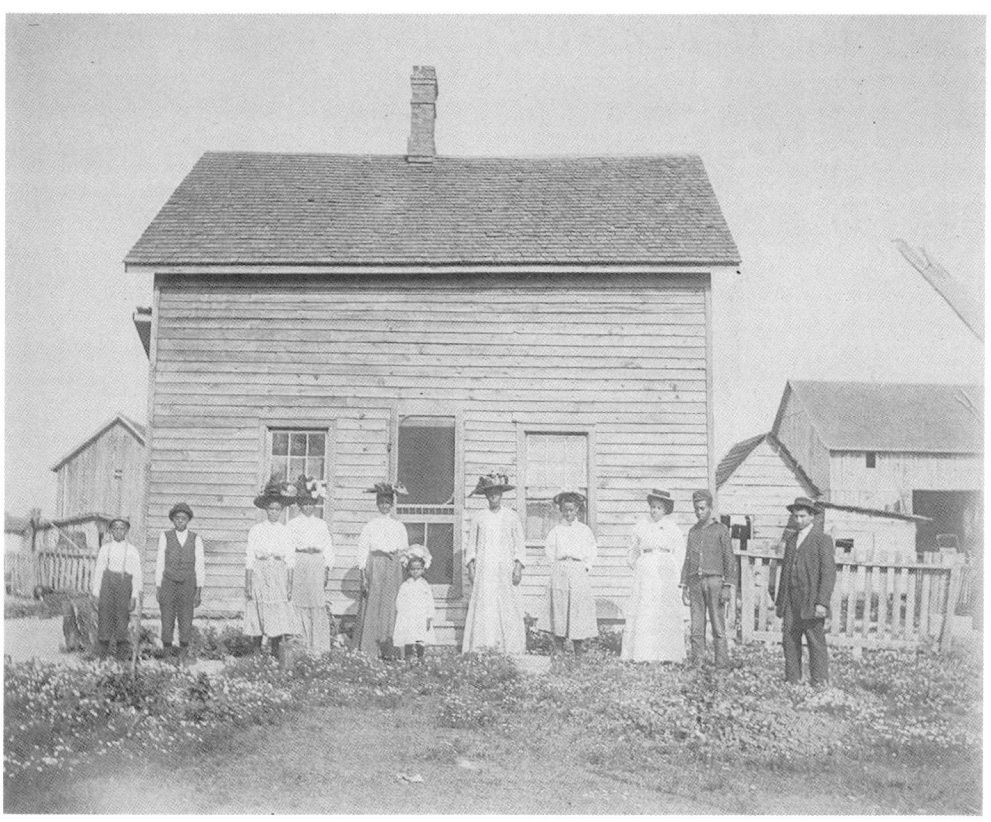

"Harris, Hill, and Holland families in front of homestead, possibly in Essex County", ca. 1900. Alvin D. McCurdy fonds, Archives of Ontario

well accessorized, and while the shadow of the photographer can be seen in the foreground, the lighting of the shot permits a clear rendering of both subjects. Similarly organized is a photograph of a young child dressed in a petticoat and bonnet with immaculate white shoes and matching lace socks, standing in front of the steps of a home [Figure 8]. Again the subject is facing the bright sunlight, casting a shadow into the frame that can clearly be identified as a woman based on the silhouette of her hat and coat. Likely the child's mother, the woman has carefully crafted this representation. The compositional structure of these photographs is such that both the subjects and the background take up significant space within the frame, suggesting that inclusion of the housefront was an intentional act. Just as backdrops used in commercial portrait studios contribute to the meanings produced in photographic space, within vernacular photograph the background plays an equally important role in elevating and animating its subjects. Here domestic space functions via its

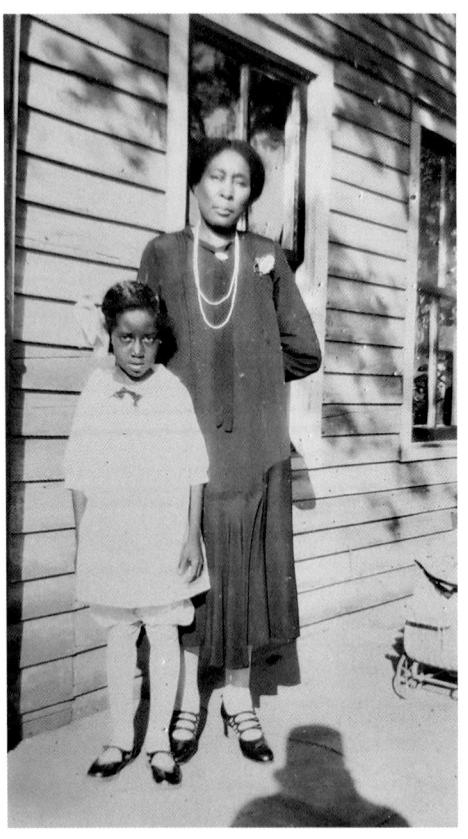

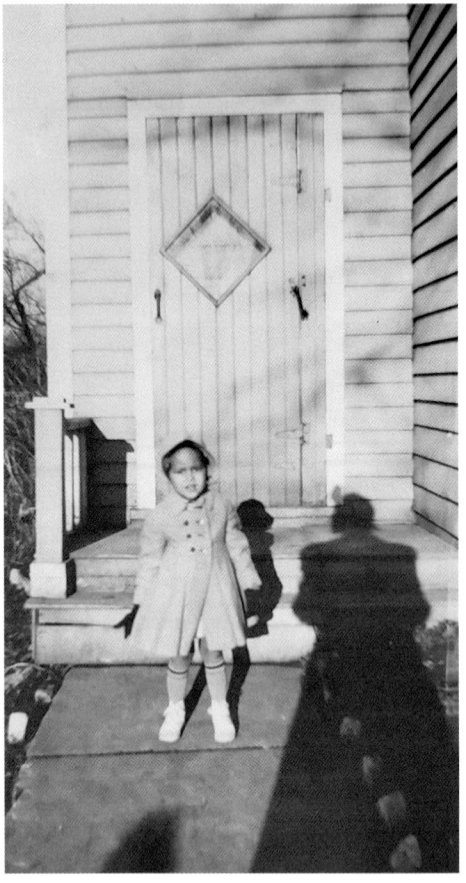

"Phillis Allen and Mrs. Allen, Amherstburg, Ontario", ca. 1920. Alvin D. McCurdy fonds, Archives of Ontario.

"Joan taken outside door of Mom's house on Seymour St., Amherstburg", ca. 1930. Alvin D. McCurdy fonds, Archives of Ontario.

associative qualities able to engage different modes of seeing and inscribe social identities codified by socio-political aspects of the domestic.

Though mothering practices and relations varied enormously within specific historical moments, the reliance on these mythical ideals of the mother rests on the importation of European ideologies. In particular, the home becomes a metaphor for the nation-state, stratified and contingent on shared beliefs of common goals. As Hirsch remarks (1981: 21): "The image of the family as a spiritual assembly overlaps with the image of the state. While the latter describes the family's relationship to the physical world, the former describes its shared eternal values". As illustrated by photographs and oral histories within the fonds, long-standing Black communities in Canada built their own schools, homes and churches, and raised their own barns all while experiencing violent backlash from neighboring white communities. Indicative of this sentiment, in the October 27, 1849 issue of the *Amherstburg Courier* a local white resident declared that "there is but one feeling, and that is of disgust and hatred, that they (the Negroes) should be allowed to settle in any township where there is white settlement" (Landon 1925: 6). In this way, these photographs have a resistive quality—demonstrating situated knowledges of communities, and their contributions to both real and imagined human geographies (McKittrick and Woods 2007: 4). At the time these photographs were taken formal and informal segregation policies were enacted across all facets of Canadian society, "one of Canada's foremost strategies for maintaining white dominance" (Maynard 2017: 32–33). Segregated residentially, and subject to practices of containment, Black presence itself was heavily surveilled and resisted (37). The 1920s through the end of the Second World War—the decades in which these photographs were taken—saw an expanded focus on restricting Black presence in public space through "sundown laws", curfews, and bylaws (Ibid.). When read alongside the local histories of Amherstburg, a place where Black settlers struggled with and resisted against racism on a daily basis, the inclusion of outer and inner spaces of family experience within these photographs suggest a mode of claiming presence. While formal mapping practices may, as Katherine McKittrick and Clyde Woods (2007) maintain, overlook, erase or segregate Black geographies, here we see a reorienting of social-spatial dynamics in favor of commemorating distinctive local identities. In this way the photographs articulate the locally derived material experiences of both Black women, and the larger Black community of Amherstburg, Ontario—geographic subjects under erasure within Canada's nation building project.

The photographs analyzed here are a feminized form of cultural production that validate the historical experiences of Black women in Canada. Moreover, they are objects that give materiality to their own specific desires and pleasures, and are a fruitful site for examining entrenched ideologies of womanhood. Though the production of such portraits required careful adherence to tropes of gendered familial structures and middle-class national subjects, these amateur photographs are also capable of reorienting the gaze and actively producing new subjectivities. They radically transgress the conceptions of Black womanhood that have been normalized through the proliferation of negative stereotypes and assumptions via print culture. These hegemonic constructions of Black racial identity, which have their basis in histories of enslavement, shape the contours of popular memory and influence how images of Black woman-hood are perceived and interpreted. Despite their ephemerality, anonymity and partiality, the photographs under examination here give critical insight into how Black women used this technology to create representations that corresponded to the realities, hopes, and aspirations within their own lives.

Notes

1   Alvin D. McCurdy was born in 1916 in Amherstburg, Essex County, Ontario—a major terminus of the Underground Railroad. Like many Black communities formed at the borderlands of Southwestern Ontario, McCurdy's family history is linked to the processes of migration that defined the African Diaspora in the nineteenth century. Interested in his family's genealogy and the broader history of Black settlement in southwestern, Ontario, Alvin McCurdy collected material throughout his life in order to preserve his community's heritage (Crooks 2019, 77). He believed this archival labour necessary, as these histories were largely ignored by traditional cultural institutions and were in danger of erasure. Through donations and voracious collecting, his personal collection blossomed into one of the richest sources of African-Canadian archival material in Ontario, containing roughly 3,000 photographic objects, as well as textual files, oral history interviews, and literary works, with materials that pre-date the founding of the province in 1791, and extend through the mid-twentieth century. McCurdy worked professionally as a carpenter and was a long-time member of the Carpenters and Joiners Union, as well as a Freemason and active member of local anti-discrimination groups.

Works Cited

Anderson, K. (2009). "The Mother Country: Tracing Intersections of Motherhood and the National Story in Recent Canadian Historiography," *Atlantis* 34, 1: 121–131.

Arat-Koç,S.(1989). "In the Privacy of Our Own Home: Foreign Domestic Workers as Solution to the Crisis of the Domestic Sphere in Canada." *Studies in Political Economy* 28 (Spring 1989): 33–58.

Braithwaite, R. and T. Benn-Ireland (1993). *Some Black Women, Profiles of Black Women in Canada*. Toronto: Sister Vision Press.

Brand, D. (1991). *No Burden to Carry: Narratives of Black Working Women in Ontario, 1920s to 1950s*. Toronto: Women's Press.

———(1994). "'We Weren't Allowed to Go into Factory Work until Hitler Started the War': The 1920s to the 1940s." In *We're Rooted Here and They Can't Pull Us up: Essays in African Canadian Women's History*, edited by Peggy Bristow et al., 171–192. Toronto: University of Toronto Press.

Brown, K. J. (2015). *The Repeating Body: Slavery's Visual Resonance in the Contemporary*. Durham: Duke University Press.

Campt, T. (2012). *Image Matters: Archive, Photography, and the African Diaspora in Europe*. Durham: Duke University Press.

Chambers, D. (2001). *Representing the Family*. London; Thousand Oaks; New Delhi: Sage.

Crooks, J. (2019). "Exerting and Cultivating Selves: Nineteenth-Century Photography and the Black Subject in Southern Ontario." In *Towards an African Canadian Art History: Art, Memory, and Resistance*, ed. Charmaine Nelson, 63–68. Concord: Captus Press.

Davis, A. Y. (2011). *Women, Race, & Class*. New York: Random House US.

Estrin, J. (2016) "Honoring the Legacy of African-American Women." *The New York Times*, (May. 26, 2016), https://lens.blogs.nytimes.com/2016/05/26/honoring-the-legacy-of-african-american-women/ (accessed July 13, 2020).

Evans, J. and S. Hall (2007). *Visual Culture: The Reader*. Los Angeles, CA.: Sage Publications.

Farmer, A. D. (2018). "Into the Stacks: In Search of the Black Women's History." *Archive Modern American History* 1: 289–293.

Gilroy, P. (2007). *The Black Atlantic: Modernity and Double Consciousness*. London: Verso.

Green, H. (2017). "The Rise of Motherhood: Maternal Feminism and Health in the Rural Prairie Provinces, 1900-1930." *Past Imperfect* 20, 1: 48–70.

Gregson, N. (2011). *Living with things: ridding, accommodation, dwelling*. Wantage: Sean Kingston.

Hall, C. (1992). *White, male and middle-class: explorations in feminism and history*. Cambridge: Polity Press.

Hamilton, S., C. Prieto, and S. Mackenzie (1989). *Black Mother, Black Daughter* Montreal: National Film Board of Canada.

Hamilton, S. (1994). "Naming Names, Naming Ourselves: A Survey of Early Black Women in Nova Scotia." In *We're Rooted Here and They Can't Pull Us up: Essays in African Canadian Women's History*, edited by Peggy Bristow et al., 13–40. Toronto: University of Toronto Press.

Harris, R. L. (1988). "The Transformation of Canadian Policies and Programs to Recruit Foreign Labor: The Case of Caribbean Female Domestic Workers, 1950's-1980's." Michigan State University, Ph.D.

Hirsch, J. (1981). *Family photographs: content, meaning and effect*. New York: Oxford University Press.

hooks, bell (1994). "In Our Glory: Photography and Black Life." in *Picturing Us: African American Identity in Photography*, edited by Deborah Willis, 54–64. New York: The New Press.

———— (2016). *Images of Black History, Exploring the Alvin McCurdy Collection*. Archives of Ontario, North York.

Kuhn, A. (2002). *Family secrets: acts of memory and imagination*. London: Verso.

Maynard, R. (2017). *Policing Black Lives: State Violence in Canada from Slavery to the Present*. Halifax: Fernwood Publishing.

McClintock, A. (2015). *Imperial Leather Race, Gender and Sexuality in the Colonial Contest* .New York: Routledge.

McKittrick, K. and C. A. Woods eds. (2007). *Black Geographies and the Politics of Place*. Toronto: Between the Lines.

Rose, G. (2016). *Doing Family Photography: The Domestic, the Public and the Politics of Sentiment*. London: Routledge.

Singh, N. (2005). *Black is a Country: Race and the Unfinished Struggle for Democracy* Cambridge, Mass.: Harvard University Press.

Spence, J. (1986). *Beyond the Family Album*. London: Virago.

Thobani, S. (2007). *Exalted Subjects: Studies in the Making of Race and Nation in Canada* Toronto: University of Toronto Press.

Walkerdine, V. (1990). *Schoolgirl Fictions*. London; New York: Verso.

7. "I LIKE TO MAKE PICTURES OF CHILDREN"

African American Women Photographers and Wielding
the Weapon of 'Motherhood'

EMILY BRADY _____

In 1944, Eslanda Goode Robeson delivered an address for the Pro Merito Club Convention at Tech High School in Springfield, Massachusetts—her son's high school. Robeson was an activist, author, actress, and anthropologist, whose book *African Journey* (1945) offered a rare African American woman's perspective on the African continent. She used her platform at this address to criticize the United States government's focus on "total war," which had caused people to lose focus on a world in which children "are intelligently, comprehensively educated, physically, mentally, and morally" (Castledine 2012: 93). Jacqueline Castledine cites this speech in her text *Cold War Progressives: Women's Interracial Organizing for Peace and Freedom* (2012) as an example of how African American activists used their roles as mothers to further their political agendas. Castledine asserts that Robeson's experiences delivering public speeches at this time "offered Robeson the opportunity to develop her own concept of activist motherhood" (Castledine 2012: 93). Furthermore, Castledine suggests that this could be seen in the ideology of the Black women—including Robeson—who formed the Progressive Party in 1948, as their "civil rights agenda would intersect with Progressive motherhood, as understandings of maternal peace activism were informed by the concept of 'mothering the race,'" as the African American women involved in forming the party "integrated issues of race and maternalism, making motherhood both a peace and civil rights issue" (Castledine 2012: 85). As such, Castledine reveals how Robeson effectively weaponized the role of motherhood for her activism. Yet, Castledine overlooks a vital component of Robeson's activist identity: her passion for photography. Extending the idea of activist motherhood into not just the realm of Robeson's photographic work, but also into the realm of several other African American women photographers who worked within the realm of portraiture, reveals how the label of motherhood was effectively weaponized and wielded by African American women photographers in the decades prior to World War Two.

Robeson and other African American women photographers utilized the label of motherhood within their photographic work to their advantage in multiple ways. In some cases, such as for professional portraitists, the advantage was economic and indirectly activistic. Portraitists such as Wilhelmina Pearl Selina Roberts, Elnora Teal, and Florestine Collins would all wield the tool of motherhood in their portrait studios to enable their, at the time, unusual careers, and to provide their communities with aesthetically desirable images of their children in ways which combatted white-held racist stereotypes. For these three women, this was in part due to their situation in the American South, where gendered labor took on more conservative forms which more clearly evoked the theme of motherhood, specifically in the era before World War Two.[1] In other cases, such as in Robeson's anthropological work, the advantage was educational and overtly activist. Robeson used her label as a mother to create familial ties to Africa, championing a deeper diasporic connection between people of African descent. In using motherhood as a tool, these women—some mothers, some not—were able to effectively promote racial pride and protest against white supremacy. African American women across multiple photographic modes used their role—or implied role based on gendered expectations—as mothers with innate sensitivities to children to further their careers and add greater moral weight to their photography. By adhering to the problematic ideals of the 'politics of respectability' and speaking to ideals of pictorialism, these photographs advocate for the dignity and humanity of those captured in their lens. In this way, the label of 'motherhood' served to disrupt a masculinized field of work. Although the label of 'motherhood' could be one with limitations, in occupying this space these women created photographs that not only advocated a familial perspective, but also protested against white-held racist notions of Black inferiority.

Thanks to the research of academics such as Jeanne Moutoussamy-Ashe (1985), Deborah Willis (2000), and Arthé A. Anthony (2012), the works and lives of African American women photographers have become more visible than ever before. A powerful canon of imagery produced by African American women reflecting the realities of life in the 20th century is emerging and revealing a history that combines race, gender, and photographic areas of study. Building on this recovery work, this chapter seeks to expand the groundwork on which it is necessary to consider the role of 'motherhood' in African

American women's photography before World War Two. For many of these photographers, the role of motherhood was an aesthetic device, a network through which to access new audiences, and a marketing device that simultaneously increased and decreased their reach. As such, this paper will offer a new framework which expands our understanding of "motherhood" as a tool which opened doors for African American women photographers in this era.

"She and My Father Started a Mission": Motherhood and Portraiture in the American South

Maternalism and the notion of motherhood often formed a key part of a white women's role in the Progressive Era (Ladd-Taylor 1993). For African American women, however, the Progressive Era was a complicated landscape to navigate, as they were confronted with both racism and sexism, and would not officially be able to exercise their right to vote until the Voting Rights Act of 1965. Nevertheless, the idea that women possessed a unique set of qualities that made them better suited to some kinds of public work and activism took root. African American women were involved in maternalistic reform cultures, as both reformers and targets of reform, commonly within the Church. Some practices that by modern standards we can recognize as problematic were embraced. Evelyn Brooks Higginbotham spoke of a "politics of respectability" that was adopted by the Women's Convention of the Black Baptist Church during the Progressive era (Higginbotham 1993: 14). This was the idea that by following Victorian ideals of behavior and conduct, "reform of individual behavior [functioned] as a goal in itself and as a strategy for reform" (Higginbotham 1993: 187). By policing their conduct in such a way, these women also attempted to protect themselves and their communities from brutality and violence. This not only enforced the idea of progressive values and "dignified" conduct among African Americans themselves, but also challenged the racist stereotypes commonly held by white people. Floris Barnett Cash noted this in her analysis of African American clubwomen from 1896–1936, as they "looked to progress and respectability to bring the masses in step with the values and attitudes of the middle class. [...] The politics of respectability was a means of expressing Black women's identity, discontent, and agenda for social action." (Cash 2001: 4) By evoking the idea of 'motherhood' in their photography, the women in this essay engaged with this longer tradition of class aspirations as a route to racial pride.

It would be easy to fall into a discussion of the merits of the "politics of respectability" as a strategy for reform, and indeed the approach has been roundly criticized. E. Franklin Frazier vocally criticized ideas of respectability through a class lens. He argued that the Black bourgeois have "accepted unconditionally the values of the white bourgeois world: its morals and its canons of respectability, its standards of beauty and consumption" (Frazier 1965: 26). In so doing, Frazier argues that the politics of respectability hinges on the wholehearted rejection of the African American "folk" culture. This view may certainly be supported by the pictorialist techniques which the women in this chapter adopt, a form generated by white people. Indeed, they do seek to emulate a middle class standard, to the exclusion of a more working class "folk" identity. The same can be said of the women in this chapter themselves—they belonged to the Black upper and middle class, which afforded them a degree of social mobility and enabled them to progress in their unusual careers as photographers. However, although the idea of the "politics of respectability" was problematic for holding its class aspirations to white standards and rejecting the culture of the African American working class, the women in this chapter arguably did not possess the social capital to either problematize this idea or present an alternative aesthetic. To argue the righteousness of such an approach does not erase the fact that these images were produced, and that they were effective tools to challenge white, racist stereotypes in the private and public sphere. The influence of progressive ideals can be seen in the field of pictorialist photography, which early African American women's photography evoked in significant ways.

Pictorialism was a mode of photography for which women were thought to be especially well suited, based on their inherent feminine qualities. Although there is no precise definition of pictorialism, Davidov writes that "Pictorialist photographers, one might say, wished to preserve in their carefully crafted pictures the very thing Walter Benjamin would declare dead after the invention of photography: the *aura*, the unique and irreproducible quality that made a pictorial work 'art'" (Davidov 1998: 52). Within this field, and for the first time in photographic history, women's femininity was a desirable trait. Rosenblum writes that "women were supposed to have an intrinsic artistry that enabled them to convey each individual's character and to understand the virtue of indefiniteness, which brought the camera image closer to handmade art" (Rosenblum 1994: 75). Davidov notes that "Käsebier's special interest in studies of mothers and children had to do with her interest in progressive child-raising methods" (Davidov 1998: 60), as can be seen by her images.

However, these women explored pictorialism in the late nineteenth and early twentieth centuries in the early stages of the Progressive Era, and it would take African American women until at the earliest the 1920s to meaningfully engage with pictorialism due to the lack of accessibility to the camera. The notable work of the Black women portrait photographers discussed in this chapter—Wilhelmina Roberts, Elnora Teal and Florestine Collins—should be considered as part of this canon.

Alongside the mode of pictorialism, the emergence of portraiture as a component of African American family life was significant. Portraits of loved ones, friends, and even admired celebrities became commonplace in African American homes in the 20th century.[2] Arthé A. Anthony argues that the photographs Florestine Collins produced were "examples of the visual weapons African Americans used in their fight for self-representation in the 1920s era of the 'New Negro,'" an analysis which extends to Roberts and Teal's images as well. The idea of photography as "visual weapons" in combatting white supremacy within the private realm of the home has been well-documented, as photography promoted African American racial pride (Anthony 2002:167–168). In the contemporary moment, Ayana V Jackson's work can be seen as a powerful example of this approach.[3] Jackson echoes figures such as W. E. B. Du Bois and bell hooks when she comments that, "the photos on my grandfather's wall were propaganda meant to counter all the other negative propaganda I was bombarded with every day" (Estrin 2016). Almost a hundred years ago, W. E. B. Du Bois (1926: 295) famously stated that:

> All art is propaganda and ever must be, despite the wailing of the purists. I stand in utter shamelessness and say that whatever art I have for writing has been used always for propaganda for gaining the right of black folk to love and enjoy. I do not care a damn for any art that is not used for propaganda.

That Du Bois took this attitude is notable given the prominent role of photography and portraiture in *The Crisis* magazine. On multiple occasions, portraits of children would appear on the front cover, which suggests that Du Bois (1912: 261–312) viewed these seemingly domesticated images as tools, or "propaganda," through which to challenge the racism of the white population. Contemporary academics such as bell hooks have expanded on Du Bois' understanding of the correlation between activism and portraiture, arguing that the photography which seemingly should exist in a private sphere can have a powerful impact on the audience. In Southern African American homes, bell hooks noted the prominence of images on the walls, functioning as "sites of resistance" and "a space where... dehumanization could be countered" (hooks 1995: 59). hooks notes that these images opposed "the degrading images of blackness that emerged from the racist white imagination and that were circulated widely in the dominant culture" (hooks 1995:59). In this way, extending the ideologies of hooks and Du Bois, the images produced by African American women in this chapter served as weapons to protest against the racist stereotypes of the era. The work of Deborah Willis is further testament to this, particularly *Family History Memory: Recording African American Life* (2005). In this text, Willis explores her own photography and the lives and works of many other photographers. She notes the work of three photographers whose "personal art interrogates or overturns social ideas to make powerful statements about race and gender in American culture" (Willis 2005: 188). Therefore, Willis asserts that family photography can function outside of a purely domestic sphere, suggesting that it can serve activist functions that challenge the widely held racist beliefs of the time.

Both the pictorialist aesthetic and the role of portraiture in family life suggest the role of motherhood in the photography of African American women portrait photographers. This relationship is exemplified in their work. An important example includes their images of young children, including those taken by Wilhelmina Pearl Selina Roberts. A college-educated, family-orientated woman, Roberts was one of only 101 African American female photographers by 1920 according to census statistics (Rosenblum 1994: 31). Roberts took photographs within the studio which her husband ran; following their marriage in 1902, they moved to Columbia, South Carolina with their eight children in 1920. Here, Richard opened a photographic studio, named The Roberts' Art Studio (Wynn unpublished interview). Despite the studio being Richard's venture, Roberts "learned from her husband the mechanics of the camera," as she managed the studio and took photographs when he was at work (Moutoussamy-Ashe 1985: 40). Roberts took the initiative to read photographic books, thus gaining her own knowledge on the subject, despite having no formal training or instruction aside from that which her husband taught her (Moutoussamy-Ashe 1985: 40). She followed her passion for motherhood, as her daughter noted that: "my mother was crazy about babies," and that she would often combine her own childcare with her work as a photographer, stating "she was sort of minding her own baby while she was taking the picture of this other child"

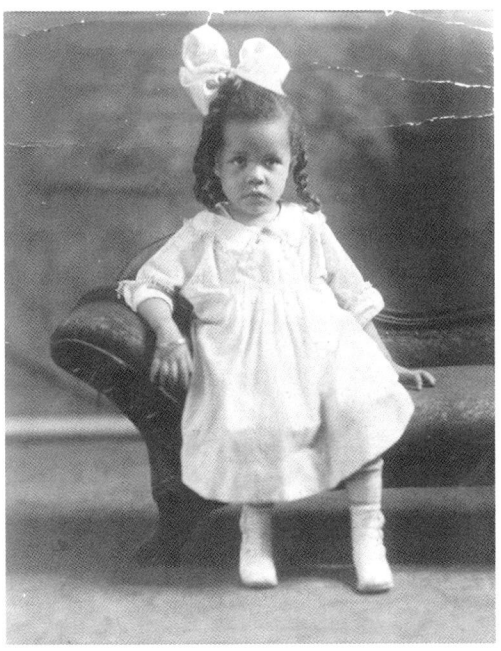

Figure 1. Wilhelmina Roberts, Wilhelmina Robert's daughter, date unknown. Courtesy of the South Caroliniana Library, University of South Carolina, Columbia, SC

(Wynn unpublished interview). These images of children became Roberts' area of expertise.

Roberts' images of children demonstrate not just the centrality of motherhood to her work, but her focus on respectability. Indeed, the photograph Roberts took of her own daughter underlines the notions of respectability within pictorialism (Fig. 1). In this image, the young girl wears a white dress framed against a dark background. The notion of pictorialism is apparent with the use of feminine props, such as the chaise longue, which performs the dual function of creating a stylish portrait and suggesting affluence. In this way, the image of a young child performs the respectability and middle class aspirations of the family. This is an aspiration that, according to her daughter, Roberts understood all too well, as the fact that her mother was once enslaved meant that she "was trying very hard to become educated and move away from slavery and I think it was important to her how people looked" (Moutoussamy-Ashe 1985: 15). As Roberts's daughter maintains, "she felt photography was an important record. She and my father started a mission" (Moutoussamy-Ashe 1985: 15). This idea of photography as a "mission" speaks to the activist connotations raised by Willis, as well as her emphasis on creating an archive of her family images. To record one's family at their best, and fulfil middle class aspirations, was a desire that the Roberts family's slave past perhaps entrenched in Roberts' photographic staging.

Nor was Roberts alone as an African American woman evoking pictorialist styles in the early 20th-century portrait photography; figures such as Elnora Teal were active as well. Teal and her husband Arthur C. Teal both became established photographers in their own right, but at the time of their marriage, Arthur was an itinerant photographer who travelled and took images. Upon their marriage in 1919, Arthur taught Teal the basics of photography and opened a studio in Houston, Texas at 111 Andrews Street (Moutoussamy-Ashe

1985: 44). Initially they worked together as photographer and photographic assistant, but as the business expanded, so too did Teal's role, as "she grew to love developing photos in the studio." (44) Within a few years, the Teals had opened two studios: one at 411 ½ Milan in downtown Houston, and another on Dowling Street in the heart of the Black residential community. When Arthur purchased the second studio, Teal became the sole runner of the Milan studio, entirely independent of her husband. Although they shared the same name—The Teal Portrait Studio—and they considered their businesses one, Teal had complete creative control over her studio.

Teal's studio proved particularly popular with women and children. Her images display many of the conventions of portraiture that African American women adhered to during the early 20th century. Her female clients saw Teal's gender as an advantage, as she "paid such close attention to detail" and "bought photography supplies the way some women bought materials for their fine dresses" (Moutoussamy-Ashe 1985: 45). The gendered language of this assertion reveals the key role that Teal's own gender played in her clients' assessments of her. Teal's photography, including one portrait of an unidentified young child, adhered closely to the principles of pictorialism. Like the

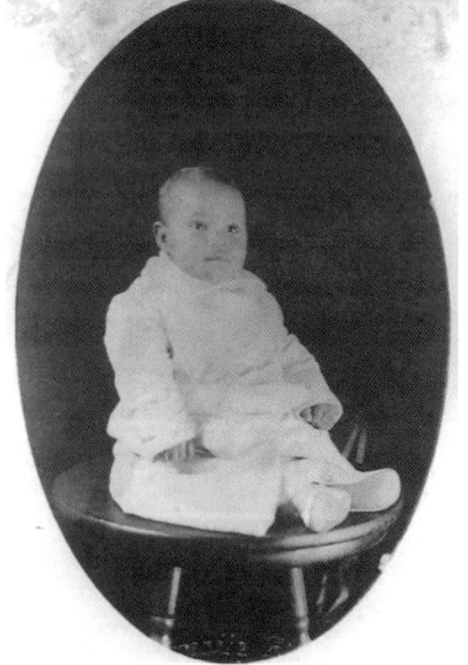

Roberts image, Teal contrasted white cloth on dark backgrounds, with a soft focus, and a use of theatricalized staging (as evidenced by the chair that the child is leaning on and the bonnet they are wearing). Furthermore, the fall of the fabric and the age of the child, coupled with the child's upright pose, suggest that there may be someone or something behind the infant holding them up.[4] Whilst it is difficult to say for certain, the conventions of child portraiture during the early 20th century suggest that this is likely, and illustrates Teal's professional handling of her youngest clients. In this way, Teal

Figure 2. Florestine Collins, Joseph Sordelet, Jr., 1923.
Used with the permission of Arthé A. Anthony.

captured an image of a child most likely in their Sunday best, reflecting the ideals of the period that the family wished to project. Features of this image can also be seen in the work of Florestine Collins.

Florestine Collins was born in New Orleans in 1895 and was of Creole descent. Collins had to leave school in 1909 at age fourteen to support her family, and took the dangerous decision to pass for white in order to work in photographic studios. In the Jim Crow era, this practice was one of the ways to avoid racialized domestic work that often left women vulnerable to exploitation or sexual assault from their white employers (Anthony 2012: 26). In the 1910s she worked as a clerk for finisher Jerome Hannafin, as a finisher for Herbert J. Harvery, and as a developer for the Eastman Kodak Company (Anthony 2002: 170). She would open her first studio in 1920 in the domestic space of her own living room, before expanding into her own studio space. Yet despite her different circumstances to those of Roberts and Teal, who started careers with their husbands, Collins' images of children would mirror them in many ways. Her photographs of young babies evoke many of the same pictorialist techniques as her contemporaries (Fig. 2). For example, the baby in this image is positioned on a piece of furniture, in pale clothing, against a dark background. The combination of white, respectable clothing and props conveys the pictorialist tradition in this image, enacting the class aspirations of the baby's parents as a route to racial dignity and pride in line with the "politics of respectability." The image could go on to function as a "site of resistance" within the family home, as advocated by bell hooks, and also as "propaganda" to challenge white-held notions of Black inferiority, as advocated by Du Bois. Hence, producing images of this nature effectively challenged racist stereotypes, as African Americans were able to present themselves as they wished to be seen, and display them as they saw fit.

That Collins directly linked her own gender, and therefore her capacity for inherent motherly skills, to her work can be seen by examining her advertisements. A *New Orleans Herald* advertisement from 1925 stated:

WHY NOT A PICTURE OF THE CHILD
With the First Book Bag, on the Way to
School for the First Time
Preserve That Wonderful Event
BERTRAND'S STUDIO
I Like to Make Pictures of Children

(Anthony 2012: 41)

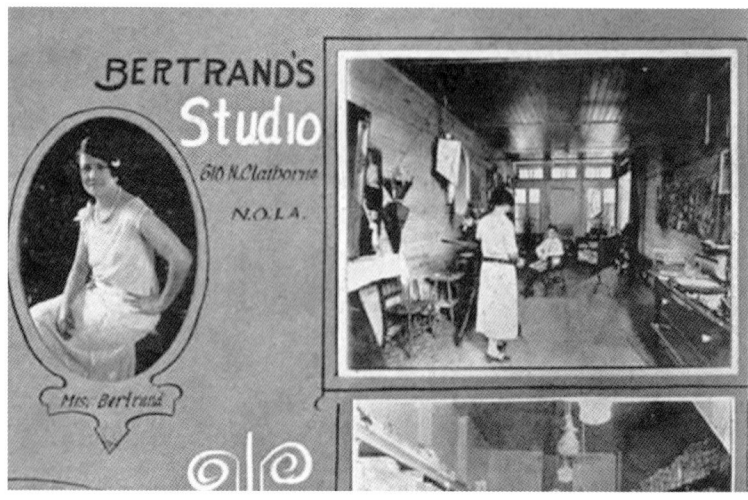

Figure 3. OCW Taylor, The Crescent City Pictorial, 1926. Source: Digital Library Website, Amistad Research Center, New Orleans, LA

Arthé A. Anthony maintains that this advertisement "appeals to mothers with its implications that as a woman photographer, she had special skills for understanding the importance of critical moments in a child's development" (41). Although Collins never had any children herself, she used her gender and the assumptions that people made at the time to directly compound her status as a businesswoman. In this way, Collins signified her gender through her advertising to imply that she had innate motherly instincts which would produce a better photograph of children than her male competitors. In other words, Collins utilized the label of motherhood for a competitive advantage.

Collins takes this even further in her 1926 advert in *The Crescent City Pictorial*, as she makes an image of herself central to the advertisement (Fig. 3). We can see that Collins (then named Bertrand) makes herself the focal point of the advertisement. Within the context of the wider page, the self-portrait of Collins sits centrally, her direct gaze emphasized by the fact that it is the only portrait on the page. Hence, it immediately catches the reader's eye. Collins' gesture and body language suggest confidence, as she sits with one hand on her hip. Once the portrait has caught the reader's attention, however, it is the second image on the right that asserts her identity as a businesswoman. A small boy sits in the center of the frame, as the high ceilings dwarf him, and a downward angle is created by the perspective of the room. Collins, standing to the viewer's left, contrasts this image in her pale dress, and frames the boy both literally within the scene and spatially within the photograph. Here, we see Collins at work, not looking at the camera. In the potentially intimidating space of the studio, Collins bridges the gap between the viewer and the boy she photographs. In so doing, she

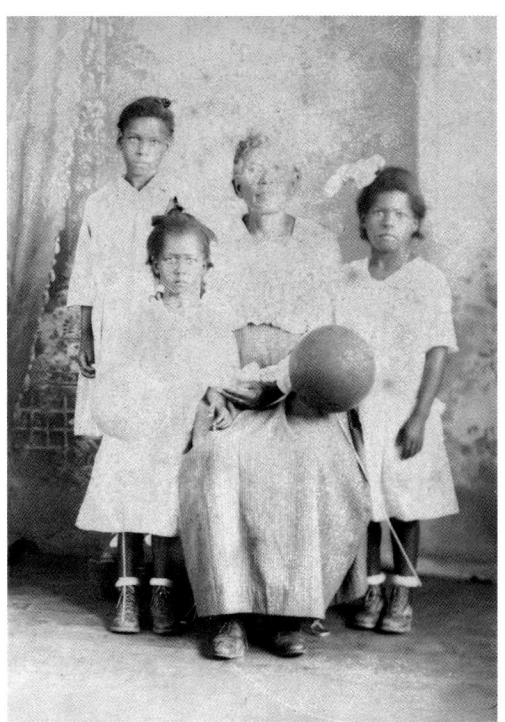

Figure 4. Wilhelmina Roberts, Grandmother with three children, date unknown. Courtesy of the South Carolina Library, University of South Carolina, Columbia, SC

casts herself as a protective, motherly force in these images. Unlike many white female photographers, who by the 1920s were able to take their cameras into outside spaces, Collins creates a physically safe, interior domestic space in both her advertising and her images. When reaching out to her community, Collins orientates herself around her gender, using it to generate business for herself and establish her unique identity compared to her male counterparts. Thus, signifying the language and imagery of 'motherhood' was crucial to this success.

Due to the collaborative nature of their studios, there are no similar advertisements that pinpoint a similar attitude in the marketing of Roberts or Teal. Yet this evocation of family dynamics can be seen in the content of their photographs, and specifically within their images of familial groups. Roberts's image *Grandmother with three children* exhibits this, as it draws on notions of pictorialism (Fig. 4). The contrast between the white dresses and the dark background, use of props in the form of balloons, and soft focus creates a feminine quality to this image. In addition, what little can be seen of the painted backdrop suggests flowers, curtains, and a painted bay window, which is again consistent with the romantic qualities of pictorialism within a domestic setting. Whilst in portraiture it was common for subjects to hold objects of symbolic significance—for instance, a man seeking to appear intelligent might hold a book—here the grandmother at the center of the image is holding the hands of her granddaughters in her lap. We can also see that she rests one of her hands on the shoulder of her granddaughter. In this way, Roberts creates an image that cultivates a sense of a close, interlinked family. Teal created images of a similar ilk, including one of Mrs. Irene Frazier which appeared in Jeanne Moutoussamy-Ashe's *Viewfinders* (1985). This image, likewise, typifies many of the conventions of pictorialism and children's portraiture. The framing of the photo places the entwined hands of baby and mother in the center of the photograph, and by emphasizing the literal interconnectedness of their hands, Teal emphasizes the closeness of their relationship. In this way, the aesthetics of these images reflect notions of motherhood and intergenerational connectedness.

Yet it was not just aesthetically that the theme of motherhood factored into the careers of African American women portrait photographers. The network of motherhood played a role as well. Wilhelmina Roberts did not enter the world of photography until she married her photographer husband in 1902 at the age of nineteen and did not become an active photographer until her husband opened his own studio in South Carolina in 1920. Richard worked a day job as a custodian, leaving his wife to run the studio in his absence. Outside of the studio, Richard did not permit his wife and daughters to work because, according to Wilhelmina and Richard's daughter, "he knew that segregation would be too much. He didn't want us to experience that" (Wynn unpublished interview). However, within the context of his studio, Wilhelmina Roberts was able to experience working life and develop her own artistic voice. What began as Roberts selling homemade cookies in the waiting area of the studio, in a classically gendered form of labor, soon evolved into a more photographic role. When asked what her mother's most important contribution to the studio was, Roberts's daughter stated:

> I think it was in meeting the people who came there, and they had confidence in her, and I think they were then able to be more relaxed when Dad took the pictures. Also, she was the one who designed a little dressing room and kept it supplied with things that people would use to comb and brush their hair when they came in. (Wynn unpublished interview)

Roberts also helped pose the subjects whilst her husband took their pictures and adjusted their clothing and appearance accordingly. Roberts' role in the studio can be read as a traditionally maternal one—setting subjects at ease, undertaking gendered labor.

Even where the photographer herself did not fit the archetype of motherhood, there remained gendered restrictions on the kind of work she could undertake. Florestine Collins would remain a photographer in a studio setting throughout her career. At times she was frustrated by her lack of mobility and found her efforts to photograph outside of a domesticated studio space rebuffed. For instance, when Collins was not selected to photograph a group picture of the local bridge club Entre Nous, Collins' friend Marguerite Perez "vividly recalled how angry she was that she was not chosen as the group's photographer" (Anthony 2012: 67). Collins actively sought to educate and train her family and friends in the art and business of photography as well. Her sister Thelma Lombard was a saleswoman, her other sister Mildred Gardina and family friend Walterine Celestine co-managed the establishment, and her brother Arthur became a photographer in his own right. Indeed, Anthony mistakenly assumed that Collins had learned photography from her brother, but Collins "corrected the mistaken assumption in no uncertain terms, making it clear that she, the oldest, had introduced her younger siblings to photography" (Anthony 2012: 6). Ironically, her brother would be able to journey outside of the studio and town to take photographs further afield, something that Collins was rarely able to do. Collins' networks were inherently familial and domestic in nature and reflected both the opportunities and limitations of that approach.

Likewise, despite Elnora Teal's artistic prowess and the independent nature of her business, it is significant that Teal was very rarely able to photograph outside of a studio setting. Jeanne Moutoussamy-Ashe notes that "Elnora Teal never photographed outside of her downtown studio, but because of its location, she was always busy" (Moutoussamy-Ashe 1985: 44). Whilst Arthur travelled around the state and established his own photography school, Teal remained restricted to a studio setting for most of her career. Nevertheless, following Arthur's death, Elnora was able to maintain both studios and their photography school for over a decade. Motherhood, therefore, became a tool to emphasize Roberts', Teal's and Collins' roles as businesswomen in their local communities. Whilst more masculinized forms of labor would have been frowned upon, particularly in the early part of the 20th century, these three women utilized the aesthetics, networks, and marketability of motherhood in order to work an unusual career in a way that would have been deemed societally respectable.[5]

The role of motherhood in portrait photography, therefore, reveals the complex aesthetic and social lines which African American women photographers had to navigate. Their studios were expected to be domesticated, homely spaces that reflected their femininity. Likewise, their imagery was desirable for the inherent delicacy and mothering instincts which they were anticipated to bring to the frame. Both behind the camera and within the images themselves, the idea of motherhood remained a powerful theme in the lives and works of these women. Yet through these photographs, these women were able to create powerful and beautiful images which celebrated the lives of those within the frame. In so doing they not only advocated for the dignity and humanity of African American communities, but created studios that functioned as a fantasy space for families to present themselves as they wished to be seen—and that space was inherently gendered and domesticated according to the ideals of conventional motherhood.

"For the brothers and sisters, who will know whom I mean:" Photography, Family, and Anthropology in African Journey (1945)

Even outside of a studio space, African American women photographers engaged with the concept of motherhood. Robeson's dedication to her 1945 anthropological text *African Journey* is an immediate call for a diasporic familial connection, as she writes "for the brothers and sisters, who will know whom I mean" (Robeson 1945). In so doing, from the very start of this text Robeson cultivates a sense of family in her work. This builds on the idea of "activist motherhood," and what Nicholas Grant called "the idea of the Pan-African family" (Grant 2017: 162). Grant furthers the perspective of Castledine as he argues that Robeson frequently used the metaphor of family when speaking about Pan-African solidarities, as "Robeson strategically transferred the politics of the home to the global political arena, a rhetorical move that collapsed the divides between the domestic and the public, the local and the global" (162). Yet this was not just a rhetorical move—it was a photographic one as well.

Although Robeson was an impressive activist and writer, who championed the rights of African Americans for decades, her work as an anthropologist is often underdeveloped in discussions of her life and work. Born in 1895, and travelling extensively around the world, Robeson spent decades campaigning for racial equality and decolonization in Africa. Anthropological thought was a key aspect of Robeson's photographic approach, as she studied anthropology at the London School of Economics. Here, Robeson developed her own thesis: anthropology as "dynamic interpretation," and the study of "man and his relation to his fellow man, and to his changing environments. Thus, it includes the study of primitive man under primitive conditions, of modern man under modern conditions, of human relations, race relations, of education, of social institutions" (Raiford 2017: 139). Combining her passion for decolonization with her own assertive voice, *African Journey* was a powerful infusion of anthropological work, travel writing, and protest literature.

African Journey was the product of Eslanda Robeson's first anthropological trip to South Africa in 1936. The difficulty of travelling to Africa at this time cannot be understated, as "there were unique emotional, psychological, and even logistical challenges. European colonialism still dominated the continent" (Ransby 2017: 100). Many Americans at this time had their cultural understanding of Africa from fictionalized and problematic sources, such as "Tarzan comic books and stories about cannibalism" (Ransby 2017: 100). Although Black nationalists such as Marcus Garvey advocated for pride and a return to Africa in the 1920s, many African Americans remained unaware of the reality of life on the continent. Within *African Journey*, Robeson takes photographs that challenge stereotypical and racist views by presenting her subjects with dignity. Although Eslanda was unable to obtain a visa, she decided to travel to South Africa with her son Pauli regardless. She used her friends in Africa as a network in order to get off the boat at Cape Town and receive her visa, as influential members of the community met her. The role of her husband is also crucial; at various points in *African Journey* Eslanda speculates that Paul Robeson has assisted behind the scenes, noting that "I sense Paul's hand somewhere" (93). Although Robeson was an influential figure in her own right, the additional clout provided by being the wife of famous actor and activist Paul Robeson helped her to attain an increased, though still limited, freedom of movement that may have otherwise been denied her. Robeson wielded the privilege afforded to her by being upper middle class, being both a respected activist in her own right and the wife of a well-known celebrity, and being the mother of Paul Robeson's child in order to produce her ground-breaking work. From this trip in 1936, Robeson would produce the text *African Journey* a decade later in 1945.

Robeson's photographs form a key facet of this text, as Maureen Mahon argues that she utilized photography in order to reflect her "diasporic politics of identification" (Mahon 2006). With over sixty images included in the text, with topics ranging from people to objects, Mahon (2006) writes of the images:

> Here, she followed the anthropological process of providing information to make "the exotic" seem familiar, selecting photographs that attacked dominant representations of "primitive Africa." Many of the photo captions identify people by name or occupation, individualizing them and creating a feel of informal snapshots from a vacation rather than of scientific data.

Robeson blended informal snapshots with anthropology to preserve the everyday dignity of her subjects whilst still providing factual evidence. The very notion of a feel of "informal snapshots" to the anthropological data Robeson cultivated conveys an immediate sense of familial connection—as though one is looking at the travel photographs of a family on holiday. Indeed, key to this "familiarization" of "the exotic" was the role of motherhood and creating diasporic family ties.

In *African Journey*, there is an image of four figures standing side by side: Eslanda Robeson, her son Pauli, the *Mulamuzi* (the chief justice of Buganda) and an unknown second boy. The positioning of the figures—with the two boys separating the two adults—serves as a bridge between the African and African American identities of the adults. The four individuals stand close together, as a single unit. Robeson's arm disappears behind her son Pauli, suggesting that her arm is around him, and suggesting her role as a mother within this image. By portraying the African American identity in herself and her son alongside the African identity of the *Mulamuzi*, Robeson advocates what Maureen Mahon has dubbed a "diasporic politics of identification," clarifying that, "this viewpoint recognizes, creates, and extends cultural and political connections among people of African descent" (Mahon 2006.) Robeson's book dedication further cultivates these diasporic links. Leigh Raiford writes of this image that "if anthropology photography finds pleasure in difference, family snapshots locate joy in sameness..." and that the inclusion of Pauli is "clearly hailing Africans as family" (Raiford 2017: 146). In this way, Robeson evokes the idea of motherhood by including her son in this image and having body language which suggests embrace. This serves as a tool to suggest a familial, diasporic connection.

In sum, in *African Journey*, Robeson looked to counter inaccurate stereotyping of the African continent and educate American and European readers. One of the key ways Robeson did this was by using photography to invoke diasporic familial ties which suggested commonality between Africans and African Americans. The role of motherhood was prominent in this, as she positioned herself in her image to cultivate the impression of a familial relationship in her photography. Through this method, Robeson advocated for a better understanding of and closer relationships with the people in her images and presented a version of Africa which combatted stereotypical images that painted an inaccurate and racist picture. The photography forms a critical part of Robeson's "activist motherhood," which in turn becomes a vital tool to advocate for diasporic, familial ties.

Over the course of this chapter, I have demonstrated how the idea of motherhood was presented, utilized, and coded into African American women's photography during the early 20th century. For portraiture, evoking the ideals of motherhood both in the content and context of producing photographs helped to support women who sought out their unusual careers. By presenting themselves through the language of motherhood, these women presented their work as something different to their male competitors and emphasized the (perceived) innate feminine qualities present in their photography. Even within the more scientific field of anthropology, utilizing the language and subtext of motherhood enabled early African American women photographers such as Eslanda Goode Robeson to bolster their anthropological claims. What unites these fields of study is the presentation of their African American subjects with dignity and respectability. Although a field limited to middle class women, who were able to portray middle class ideals of motherhood, these images nevertheless became powerful tools to combat racist stereotypes. Privately, these portraits would hang in African American homes as symbols of respectability and self-worth. Publicly, these anthropological images would act as a call to action and unity, advocating for the increased connection of a diasporic family.

Notes

1   In New York, Winifred Hall Allen was able to take dynamic shots of African American businesses and streets alongside her portraiture during the Harlem Renaissance. Allen did not overtly evoke the theme of motherhood in most of her images. The more conservative values of the South during this era meant that for women to work in the public sphere, they had to clearly link their work to domestic, private life.

2   The most well-known photographer from this period is James VanDerZee from Harlem, New York (Willis-Braithwaite, 1993).

3   Ayana V Jackson explores 19th and 20th century depictions of portraiture, and what they mean in terms of African American identity and body politics. See her collection 'Archival Impulse.' https://www.ayanavjackson.com/archival-impulse

4   At this time, it was not uncommon for clamps to be used to hold up children for portraits.

5   For further discussion of African American women as businesswomen in the early 20th century, see: Tiffany M. Gill, *Beauty Shop Politics: African American Women's Activism in the Beauty Industry* (Chicago: University of Illinois Press, 2010).

Works Cited

Anthony, A. A. (2002). "Florestine Perrault Collins and the Gendered Politics of Black Portraiture in 1920s New Orleans." *Louisiana History: The Journal of the Louisiana Historical Association* 43, 2 (Spring): 167–188.

———(2012). *Picturing Black New Orleans: A Creole Photographer's View of the Early Twentieth Century*. Berkley: University Press of Florida.

Castledine, J. (2012). *Cold War Progressives: Women's Interracial Organizing for Peace and Freedom*. Urbana, Chicago and Springfield: University of Illinois Press.

Cash, F. B. (2001). *African American Women and Social Action: The Clubwomen and Volunteerism from Jim Crow to the New Deal, 1896-1936*. Greenwood Press.

Davidov, J. F. (1998). *Women's Camera: Self/Body/Other in American Visual Culture*. Durham: Duke University Press.

Du Bois, W.E.B. (1926). "Criteria of Negro Art." *The Crisis* 32, No. 6.

Estrin, J. (2016). "Honoring the Legacy of African-American Women." *The New York Times, Kolumn Magazine*, May 26. http://www.kolumnmagazine.com/2016/05/26/honoring-legacy-african-american-women/.

Frazier, E. F. (1965). *Black Bourgeois*. Free Press.

Gill, T. M. (2010). *Beauty Shop Politics: African American Women's Activism in the Beauty Industry*. Chicago: University of Illinois Press.

Grant, N. (2017). *Winning Our Freedoms Together: African Americans and Apartheid, 1945–1960*. Chapel Hill: University of North Carolina Press.

Higginbotham, E. B. (1993). Righteous Discontent: The Women's Movement in the Black Baptist Church, 1880–1920. Harvard University Press.

hooks, bell. (1995). *Art on My Mind: Visual Politics*. New York: The New Press.

Jackson, A. V. "Archival Impulse." Ayana V. Jackson. Accessed June 20, 2020. https://www.ayanavjackson.com/archival-impulse

"Jeanne Moutoussamy-Ashe interview with Wilhelmina Roberts Wynn." Box 2, Folder 9. Jeanne Moutoussamy-Ashe manuscript and research collection. Schomburg Center for Research in Black Culture, Manuscripts, Archives and Rare Books Division, The New York Public Library, New York, New York.

Ladd-Taylor, M. (1993). "Towards Defining Maternalism in U.S. History," in "Maternalism as a Paradigm." *Journal of Women's History* 5, no. 2 (Fall 1993): 95–130. https://doi.org/10.1353/jowh.2010.0143.

Mahon, M. (2006). "Eslanda Goode Robeson's African Journey: The Politics of Identification and Representation in the African Diaspora." *Souls, A Critical Journal of Black Politics, Culture, and Society* 8, no. 3 (December 2006): 101–118.

https://www.marxists.org/history/usa/workers/civil-rights/crisis/1000-crisis-v04n06-w024.pdf.

Moutoussamy-Ashe, J. (1993). *Viewfinders: Black Women Photographers*. New York & London: Writers & Readers Publishing, Inc.

Ransby, B. (2013). *Eslanda: The Large and Unconventional Life of Mrs. Paul Robeson*. New Haven and London: Yale University Press.

Robeson, E (1945). *African Journey*. London: Victor Gollancz Ltd.

Rosenblum, N. (1994). *A History of Women Photographers*. London, New York, Paris: Abbeville Press.

Taylor, O. C. W. (2016). "The Crescent City Pictorial." *Tulane University Digital Library*. Accessed December 2, 2016. http://cdm16313.contentdm.oclc.org/cdm/compoundobject/collection/p16313coll63/id/35

The Crisis 4, No. 6, (October 1912): 261–312.

Willis, D. (2000). *Reflections in Black: A History of Black Photographers, 1840 to the Present.* New York & London: W.W. Norton.

———— (2005). *Family History Memory: Recording African American Life.* New York: Hylas Publishing.

Willis-Braithwaite, D. (1993). *VanDerZee, Photographer, 1886-1983.* New York: Harry N. Abrams, Inc. Publishers.

Wynn, W. R. "Wilhelmina Roberts: Black Woman Photographer." Box 2, Folder 9. Jeanne Moutoussamy-Ashe manuscript and research collection. Schomburg Center for Research in Black Culture, Manuscripts, Archives and Rare Books Division, The New York Public Library, New York, New York.

8 LOSSES NOT TO BE PASSED ON

Paula C. Johnson's and Sara Bennett's Portraits Rewriting
(Ex-) Incarcerated Black Mothers

ATALIE GERHARD ⎯⎯⎯⎯⎯⎯⎯⎯⎯⎯⎯⎯⎯⎯⎯⎯

This essay analyzes how portraits from *Inner Lives: Voices of African American Women in Prison* by Paula C. Johnson (2003) and photographs by Sara Bennett from her series *Life After Life in Prison* (2016) and *Spirit on the Inside* (2013) create opportunities for currently and formerly incarcerated women to contribute their experiences to critiques of mass incarceration. The impressions that Paula C. Johnson and Sara Bennett gather testify to the lasting personal and collective impact of incarceration while articulating subversive perspectives through the faces of mothers whose life stories connect them to larger struggles against racism in the U.S. To allow this interpretation to emerge, they navigate both, stereotypes according to which certain women are disproportionately prone to criminal behaviors ("bad Black mothers") as well as perspectives which sensationalize mothers' suffering to the point of detaching it from systemic oppression ("mammies"). Instead, photographs from *Inner Lives*, *Life After Life in Prison*, and *Spirit on the Inside* highlight the creative and complex ways in which women reclaim their identities within their personal spaces where they perform crucial social functions.

Given their declared aspirations for their projects, Paula C. Johnson's collection and Sara Bennett's exhibitions relate to bell hooks' call for searching for truly inclusive Feminist practices of empowerment at the margins of U.S. society, since they shed light on the particular significance of motherhood in and after prison. By delivering critiques through the testimonies of women, they display their subjects' unique perspectives, which derive from a lack of privilege vis-à-vis fellow members of their society, according to bell hooks.[1] In her book *From the Margins to the Center* (1984), bell hooks recounts her experience of how, in a women's studies class at university, her white classmates condemned her for criticizing their oblivion to how women in her Southern working-class community supported each other as a model of Feminist empowerment.[2] Echoing bell hooks' emphasis on the strategies already at the disposal of women to resist patriarchal oppression, both Paula C. Johnson and Sara Bennett reveal how their subjects negotiated their identities with the help of Black Feminist culture beyond the institution of the prison. Thereby, their criticism of the dehumanizing effects of incarceration supplements legal notions of freedom based in body-centered discourses that the women activate. Especially when they depict criminalized women who identify as mothers and/or perform maternal care, Paula C. Johnson's and Sara Bennett's photographs produce visions of resistance that cast prisons as obsolete when it comes to promoting personal rehabilitation and public security.

Paula C. Johnson lets the faces and voices of women who are legally prevented from educating their children and participating in society testify to both their ongoing struggles to resist domestic and institutional violence as well as to overcome isolation by practicing meaningful care within their surroundings. Combining legal research with personal interviews as a law professor, Paula C. Johnson explains in the introduction to *Inner Lives* that legal and workplace discrimination have targeted Black women since the abolition of slavery but that these practices have always been countered by women's resistance against stereotypes and struggle for human rights.[3] Guided by her interviews with currently and formerly incarcerated women in the U.S. East, Midwest, South, and West, she decided to publish the portrait photographs that she took of them while recording their life stories for later transcription and editing with the real names that they gave.[4] In her role as an advocate for (ex-) incarcerated women, she includes the story of Janneral Denson whom customs officers from Fort Lauderdale detained in 1997 for drug trafficking suspicions and urged to take laxatives despite her advanced pregnancy.[5] The words of Janneral Denson's congressional testimony demonstrate the negative consequences of racial profiling for an affected woman's perception of her society,

> The very fact that I am here, speaking before you, points to the greatness of our country. But what I, and many other African Americans, have gone through, points to a great failure in our country. Conduct such as this is both illegal and Un-American, and, in the long run, can only serve to drive a wedge between you, the government, and the citizens of the country.[6]

Although no picture of her appears, Janneral Denson's story in *Inner Lives* inspires criticism of U.S. policing practices by invoking the trope of motherhood as an act of creating communal continuity that gains a subversive potential when threatened by institutional violence, in this case due to racial profiling and suspect detention. The narratives in *Inner Lives* argue for the mothers' rights to inspire and care for their children despite their incarcerations as they represent their views to the outside population and promote empathy. The portraits aesthetically resist an institution that produces what Alexander G. Weheliye refers to as "racializing assemblages". Alexander G. Weheliye employs this term in his book, *Habeas Viscus. Racializing Assemblages, Biopolitics, and Black Feminist Theories of the Human* (2014) to describe how the status of oppressed people in Western modernity is not determined by how their bodies are perceived by others alone, but most importantly, by the violence that they experience as a result.[7] The effects of his shift of focus are that any one racialized group's claims to the singularity of their suffering may be challenged as well as that oppressed people may unite across their differences based on their lived experiences. In the tradition of Black Feminism, he traces strategies of survival that racialized, gendered subjects develop under inhumane corporeal violence, and which I recognize as performed in Sara Bennett's photographs documenting women's lives following their releases from prison as well. Her projects advocate for public understanding for formerly incarcerated women. The photographs could suggest that the women transfer to their children a particular knowledge of U.S. society resulting from their experiences. This knowledge might evade verbal explication but results in lived resistance that shapes future generations. The complex ways in which formerly incarcerated women perform agency challenges post-Enlightenment notions of freedom, as in the case of the character Sethe from Toni Morrison's novel *Beloved* (1987) who kills her daughter so that she may escape slavery in spirit if not in body, but is haunted by the girl's ghost in the future.[8] By exhibiting photographs of mothers caring for their children in everyday settings, such as playing in the street and only alluding to their past incarcerations in captions, Sara Bennett destigmatizes this period of their lives and emphasizes their identities beyond the label of "ex-convict". Reflecting on her work as a defense attorney for domestic abuse victims, Sara Bennett explains that she hopes her photographs will inspire judges to reconsider their sentencing practices.[9] In the following citation from a *Huck Magazine* article on her work, she discusses her own method of listening to the stories of women while trying to capture distinct aspects of their self-representations,

> Before I bring out my camera, I talk to the women at length, listen to their stories, and hear what they've been through [...] One of my challenges is that the women talk to me so much that it's hard for me to get a shot where they're not mid-sentence.[10]

When the press advertises her exhibitions, journalists emphasize that Sara Bennett is a white defense attorney and that she hopes to challenge stereotypes through photography. However, she prefers to explain her choice of medium by citing the empathy that it produces,

> So I hope my photos make the formerly incarcerated women relatable, and then your empathy for them sort of kicks in. That's what I was trying to do in the re-entry project. I show people at work or socializing or with grandchildren or just interacting. I mean you can't just help but feel the humanity in the women, and that's what I was going for. I mean, even if they have struggles in their lives, which they do, there's a lot of poverty and homelessness. But even with all of that, you can still feel their inner strength or their ability to overcome whatever is put in their way. I think those are the kinds of things that humanizes my subjects. It's just like that saying that a photo is worth a thousand words; it's really true.[11]

Despite her efforts to improve public perceptions of the women she photographs, her description of them as essentially resilient could still marginalize them further, if viewers take their strength for granted rather than acknowledge their suffering. However, Susan Sontag warns that photographs of struggling civilians, albeit in warzones, can affirm colonial divides of power if they sensationalize suffering for the entertainment of First World audiences rather than raise awareness for the roots of violent conflicts.[12] Although her essay *Regarding the Pain of Others* (2003) deals with documentary war photography, I refer to it to reaffirm that even photographs advocating empathy can normalize the suffering of human subjects if they represent it in the form of depoliticized spectacles.[13] As a white public defender, Sara Bennett is more privileged than the women she photographs and this could lead to intense emotional responses to their suffering that could prevent them from conveying resistance against the penal system in her photographs.

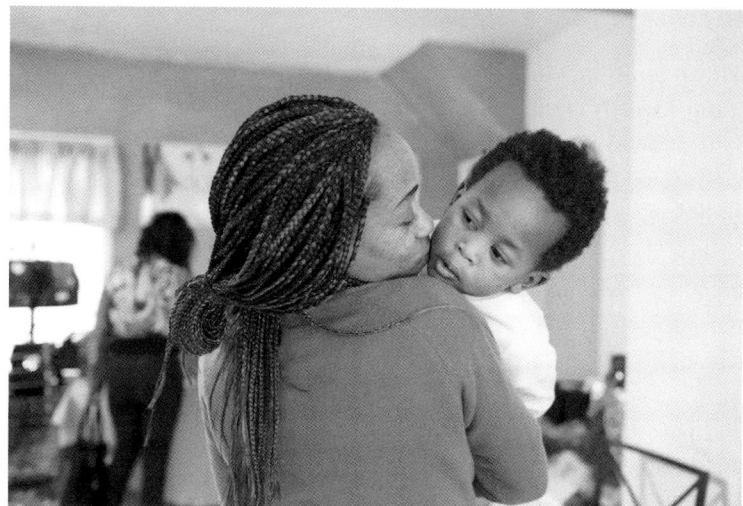

However, Sara Bennett's dedication to defending accused women and her usage of documentary photography to humanize her subjects, materialize in a photograph such as the one of the ex-incarcerated Tracy with her grandson Joshia. The scene invites a reading of Tracy's care practices as resistance against her stigmatization within the criminal justice system. Among Sara Bennett's photographs of Tracy's reintegration into society, this photograph highlights the healing power that she could derive from her love for Joshia. According to Celeste-Marie Bernier, domestic life historically constituted a site of creative resistance for women, as in her example of the enslaved artist Harriet Powers, who told Biblical stories of liberation with the help of her handmade quilts.[14] While Tracy's loving embrace in Sara Bennett's photograph could suggest that domesticity can be empowering, this scene's limited focus on the common theme of family could normalize Tracy's past incarceration as meaningless. In this sense, Rebecca Wanzo criticizes how stereotypes of Black women's suffering as common lead to a view of violence against them as meaningless.[15] In the case of Sara Bennett's photograph, the relatability of Tracy's love for Joshia should not overshadow the context of rehabilitation in the eyes of viewers who should not accept her marginalization as common.

So far, I have argued that Paula C. Johnson as well as Sara Bennett criticize incarceration by emphasizing the personal lives of women in an age of mass incarceration. The women's self-expressions in photographs, edited narratives, and captions underline the impact of incarceration on families as they call for empathy. Paula C. Johnson's and Sara Bennett's representations of their subjects perform multiple strategies that I connect to Black Feminism, intersectionality, and identity politics which manifest visually. While Sara Bennett asks judges to reconsider how they sentence women in light of their personal living conditions, Paula C. Johnson's book lets her interviewees testify to the roots of incarceration within their lives as they face their viewers. Paula C. Johnson's and Sara Bennett's projects must counter stereotypes of incarcerated women and avoid sensationalist tropes while placing the faces and bodies of their subjects at the center of their critiques. With regard to a photograph such as the one of Tracy with Joshia, for example, this means neither emphasizing her suffering as a grandmother who was separated from her family over her past stigmatization as an incarcerated woman nor vice versa. Therefore, the challenge and opportunity of projects like Sara Bennett's is to celebrate women's survival despite incarceration without universalizing their experiences or catering to stereotypes of "criminally deviant" womanhood. On the one hand, it is impossible to mistake the intentions of Paula C. Johnson and Sara Bennett, since they add edited narratives and captions, respectively. On the other hand, their reliance on photographs suggests that they aim to provide evidence of their subjects' identities as part of their critiques of mass incarceration. In this sense, Paula C. Johnson explains that photography has historically served women's cultural resistance in the past. As an example, she refers to Renée Cox's nude self-portrait, *Yo Mama's Last Supper* (1996).[16] She argues that because of the hope and pride that this photograph communicates by associating a Black woman's body with divinity, it provoked threats by then-mayor of New York City, Rudy Giuliani to defund the Brooklyn Museum of Art that exhibited it in 2001.[17] According to Paula C. Johnson, Rudy Giuliani's attempt at censorship affirms the culturally transgressive potential of celebratory representations of Black women that are rare but also important in terms of promoting positive self-images for them.[18] When Paula C. Johnson and Sara Bennett emphasize the faces and bodies of (ex-) incarcerated women alongside their edited narratives or statements in captions, respectively, they symbolically perform the legal principle of *habeas corpus*. In the U.S. Constitution, *habeas corpus* demands a fair trial for accused subjects. Paula C. Johnson and Sara Bennett imply that their subjects deserve unbiased and empathetic sentencing. By using black-and-white instead of multicolor settings, their photographs could aesthetically allude to racialized disparities that underwrite discrimination, as discussed by Alexander G. Weheliye.[19] In the following, I will bear this notion in mind while I analyze selected representations.

Paula C. Johnson's Inner Lives (2003): Through the Mirror of Black Motherhood

Paula C. Johnson places portrait photographs of her interviewees ahead of their edited narratives in her book *Inner Lives*. Eighty-eight percent of her (ex-) incarcerated interviewees are mothers and seventy percent experienced physical and sexual abuse before their incarcerations.[20] During her interviews, she photographed the women in their institutions or homes in the way they styled themselves—this could explain their comfortable poses and their direct gazes into her camera.[21] The minimalistic accessorizing of Rae Ann, who drapes glasses over her shirt,[22] DonAlda's tiny ear hoops,[23] or Mamie's tight curls[24] could represent minor acts of resistance against institutional structures designed to produce conformity. Although their uniforms with tags remind viewers of their incarcerations, the women perform agency in their interactions with the camera and in their fashion choices. In contrast to the institutional limits to self-expression that shape the incarcerated women's identity performances, the ex-incarcerated women appear confident as they wear shell jewelry (Ida P. McCray)[25] or surround themselves with awards and photographs (Donna Hubbard Spearman),[26] to mention a few examples. The postures of the ex-incarcerated activists Ida P. McCray and Donna Hubbard Spearman are also more relaxed and their smiles are broader. As they directly face the camera in their homes, they express a willingness to represent their survival.

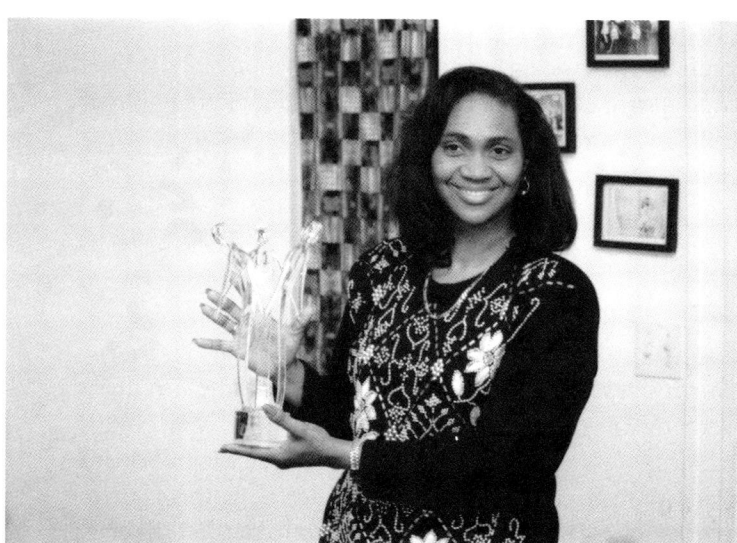

Paula C. Johnson, "Donna Hubbard Spearman," in *Inner Lives: Voices of African American Women in Prison: With a Foreword by Joyce A. Logan and an Afterword by Angela J. Davis* (New York and London: New York University Press, 2003), 195. © Paula C. Johnson

While Hortense J. Spillers warns that motherhood can only provide insights into womanhood but not define it,[27] the struggles of Paula C. Johnson's interviewees against stereotypes could already represent their maternal legacies. In her edited narrative in *Inner Lives*, DonAlda reveals she is her children's only surviving parent after defending herself against their violent father—her act of shooting him in self-defense is the reason for her incarceration which she struggled to accept at first.[28] In her photograph, she seems to pursue visibility as she turns toward the camera in front of a blurred wire fence.[29] Hortense J. Spillers criticizes how Black mothers are exclusively identified with biological reproduction but not with personal legacies in the footsteps of slavery, under which women were sexually exploited with economic motives.[30] By facing the camera alone while their children are mentioned in their edited narratives, Paula C. Johnson' interviewees, including DonAlda, could resist such simplistic definitions of their roles as mothers. According to Hortense J. Spillers, the racist refusal to recognize institutionally contained women as human and as mothers legitimated their rape and exploitation.[31] However, Paula C. Johnson's portrait photographs of the women's faces omit the trope of corporeal exploitation. By choosing how much of their bodies to reveal to the lens, both the incarcerated Marilyn, whose eyes peep out under her fringe,[32] or the released Bettie Gibson, whose broad smile reveals her partially broken teeth,[33] control viewers' perceptions of their unique lives. Paula C. Johnson's portrait photographs also contrast the function of mugshots. Mugshots constitute the photographic genre that is most commonly associated with incarceration following in the footsteps of Orientalizing ethnographic headshots, since both styles attempt to produce knowledge about a group based on standardized representations of its members.[34] Paula C. Johnson's portrait photographs of incarcerated women may subversively allude to this genre by emphasizing the women's faces and partially representing them in standardized uniforms with tags. However, the women's free choice on how to pose contrasts the principle of standardization. Thus, the women perform agency despite institutional containment when they determine their own visual representation to outside society.

Women's performances of agency constitute resistance against racist stereotypes of passivity, especially with regard to motherhood. Such racist stereotypes permeate the Moynihan report from 1965 that falsely attributed high incarceration rates to an absence of strict fathers within disenfranchised woman-led families.[35] With regard to the forced absence of mothers due to incarceration, Donna Hubbard Spearman narrates in *Inner Lives* that she aims to help mothers pursue emotional connections with their children despite their physical separation,

> I realized at that point that a large part of what I had to do when I got out was to work with making the process of motherhood easier to deal with during incarceration. This is where our organization's parenting program comes from. During my pregnancy, I talked to many women who were incarcerated about their experiences with their children. I actually took notes and I took all those experiences and put it into our program once I was released. We have a parenting program that directly addresses the challenges that incarcerated women face as mothers, and helps them to remain parents in spite of the incarceration. What I realized, as an addict myself, is that parenting wasn't presence, it's participation. Even when I was present in my children's lives, I didn't participate. For most of us, just before our prison sentence that was true.[36]

The activist Ida P. McCray is another interviewee in *Inner Lives* who aims to prevent familial disintegration by helping incarcerated women receive visits from their children through her organization, Families with a Future.[37] In her edited narrative, Ida P. McCray narrates that her own son delivered her to the police for air piracy during a fight but has since become her "ally".[38] In her photograph, her shell necklace could reflect nostalgia for the solidarity that

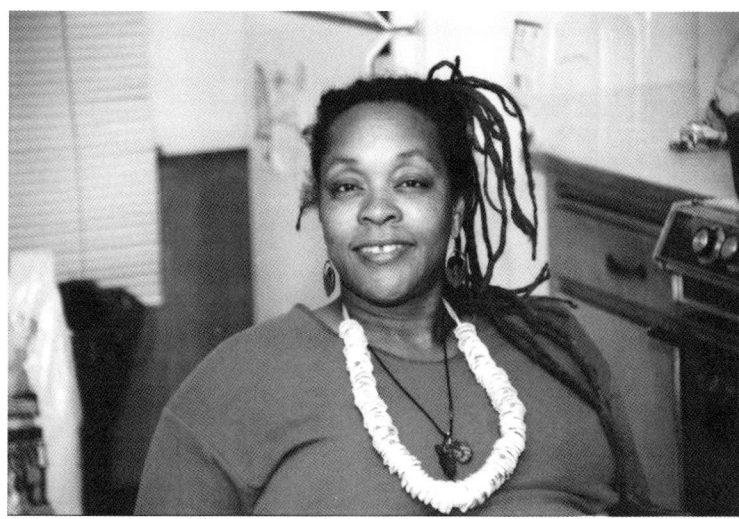

Paula C. Johnson, "Ida P. McCray," in *Inner Lives: Voices of African American Women in Prison: With a Foreword by Joyce A. Logan and an Afterword by Angela J. Davis* (New York and London: New York University Press, 2003), 175. © Paula C. Johnson.

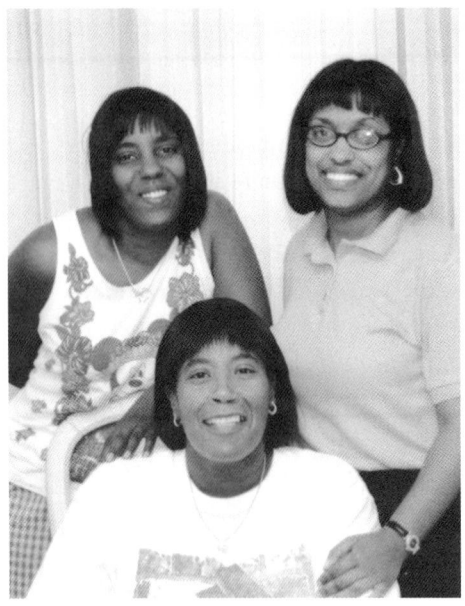
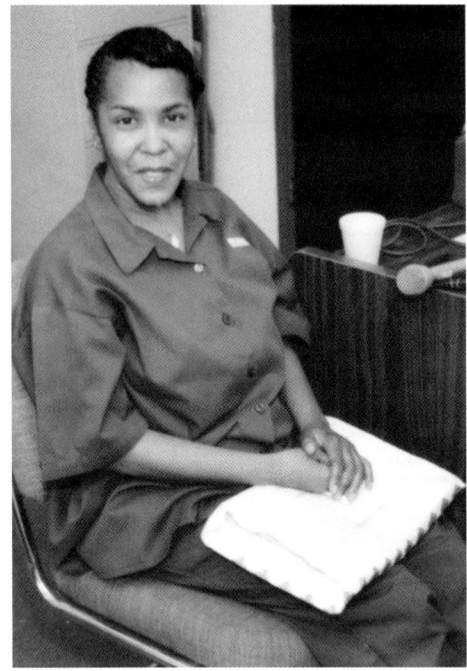

Paula C. Johnson, "Debbie, Judy, and Kito," "Renay," in *Inner Lives: Voices of African American Women in Prison: With a Foreword by Joyce A. Logan and an Afterword by Angela J. Davis* (New York and London: New York University Press, 2003), 261. © Paula C. Johnson

she narrates about having experienced as a single mother during her time in Cuba.[39] Her narrated struggles while negotiating with the mothers' penal institutions and the children's orphanages or foster homes reveal how the criminal justice system prevents incarcerated women from exercising their maternal rights.[40] Ida P. McCray narrates that before her own incarceration for her involvement with Black Liberationist movements, she received more solidarity as a single mother in Cuba than in the U.S., where single mothers are socially marginalized.[41] Both Ida McCray's photograph and her edited narrative hold the mirror to the society that marginalized her further by incarcerating her. Her representation rewrites her experiences as a mother before, during, and after incarceration as critical sites of knowledge formation. By representing herself in her photograph as well as her experiences and activism in her edited narrative, Ida P. McCray underlines the political relevance of her engagement with the issue of motherhood for her community.

Paula C. Johnson prevents any stereotypical perceptions of her interviewees as either "Jezebels" or "mammies" and instead emphasizes their forced separation from their children as a loss by depicting them in their portrait photographs without their children. In this sense, Madina V. Tlostanova recognizes women's corporeal experiences as sources of knowledge about, for example, racial inequality in the U.S.[42] At this point, I would like to emphasize that the racist stereotypes legitimating inequality in the U.S. often target women's motherhood practices. According to Carla Rice, four types of Black women exist in the racialized imagery derived from the time of slavery: the hypersexualized "breeder", the disenfranchised bad mother who abuses her children, the desexualized mammy who is allegedly content to sacrifice herself for her oppressors, and the highly moral superwoman who is selflessly dedicated to her work.[43]

Judy, and their mother Renay resists such stereotypes while visualizing their separation. Firstly, there is a photograph of each sister and their aunt alone, secondly, there is a group photograph on the next page and thirdly, there is a portrait photograph from a slightly elevated angle of Renay alone.[44] Although Renay is wearing her prisoner's uniform with a tag, her graceful posture with her hands folded in her lap, her hair neatly pulled back, and her slight smile are more reminiscent of a James Van der Zee portrait photograph of a bourgeois family than of the social marginalization of incarcerated mothers.

Since incarcerated mothers have historically experienced the impact of racist and sexist stereotypes, they may also be aware of how the trope of the "welfare queen" could harm them. According to Anita Hill, the trope of the "welfare queen" emerged in the 1960s to stigmatize disenfranchised single mothers and was famously invoked by then-candidate Ronald Reagan during his 1976 presidential campaign with the effect of mobilizing bias against women receiving public welfare.[45] Dorothy Roberts criticizes how this rhetoric resurfaced in the Personal Responsibility and Work Opportunity Reconciliation Act of 1996 that advocated the reproductive policing and punitive incarceration of single mothers on welfare while targeting their familial care practices as public threats.[46] In contrast, many of Paula C. Johnson's interviewees in *Inner Lives* defend how they cared for their relatives before their incarcerations. In her edited narrative, Karen Michelle Blakney, for example, narrates about not regretting refusing to snitch on her sister after she was arrested for cooking crack cocaine for undercover police officers.[47] Karen Michelle Blakney further implies criticism of the criminal justice system when she narrates that instead of mandatory rehabilitation programs, her faith helped her overcome addiction.[48] Her narrated adherence to personal values emphasizes her agency and prevents any perceptions of her as passive. In her photograph, her smiling appearance with her hair pulled back, her

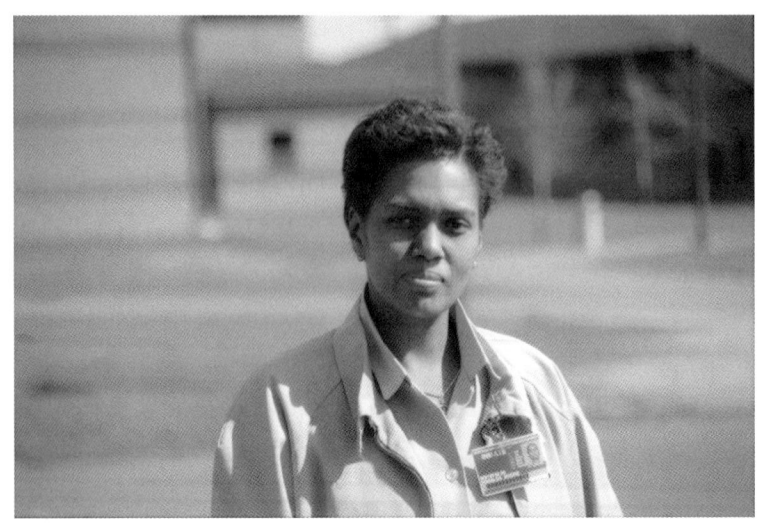

sleek shirt, and her shiny watch could symbolically allude to her success in life with the help of her personal resources.[49]

Stephanie Walker and Anne Worrall note that incarcerated women often pursue agency by learning about the legal system on their own terms.[50] In *Inner Lives*, DonAlda's edited narrative describes how she bonds over shared knowledge about incarceration with one of her daughters outside despite their physical separation,

> Both of my daughters have been to jail. One daughter was there for disturbing the peace. She was in a fight somewhere and they arrested her. Just recently, my other daughter went to school with a utility knife in her purse. She says she carries it—we live in a bad neighborhood— she carries it in her purse at night, and she forgot to take it out at school and it beeped the metal detector. They took her to jail, so she's been to court. She came out of it fine. She's made the honor roll since. She didn't let it deter her, but she realized a lot of things by those six hours in jail. She realized, 'Mom, I see what you go through now.'[51]

In her photograph, DonAlda is wearing a buttoned shirt and has short hair, as her tilted face emerges into the sunlight. The photograph implies self-improvement while emphasizing DonAlda's identity as a woman and a mother with a legacy. In her speech "Ain't I a Woman?" in 1851, Sojourner Truth famously expresses a concern for recognition as a woman due to institutional containment under slavery. She contrasts her emotional suffering after every forced separation from her children with her physical strength and demands polite treatment despite her social status.[52] In the footsteps of Sojourner Truth's speech, the aesthetics of Paula C. Johnson's representations of (ex-) incarcerated mothers challenge how their identities could have been targeted during their physical containment. The theme of corporeality surfaces on the cover of *Inner Lives* as well, as it shows a woman's face marked by stripes, or bars. These lines constitute the only visual allusion to the book's focus on the issue of women's incarceration—which is humanized with the help of portrait photographs, interviews, and edited narratives.

Sara Bennett's Life After Life in Prison (2016) and Spirit on the Inside (2013): Black Women's Survival through Motherhood

Sara Bennett's series *Life After Life in Prison* includes photographs of a woman named Tracy in her everyday life following her release from prison. For her series *Spirit on the Inside*, Sara Bennett photographed several women as they recalled their incarcerations alongside the Communist activist Judith "Judy" Clark in captions under their own black-and-white photographs with their children. Their representations could express that motherhood represents a

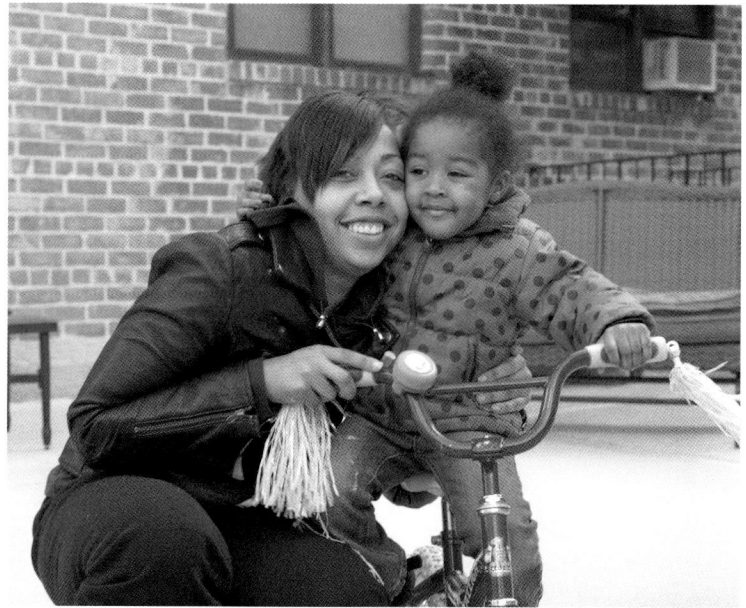

Sara Bennett, "Anael, 29 and Rayne, 2. Served 8 years. Released: 2012. Judy's great. She's so insightful. In prison, I always said, 'I don't care, I don't care, I don't care,' and she would say, 'you do care.' Judy taught all of the mothers on the nursery the same thing—we have to learn how to love ourselves because we're no good to anyone if we're not good to ourselves. I carry that with me," *Spirit on the Inside*, 2013, https://sarabennett.org/spirit/7ipgprwl3tekn-lt8qy1fyz1szhei5a (accessed July 12, 2021). © Sara Bennett

site of practicing agency for them compared to the time of their incarcerations. They imply that there is hope for the next generation—a revolutionary view for Black women in light of their historical oppression in the U.S. For example, Margaret Garner, whose story is loosely represented in Toni Morrison's novel *Beloved*, killed her own daughter to prevent her from being enslaved and thus suffering like herself. Her famous act of filicide signifies both agency and despair to a shocking extent. In contrast, Sara Bennett's photographs of ex-incarcerated women with their children highlight strength and survival. They do not emphasize maternal isolation like some of Paula C. Johnson's portrait photographs of (ex-) incarcerated women.

For example, Sara Bennett photographs Anael while she supports her daughter Rayne in learning to ride her tricycle. The way Anael smilingly crouches beside Rayne, who clings to her at eyelevel, could symbolically reflect Rayne's reliance on her mother as well as Anael's willingness to support her daughter as an equal in pursuing her path in life. Anael's emphasis on caring for others challenges stereotypes of incarcerated women as useless for society. Her care for her daughter could further prevent the cycles of social marginalization within families and communities that Michelle Alexander warns of as an effect of mass incarceration.[53]

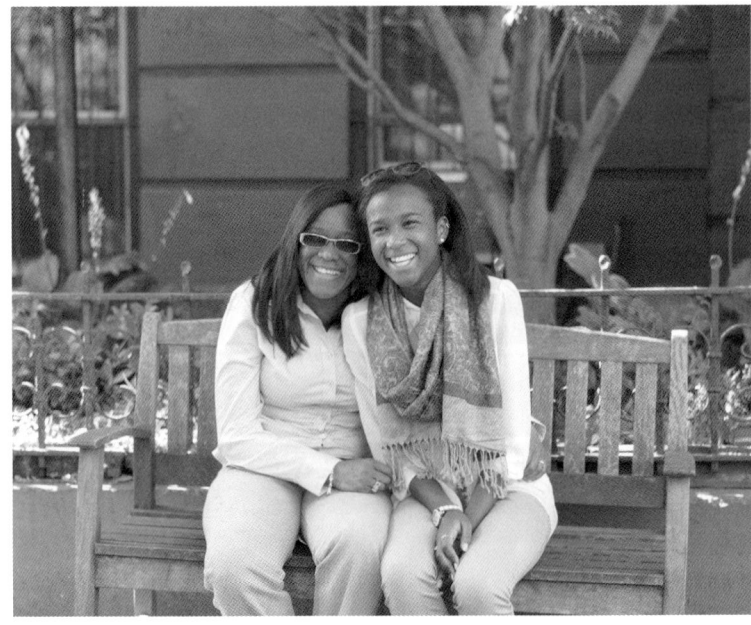

Sara Bennett, "Monique, 49 and Joy, 16. Served almost 10 years. Released: 2007. I was known as a crier in prison—I always cried a lot because I was separated from my infant daughter, Joy. And people thought there was something the matter with me, but Judy never made me feel as though there was anything wrong with being a mother missing her child," *Spirit on the Inside*, 2013, https://sarabennett.org/spirit/mbzgp6qkvqvynr6f9s-rn55oti6o9ag (accessed July 12, 2021). © Sara Bennett

Sara Bennett's photograph of another ex-incarcerated mother, Monique, who wraps her arm around her teenage daughter Joy, who is wearing an out-fit that matches her mother's, as well as the accompanying caption, could emphasize both maternal love and (self-)acceptance as strategies of resisting the judgments of others as well.

Overall, Sara Bennett's representations of her subjects outside penal institutions underline the survival strategies that circulate within their communities, as in the case of Tracy from the series *Life After Life in Prison*. The series *Spirit on the Inside*, however, could inspire questions about underlying power relations, since it features a white public defender's representations of ex-incarcerated Black women expressing how an incarcerated white activist supported them in surviving their incarcerations. On the one hand, the white privilege of Sara Bennett and Judith Clark could risk overshadowing the strength that Black mothers, such as Anael and Monique already possessed before their incarcerations. Their own power to (re)claim their roles as mothers may manifest throughout their lives and not in any singular spectacle alone. On the other hand, photographs from the series *Life After Life in Prison* like the one of Tracy lying on the bed that a male relative provided for her in a room full of stuffed animals and pictures of children could project imaginations of childlike innocence and vulnerability upon her.

Sara Bennett's photographs of Tracy do not emphasize her care practices alone but could point to the central role of family in her life that is evidenced by the pictures surrounding her as well. By representing Tracy's connection

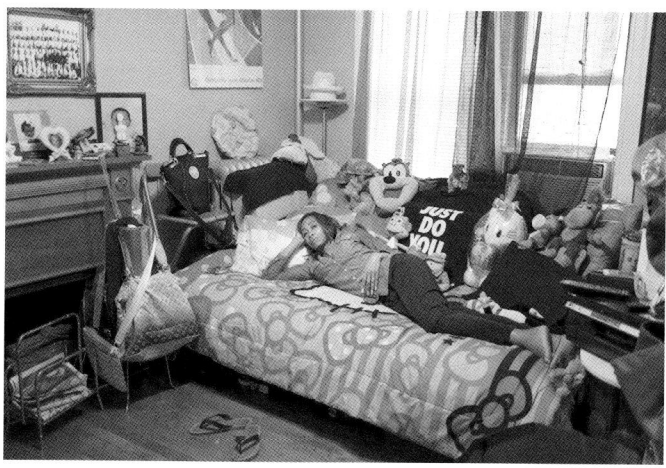

Sara Bennett, "Tracy six months after her release. East Harlem, NY (2014). 'This is my third home in six months. I was at Providence House [a halfway house]. But my time was up after four months and I ended up at a three-quarter house. It was horrible. Then the uncle of my grand-children, not related to me, took me in,'" *Life After Life in Prison*, July 17, 2016, https://sarabennett.org/life-after-life/2016/7/17/2016/7/17/tracy-six-months-after-her-release-east-harlem-ny-2014 (accessed July 12, 2021). © Sara Bennett

to her family through visual references, Sara Bennett emphasizes the difficulties of Tracy's life in light of her ongoing separation from her family during her rehabilitation process. However, the photographs could attribute a legacy to Tracy, since she is shown actively rebuilding her life and could thus echo Hortense J. Spillers' appeal to Black people to remember and embrace the legacies of their mothers despite their social marginalization.[54] In this sense, the aspect of gender could connect Sara Bennett's representations of Tracy desiring closeness with her family to the Black Lives Matter movement (2013—). The Black Lives Matter movement performs intersectional Black Feminist politics by giving voice to women who demand justice for young women and men.[55] Intersectionality, as defined by the legal scholar Kimberlé Crenshaw, demands that people develop solidarity based on comparisons of their experiences of discrimination.[56] As an ex-incarcerated civil rights activist, Angela Y. Davis traces her criminalization to prejudices against Black people and women that legitimate violence against others as well.[57] In contrast, U.S. liberalism posits that every person can determine their condition in society. However, this opportunity has historically been denied to people who deviate from the white, middle-class, Christian, heterosexual, cisgender, able-bodied ideal citizen. Sara Bennett's photographs of (ex-) incarcerated women must consider

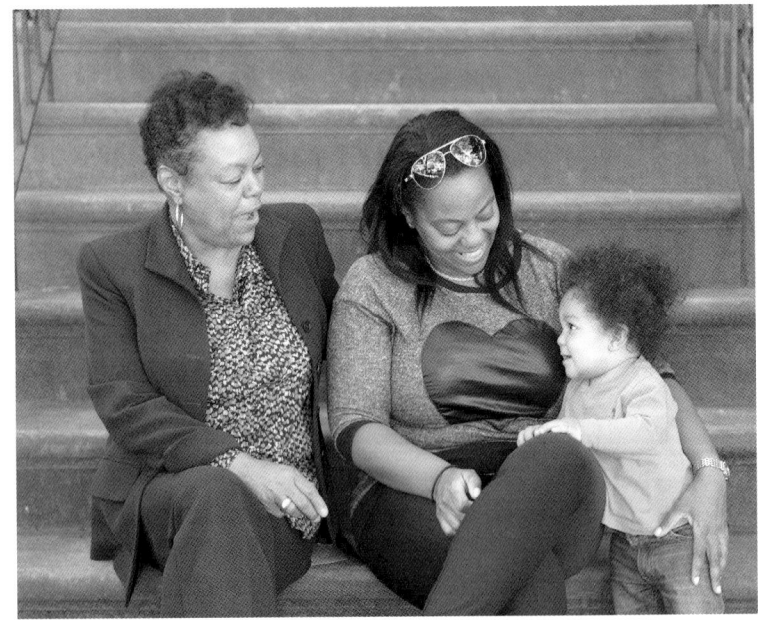

Sara Bennett, "Toni, 65, Leah, 45, and Liam, 11 months. Toni: Served almost 25 years. Released: 2011. Leah: Served almost 10 years. Released 2001. Toni: When my daughter, Leah, came to Bedford it was really difficult. Judy mediated disputes between us. Today, my daughter, 3 grandkids, and my great grand have a close loving relationship. I give thanks to Judy for this," *Life After Life in Prison*, 2013, https://sarabennett.org/spirit/z32cu49hme6bnfz3t2i-ue7i4e8qkri (accessed July 12, 2021). © Sara Bennett

both the specific discrimination that they face even after being released from prison and the universal relatability of their suffering in order to advocate empathy. Her photographs in *Spirit on the Inside* pursue empathy by representing mothers alone with their children in blurred public spaces such as in streets or on doorsteps; therefore, the women's and the children's bodies are the only ones that viewers can identify with despite any markers of difference.

Sara Bennett's photograph of Leah with her mother Toni and her son Liam exemplifies Audre Lorde's intersectional concept for women's resistance that she described in her speech, "The Master's Tools will Never Dismantle the Master's House" (1979). The photograph shows three generations that are affected by incarceration and its legacies. Leah, Toni, and Liam share laughs and smiles while they look away from the camera. The photograph emphasizes the joyful relationship that only a grandmother, mother, and son share with each other. The photograph could symbolically imply that the relationship between Leah and Toni is egalitarian and admirable, since the mother and the daughter are sitting on the same level of steps while Liam looks up at them smiling. Neither the women's joyful expressions nor their fashionable clothing refers to their past incarcerations. Instead, Leah and Toni appear to be content in their roles and to have distanced themselves from their experiences of incarceration. However, both Leah's performance of daughterhood toward Toni and Toni's performance of motherhood toward Leah could be informed by their shared experience. The caption, which reveals that both mother and daughter were incarcerated, underlines the high risk of incarceration within their community.

Performances of unity among (ex-) incarcerated women and performed care for their children could represent political resistance in light of their isolation within institutions as well as their frequent victimization by the police. Mothers who transform their love for their children into a cause of activism, for example, within the Black Lives Matter movement, emphasize how remembrance instead of loss defines their collective identity. In 2019, Sheila Pree Bright's black-and-white mural that portrays a group of mothers who lost their sons to police violence makes this point by foregrounding the bodies of the women, who are standing up and facing the camera directly—a visual reference to how Richard Avedon famously photographed the members of the Student Nonviolent Coordinating Committee in 1963.[58] In her urban art installation in Atlanta, Sheila Pree Bright's juxtaposition of her photograph with Richard Avedon's photograph commemorates how the mothers transfer the legacy of the Civil Rights movement into the present.[59] Sara Bennett's photograph of Leah and Toni implies that they embody their community's historical knowledge of the U.S. criminal justice system and transfer their perspectives to future generations as well.

Sara Bennett's photographs could inspire criticism of the notion that incarceration is necessary for all offenders in order to mold them into law-abiding citizens. According to Michel Foucault, modern Western practices of incarceration are rooted in a post-Enlightenment belief in the value of isolation, critical introspection, and routine physical labor.[60] In contrast, Sara Bennett's photograph of Denisha emphasizes her bond with her daughter Zeiyana, happiness, and laughter as sources of her wellbeing and as evidence for her recovery from any past criminalization. Denisha challenges stereotypes of (ex-) incarcerated womanhood with her fashionable short dress and slippers, while she smiles and cradles Zeiyana on her knees, as their hands overlap. The caption alludes to her joyful practice of motherhood as an indicator of her rehabilitation. Sara Bennett therefore highlights Denisha's agency in her private life instead of her past incarceration. The aesthetics of Sara Bennett's photograph could further reflect her emphasis on Denisha's present role as a mother, since their urban setting is blurred and seen only from their eyelevel. Similar to the photograph of Leah and Toni, Denisha's and Zeiyana's postures and expressions almost

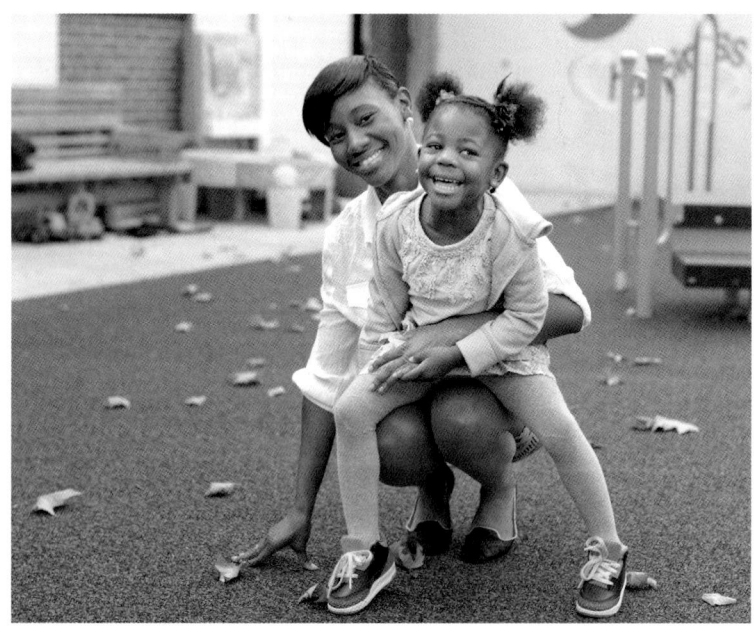

Sara Bennett, "Denisha, 23 and Zeiyana, 3. Served less than 1 year. Released: 2010. Because of Judy, I'm more grateful for my life. I'm home, I'm raising my daughter, I'm being a good mom, and I've learned to take anything negative and turn it into a positive. I wish I could have put Judy in my bag and taken her through the gate with me," *Spirit on the Inside*, 2013, https://sarabennett.org/spirit/81h-w97qm9n39gpdu1zm2sc-9c7wvdqt (accessed July 12, 2021). © Sara Bennett

mirror each other and could underline their emotional connectedness. Since generations of women with experiences of incarceration and a commitment to their children constitute Sara Bennett's subjects, her photographs evidence that motherhood represents a site of knowledge formation as well as political resistance in their lives.

Revolutionary Implications of Paula C. Johnson's and Sara Bennett's Pictures of (Ex-) Incarcerated Black Mothers

In this essay, I analyzed the aesthetics and discourses of Paula C. Johnson's and Sara Bennett's representations of (ex-) incarcerated women with a focus on how they express timely and urgent criticism of U.S. racism, sexism, and mass incarceration. The photographs, edited narratives, and captions give women opportunities to represent their agency and survival in their private lives and thereby challenge the primary association of incarceration with rehabilitation in society. The women appear both powerful and vulnerable in their everyday performances of motherhood in light of racialization, discrimination, and institutional containment. Paula C. Johnson and Sara Bennett do not define the women by their incarcerations but emphasize their subjectivities in the titles of their projects, *Inner Lives*, *Life After Life in Prison*, and *Spirit on the Inside*. The women identify themselves as Black women, (grand)mothers, and daughters in their edited narratives or captions. Paula C. Johnson's and Sara Bennett's projects seem to illustrate Alexander G. Weheliye's argument that the gendered racialization of people is related to their experiences of dehumanizing victimization in institutions.[61] However, Paula C. Johnson's and Sara Bennett's projects imply a revolutionary potential in the women's performed connectedness to their community's past, present, and future. Their politics of representation could elevate (ex-) incarcerated women's performed care practices in their private lives to sites of knowledge formation about their communities with the potential to reduce incarceration rates in the future. Celeste-Marie Bernier points out that enslaved women in the U.S. devised plots of resistance and escape while they practiced traditionally feminine labor in the household, such as quilting, embroidering, and sewing.[62]

When Paula C. Johnson gives women the opportunity to (re)write their lives with the help of photographs and interviews, she echoes Audre Lorde's understanding of marginalized women as experts on how to overcome their oppression by deriving strength from their own identities.[63] For example,

Donna Hubbard Spearman contrasts how she hated being a parent when she was an incarcerated drug addict with how she loved being a mother while she holds her award that she won for her activism on behalf of incarcerated mothers, underlining the connection between her experiences as a mother and her self-image.[64] In her photograph, Donna Hubbard Spearman's physical appearance with her broad smile, bejeweled sweater, and perfect hairstyle and manicure could challenge stereotypes of ex-incarcerated women. However, her award directly references her organization, Revelation Seed, which she founded following her pregnancy during her incarceration, when she experienced how incarcerated mothers comforted each other after forced separations from their babies after delivery.[65] In her edited narrative, Donna Hubbard Spearman advocates recognizing the opportunity to practice motherhood as a condition for criminalized women's rehabilitation,

> It's going to take a community's support. It's going to take some innovative ideas. It's going to be criminal justice folks being willing to take some chances and take some risks. Granted, there are those of us that need to be in prison. I'm not going to lie, but there is a larger majority of women who don't need to be in prison and who would be better served by being in a program with their children. We're talking about rehabilitation. How about talking about *habilitation*. If you've never had a healthy life or a productive life, then you can't return somebody to something they never had.[66]

Donna Hubbard Spearman does not foreground the act of childbirth but connects the condition of being together with own children with wellbeing and rehabilitation. With regard to motherhood, she invokes her mother's expectation of early marriage and motherhood after joining the Nation of Islam, her own perception as a drug addict that her children would benefit from her absence, and her later realization that she had to care for her health in the interest of her children.[67] On the one hand, Donna Hubbard Spearman's edited narrative implies that (ex-) incarcerated mothers can choose to practice care toward each other and thereby empower each other in (re)claiming their roles as mothers. On the other hand, Sara Bennett's representations of Tracy's rehabilitation process in *Life After Life in Prison* criticize her limited opportunities for self-determination, since the Salvation Army was the only employer to hire her, as a bell ringer at first[68], and she could only afford to live in a three-quarter house or with a friend.[69] Sara Bennett's photograph of Tracy with Joshia implies that she desires closeness with him and that the love she shares within this familial relationship contrasts with the surveillance and marginalization that she experienced within the criminal justice system. Accordingly, Tracy's representation from behind as she cradles Joshia does not yield her body to external gazes.

Both examples, Sara Bennett's photographs of Tracy and Paula C. Johnson's photograph and edited narrative of Donna Hubbard Spearman could represent care as resistance against women's physical containment and thereby posit their private lives as possible sites of identity (re)negotiation in light of histories of racism and sexism in the U.S. Under slavery, Black women were prevented from creating their own homes for their families, since their familial ties were denied any legal recognition. After the abolition of slavery, Black women who were incarcerated for alleged crimes were less likely to be considered as "'fallen sisters'" and assigned to women's reformatories.[70] On the one hand, Michael Welch contrasts the custodial institutions that dominantly held disenfranchised women of color with the reformatories for middle-class women that aimed to transform inmates into submissive housewives until the 1930s.[71] On the other hand, Paula C. Johnson refers to the public rape and lynching of the accused Laura Nelson in Oklahoma in 1911 as an example of how Black women were historically punished for alleged crimes in the U.S. South.[72]

Paula C. Johnson and Sara Bennett could symbolically support (ex-) incarcerated women in expressing their agency and subjectivity when they photograph them according to their own wishes. By representing how the women express maternal love or experience separation from their families, they challenge stereotypes of criminalized womanhood and advocate understanding. In contrast, Paul Gilroy explains that stereotypes of violent mothers from the U.S. South do not consider the women's fears in light of Jim Crow laws that their children had to internalize in order to survive.[73] However, Paula C. Johnson's and Sara Bennett's representations of confident women and loving mothers advocate resistance against discrimination by humanizing their subjects. The women's performances of confidence despite their (past) incarcerations underline the historical knowledges and survival strategies that circulate within their communities and which they could transfer to their children. The women's performances of motherhood both resist stereotypes of their stigmatized identities in the eyes of viewers and positively influence their children's perceptions of them in the future.

To conclude, the analyzed representations by Paula C. Johnson and Sara Bennett prioritize the performances of agency of (ex-) incarcerated women over their experiences of incarceration as sites of knowledge formation about their lives. Firstly, Paula C. Johnson's portrait photographs and edited narratives in *Inner Lives* criticize mass incarceration with the help of perspectives of women who already experienced violence before their criminalization and who often discuss how motherhood inspired them to change their lives. Secondly, Sara Bennett's photographs in *Life After Life in Prison* and *Spirit on the Inside* could juxtapose women's care practices with their stigmatization within the criminal justice system, since the politics of mass incarceration perpetuate racist and sexist discrimination against Black women, including mothers. Thus through these representations, (ex-) incarcerated women who perform their identities as mothers could practice resistance against forced absence from their children's lives and emphasize their experiences as critical sites of knowledge formation about their societies.

Notes

1   hooks, bell (1984) *Feminist Theory from Margin to Center.* Boston: South End Press, 15.
2   hooks, *Feminist Theory from Margin to Center*, 11.
3   Johnson, P. C. (2003) *Inner Lives: Voices of African American Women in Prison: With a Foreword by Joyce A. Logan and an Afterword by Angela J. Davis.* New York and London: New York University Press, 26.
4   Johnson, *Inner Lives*, 16.
5   Johnson, *Inner Lives*, 41–43.
6   Denson, J. (1999) "Testimony before the Subcommittee on Oversight, of the House Committee on Ways and Means," *Hearing on the U.S. Customs Service Passenger Inspection Operations*, May 20, 1999, https://www.govinfo.gov/content/pkg/CHRG-106hhrg66023/html/CHRG-106hhrg66023.htm.
7   Weheliye, A. G. (2014) *Habeas Viscus: Racializing Assemblages, Biopolitics, and Black Feminist Theories of the Human.* Durham and London: Duke University Press, 112, 126.
8   Wanzo, R. (2009) *The Suffering Will not Be Televised: African American Women and Sentimental Political Storytelling* Albany: State University of New York Press, 72–73.
9   Clifford, E. (2018) "Formerly Incarcerated Women on Life after Life in the Bedroom," *Huck Art & Culture*, November 15, 2018, https://www.huckmag.com/art-and-culture/photography-2/formerly-incarcerated-women-on-life-after-life/.
10   Clifford, "Formerly Incarcerated Women on Life after Life in the Bedroom".
11   Mattila, H. (2018) "Lawyer, Photographer, and Activist Sara Bennett Talks Prison System and Life after Parole," *Merion West*, March 7, 2018, https://merionwest.com/2018/07/03/lawyer-photographer-and-activist-sara-bennett-talks-prison-system-and-life-after-parole/.
12   Sontag, S. (2003) *Regarding the Pain of Others.* New York: Picador, Chapter 8.
13   Sontag, *Regarding the Pain of Others*, Chapter 6.

14   Bernier C-M. (2008) *African American Visual Arts from Slavery to the Present*. Chapel Hill: The University of North Carolina Press, 41–42.

15   Wanzo, *The Suffering Will not Be Televised*, 176.

16   Johnson, *Inner Lives*, 10.

17   Ibid.

18   Ibid.

19   Weheliye, *Habeas Viscus*, 26–27.

20   Johnson, *Inner Lives*, 51.

21   Johnson, *Inner Lives*, 16.

22   Johnson, *Inner Lives*, 96.

23   Johnson, *Inner Lives*, 57.

24   Johnson, *Inner Lives*, 78.

25   Johnson, *Inner Lives*, 175.

26   Johnson, *Inner Lives*, 195.

27   Hortense J. Spillers, "Mama's Baby, Papa's Maybe: An American Grammar Book," *Culture and Countermemory: The 'American' Connection*, Spec. Issue of *Diacritics*, 17, 2 (Summer 1987): 64–81, 78.

28   Johnson, *Inner Lives*, 62.

29   Johnson, *Inner Lives*, 57.

30   Spillers, "Mama's Baby, Papa's Maybe," 74.

31   Spillers, "Mama's Baby, Papa's Maybe," 77–78.

32   Johnson, *Inner Lives*, 124.

33   Johnson, *Inner Lives*, 133.

34   Barson, T. (2010) "Introduction: Modernism and the Black Atlantic," in *Afro Modern: Journeys through the Black Atlantic*, eds Tanya Barson and Peter Gorschlüter. Liverpool: Tate, 8–25, 21.

35   Spillers, "Mama's Baby, Papa's Maybe," 65.

36   Johnson, *Inner Lives*, 202.

37   Johnson, *Inner Lives*, 175.

38   Johnson, *Inner Lives*, 179.

39   Johnson, *Inner Lives*, 177.

40   Johnson, *Inner Lives*, 181–182.

41   Johnson, *Inner Lives*, 177.

42   Tlostanova,M. V. (2010) *Gender Epistemologies and Eurasian Borderlands*. New York: Palgrave Macmillan, 39–40.

43   Rice, C. (2014) *Becoming Women: The Embodied Self in Image Culture*. Toronto, Buffalo, and London: University of Toronto Press, 85.

44   Johnson, *Inner Lives*, 260–261.

45   Hill,A. (2011) *Reimagining Equality: Stories of Race, Gender, and Finding Home* Boston: Beacon Press, 69, 71.

46   Roberts, D. (1997/2016) *Killing the Black Body: Race, Reproduction, and the Meaning of Liberty*. New York: Vintage Books, xvi.

47   Johnson, *Inner Lives*, 170–171.

48   Johnson, *Inner Lives*, 171–174.

49   Johnson, *Inner Lives*, 167.

50   Walker, S. and A. Worrall, (2006) "Life as a Woman: The Gendered Pains of Indeterminate Imprisonment," in *Prison Readings. A Critical Introduction to Prisons and*

Imprisonment, eds Yvonne Jewkes and Helen Johnston. London and New York: Routledge, 253–267, 255–256.

51 Johnson, *Inner Lives*, 63.

52 Truth, S. (1851), "Ain't I a Woman?" in *The Norton Anthology of Literature by Women: The Traditions in English*, vol. 1, eds Sandra M. Gilbert and Susan Gubar. New York: W.W. Norton, 1985/2007, 510–511, 510.

53 Alexander, M. (2010) *The New Jim Crow: Mass Incarceration in the Age of Color Blindness*. New York: The New Press, 12–13.

54 Spillers, "Mama's Baby, Papa's Maybe," 80.

55 Maraj, L. M, P. Prasad, and S. V. Roundtree (2018) "#Black Lives Matter: Pasts, Presents, and Futures," *Prose Studies*, 40, 1-2: 1–14, 5, 12.

56 Crenshaw, K. (1989) "Demarginalizing the Intersection of Race and Sex: A Black Feminist Critique of Antidiscrimination Doctrine, Feminist Theory and Antiracist Politics," *University of Chicago Legal Forum*, 1, 8: 139–167, 161–162.

57 Davis A. Y. and E. Mendieta (2005) *Abolition Democracy: Beyond Empire, Prisons, and Torture: Interviews with Angela Y. Davis*. New York: Seven Stories Press, 17, 113–114.

58 Shakur, F. (2019) "From the Civil Rights Movement to Black Lives Matter: Honoring Black Mothers Who Lost Their Sons," *New York Times*, January 29, 2019, https://www.nytimes.com/2019/01/29/lens/sheila-pree-bright-civil-rights-Black-lives-matter-mothers-atlanta.html.

59 Shakur, "From the Civil Rights Movement to Black Lives Matter".

60 Foucault M. (1975), *Surveiller et punir: Naissance de la prison*. Paris: Gallimard, 152.

61 Weheliye, *Habeas Viscus*, 2, 96.

62 Bernier, *African American Visual Arts from Slavery to the Present*, 43.

63 Lorde, A. (1979), "The Master's Tools Will Never Dismantle the Master's House," in *Sister Outsider: Essays and Speeches*. Freedom, CA: The Crossing P, 1984, 110–113, 111–112.

64 Johnson, *Inner Lives*, 195, 197.

65 Johnson, *Inner Lives*, 202.

66 Johnson, *Inner Lives*, 204.

67 Johnson, *Inner Lives*, 201.

68 Bennett, S. (2014) "Tracy Working as a Bell Ringer for the Salvation Army: New York City," *Life After Life in Prison*, July 17, 2016, https://sarabennett.org/life-after-life/2016/7/17/tracy-working-as-a-bell-ringer-for-the-salvation-army-new-york-city-2014

69 Bennett, S. (2015) "Tracy Living Back in the Three-Quarter House for a Few Months Before She Moved to a Friend's Apartment: Bronx, NY," *Life After Life in Prison*, July 17, 2016, https://sarabennett.org/life-after-life/2016/7/17/2016/7/17/tracy-living-back-in-the-three-quarter-house-for-a-few-months-before-she-moved-to-a-friends-apartment-bronx-ny-2015.

70 Welch, M. (1995/2011) *Corrections: A Critical Approach*. London and New York: Routledge, 163.

71 Welch, *Corrections*, 164.

72 Johnson, *Inner Lives*, 24.

73 Gilroy, P. (1993) *The Black Atlantic: Modernity and Double Consciousness*. Cambridge: Harvard University Press, 174–175.

Works Cited

Alexander, M. (2010). *The New Jim Crow: Mass Incarceration in the Age of Color Blindness* New York: The New Press.

Barson, T. (2010). "Introduction: Modernism and the Black Atlantic," in *Afro Modern: Journeys through the Black Atlantic*, eds Tanya Barson and Peter Gorschlüter, 8–25. Liverpool: Tate.

Bennett, S. (2014). "Tracy Working as a Bell Ringer for the Salvation Army. New York City"
——— (2015). "Tracy Living Back in the Three-Quarter House for a Few Months Before She Moved to a Friend's Apartment. Bronx, NY"
——— (2016). *Life After Life in Prison*, July 17, https://sarabennett.org/life-after-life/2016/7/17/2016/7/17/tracy-living-back-in-the-three-quarter-house-for-a-few-months-before-she-moved-to-a-friends-apartment-bronx-ny-2015 (accessed July 12, 2021).
——— (2016). *Life After Life in Prison*, July 17, https://sarabennett.org/life-after-life/2016/7/17/tracy-working-as-a-bell-ringer-for-the-salvation-army-new-york-city-2014 (accessed July 12, 2021).

Bernier, Celeste-Marie (2008). *African American Visual Arts from Slavery to the Present*. Chapel Hill: The University of North Carolina Press.

Clifford, E. (2018). "Formerly Incarcerated Women on Life after Life in the Bedroom," *Huck Art & Culture*, November 15, 2018, https://www.huckmag.com/art-and-culture/photography-2/formerly-incarcerated-women-on-life-after-life/ (accessed July 3, 2021).

Crenshaw, K. (1989). "Demarginalizing the Intersection of Race and Sex: A Black Feminist Critique of Antidiscrimination Doctrine, Feminist Theory and Antiracist Politics." *University of Chicago Legal Forum*, 1, 8: 139–167.

Davis, A. Y. and E. Mendieta (2005). *Abolition Democracy: Beyond Empire, Prisons, and Torture: Interviews with Angela Y. Davis*. New York: Seven Stories Press.

Denson, J. (1999). "Testimony before the Subcommittee on Oversight, of the House Committee on Ways and Means." *Hearing on the U.S. Customs Service Passenger Inspection Operations*, May 20, https://www.govinfo.gov/content/pkg/CHRG-106hhrg66023/html/CHRG-106hhrg66023.htm (accessed July 3, 2021).

Foucault, M. (1975). *Surveiller et punir: Naissance de la prison*. Paris: Gallimard.

Gilroy, P. (1993). *The Black Atlantic: Modernity and Double Consciousness*. Cambridge: Harvard University Press.

Hill, A. (2011). *Reimagining Equality: Stories of Race, Gender, and Finding Home*. Boston: Beacon Press.

hooks, bell, (1984). *Feminist Theory from Margin to Center*. Boston: South End Press.

Johnson, P. C. (2003). *Inner Lives: Voices of African American Women in Prison: With a Foreword by Joyce A. Logan and an Afterword by Angela J. Davis*. New York and London: New York University Press.

Lorde, A. (1979). "The Master's Tools Will Never Dismantle the Master's House," in *Sister Outsider: Essays and Speeches*, 110–113. Freedom, CA: The Crossing Press.

Maraj, L. M., P. Prasad, and S. V. Roundtree (2018). "#Black Lives Matter: Pasts, Presents, and Futures," *Prose Studies*, 40, 1-2: 1–14.

Mattila, H. (2018). "Lawyer, Photographer, and Activist Sara Bennett Talks Prison System and Life after Parole," *Merion West*, March 7, 2018, https://merionwest.com/2018/07/03/

lawyer-photographer-and-activist-sara-bennett-talks-prison-system-and-life-after-pa-role/ (accessed July 3, 2021).

Rice, C. (2014). *Becoming Women: The Embodied Self in Image Culture.* Toronto, Buffalo, and London: University of Toronto Press.

Roberts, D. (1997/2016). *Killing the Black Body: Race, Reproduction, and the Meaning of Liberty.* New York: Vintage Books.

Shakur, F. (2019). "From the Civil Rights Movement to Black Lives Matter: Honoring Black Mothers Who Lost Their Sons." *New York Times*, January 29, 2019, https://www.nytimes.com/2019/01/29/lens/sheila-pree-bright-civil-rights-Black-lives-matter-mothers-at-lanta.html (accessed July 3, 2021).

Sontag, S. (2003). *Regarding the Pain of Others.* New York: Picador.

Spillers, H. J. (1987). "Mama's Baby, Papa's Maybe: An American Grammar Book," *Culture and Countermemory: The 'American' Connection*, Spec. Issue of *Diacritics*, 17, 2: 64-81.

Tlostanova, M. V. (2010). *Gender Epistemologies and Eurasian Borderlands.* New York: Palgrave Macmillan.

Truth, S. (1851), "Ain't I a Woman?" In *The Norton Anthology of Literature by Women: The Traditions in English*, vol. 1, edited by Sandra M. Gilbert and Susan Gubar, 510–511. New York: W.W. Norton.

Walker, S. and A. Worrall (2006). "Life as a Woman: The Gendered Pains of Indeterminate Imprisonment." In *Prison Readings. A Critical Introduction to Prisons and Imprisonment*, edited by Yvonne Jewkes and Helen Johnston, 253–267. London and New York: Routledge.

Wanzo, R. (2009). *The Suffering Will not Be Televised: African American Women and Sentimental Political Storytelling.* Albany: State University of New York Press.

Weheliye, A. G. (2014). *Habeas Viscus: Racializing Assemblages, Biopolitics, and Black Feminist Theories of the Human.* Durham and London: Duke University Press.

Welch, M. (1995/2011). *Corrections: A Critical Approach.* London and New York: Routledge.

9 SPEAKING OF "UNSPEAKABLE THINGS UNSPOKEN"[1]

Sasha Turner ———————————————————————

"Imperialist. White Supremacist. Capitalist. Patriarchy."[2]

Say its name.

Imperialist. White Supremacist. Capitalist. Patriarchy. The intersecting systems of domination and oppression.

Say its name.

Imperialist. White Supremacist. Capitalist. Patriarchy.

Not race. Not gender. Imperialist. White Supremacist. Capitalist. Patriarchy. Dominating together. Intertwined. Roped. Simultaneously.

Say its name.

Imperialist. White Supremacist. Capitalist. Patriarchy.

Name how it hurts.

Original violence. They kill our children. We kill our children. Our children kill themselves. Grieving mothers. Broken families. Broken hearts.

December 18, 1780. Last night Abba miscarried of a boy. Mary Ann was delivered of twins both died. Rosetta's child not named, dead.[3]

Say their names. Abba. Mary Ann. Rosetta.

Margaret Garner chose death for herself and her children, Mary and Cilla, rather than suffer a life of enslavement.

"The faded faces of the negro children tell...the degradation female slaves submit[ted.] Rather than give her little daughter to that life, she killed it...who shall say she had no right? With my own teeth would I tear open my vein, and let the earth drink my blood, rather than wear the chains of slavery."[4]

Say their names. Abba. Mary Ann. Rosetta. Margaret Garner. Mary. Cilla.

"Tender sorrow for Mamie Till-Mobley," "When [I later] lost one of [my] sons, [I] thought about the grief that Mamie must have felt and grieved all the more."[5]

The dying words of Carolyn Bryant Donham confessing she did not tell the truth about Emmett Till. "That old threadbare lie."[6]

Say their names. Abba. Mary Ann. Rosetta. Margaret Garner. Mary. Cilla. Emmet Till. Mamie Till-Mobley.

The "real American carnage."[7]

May 15, 2010. Wrongfully arrested and imprisoned for 3 years for theft. Refusing a guilty plea to a crime he did not commit. Battered, beaten, and denied the protective innocence promised by childhood. Kalief Browder killed himself. Sixteen months later, his mother, Venida Browder died of a heart attack...a broken heart.

Say their names. Abba. Mary Ann. Rosetta. Margaret Garner. Mary. Cilla. Emmet Till. Mamie Till-Mobley. Kalief Browder. Venida Browder.

Says its name. Imperialist. White Supremacist. Capitalist. Patriarchy. The intersecting system of domination and oppression that kills our children, breaks our families, destroys our lives.

Say their names. Abba. Mary Ann. Rosetta. Margaret Garner. Mary. Cilla. Emmet Till. Mamie Till-Mobley. Kalif Browder. Venida Browder.

Many others, named, not named, dead.

Notes

1   Morrison, T. (1988) "Unspeakable Things Unspoken: The Afro-American Presence in American Literature," *The Tanner Lecture on Human Values at The University of Michigan*, October 7, 1988; printed in *Michigan Quarterly Review* 28, no. 1, 1989, https://quod.lib. umich.edu/m/mqrarchive/act2080.0028.001,Accessed January 8, 2020.

2   hooks, bell (2013). Writing Beyond Race: Living Theory and Pratice, New York and London: Routledge.

3   Turner, S. (2017). "The Nameless and the Forgotten: Maternal Greif, Sacred Protection, and the Archive of Slavery," *Slavery and Abolition* 38 no. 2, 232–250.

4   *Cincinnati Daily Gazette* February 14, 1856. Cited in Delores M. Walters, "Re(Dis)Covering and Recreating the Cultural Milieu of Margaret Garner," in *Gendered Resistance: Women, Slavery, and the Legacy of Margaret Garner*, edited by Mary E. Frederickson and Delores M. Walter, Urbana: University of Illinois Press, 2013, 5.

5   Carolyn to Timothy Dyson, a Duke University senior research working on Emmett Till's story cited in Breanna Edwards "Woman Who Caused Emmett Till's Death Admits to Lying," *The Root* 27 January 2017 http://www.theroot.com/woman-who-caused-emmett-tills-death-admits-to-lying-1791698393 accessed January 8, 2020.

6   *Free Speech* May 21, 1792. Cited in Jacqueline Jones Royster, ed., *Southern Horrors and Other Writings*, New York: Bedford/St. Martin's, 1997, 2016, 1.

7   Patten, D. (2017) "Time: The Kalief Browder Story' Review: Searing Docu Reveals American Tragedy," March 1, 2017, http://deadline.com/2017/03/time-the-kalief-browder-story-review-jay-z-spike-tv-documentary-video-1202030130/ accessed January 2, 2020.

PART THREE

"YOU ARE YOUR BEST THING"*: SELF-CARE AS A SITE OF RESISTANCE

* Morrison, T. (2004). *Beloved: A Novel*.15th ed. Ch.27.

10 BLACK BIRTH MATTERS

A Conversation with Andrea Chung and
D'Yuanna Allen-Robb

Nicole J. Caruth _____

In 1951, the Georgia State Department of Public Health and the Association of American Medical Colleges commissioned filmmaker George C. Stoney to create a documentary about childbirth, specifically, the practices of Black lay midwives in the Deep South. Also known as "granny" midwives, these women trained through apprenticeship and were respected healers in their communities. With the help of community liaisons, Stoney met Mrs. Mary Francis Hill Coley (1900–1966), a midwife who is said to have delivered 3,000 babies in roughly 30 years.[1] For four months, Stoney followed "Miss Mary" to her patients' homes, observing her practice and deriving inspiration for his script. Miss Mary would become the star of his film, *All My Babies: A Midwife's Own Story*, a bizarre period piece that merges reenactments by a mostly Black cast with midwifery instruction, a live birth, and a hymnal soundtrack.

All My Babies was intended to educate lay midwives in the Deep South, and Stoney was given a list of 118 teaching points to incorporate.[2] But the film found a broader audience. Advertised early on as one of the "outstanding humanist works of American cinema," *All My Babies* holds a place in the pantheons of film history: Stoney donated his outtakes to the Museum of Modern Art's Film Department, which was at one time a distributor of the film. And in 2002, the Library of Congress placed *All My Babies* on the United States National Film Registry, deeming it "culturally, historically, or aesthetically significant."[3]

In *All My Babies*, Stoney paints a familiar picture of Black subjects under the tutelage of a white "expert" doctor and nurse. What his film doesn't show is how much the American medical establishment loathed—but learned from —granny midwives, drawing from their deep well of knowledge as community birth attendants before outlawing their practices. Women have always served as birth attendants, and it stands to reason that skilled birth workers in Black communities date back to ancient societies, though the literature focuses on slavery and segregation. In the antebellum years, Black midwives served their enslaved sistren and masters' wives. Post-emancipation, they typically provided birth services to women in rural communities who lacked access to hospitals, or women who feared medical establishments due to entrenched racism and, ostensibly, the decades of nonconsensual experiments on Black bodies. As Lynne Jackson writes, doctors and nurses generally looked down on lay midwives in the Deep South, recognizing them as a "temporary and unfortunate necessity."[4] Such attitudes can be traced back to chattel slavery, when older enslaved women who served as midwives on plantations were at once needed for their health and healing knowledge and devalued because of not only race but age—older enslaved women were considered less valuable at auction.[5]

In the decade that *All My Babies* was released, the maternal mortality rate for Black women was 3.6 times greater than that for white women.[6] One could speculate that Jim Crow segregation and lacking medical technologies underlie this disparity. But now, nearly 70 years later, the statistics are not much better. According to a report from the Centers for Disease Control and Prevention (CDC) in 2020, Black women in the United States die from pregnancy-related causes at a rate 2.5 times higher than their white counterparts[7] (reports in previous years showed a rate of 3.3 to 4 times higher)[8]. Black newborns face similarly horrible odds with a mortality rate more than twice that of white newborns.[9] Why does this gap exist and persist?

Everyday "pull yourself up by your bootstraps" anti-Black rhetoric would have us believe that poor lifestyle choices by individual mothers is the reason for the disproportionate statistics. But multiple studies point to structural inequities, including differential access to healthcare, healthy foods, clean drinking water, reliable transportation, and safe neighborhoods. Researchers also recognize that the chronic toxic stress of racial discrimination takes a toll on the body, increasing the risk of physical and mental health issues. And then there is the centuries-old myth that Black people are impervious to pain, a racial bias that crosses class and influences medical care—or lack thereof—in doctor's offices and maternity wards across the country. Women's stories of neglect include rushed cesarean sections, too little anesthesia, and failure to listen when a mother senses that she or her baby may be in danger, such as the life-threatening experience recounted by the champion tennis player Serena Williams.

Despite how much time has passed since *All My Babies* was created, the film continues to be germane, especially now amid a resurging demand for Black birth workers. Recent journalism has turned the spotlight on midwives and doulas of color, noting how their involvement fosters better health outcomes for Black families[10] (as an aside, a midwife or doula wasn't even mentioned as an option when I was my sister's Lamaze partner 28 years ago). Birth workers serve as advocates for the mother but occupy different roles. Nowadays, midwives are clinically trained, licensed practitioners who deliver babies in homes and have access to hospitals if needed; whereas doulas are trained, unlicensed practitioners who provide emotional, physical, and educational support from pregnancy and labor to the postpartum period, including, for full spectrum doulas, miscarriage, planned abortion or medical termination, and stillbirth. In the past, a midwife might have done it all and in some countries or situations they still do.

George Stoney wrote two birth scenes for *All My Babies* based on what he had experienced in the homes of Miss Mary's patients. One scene was shot in a moderately well-off nuclear family home where everything was tidy and prepared. The other was shot in a shanty with the expecting couple depicted as emotionally traumatized and unprepared to welcome their child, believing it would be stillborn like their last. Swarming flies in this couple's home suggest unsanitary conditions. "A main emphasis of the film is cleanliness and hygiene practices for the midwives," writes Miriam Zoila Pérez. "But this emphasis foreshadows the eventual decline of the granny midwives and the messaging used to discredit them."[11] A combination of legislation and regulation eventually prohibited the services of granny midwives, but that was after they endured smear campaigns that portrayed them as dirty.

In contrast, Stoney made efforts to exclude anything that might imply poor Black-white race relations in the American South or that might be seen as a northerner's attempt to "exploit Southern poverty."[12] Despite—or maybe because of—what Stoney left out, *All My Babies* was lauded for its uniqueness, particularly for the way Stoney positioned granny midwives as respectable members of society. In later interviews, Stoney recalled comments that he had "heightened these people." His editor said to him, "You have shown them so that I don't think of them as Negroes, but just people."[13]

Contemporary Dialogues

Documentary film and photography have played a critical role in recent efforts to humanize Black maternal and infant mortality statistics. Take, for example, the 2021 documentary film *Bearing the Burden: Black Mothers in America*, released in collaboration with *The New Yorker*; the online photo exhibition,

Catching Light: Celebrating Black Midwives & Birth Workers, curated by Artists United for Reproductive Justice, an affiliate of the SisterSong Women of Color Reproductive Justice Collective; and the ongoing documentary film series *Giving Birth in America* from the nonprofit Every Mother Counts. These storytelling efforts, along with an influx of journalism on Black maternal health, have no doubt influenced contemporary artists. Among the most visible, perhaps, are the Chicago-based photographer LaToya Ruby Frazier and the San Diego-based multimedia artist Andrea Chung. Although their practices are vastly different, their work intersects at *how* they practice. That is, in relatively close proximity to doulaing and midwifery (rather than commentating from afar), serving as witnesses and champions not unlike Stoney.

In 2018, Frazier's photography accompanied Linda Villarosa's widely-circulated *New York Times Magazine* article, "Why America's Black Mothers and Babies Are in a Life-or-Death Crisis."[14] Frazier chronicled the pregnancy of Villarosa's main subject, Simone Landrum, a New Orleans-based mother preparing to welcome her third child after the loss of her previous child. Two photographs in particular spotlight the relationship between Landrum and her doula, Latona Giwa, co-founder of Birthmark Doula Collective, a grassroots organization in New Orleans. Working in the lineage of granny midwives, Giwa represents a life-affirming bridge in the mother-child-doctor relationship. Frazier's images suggest a kinship as the two women sitting together stare directly at the camera, with Giwa appearing to literally have Landrum's back. Frazier's images echo something that Stoney wanted to portray: a celebration of childbirth and family as opposed to a depiction of trauma.

In 2017, the year before Frazier's images were published by the *Times*, the artist Andrea Chung turned her attention to midwifery too, focusing on granny midwives of the American South and the Caribbean. Her *Midwives* series pays homage to Black birth workers of the past by combining found photographs of older women (and sometimes children) from the African diaspora with renderings of medicinal herbs used in traditional midwifery practices. The women in her collages were often made to look like queens and deities. In one image, the female reproductive system is fashioned into a golden crown. Here, Black women are not victims of discriminatory health institutions but powerful care providers who bolster their community and protect its children. *Midwives* was inspired by Chung's grandmother, a market woman and midwife in Jamaica, and the birth of her own child, a son named Kingston. Although Chung says she had a relatively non-traumatic birth experience in terms of the care she received, the challenges she faced being both an artist

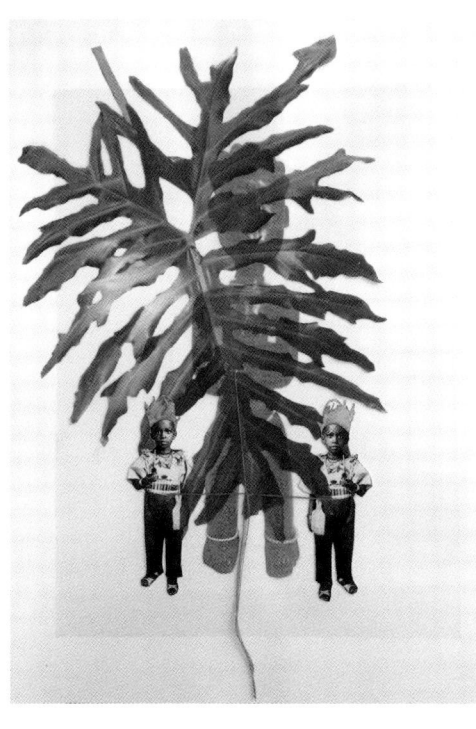

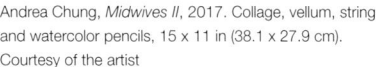

Andrea Chung, *Midwives II*, 2017. Collage, vellum, string and watercolor pencils, 15 x 11 in (38.1 x 27.9 cm). Courtesy of the artist

and new mother prompted her to creatively explore Black motherhood today.

In 2018, Chung revisited her *Midwives* photo collages, weaving them into her multimedia project *Eeny, meeny, miny, moe.* Mounted in collaboration with the public art and public health departments of Nashville, Tennessee, this three-part experience included a cookbook that paired low-cost recipes with images from *Midwives*; free cooking workshops for new and expectant mothers; and a baby-crib sculpture, all at the Lentz Public Health Center, the primary site for receiving Women, Infants, and Children (WIC) benefits. The workshops were taught by Nashville-based practitioners Taneesha Reynolds, a certified nurse-midwife, and Ashley Couse, a doula and childbirth educator, and each participant received a copy of the artist's cookbook with a free box of fresh produce. Chung's project calls our attention to an oft forgotten tenet of a healthy pregnancy: equitable access to healthy foods and health resources.

A catalyst for my research on Black maternal health, *Eeny, meeny, miny, moe* eventually lead me to Stoney's film, and, subsequently, this essay and transcribed conversation with Chung and D'Yuanna Allen-Robb, the director of Maternal Child and Adolescent Health at the Nashville Metro Public Health Department (as a guest curator for the City of Nashville, I commissioned Chung's project as part of a city-wide public art exhibition). As much as Chung was influenced by her earlier *Midwives* research, she was also motivated by Allen-Robb, who, with her vast knowledge of place, illuminated how maternal and infant mortality rates in North Nashville, a historically African American community, intersect with the displacement of young mothers today due to Nashville's real estate boom and gentrification. While Chung and Allen-Robb operate in dissimilar sectors, they intersect in their belief that art,

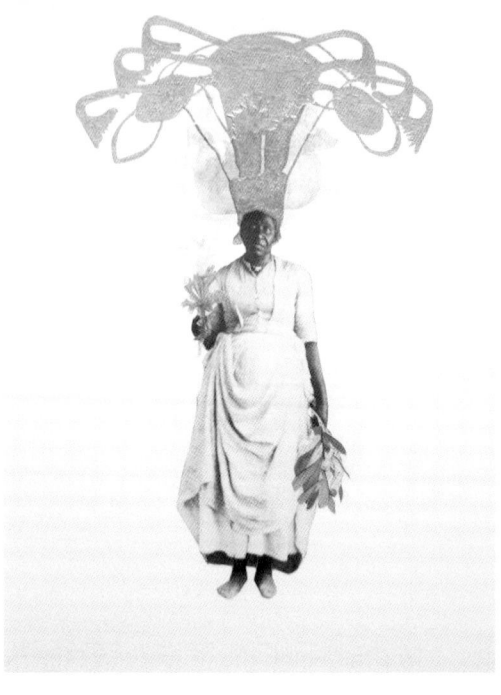

particularly photographs, can help shift consciousness, bringing audiences closer to truthful narratives on Black life and motherhood.

Chung's project serves as a rare example of the role that positive images of Black women can play not only in addressing racial health inequities, but the potential for integrating artistic practice in health systems and spaces to affect change. This begs the question: What is the role of photography (and artists in general) in contemporary movements for maternal justice? In this conversation, Chung and Allen-Robb discuss this question, as well as Black maternal and infant mortality, and the healing presence of birth workers, from their perspectives as an artist and public health leader.

A Conversation on Black Maternal Health, January 22, 2020

NICOLE J. CARUTH: Andrea, let's start with what motivated you to embark on research about Black granny midwives in the American South and Caribbean?

ANDREA CHUNG: I met Dr. Alicia Bonaparte when I was giving a lecture at the Claremont Colleges in Pomona, CA. She teaches at Pitzer College, and I was interested in her research on Black midwives in the American South. This fell in line with some interests I had around Yoruba traditions and my grandmother in Trinidad, Beryl LeCadre, who was a midwife for over thirty years. I wanted to figure out how Alicia and I could partner. After my son was born, I started thinking about birthing, the roles of mothers, and what it meant to be a mother.

I decided that to work with Alicia the most logical thing to do was a comparative study between midwifery in the Caribbean and her research on Black midwives in the American South. We wanted to compare birthing practices to see if there were any similarities or differences. We both had a lot of African retentions in midwifery that we thought were interesting. For example, using certain medicinal herbs or putting things under the bed, like axes or boots, which was supposed to reduce labor pains. I decided to start making work based on the findings of the research.

CARUTH: Andrea, how did you go about finding and selecting historical photographs for your *Midwives* series?

CHUNG: I've always worked with archives and I've always been interested in how those images have been used, specifically images from the Caribbean. When I first started using archival images, I collected them from the Schomburg Center in New York. I was really concerned about copyright and my usage of the images. However, now I source them from the Internet, often from ethnographic postcards that had circulated or posed images of the so-called "native." I've thrown caution to the wind when it comes to copyright because, as the artist Carrie Mae Weems has discussed, who has the right to own images of another culture's history?

CARUTH: D'Yuanna, before we talk about how art and photography intersect with your work, it might be helpful if you outline what you do at the Metro Public Health Department.

D'YUANNA ALLEN-ROBB: In Nashville, I serve as the director of maternal child and adolescent health at the Metro Public Health Department. We look at healthcare systems and work with partner organizations to take a public health approach to eliminating inequities. We understand that when we look at our data around the burden and distribution of disease and disability and early mortality, it is concentrated among African Americans and African American neighborhoods and communities, not necessarily through the fault of or due to the bad habits of individuals or whole communities, but rather because of systems and structures of inequity. I'm not unique in my role because I have counterparts all over the country, but I will underscore our particular focus here on eliminating those inequities by changing systems. This includes calling out the history and structure of racism, the current practices within institutions, and limiting beliefs about groups of people based on socialized identities, and then finding creative ways to help people see and understand that and start to move toward the action of dismantling it.

CARUTH: Talk more about finding "creative ways" to help people understand inequities.

ALLEN-ROBB: As an example, in 2010, Nashville's Public Health Department was selected as one of two communities nationally to be part of a W.K. Kellogg-funded initiative called Racial Healing. The idea was to collect oral histories from communities that have been suffering from inequities and present those stories either using photo archives or photography of the living individuals who shared their stories with us about what the community looked like 50 or 60 years ago versus what it looks like today, to help people, particularly in public health, understand what has changed.

We have grown in our work but there definitely have been times when we concentrated our messaging about hypertension, for example, around individual behavior. "You're eating too much salt. Or "You're eating too much sugar." Or "You're not eating healthy foods." But if you don't ever take a step back and ask, *What is the structure of the neighborhood? What is the structure of the community?* then you don't see what people actually have access to and how resources are distributed.

We recognize that the historic African American community in North Nashville, in the 37208 zip code, was once a very prosperous, well connected, and structurally resource-dense community before the historical insult of Interstate 40 being constructed through it. If you're just looking at data on a piece of paper from 2010, then all you see are negative statistics and all of these "bad behaviors" of the people who live there. That narrative has a tendency to create a story that these are individual decisions and individual behaviors as opposed to the creative way of embarking on this journey of racial healing: to look at the archival history and collect the oral histories of residents who lived in the 37208 zip code area who could talk about, from their memory, what that community was like.

For example, that sidewalks connected every house; that the majority of African American individuals who lived in that neighborhood owned their homes; that there were Black working professionals who had net worth at that time, concentrating the economic dollar within the Black community; that there was a Black grocery store, and three historically Black colleges and universities. Then Interstate 40 got constructed and it decimated and dispersed that concentration of wealth and community.

Once that narrative got to be told, it forced us as a public health department, and all of the entities we work with, to use different language and tell a different story that the health outcomes we see today and saw at that time in 2010—hypertension, high rates of cancer, high infant mortality—is not necessarily a function of individual behavior. It absolutely is a function of a living legacy of racism and structural inequity that was created. And if it was created then it can be undone.

Caruth: Did the Nashville Public Health Department use photographs from the Tennessee state archives to support the Racial Healing project research?

Allen-Robb: Yes, we used state and local archives. The Nashville Public Library archive has a Civil Rights section and the Metro Records archive has old planning maps that we pulled to see what neighborhoods looked like before Interstate 40 and afterwards. Being able to digitize one of the Metro planning maps and then do an overlay of a Google aerial view of the 37208 zip code area now was pretty powerful because we could see where there had been blocks of homes and that those areas are now flattened and no longer recognized as property or residents.

Chung: What can photography do to support movements for maternal justice now?

Allen-Robb: Photography can play a significant role in a movement around maternal justice. Or, as I would say, Black women's justice. So much imagery of Black women propagated in popular culture and media is very negative. These images reinforce stereotypes and, what's extremely important, at least in this conversation, is when those same kinds of images and ideas are subconsciously used in a healthcare setting. To give an example, when a woman goes to a doctor's office for prenatal care, there might be an image on the wall of two "families." One image is of a white woman who is pregnant and there is a white man beside her. She's smiling and he's smiling, and their hands have rings on them, so the assumption is that they are married. Then there is another image right beside it, or somewhere else in the waiting room, of an African American woman who is visibly pregnant and smiling but there ain't nobody else in the picture with her. This subconsciously reinforces the idea that we don't get married; that we don't have husbands, we somehow get pregnant by ourselves, and there's not another human being involved.

We have healthcare providers who are not checking that subconscious bias and being critical about how the brochures, pamphlets, or other materials they use make people feel welcome in a space. When you go to a provider's website to figure out where to get care and you don't see images of people who look like you, that is a critical opportunity for photography in a system, to help break down subconscious bias related to skin color and race.

Photography also has a critical role in telling stories about social cohesion and family to help offset feelings of internalized oppression and racism. There are ways to say, through photographs, "We are strong. We are supporting one another. We raise healthy children. We have this expectation for our families, and not only for our families, we have this expectation of the system around us." When we expect more, we demand more, and we hold people accountable for delivering on the more that we expect and demand. I think that photography, and images of Black women specifically, can be extremely powerful in not only systems shift, but also in helping us as a collective of individuals shift our own internalized thinking.

CARUTH: Andrea, talk about your work with photographs of Black women, specifically around midwifery and motherhood.

CHUNG: Becoming a mother changed a lot within my practice. It's made me more vocal and direct—I don't feel like I have the time to be passive—because of my experiences, including one that I had at a residency program where a white curator questioned my ability to be successful as an artist because I'm a mother. She basically called my child a distraction (my son was just three months old at the time). That made me more aware of how much harder it was going to be. It's hard enough to be a Black artist but to be a parent too... That experience made me consider what it meant to be a mother, especially a Black mother.

My use of archival images started from thinking about labor, specifically what it looks like in the Caribbean, and re-examining photos that we don't necessarily look at carefully. A lot of images of slavery in the Caribbean were not actually taken during slavery but later. People were forced to pose to project certain ideas, to make it seem like they were docile. Many stereotypes that come from the Caribbean are of exoticized women, or market women, who are often pictured in subservient positions—laying down or bending over or sitting with another figure, usually a white person, standing above them. I wanted to change the way we read these images and question who took those images and why.

My grandmother on my father's side was a market woman who had nine kids that she raised all on her own. There's power and strength in raising nine children. If you were to look at her from far away, you would judge her like, "Oh wow, a single mom with nine kids..." But she was way more than that. She was also very politically active and a Garveyite. As D'Yuanna was saying earlier, with these stereotypes of Black women, I often feel that people don't take a close look at why these women are where they are. I focus on giving the women in the [historical] photographs some power and agency. I've done things like transform them into Orishas, particularly Yemeya who protects all mothers and children.

CARUTH: Recently, there have been notable articles in *ProPublica* and the *New York Times*, for instance, about what is being called a crisis of Black maternal and infant mortality in the U.S. How do statistics in Nashville compare to national rates?

ALLEN-ROBB: I will segment out infant mortality because it continues to be our leading indicator and then I will talk about maternal mortality and maternal morbidity.

Infant mortality, or the death of an infant before their first birthday, continues to be an issue. In Tennessee, our infant mortality rate is around 6.5 per 1,000 live births, so that's about 6.5 infants that are dying for every 1,000 infants that are born. In Nashville, the rate has declined a little bit in the last year and is down to 7 infant deaths per 1,000 live births. That is still higher than the national rate and certainly higher than the Healthy People 2020 Goal. We should be nationally closer to an infant mortality rate of 5 or less. When we start to segment out infant deaths by race, that rate is about 1.5 times higher for African American families than it is for Caucasian families (Latinx families are also experiencing higher rates of infant death than Caucasian families). If you compare Tennessee to other states in terms of infant mortality rates, we're consistently around 45, so you have a better chance of surviving in 45 other states then than if you're born here. We're obviously not proud of that fact and continue doing work to drive that number down. We're seeing some success.

When it comes to maternal mortality, it's a bit more difficult, especially since maternity mortality reviews are relatively recent in Tennessee. We didn't start reviewing the deaths of women (when a death is associated and related to a pregnancy or birth and up to a year after the birth) until about two years ago and we had to pass legislation in order to do that. Some of the early information we have is that there's about 78 pregnancy associated deaths annually and about 28% of those were determined to be pregnancy-related, meaning women dying as a direct result of them being pregnant. About 63% of those deaths were not classified as being pregnancy-related, so they could have been related to a homicide. The likelihood of a lethal event when there's domestic violence increases dramatically when a woman becomes pregnant. So, it may not have been directly related to her being pregnant or how she was treated by a hospital, but she still died, and she was pregnant at the same time.

In terms of how Tennessee compares to the rest of the country, we have relatively low numbers when you think about the number of actual maternal deaths nationally. About 700 women in the United States die from a pregnancy or pregnancy-related complication every year and certainly, when we look at the racial disparities, African American women are three to four times more likely to die from a pregnancy-related or pregnancy-associated death. But in Tennessee our numbers are averaging around 73 annually. We are lower than the national average, and the disparity between African American women and Caucasian women isn't as stark, primarily because of Caucasian women who are suffering from a substance abuse disorder. We are being hit pretty hard in this state around substance use and we're helping people get into treatment. In a lot of pregnancy-related deaths among Caucasian women, a suspected overdose was the leading cause.

CARUTH: This is depressing! It makes me think of the first time that Andrea and I met you at Lentz Public Health Center. Andrea, I remember you talking that night about how hard it was to hear about women and children dying "just because they're Black." I'm wondering if and how this knowledge is affecting you?

CHUNG: I did not realize things were this bad until I met D'Yuanna. My OBGYN took really good care of me and my pregnancy went relatively smoothly until she opened me up for my C-section. I had blood vessels everywhere and it was kind of a difficult birth. I thought that was as bad as it could be. But then a friend of mine in Brooklyn had a horrible birthing experience and could have died. She's a doula now because of what she went through. And then I thought back to the fact that my mom lost a son before me primarily because the doctors waited too long to give her a C-section. Her baby couldn't live without being on a machine, so they had to make the decision at 22 months to let him die. This idea that Black women can withstand more pain and that we're not given the right to have a child like anyone else is unbelievable. How could we not be affected by reading or hearing stories like this? Everybody has the right to have a kid. Everybody has the right to proper treatment in a hospital and Black women are dying for no reason—or for lack of care.

CARUTH: Andrea, you've talked about revisiting your Nashville project, particularly the cooking workshops. What do you want this project to do going forward?

CHUNG: Sometimes books like *What to Expect When You're Expecting* aren't all that helpful; they don't give practical information about what your body's going through at certain stages and what it feels like to be a mother. There are things about being a mother that I had no idea about because no one ever told me. You just deal with it and it's very isolating when you don't have someone to talk to. I feel that when mothers come together there's possibility for sharing information; meal and clothing swaps (which is something I see happening in an Artist Mommy group I'm a part of on Facebook); and the support of knowing that you're not the only one dealing with something like postpartum depression, which I had. I would like to continue creating community among mothers so they can organize and rely on each other. I would love to continue working with women so they know how to buy food on a budget, and properly care for their bodies, not just prenatal but also postnatal to make sure the kids and family are eating healthy.

CARUTH: D'Yuanna, from a public health perspective, what are some of the benefits when a Black mother has a community of folks to talk to, seek advice from, etc.?

ALLEN-ROBB: Human beings are designed to belong and be in community. There are psychological benefits to having people that you can depend on, a support structure, which doesn't have to be a biological family. As we continue to learn more about the health impacts of living in an isolating society, the Centers for Disease Control and Prevention has released information about loneliness being a public health threat. Living in isolation increases symptoms of depression and physical ailments.

From a cultural standpoint, the African American experience and part of our DNA is rooted in the fact that we've always existed in villages and in community with the sense that I will do for you and you will do for me. And your child is my child and we will care for each other and our children collectively. We should embrace the fact that we desire a sense of belonging. There are benefits to social cohesion for us mentally and physically. When women are well, children are well. Give women the support they need. One of the best ways to do that is women taking care of women and showing up for each other as a part of a community.

CHUNG: Going back to the artist residency I mentioned, I was really lucky to have a supportive cohort and staff members who offered to babysit. You definitely need a group to lift you up and make you feel that you can do this because mothering is hard, even if you're not working a 9 to 5 job. Raising a child is the hardest thing you will ever do in your life. I would not be getting through this if I did not have people to lean on, and people who supported that parenting was something I wanted to do alongside this other dream I had of being an artist.

CARUTH: I was listening to a webinar from Black Mamas Matter Alliance the other day and one of the speakers said, "Midwifery was more than catching babies; midwives were psychologists, dieticians, loan officers, sex therapists, partners, marriage counselors, etc." I think this speaks to the various needs of mothers and also to the importance of the midwife as a community leader. My next question is for you, D'Yuanna: What are some of the documented benefits when Black mothers have a Black doula or midwife?

ALLEN-ROBB: I'm going to frame this a bit more broadly around birth support because it could be the midwife or doula or the circle of women who are your friends who form your support system. And I'm going to tie this into the benefits of group prenatal care when women are receiving education and support together during their pregnancy. Oftentimes, this model of group care is led by a midwife or a nurse practitioner or somebody who has a birthing background. What the information shows is that Black women primarily benefit from psychosocial support (and this goes back to that sense of belonging) and having a person or people who understand the unique experience of being Black.

A mother might say: "I'm being treated differently and there is another voice or set of voices in a hospital setting who are going to advocate for me. If this is the birth plan I have put together and this is what I want to experience, as long as it is safe for me and my baby, I don't have to explain myself. And there's this group of people, or my midwife or my doula, who are going to make sure my wishes are carried out within this system."

When pregnant women have a support system, they have lower incidences of experiencing hypertension. Our blood pressure naturally goes up during labor and if you have lingering high blood pressure after you deliver a baby, that's a post-pregnancy complication that can impact your next pregnancy. Women are also more likely to say they feel a sense of satisfaction in their birthing experiences because their wishes were honored, meaning they got to do things the way they wanted to do them and received more patient-centered care. The medical research will show that the impact of implementing patient-centered care includes patients reporting lower complaints of pain post-surgery, for example, and that patients are more likely to be "medically compliant," meaning they come back for their follow-up appointment.

All of these things are impacted by having a relationship with a midwife or a doula or a support system as a part of the birthing experience. And these relationships need to continue well past the postpartum period. It's a major adjustment bringing a human being home; it's an adjustment for everybody in the household or everyone who knows you. Your whole life has to change and everybody else's life changes within the family structure, whatever that is, because this new human being has arrived. Having a support system helps take some of the load off the mom or dad or immediate biological caregivers. To take it back to the African village, the child is then the collective responsibility of us all.

Caruth: D'Yuanna, what kind of policy change is necessary to reduce or eliminate the disparities in Black maternal and infant health?

Allen Robb: I sometimes struggle with this question because one policy initiative that was put in place by the American College of Gynecologists (ACOG), which is the national governing body of licensed obstetrics, is what we call "safety bundles." These are protocols that hospitals are required to follow when they are providing care to women who are in labor. For example, one complication of labor can be a postpartum hemorrhage and when we look at maternal mortality quite a few women have died from this.

A story people might be familiar with is that of Charles Johnson and his wife Kira who died at Mount Sinai hospital in Los Angeles in 2016. Charles has been traveling the country talking about the changes that are needed. He testified before a Senate committee and helped to get legislation passed that authorized the Maternal Mortality Act, which sends millions of dollars flooding into states to help address maternal mortality. But here's the issue: You can have policies all day long and at the end of the day you still have biased human beings providing care. If you have a policy and the policy is not followed, the degree of reprimand could be some type of after-action review in the hospital to try to understand what happened. A physician may lose his license or a hospital may lose accreditation but this is rare. Policies in and of themselves are not enough.

The Alliance for Innovation on Maternal Health safety bundles as supported by ACOG and other national organizations are critical because they get hospitals to actually think and have protocols in place. But you have human beings who don't follow them because when they see me or you or Andrea, they don't think we deserve the best care. When Charles's wife complained of shivering and feeling like something was wrong, and even when Charles saw the blood in his wife's catheter (I'm paraphrasing his story), it didn't matter because she was Black.

CHUNG: I mean, if Serena Williams is dealing with it then…

ALLEN-ROBB: Exactly. What I think we need are three things: Policies, yes, because there has to be some type of administrative structure that sets the standard for what an entity will and will not do in terms of care.

Two, there is a need for all kinds of training and for people to call out inequity when they see it. Every human being has biases and we've been socialized to have them. Many biases are subconscious and the fact that we have them isn't a reflection on an individual's moral character. It is simply a known fact of growing up in the Western hemisphere that you're going to have biases, so it's not something to be afraid of. But when those biases literally come down to life and death decisions, you have a practice responsibility as a licensed professional to be aware of your biases and there has to be a process in place for institutions to be able to address implicit bias.

Number three, we as consumers have to start demanding more. The internalized oppression that I think we carry sometimes as African American women may make us think, "I'm not really sure if this is what I deserve?"

Sometimes we don't know what quality looks like because if you're not white maybe you've never seen it. But we do know that something is wrong, and we have to start moving with our economic power.

Maternal mortality and infant mortality have been an issue since the first pregnancy and there's obviously been advances because of modern medicine. But in my non-researched opinion, village women have been delivering babies in sterile conditions and they have been just fine. Mom didn't die and her baby didn't die. Somebody cared about the mother, knew her name, knew her story, and was *excited* to welcome this child into the world. That is the difference. We need to be seen as human beings. Period.

CHUNG: How do you train someone to respect another person as a full human being?

ALLEN ROBB: More of us have to be willing to do the hard work of becoming aware of our biases and those of the people around us. And institutions have to be willing to create spaces where those kinds of challenges can happen. The brilliant people at Harvard recognize that there are 138 different implicit biases (and those are just the ones we know of) and this is backed up by brain science. We can reprogram our brains; we can route new pathways. The brain is plastic and it can still learn. A doctor can reroute their brain from assuming that every Black woman is aggressive and a single mother and stop to read her chart, ask her questions, and act, not based on assumption, but what she actually says. For some people it's just a matter of asking them, "If this was your wife, if this was your daughter, what would you do for her?"

CHUNG: My gynecologist is a Black woman and I told her that I'd never had a Black gynecologist before—they're like unicorns. She said most gynecologists are white males, and there's a shortage of gynecologists in general. She also mentioned that biases aren't just coming from white doctors but from Black doctors too because of their training. It's like everybody needs to be reprogrammed because they've all been trained to think that Black women can bear more pain than other patients, or they've been trained not to listen to us. It's sad and even more frustrating when the biases are coming from a doctor who looks like you.

ALLEN-ROBB: There are only two historically African American medical schools in the entire United States. One is at Howard in Washington, DC and the other one is here at Meharry Medical College in Nashville. There's not a whole lot of opportunity for Black professionals who want to pursue medicine and have an unbiased experience, and there's only so many spaces for enrollment. The threat of racism intersects with everything. If you pull one thread in this tapestry, you're going to connect to many other threads. To map it back to photography, images can help open up a conversation about how all of these things are connected. There's an opportunity for every person to see themselves as being a part of the solution.

CARUTH: Is there anything either of you want to say that feels relevant to this discussion that I haven't addressed?

ALLEN-ROBB: I would love to see more local health departments embracing creativity and using photography to tell stories, understand root cause issues, and change the narrative. The narrative that we tell in public health is that people are sick and they don't live as long because of individual decisions. The narrative we should be telling is that people are sick and don't live as long because we did this to them, because of our racist inequities that have to change. It's not solely on the individual; it is on the system and the institution that is getting rich off of the fact that people are sick and dying early. I do believe that part of the role of public health, and those of us living in this society, is to push social justice forward because we all have a functional understanding of the disparities and there's no excuse. If we aren't telling these stories, if we aren't presenting pictures and our understanding to people, then things won't change.

There is evidence that change is happening because I can see it in the data. I can see that we have more babies being born today that are celebrating their first birthday than we did last year, and that's a very promising sign. It tells me not to take my foot off the gas. I'm going to continue moving forward and building this movement. We are saving ourselves and we just need more communities to do it so that no matter where you are, you and your family have the best chance that you can have.

Notes

1   "Mary Francis Hill Coley," Georgia Women of Achievement, https://www.georgia-women.org/mary-francis-hill-coley.

2   Jackson, L. (1987) "The Production of George Stone's Film 'All My Babies: A Midwife's Own Story' (1952)," *Film History 1*, no. 4 (1987): 372, http://www.jstor.org/stable/3814989.

3   "About this collection," Library of Congress: Selections from the National Film Registry, https://www.loc.gov/collections/selections-from-the-national-film-registry/about-this-collection/.

4   Jackson, "The Production of George Stoney's Film," 387.

5   Fett, S. M. (2002) *Working Cures: Health, Healing, and Power on Southern Slave Plantations.* Chapel Hill: University of North Carolina Press, 55.

6   Centers for Disease Control (1990) "Differences in Maternal Mortality Among Black and White Women: United States," *Morbidity and Mortality Weekly Report*, no. 44 (January 13, 1995): 6–7,13–14, https://www.cdc.gov/mmwr/preview/mmwrhtml/00035538.htm.

7   Hoyert, D. L. S. F. G. Uddin, and A. M. Miniño (2020) "Evaluation of the Pregnancy Status Checkbox on the Identification of Maternal Deaths," *National Vital Statistics Reports* (January 30) https://www.cdc.gov/nchs/data/nvsr/nvsr69/nvsr69_01-508.pdf. And Dina Fine Maron, "Has Maternal Mortality Really Doubled in the U.S.?," *Scientific American* (June 8, 2015), http://www.scientificamerican.com/article/has-maternal-mortality-really-doubled-in-the-u-s/.

8   Petersen, E. E., N. L. Davis, D. Goodman, S. Cox, N. Mayes, E. Johnston, C. Syverson, K. Seed, C. K. Shapiro-Mendoza, W. M. Callaghan, and W. Barfield (2019) "Vital Signs: Pregnancy-Related Deaths, United States, 2011–2015, and Strategies for Prevention, 13 States, 2013–2017," *Morbidity and Mortality Weekly Report*, no. 68 (May 10, 2019): 423–429, http://dx.doi.org/10.15585/mmwr.mm6818e1.

9   Greenwood, B. N., R. R. Hardeman, L. Huang, and A. Sojourner. (2020) "Physician–patient racial concordance and disparities in birthing mortality for newborns," *Proceedings of the National Academy of Sciences of the United States of America* 117, no. 35 (September 1): 21194–21200, https://www.pnas.org/content/pnas/117/35/21194.full.pdf.

10   Bahadur, N. (2020) "What It's Like to Be a Midwife or Doula Fighting Black Maternal Mortality," *Self* (January 13, 2020), https://www.self.com/story/midwives-doulas-black-maternal-mortality; and Janel Martinez, "What Black Doulas Are Doing to Keep Women and Children Alive," *Well + Good* (February 27, 2020), https://www.wellandgood.com/good-advice/black-doulas/.

11   Pérez, M. Z. (2015) "Granny Midwives' of the South," *Colorlines* (March 19), https://www.colorlines.com/articles/tbt-granny-midwives-south.

12   Jackson, "The Production of George Stoney's Film," 376.

13   Jackson, "The Production of George Stoney's Film," 386.

14   Villarosa, L. (2018) "Why America's Black Mothers and Babies Are in a Life-or-Death Crisis," *The New York Times Magazine*, (April 11), https://www.nytimes.com/2018/04/11/magazine/black-mothers-babies-death-maternal-mortality.html.

11 WORTH A THOUSAND WORDS

Visualizing Black Motherhood and Health

HAILE ESHE COLE _____

Introduction

> *"Such is the power of the photograph, of the image, that it can give back and take away, that it can bind..."*
> —hooks, 1994: 44

I can see the picture so clearly in my mind. She is young—29 years old to be exact. Standing on concrete steps, her smooth, brown skin stands out against the gray and colorless brick building behind her. This is a building that I would later recognize as the local public library where she worked as a librarian and children's storyteller. It is obvious that the photographer is standing a few meters back and possibly in the street. You can see her entire body and an expansive view of her surroundings. Despite this, you can make out her facial expression clearly. She is smiling. When she smiles her round face lights up the entire frame and her dimples create beautiful, deep, dark, and bowl-shaped craters in her full cheeks. This smile is one that will forever be etched into my memory. It is a smile that has brought me comfort and joy since before I can even remember. The long navy and white-striped, ankle length dress that she wears hangs effortlessly across her body barely masking her protruding belly—a belly where I am growing and undoubtedly being nurtured by love, care, and southern soul food as she awaits the arrival of her first born child, a daughter. Her arms that cook, clean, teach, and will hold me in times of sorrow and joy, are proudly outstretched, beautiful, bold, and stately like the Christ the Redeemer statue. It is as if she is inviting the world to see her in all her glory.

*
*　*

I am unsure why this image is something that I so clearly remember. Maybe it is the joy and love in her expression that drew me in and seared itself into my mind as a young child first discovering the photo. Maybe it is because it was one of our first photos together—the embodiment of all that she is to me and the documentation of the beginning of our dear and intimate relationship. This image of my mother is one of many images that exists in my early mental curation of Black motherhood. The image serves as an example of how a photo can help construct a narrative about oneself and those close to them. As I began to write this piece on Black motherhood, health, and photography, this image of my mother immediately came to mind. Fully understanding the reason why requires a bit of additional context.

Recently, my mother recovered from an acute health condition that resulted in months of ongoing hospitalizations, procedures, and therapies. As an engaged scholar with experience and community work around health care access and justice, I was prepared to advocate fiercely for her needs. I was acutely aware of the variability of Black folks' experiences in hospital settings and as a trained doula[1] and women's health advocate, I had witnessed the spectrum of treatment given to Black women from good to terrifying. I could not help but wonder (and fear) how my mother would be treated during this vulnerable time. Would the doctors and medical staff validate her knowledge about her own body and her needs? Would they acknowledge and hear her cries of pain?[2] Would they understand her questioning as a patient's right to information and self-advocacy or would she be labeled as difficult and non-compliant? Moreover, as her primary caretaker, I wondered how they would perceive *me*? I have written about the fear of being perceived as an uneducated, single, Black mother and its impact on my care. I also reflected on the practice of touting my education and credentials with the hopes that the medical staff and doctors will listen to me (Cole 2015: 127). Looking back, I see this as a desperate attempt to play on respectability to grasp, on the most basic level, a miniscule amount of compassion or as Evelyn Brooks Higginbotham might say a "measure of esteem from White America" (Higginbotham 1993: 14). Deep down I knew, and history has taught us, that respectability is never enough to save us. Nevertheless, the truth of the matter was that my fears boiled down to one thing—legibility. How did the folks who held my mother's life in their hands *see* her? Did they see her the way that I did, as a loving and fierce Black woman, daughter, mother, teacher, and human being? Or did they see age-old stereotypes that have historically and unjustly dehumanized Black women? In the end, one of the most essential questions at hand is what is being seen when the white dominant gaze is directed at the Black body and what are its implications. This is important when considering the issue of Black Motherhood, photography, and health.

Taking this into account, this essay seeks to highlight the intersections between the visual and concrete life experiences of Black women and mothers. The essay will examine the legacies of visual representation of the Black reproductive body—and more importantly Black motherhood—to demonstrate the ways in which visual culture creates powerful narratives that directly impact Black mother's experiences. Overall, this essay argues that visual representations of Black motherhood that pigeonhole, criminalize, and perpetuate harmful stereotypes have far-reaching and direct impacts on Black life, including, but not limited to, issues of health and wellness. Moreover, these images contribute to a longstanding history of racialized, gendered, and sexed ideologies that serves as the basis for the systems and structures that create racial inequities in health and otherwise. The current epidemic of Black maternal and infant mortality, deeply rooted in the interminable experience of racism-induced stress, explored here briefly, serves as one chilling example. On the other hand, this essay also suggests that one seriously considers the powerful and transformative potentialities of visual media—that of photography and film—as a mechanism of liberation and power to write new self-determined narratives.

My Lens

In an attempt at transparency and reflection, I would like to take a moment to briefly examine my lens as I begin this piece. First and foremost, it would be remiss not to mention that this piece feels pressing and timely in a very personal way. After the murder of George Floyd at the hands of the police in Minneapolis, Minnesota, Black Lives Matter protests have erupted around the world calling for the defunding of the police and justice for the many lives lost to anti-Black, state-sanctioned violence. In these moments, while I find the toll on Black communities monumental, the centrality of Black motherhood remains significant. We painfully recall George Floyd's final words as he calls for his mother during his last breaths. We also see how the mothers of those lost (Trayvon Martin, Michael Brown, and Tamir Rice to name a few) continue to fight and demand justice. Others, see Erica Garner and Venida Browder for example, suffer fatal heartbreaks under the weight of pain and loss. As a Black

Mother myself, these recurring instances painfully resonate in ways that, at times, render me speechless and paralyzed.

Then there is the issue of health. The recent struggles with my mother's health are only one piece of it. As I sit at my computer penning this chapter, the world is attempting to survive a global pandemic. The pandemic has brought to light yet again the issue of health disparities as mortality rates for Black folks have far outpaced other racial and ethnic groups (AMP Research Lab Staff 2020). The health outcomes of the COVID-19 pandemic reveal, again, how experiences of systemic racism, discrimination, and stress impact health.

Much of my work over the years—academic, professional, and community—has focused on experiences of Black motherhood but more specifically, the current maternal and infant health disparities in the United States. Black motherhood and maternal and infant health disparities is a key marker of community health. With Black women three to four times more likely to die from pregnancy related complications and Black infants 2.5 times more likely to die before their first birthday, these stark differences in outcomes have raised alarm bells in maternal health around the nation.[3] Most important, the scientific findings about racism-induced stress over the life-course as a primary cause for negative birth outcomes has been impactful.[4] Although documented largely in public health and medical research, much of the media attention around the issue that has spread like wildfire after celebrities such as Serena Williams and Beyonce began to speak out about their experiences (Howard 2018; Scutti 2018; Williams 2018), failed to fully acknowledge the role of racism in these fatal outcomes.

It is important to make the connection between police brutality, anti-Black violence, and health. Calls to defund the police, for example, are inextricably linked to the health and wellness of Black communities. I find the definition of reproductive justice useful for understanding these dynamics. Founded by Black women, reproductive justice has been described in its most basic sense as "the human right to maintain personal bodily autonomy, have children, not have children, and parent the children we have in safe and sustainable communities" ("Reproductive Justice"). Most notable to me, is that this definition asks us to consider what it might require to create safe and sustainable communities. Based on this definition, to accomplish justice and equity requires that we look comprehensively at our definitions of health while rooting them in a deep understanding of history, structures, and systems. On this point, my definition and understanding of health is not measured in trips to the doctor or physiological measures of wellness. While these are important indicators,

I am thinking of a construction of health in which Black women and mothers, their children, families, and communities can access the resources to live safe, healthy, and fully realized lives.

So, what does this have to do with photography? In a previous article, I examined the contribution of media attention to the problematic narratives around Black women in their coverage of maternal and infant health disparities. My argument maintained that the erasure of racism from the narrative of maternal mortality redirects blame away from social structures and conditions and continues to not only seek solutions in behavioral interventions that place the onus and blame on Black women but also perpetuates existing narratives of the unredeemable and diseased Black body (Cole 2018: 90–91). This article on Black motherhood and photography picks up, for me, where that article left off. Interrogating health disparities themselves is only one piece of the pie. Also questioning notions of narrative and representation is central to fully understanding the social, economic, and political context

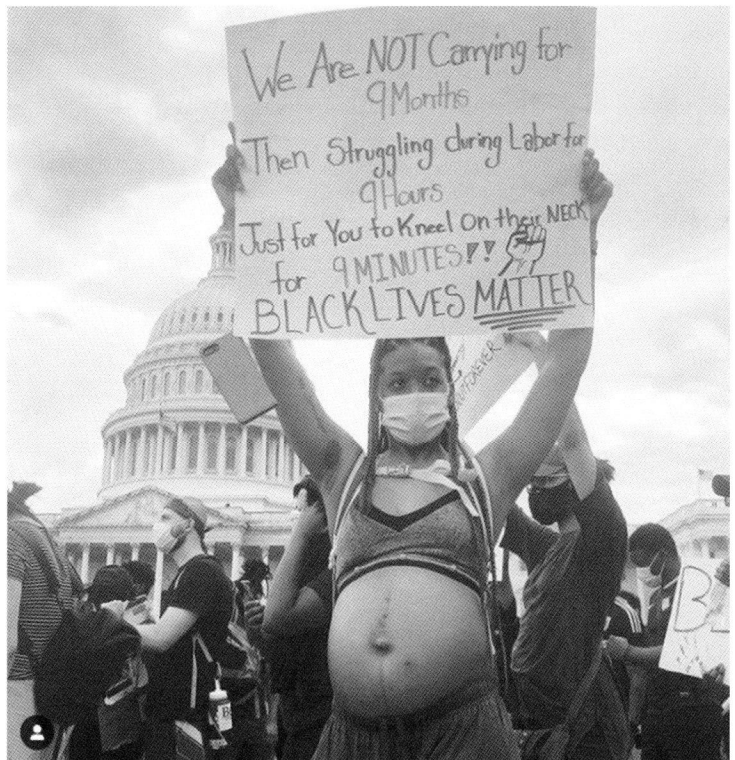

Thema (@Uluvmylovefaces), "I SAID WHAT I SAID!!" #BLACKLIVESMATTER #BLACKOUTEVERYDAY #STOPKILLINGOURKIDS #VIRAL #FREEDOMFIGHTERS #justiceforgeorgefloyd #justiceforbreonnataylor #nojusticenopeace #washingtondc #Thema. Sign reads "*We are not carrying for 9 months then struggling for 9 hours in labor just for you to kneel on their neck for 9 seconds!! BLACK LIVES MATTER*," Instagram photo, June 2020, https://www.instagram.com/p/CA_Xfh-BXl4/

surrounding health and wellness for Black women and mothers. In digging into notions of representation, we begin to uncover and fully see the ideological foundations that inform problematic belief systems that marginalize and harm communities. If you want to answer the question of what the dominant gaze sees when they see us, then interrogating the visual is an important and critical step. Moreover, in our attempts to shift narratives, imagine new worlds and live healthy (fully realized) lives, how does the visual lend itself as a tool in this process of creation?

Seeing is Believing: The Visual as Power

"One thing is obvious: film and television images in America are greatly influenced by the political conditions of the times, and these images tend to serve the psychological needs of the people who create them..."
—St. Claire Bourne, 1994: 145

As the opening reflection of my mother reveals, the visual is inextricably linked to one's capacity to make meaning out of personal experience. Images and photos serve as critical sites of memory. They are indexical tools that link us back to a person, place, time, moment, or even an emotion. On the other hand, visuals can also be used to create powerful narratives that define and shape realities. In fact, visuals have served as important components contributing to the ideological foundations that have supported systems of power and racial oppression.[5] bell hooks in her introduction to *Black Looks: Race and Representation* states that

> There is a direct and abiding connection between the maintenance of white supremacist patriarchy in this society and the institutionalization via mass media of specific images, representations of race, of blackness that support and maintain the oppression, exploitation, and overall domination of all black people. Long before white supremacists ever reached the shores of what we now call the United States, they constructed images of blackness and black people to uphold and affirm their notions of racial superiority, their political imperialism, their will to dominate and enslave. From slavery on, white supremacists have recognized that control over images is central to the maintenance of any system of racial domination. (hooks 2014: 2)

While the tools of power and domination evolved over time, taking hooks' assertion into account maintains that image making helped to build the foundation for racial and gendered oppression. Ideology served as an important piece of the skeleton for the structure of powerful racial hierarchies. While pseudo-science, such as phrenology and craniology, served as a supposed objective and scientific justification for racist beliefs and anti-Blackness, many of these unfounded assertions were also supported by visuality, namely photography.

Photography and other forms of visual media become powerful tools whereby they enact the idea that seeing, as opposed to other senses, is truly believing. Photographic technologies served as a source of "proof" to justify problematic and racist assumptions. For Black motherhood, these images supported not only the ideal of the hypersexual and pathological Black mother but also her inability to access womanhood and motherhood.

Controlling Images

Patricia Hill Collins in her book, *Black Feminist Thought: Knowledge, Consciousness, and the Politics of Empowerment* (2002), examines the issue of "controlling images" of Black women. She maintains that

> "As part of a generalized ideology of domination, stereotypical images of Black womanhood take on special meaning. Because the authority to define societal values is a major instrument of power, elite groups, in exercising power, manipulate ideas about Black womanhood.... These controlling images are designed to make racism, sexism, poverty, and other forms of social injustice appear to be natural, normal, and inevitable parts of everyday life. Even when the initial conditions that foster controlling images disappear, such images prove remarkably tenacious..." (Collins 2002: 69)

Various controlling images and stereotypes get regurgitated in visual and popular media—the mammy, the sapphire, the jezebel, and the welfare queen are some of the most widely utilized. These stereotypes offer problematic and racist commentary on not only Black female sexuality, both hyper and/or asexual, but also mothering capabilities. While these images get reused and repurposed contemporarily, it is also important to note the ways that these ideas presented themselves early on and how these ideas were supported visually. Missionary and colonial photography as well as the daguerreotypes of enslaved individuals during the 1800s serve as important early examples.

The Black Woman, Health and Pathology

Ideas of Black women's lasciviousness is reflected in modern-day representations of the sapphire and jezebel, for example. The broader implications of this is not only the idea of a hypersexual Black woman but also one that is inherently pathological. Several authors have done work to historicize the conception of the pathological Black woman and mother as well as the ideological work that sought to explicitly delineate the space between white women's virtuous womanhood and Black women.[6]

Most importantly, these stereotypes had huge implications for conceptualizations of health. In fact, Janell Hobson pinpoints the conflation of racialized ideas of beauty and perfection and beliefs about health and disease (Hobson 2003: 88–89). Jean Comaroff's work *The Diseased Heart of Africa* explores the ways in which ideologies about disease and illness began during early imperialist expansion in Africa. These ideologies about the diseased Black body were often both raced and gendered. She asserts that in the European imagination, Africa was a "hothouse of fever and affliction" and Black women were thought to be carriers of venereal disease (Comaroff 1993: 305). According to Comaroff, central to the early missionary and colonialist expansion was this idea of the "healing mission" both as a means of addressing what they perceived to be not only physical ailments but also spiritual and moral ones (313).

Missionary work often occupied an interesting and conflictual role of supposed altruistic aims alongside colonial expansion. These same conflictual sentiments were also reflected in missionary documentary photography. Thomas Hendriks in his piece *Erotics of Sin: Promiscuity, Polygamy and Homo-Erotics in Missionary Photography from the Congolese Rainforest* asserts that

> "Black women were clearly aestheticized and eroticized as exotic "types" whose essentially 'tribal' nature resulted in an excessive and bestial sexuality seducing both black and white men and constituting an obstacle to moral reform and Christianization. Young girls were equally aestheticized, but their aestheticization was based on the "perverted" system of commercialized polygamy that corrupted their innocence and would eventually transform them into over-sexualized

women. The representation of women and girls was thus strongly informed by a moral rejection of what missionaries thought to be sinful sexuality." (Hendriks 2013: 378)

Overall, he argues that these images served to perpetuate racialized ideologies and exoticized and othered the Black body in a coalescence and duality of desire and repulsion, "morality and pornography"[7] (Hendriks 2013: 355). Exploring missionary and colonial photography in Africa is central to the historic excavation to unearth the relationship between photography and constructions of race and health.

Erasing the Black Mother

Given the historical ideas of Black women being less than women and pathological, it follows these ideologies also have an impact on the views of Black motherhood. Consumers of such racist ideals would undoubtedly question how a woman so unredeemable can be fit to be a mother. Interestingly, the idea of the neglectful and culpable Black mother goes back a way as well, as previously mentioned, the difficulty for Black women and mothers from slavery and into the present to access the ideas of virtuous womanhood and motherhood afforded to white women in the dominant imagination. In thinking this through visually, some of the early daguerreotypes of the enslaved come to mind. The widely consumed image of the Black wet nurse epitomizes the image of the mammy. Furthermore, "the mammy typifies the Black mother figure in white homes" (Collins 2002: 75). Unfortunately, this image is painfully symbolic in several ways.

In many of these early images of the enslaved, rarely do we see Black women nurturing and caring for their own children. Of course, this is an outcome of a brutal system that delegitimized and criminalized Black motherhood. From the separation of families, to the auction block and the rape and breeding of Black women, Black motherhood was a phenomenon that was not allowed to exist. Dorothy Roberts in her work *Killing the Black Body: Race, Reproduction, and the Meaning of Liberty* (1997) explores the historical relationship between slavery and Black motherhood and how these histories have continued into the present. She states that

> The domination of slave women's reproduction continued after their children were born. Black women in bondage were systematically

denied rights of motherhood. Slavery so disrupted their relationship with their children that it may be more accurate to say that as far as slaveowners were concerned, they 'were not mothers at all' (Roberts 1997:33)

The image of the wet nurse feeding the white child or the Black mammy posing with white children is telling. This structure of slavery laid the groundwork for the ideology of the Black mother, whose responsibility is to labor for others and yet neglects her own children. It is unsurprising that the images from this period failed to reflect the loving and caring nature of Black mothers who, in actuality, resisted in diverse ways and fought to keep their families intact. In this way, just as the ideology, socio-political and economic structures of the time attempted to erase Black mothers, visual representations mirrored the dominant assumptions and ultimately contributed to the erasure of Black mothers as well.

What is most important to consider, when grappling with the stereotypes, is the fact that these ideals and images have power and concrete impacts on women's lives. In returning to Collins, she asserts that "African-American women encounter these controlling images, not as disembodied symbolic messages but as ideas designed to provide meaning in our daily lives." In this way, these images are more than symbolic. They are meant to impact and structure the conditions of Black women and mothers' experiences.

Despite the power and persistence of these problematic narratives, Black women's "acts of resistance, both organized and anonymous, have long existed" (Collins 2002: 97). They have fought not only to improve the material conditions of their lives, but also challenged stereotypes visually and artistically by crafting their own representations of themselves and the communities around them. Robert A. Hill states that "the communication from the photograph is visual and vocal..." (Hill 1994: 181). Photography, despite its usage to dehumanize, also became a powerful tool in the fight to raise the collective voices and highlight the experiences of Black communities.

Re-Imagining the Narrative

"To capture the attitude of black women on film, without characterizing their posture as sassy, docile, and/or threatening, is a transformative act."
—Willis, 1994: 10

As access to photographic technology increased, Black folks began to realize the power of the visual and photography as not only a means of documentation but as a powerful storytelling tool. Frederick Douglass' speech "Pictures and Progress" identified photography as an important tool towards progress for Black people. We see its usage over time not only as a mechanism for creative outlet but as a documentary tool in, for example, the civil rights photography as a radical political outlet for Black folks to have their voices heard and document their movements.[8] Most importantly, photography (and other forms of visual media) allowed Black folks access to a key technology to write their own narratives and potentially shift existing ones. bell hooks again asserts that

"Cameras gave to black folks, irrespective of our class, a means by which we could participate fully in the production of images. Hence, it is essential that any theoretical discussion of the relationship of black life to the visual, to art making, make photography central. Access and mass appeal have historically made photography a powerful location for the construction of an oppositional black aesthetic..." (hooks 1994: 45)

In this way, early Black photography possessed a vindicationist spirit. It became a tool for as Leigh Raiford calls it "critical *Black* memory" or (re)memory to use Toni Morrison's term (Raiford 2009: 113; Morrison 1987: 43). On the one hand, we see Black photographers documenting their families, communities, and their day-to-day lives. On the other hand, we see more explicit photographic responses such as Carrie Mae Weems's repurposing of Louis Agassiz's daguerreotypes in *From Here I Saw What Happened and I Cried.* Whether or not Black photographers were intentionally trying to respond to racism, the act of crafting these new narratives was radical. Ultimately, articulating one's own self-determined perspective is and continues to be transformative. Consequently, as Black photographers began to document Black life, images of motherhood, families, and children were also reflected. As the important work of Jeanne Moutoussamy-Ashe and Deborah Willis reveal, Black women photographers played vital roles in this process.

A New Aesthetic of Black Motherhood

Thus far, I have provided a few brief examples of the ways in which stereotypes of Black women were important in creating structures of power and control and how narratives of health and reproduction were closely intertwined to these structures of power. Furthermore, I have attempted to illustrate how images and visuals aligned with the ideology of the times.

The theoretical framework employed thus far is closely aligned with other Black Feminist theorists who have examined the representation of Black women in visual culture. In fact, Jennifer Nash's book *The Black Body in Ecstasy: Reading Race, Reading Pornography* (2009), traces the Black Feminist theoretical archive as she calls it by drawing attention to the various approaches to the topic of representation including pedagogy, epistemology, temporality, metonymy, and recovery. In this way, Black Feminist examinations of representation center on historical readings of injury and harm to the Black female body and that "Black women must be outside of this dominant economy because they are often injured by it. It is in this outsider space—this self-authored space—that Black women can heal the wound..." (Nash 2009: 57). For this piece, I find the historical connections made here important to pinpoint. Yet, I hope to depart from this trajectory to consider more intently the broader possibilities for Black motherhood outside of the work of recovery.

Returning to Nash's work, she focuses on a "reading of ecstasy rather than injury" whereby she refers "...both to the possibilities of Black female pleasures within a phallic economy and to the possibilities of Black female pleasure within a white dominated representational economy..." (2). Although Nash explores pleasure within the context of pornography, I find this framing useful in thinking through the potentialities of Black motherhood and photography.

Audre Lorde in her piece "Uses of the Erotic: The Erotic as Power" defines the erotic as something that can encompass sexuality but is much more than that. Instead, she maintains that the erotic

"is a measure between the beginnings of our sense of self and the chaos of our strongest feelings. It is an internal sense of satisfaction to which, once we have experienced it, we know we can aspire..." (Lorde 1984: 54)

She continues later to say that

> "when I speak of the erotic then, I speak of it as an assertion of the life-force of women; of that creative energy empowered, the knowledge and use of which we are now reclaiming in our language, our history, our dancing, our loving, our work, our lives..." (55)

With this definition in mind alongside Nash's framework of ecstasy, it begs the question how can we imagine an aesthetic of erotic Black motherhood through the visual? Rephrased, this question posits how we can envision a visual representation of Black motherhood that is expansive, makes space for more than just a (re)writing, but rather reimagines a visuality that can hold the vast and complex nuances of Black motherhood.

While I would argue that a move towards an aesthetic of erotic Black motherhood is important in and of itself both for its potential impacts on representation and expression for Black mothers, I also believe that such visual shifts would also have concrete impacts on health. If racist structures, systems, and social conditions—of which the visual are a significant part—negatively impact the health of Black communities and in this case Black mothers, then couldn't a radical aesthetic shift help move the needle towards less toxic and harmful environments and ultimately conditions?

(Re)Visiting Black Maternal Health

In closing, I seek to examine examples of photographic explorations of Black motherhood via the issue of health—namely maternal health. The works listed below, though largely focused on pregnancy and birth, do not represent the totality of issues related to Black motherhood, but serve as noteworthy examples of more contemporary visual responses to the issue of Black motherhood and health. I also believe that they can help with beginning to think through and towards an aesthetic of erotic Black Motherhood.

Black Birth

Cary Beth Cryor's series of images entitled *Rites of Passage* (1979) beautifully documents the birth of her child. Photographing her birth in between contractions, Cryor's effort's result in a beautiful montage that pays homage to Black birth and motherhood. Instead of depicting Black death, illness, or pathology, it powerfully reveals the entree of Black life in action. In speaking of this work, Cryor states that "it is my hope that this will serve as inspiration to other women who may want to do the unthinkable, the unfathomable, the utterly ridiculous" (Moutoussamy-Ashe 1993: 154). This series not only exhibits a self-authored and self-defined depiction of Black motherhood and birth, but it also explicitly calls for Black mothers to be empowered to think, create, and I believe live, outside of the dominant conventions.

Black Mothers and Miscarriage
In 2018, the New York Times published an article that examined pregnancy discrimination and miscarriages (Silver-Greenberg and Kitreoff 2018). The editorial included images depicting Black women taken by photographer Miranda Barnes. The beautiful images, although reflecting the experience of miscarriage in this case, also offer an opportunity to see the humanity of Black mothers in the wake of maternal loss.

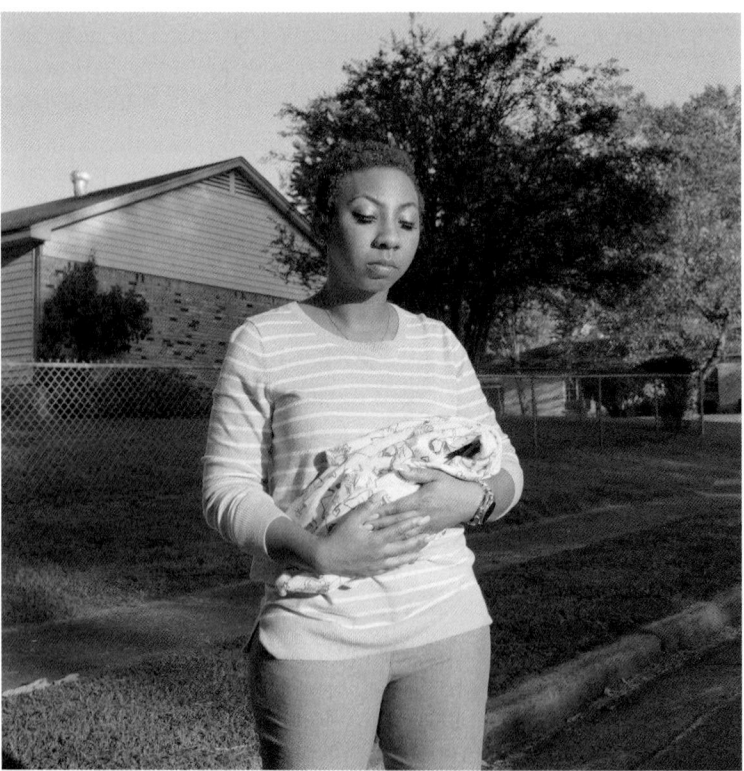

Miranda Barnes, Chasisty Bee from the essay "Miscarrying at Work: The Physical Toll of Pregnancy Discrimination," first published in *The New York Times* on October 21th, 2018. Photo courtesy of the artist

Black Mothers with Their Children

Solana Cain's work entitled "The First + The Last: Black Motherhood" was published online by Womanly magazine in honor of Black maternal health. The black and white images depict Black mothers with their children donning all white attire. The images are also accompanied by quotes from the women who are pictured. According to Cain's website,

> "The portraits and statements from each mother, honor and celebrate Black Motherhood, with the additional intent of shedding light on racial inequality in the maternity ward and the meaning of Black reproductive justice."

Cain's series raises awareness about racial inequality but also holds space for both joy and pain. The images depict for the most part Black women holding, hugging, and loving their children while also recalling their pregnancy and birth experiences—both trying and triumphant. In this way, visuals of Black motherhood can acknowledge painful and problematic racial histories or experiences in parallel to self-defined representations of even joy and pleasure.

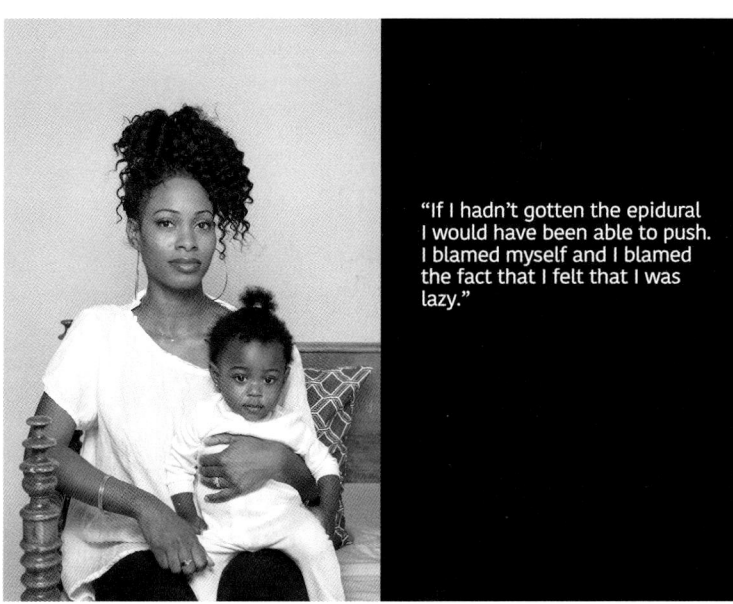

"If I hadn't gotten the epidural I would have been able to push. I blamed myself and I blamed the fact that I felt that I was lazy."

Solana Cain, from the series The First + The Last: Black Motherhood (2018). Photo courtesy of the artist

Although not tied to one photographer, there is a growing visual celebration of Black breastfeeding. Celebrating its 7th year in 2020, the founders of Black Breastfeeding Week identified five key reasons for the annual event: 1) high Black infant mortality rates, 2) high rates of diet-related disease, 3) lack of diversity in the lactation field, 4) cultural barriers among Black women, and 5) and food desserts in Black communities ("Top Five Reasons We Need a Black Breastfeeding Week").

Black Breastfeeding Week has inspired images of Black mothers breastfeeding their children that have inundated the internet and social media. The visual accessibility of the movement is noteworthy and powerful with Black women sharing both professionally photographed images as well as snapshots and selfies of themselves breastfeeding. Part of the effort is to not only normalize breastfeeding but also celebrate Black women's bodies, Black children, and Black motherhood in general. On the one hand we see here the juxtaposition to the image of the Black wet nurse. We also see an exhibition of the Black reproductive body that seeks to redefine Black beauty, sexuality and maternal culpability and present an image of a beautiful and nurturing Black mother.

At the crux of this piece is the assumption that shifting ideologies can also shift structures and therefore the lived realities and material conditions of people's lives. This is where we see the concrete impacts on health and

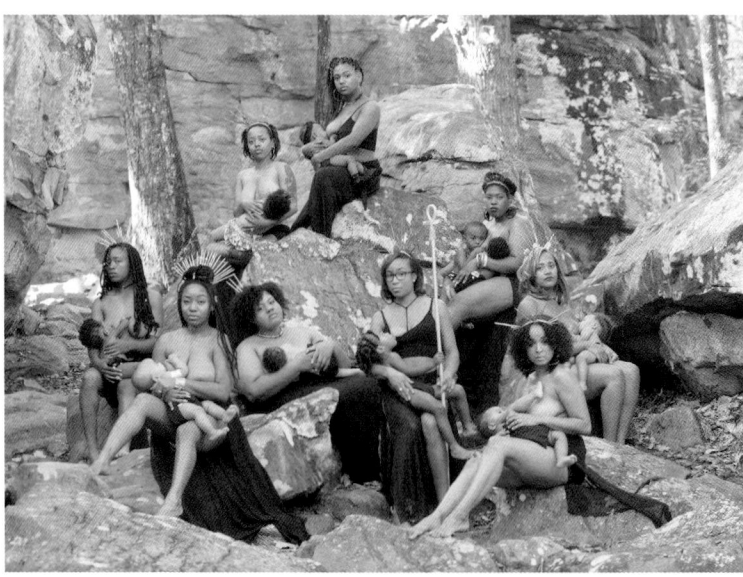

Lakisha Cohill, 2017. Created by Lakisha Cohill, Founder of The Cohill Foundation. Photo courtesy of the artist

otherwise. Grappling with the visual, media, and popular culture will be central to this ideological shift.

Additionally, the contemporary photographic examples shared here might still undoubtedly be read as a vindicationist approach to recover and repair an injurious history. My hope is that this is only the beginning of the conversation for how to create an aesthetic of the erotic for Black motherhood that allows the freedom and autonomy to creatively explore the depths of joy, pleasure, pain, knowledge, and power. Moreover, this evolving visual space can also contribute to the imagining of new worlds and existences that not only allow for but foster holistic, thriving, and healthy Black mothers and Black lives.

Notes

1   According to DONA International, a doula is a trained professional who provides continuous physical, emotional, and informational support to a mother before, during and shortly after childbirth to help her achieve the healthiest, most satisfying experience possible. https://www.dona.org/what-is-a-doula/
2   Research has shown that racial bias in health care providers impacts beliefs about how Black people experience pain and therefore their pain treatment. See, for example Anderson et al; Bonham et al; Campbell and Robert; Cintron and Morrison, Green et al; and Meghani et al.
3   Amnesty International released a report in 2009 entitled "Deadly Delivery: The Maternal Health Crisis in the USA." Since then, there has been a slew of articles in the news and media over the last few years addressing this issue including pieces by major outlets such as the New York Times, NPR, and most recently NBC News.
4   For more on this topic, see the work of Carty et al; Giscombe and Lobel; Hogue and Bremner; Jackson et al; Parker Dominguez et al; Rich-Edwards et al; Rosenthal and Lobel (2011).
5   The works of Elizabeth Able, Patricia Hill Collins, bell hooks, and Nicole Fleetwood provide additional reading on this topic.
6   See for example, Dorothy Roberts' *Killing the Black Body*, Patricia Hill Collins' *Black Feminist Thought*, Saidiya Hartman's *Scenes of Subjection*, Barbara Christian's *Black Feminist Criticism*, Hortense Spillers' *"Interstices"*, to name a few.
7   For more on missionary photography in Africa, also see the body of work from Jack Thompson, Christraud Geary, Elisabeth Engels, Elizabeth Edwards, and Paul Landau, for example.
8   For additional reading on Civil Rights photography, see Elizabeth Abel's work *Skin, flesh, and the affective wrinkles of civil rights photography*, Martin Berger's *Seeing Through Race: A Reinterpretation of Civil Rights Photography* and Leigh Raiford's *Come Let Us Build a New World Together: SNCC and Photography of the Civil Rights Movement*.

Works Cited

Abel, E. (2010). *Signs of the times: the visual politics of Jim Crow*. Univ of California Press.

——— (2012) "Skin, flesh, and the affective wrinkles of civil rights photography." *Qui Parle: Critical Humanities and Social Sciences* 20.2: 35–69.

Amnesty International. (2010). *Deadly Delivery: The Maternal Health Care Crisis In the USA*. Amnesty International Publications.

Anderson, K. O., C. R. Green, and R. Payne (2009). "Racial and ethnic disparities in pain: causes and consequences of unequal care." *The Journal of Pain* 10.12: 1187–1204.

APM Research Lab Staff. (2020). "The Color of Coronavirus: COVID-19 Deaths by Race and Ethnicity in the U.S." apmresearchlab.org. *AMP Research Lab*. 5 Aug. 2020. https://www. apmresearchlab.org/covid/deaths-by-race. Accessed Aug. 19, 2020.

Berger, M. A. (2011). *Seeing through race: A reinterpretation of civil rights photography*. Univ of California Press.

Best, S. (2011). "Neither lost nor found: Slavery and the visual archive." *Representations* 113.1: 150–163.

Bonham, V. L. (2001). "Race, ethnicity, and pain treatment: Striving to understand the causes and solutions to the disparities in pain treatment." *The Journal of Law, Medicine & Ethics* 28: 52–68.

Cain, S. (2020). "The First + The Last of Black Motherhood." solanacain.com. http://www. solanacain.com/the-first-the-last-black-motherhood-2019. Accessed Aug. 19, 2020.

Campbell, C. M., and R. R. Edwards. (2012). "Ethnic differences in pain and pain management." *Pain management* 2.3: 219–230.

Carty, D. C., et al. (2011). "Racism, health status, and birth outcomes: results of a participatory community-based intervention and health survey." *Journal of Urban Health* 88.1: 84-97.

Chatterjee, R. and R. Davis. (2017). "How Racism May Cause Black Mothers to Suffer the Death of Their Infants." *NPR*. 20 Dec. 2017. www.npr.org/sections/ health-shots/2017/12/20/570777510/how-racism-may-cause-black-mothers-to-suffer-the-death-of-their-infants. Accessed 20 Aug. 2020.

Christian, B. (1985). *Black feminist criticism: Perspectives on black women writers*. Pergamon.

Chuck, E. (2020). "The U.S. finally has better maternal mortality data. Black mothers still fare the worst." Nbcnews.com. *NBC News*. Jan. 30, 2020. Accessed Aug. 18, 2020. https:// www.nbcnews.com/health/womens-health/u-s-finally-has-better-maternal-mortality-data-black-mothers-n1125896.

Cintron, A. and R. S. Morrison. (2006). "Pain and ethnicity in the United States: A systematic review." *Journal of palliative medicine* 9.6: 1454-1473.

Cobb, J. N. (2015). *Picture Freedom: Remaking Black Visuality in the Early Nineteenth Century*. Vol. 20. NYU Press.

Cole, H. E. (2015). "A Love Letter to My Daughter Love as a Political Act." *Birthing Justice: Black Women, Pregnancy, and Childbirth*. Taylor and Francis Inc. 126–130.

——— (2018). "Reproduction on Display: Black Maternal Mortality and the Newest Case for National Action." *Journal of the Motherhood Initiative for Research and Community Involvement* 9.2.

Collins, P. H. (2002). *Black feminist thought: Knowledge, consciousness, and the politics of empowerment*. Routledge.

Comaroff, J. (1993). "The diseased heart of Africa." *Knowledge, power and practice: The anthropology of medicine and everyday life*: 305–329.

Dominguez, T. P. et al. (2008). "Racial differences in birth outcomes: the role of general, pregnancy, and racism stress." *Health psychology* 27.2: 194.

Douglass, F. (1986). "Pictures and Progress." *The Frederick Douglass Papers, Series* 1: 1855–1863.

Duganne, E. (2013). "Pictures and Progress: Early Photography and the Making of African American Identity." edited by Maurice O. Wallace and Shawn Michelle Smith, 370–374. Durham NC: Duke University Press.

Engel, E. (2018). "Southern Looks? A History of African American Missionary Photography of Africa, 1890s-1930s." *Journal of American Studies* 52.2: 390.

Faisst, J. (2012). "Degrees of Exposure: Frederick Douglass, Daguerreotypes, and Representations of Freedom.": 71–100.

Fleetwood, N. R. (2011). *Troubling vision: Performance, visuality, and blackness*. Chicago: University of Chicago Press.

Geary, C. M. (1990). "Impressions of the African past: Interpreting ethnographic photographs from Cameroon." *Visual Anthropology* 3, no. 2–3 (1990): 289–315.

——— (1991). "Missionary photography: Private and public readings." *African Arts* 24, no. 4: 48.

——— (1995). "Photographic practice in Africa and its implications for the use of historical photographs as contextual evidence." *Alessandro Triulzi*: 103–30.

——— (1997). "Early images from Benin at the National Museum of African Art, Smithsonian Institution." *African Arts* 30, no. 3 (1997): 44.

——— (1998). "Different visions? Postcards from Africa by European and African photographers and sponsors." *Delivering views: Distant cultures in early postcards*: 147–177.

——— (2010). "Through the Lenses of African Photographers: Depicting Foreigners and New Ways of Life, 1870-1950." *Through African Eyes: The European in African Art, 1500 to Present*: 86–99.

Geary, C. M., and K. Pluskota. (2003). *In and out of focus: images from Central Africa, 1885-1960*. New York: Palgrave Macmillan.

Giscombé, C. L., and M. Lobel. (2005). "Explaining disproportionately high rates of adverse birth outcomes among African Americans: the impact of stress, racism, and related factors in pregnancy." *Psychological bulletin* 131.5: 662.

Glenn, E. N. (2016). "Social constructions of mothering: A thematic overview." *Mothering*. Routledge, 1–29.

Green, C. R., et al. (2003). "The unequal burden of pain: confronting racial and ethnic disparities in pain." *Pain medicine* 4.3: 277–294.

Hartman, S. V. (1997). *Scenes of subjection: Terror, slavery, and self-making in nineteenth-century America*. Oxford University Press.

Hendriks, T. (2013). "Erotics of Sin: Promiscuity, Polygamy and Homo-Erotics in Missionary Photography from the Congolese Rainforest." *Visual Anthropology* 26.4: 355–382.

Higginbotham, E. B. (1993). *Righteous discontent: The women's movement in the Black Baptist church, 1880-1920*. Vol. 14. Cambridge, MA: Harvard University Press.

Hight, E, and M. Rogers. (2011). "Delia's Tears: Race, Science, and Photography in Nineteenth-Century America." *Journal of American Studies* 45.4.

Hill, R. A. (1994). "Making Noise: Marcus Garvey Dada, August 1922." *Picturing Us: African American Identity in Photography*, ed. Deborah Willis. New York: New Press: 43–53.

Hobson, J. (2003). "The 'batty' politic: Toward an aesthetic of the black female body." *Hypatia* 18.4: 87–105.

Hoffman, K. M., et al. (2016). "Racial bias in pain assessment and treatment recommendations, and false beliefs about biological differences between blacks and whites." *Proceedings of the National Academy of Sciences* 113.16: 4296–4301.

Hogue, C., J. Rowland, and J. D. Bremner. (2005). "Stress model for research into preterm delivery among black women." *American journal of obstetrics and gynecology* 192.5: S47–S55.

hooks, bell. (1994). "In our glory: Photography and black life." *Picturing Us: African American Identity in Photography*, ed. Deborah Willis. New York: New Press: 43–53.

————— (2014). *Black looks: Race and representation.* Taylor & Francis.

Howard, J. (2018). "Beyoncé, Serena Williams bring attention to risks of childbirth for black women." cnn.com. *CNN.* 6 Aug. 2018. www.cnn.com/2018/08/06/health/beyonce-vogue-pregnancy-complication-bn/index.html. Accessed 19 Aug. 2020.

Jackson, F. M, et al. (2001). "Examining the burdens of gendered racism: Implications for pregnancy outcomes among college-educated African American women." *Maternal and Child Health Journal* 5.2: 95–107.

Jenkins, P. (1993). "The earliest generation of missionary photographers in West Africa and the portrayal of indigenous people and culture." *History in Africa* 20: 89–118.

Killingray, D., and A. Roberts. (1989). "An outline history of photography in Africa to ca. 1940." *History in Africa* 16: 197–208.

Landau, P. S. (2002). "Empires of the visual: photography and colonial administration in Africa." *Images and empires: visuality in colonial and postcolonial Africa*: 141–171.

————— (2013). "Photography in Africa: Ethnographic perspectives." 693–694.

Landau, P. S., and D. D. Kaspin, eds. (2002). *Images and empires: visuality in colonial and postcolonial Africa.* Univ of California Press.

Lorde, A. (1984). *Sister outsider: Essays and speeches.* Crossing Press.

Maxwell, D. (2011). "Photography and the religious encounter: ambiguity and aesthetics in missionary representations of the Luba of south east Belgian Congo." *Comparative Studies in Society and History* 53.1: 38–74.

Meghani, S. H., E. Byun, and R. M. Gallagher. (2012). "Time to take stock: a meta-analysis and systematic review of analgesic treatment disparities for pain in the United States." *Pain Medicine* 13.2: 150–174.

Morrison, T. (1988). "Beloved." *New York: Plume* 252.

Moutoussamy-Ashe, J. (1993). *Viewfinders: black women photographers.* Writers & Readers Publishing.

Murray, Y. M. (2013). "From Here I Saw What Happened and I Cried: Carrie Mae Weems' Challenge to the Harvard Archive."

Nash, J. C. (2009). *The black body in ecstasy: Reading race, reading pornography.* Harvard University.

Raiford, L. (2009). "'Come Let Us Build a New World Together': SNCC and Photography of the Civil Rights Movement." *American Quarterly* 59. 4: 1129–1157.

————— (2009). "Photography and the practices of critical black memory." *History and Theory* 48.4: 112–129.

Rich-Edwards, J, et al. (2001). "Maternal experiences of racism and violence as predictors of preterm birth: rationale and study design." *Paediatric and perinatal epidemiology* 15: 124–135.

Roberts, D. E. (1999). *Killing the black body: Race, reproduction, and the meaning of liberty.* Vintage.

Rogers, M. (2006). "The slave daguerreotypes of the Peabody Museum: scientific meaning and utility." *History of photography* 30.1: 39–54.

Silver-Greenberg, J. and N. Kitreoff. (2018). "Miscarrying at Work: The Physical Toll of Pregnancy Discrimination." *The New York Times.* 21 Oct. 2018. https://www.nytimes.com/interactive/2018/10/21/business/pregnancy-discrimination-miscarriages.html. Accessed 20 Aug. 2020.

Schneider, J. (2010). "The topography of the early history of African photography." *History of Photography* 34, no. 2: 134-146.

Scutti, S. (2018). "After Serena Williams gave birth, 'Everything went bad'." cnn.com. *CNN.* Jan. 11, 2018. Accessed Aug. 19, 2020. https://www.cnn.com/2018/01/10/health/serena-williams-birth-c-section-olympia-bn/index.html

Silver-Greenberg, J. and N. Kitreoff. (2018). "Miscarrying at Work: The Physical Toll of Pregnancy Discrimination." www.nytimes.com. The New York Times. Oct. 21, 2018. Accessed July 18, 2021. https://www.nytimes.com/interactive/2018/10/21/business/pregnancy-discrimination-miscarriages.html

Smalley, M. L. (2007). "Communications from the Field: Missionary Postcards from Africa." *African Research & Documentation* 104: 15.

Smith, C. (2019). "Carrie Mae Weems: Rethinking Historic Appropriations." *Nka: Journal of Contemporary African Art* 2019, no. 44: 38–50.

Spillers, H. (1984). "Interstices: A small drama of words." *Pleasure and danger: Exploring female sexuality*: 73–100.

St. Clair B. (1994). "The Continuing Drama of African American Images in American Cinema." *Picturing Us: African American Identity in Photography*, ed. Deborah Willis. New York: New Press: 43–53.

"The First + The Last: Black Motherhood." (2019). Womanlymag.com. *Womanly Magazine.* May 4. Accessed Aug. 19, 2020. https://www.womanlymag.com/black-maternal-health/the-first-the-last-black-motherhood

Thompson, T. J. (2004). "Images of Africa." *Missionary Photography in the Nineteenth Century an Introduction. Copenhagen: University of Copenhagen.*

———— (2007). *Capturing the Image: African Missionary Photography as Enslavement and Liberation.* Yale Divinity School Library.

———— (2012). *Light on Darkness: Missionary Photography of Africa in the Nineteenth and Early Twentieth Centuries.* Wm. B. Eerdmans Publishing.

"Top Five Reasons We Need a Black Breastfeeding Week." *Blackbreastfeedingweek.org.* blackbreastfeedingweek.org/why-we-need-black-breastfeeding-week/. Accessed Aug. 19, 2020.

Villarosa, L. (2018). "Why America's Black Mothers and Babies are in a Life or Death Crisis." *New York Times.* 11 April, 2018. www.nytimes.com/2018/04/11/magazine/black-mothers-babies-death-maternal-mortality.html. Accessed 20 Aug. 2020.

Williams, S. (2018). "Serena Williams: What my life-threatening experience taught me about giving birth." cnn.com. *CNN.* 20 Feb. 2018. www.cnn.com/2018/02/20/opinions/protect-mother-pregnancy-williams-opinion/index.html. Accessed 19 Aug. 2020.

Willis, D. (1994). "Introduction: Picturing Us." *Picturing Us: African American Identity in Photography*, ed. Deborah Willis. New York: New Press: 3–28.

————(2000). *Reflections in black: A history of black photographers, 1840 to the present.* New York & London: WW Norton.

12 THREE BLACK MOTHERS IN A CLEVELAND CABARET

RHAISA WILLIAMS

Three Black Mothers in a Cleveland Cabaret

There's a photograph of my mother, grandmother, and great-aunt sitting regally in front of a burgundy red backdrop that looks as though it were made of velvet. The floor is a large checkerboard pattern of burnt red and cream slate tile, accented by black scuff marks. This photoshoot is set on a makeshift stage, them posing in a place evident of heavy foot traffic. All three women wear bell bottom pant suits where the hemline hits strapped heels. The extra fabric gathered around their legs remain ordered by a deep crease struck perfectly down the middle of the pant leg. My mother insists on ironing her pants this way still. In the center sits my grandmother, Lillie Mae, smiling wide, head slightly cocked to the left, hands delicately laid over the other in her lap, her hair permed, pressed, and curled at the ends. She mothered eight children alone once her husband abdicated his familial responsibilities because it no longer fit with the love he found elsewhere. To my grandmother's left is her older

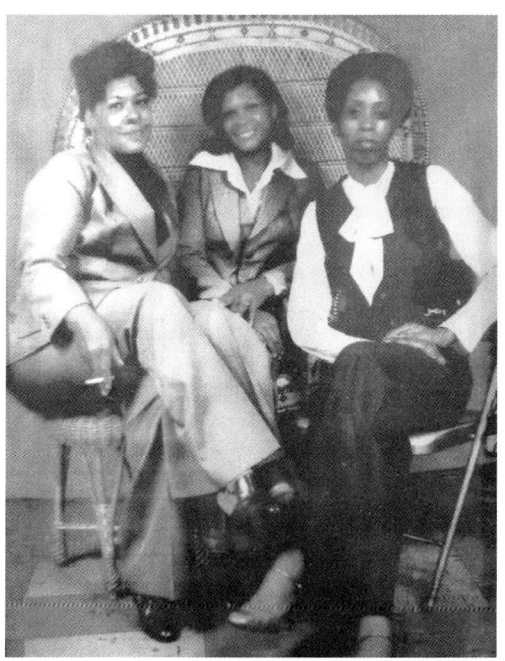

From the personal collection of Rhaisa Williams. Photographer unknown, (left to right) Dazelle Johnson, Lillie Mae Johnson, Helen Johnson; at a cabaret party held at Queen Esther Hall, 3161 E. 93rd St, Cleveland, OH, 1977

sister, Dazelle. She's perched on a rattan stool, legs crossed. A lit cigarette juts delicately between her index and middle fingers, the smoke held at a distance from her sister through the positioning of her hand, made more distant by the width of her hips (*She's a brick...HOUSE*).[1] Two sisters married two brothers and migrated with their partners from Tuskegee, Alabama to Cleveland, Ohio. Both believed deeply in the power of hoodoo, with Dazelle blaming her life-long affliction of migraines on her mother-in-law throwing an unknown powder onto her scalp while walking through a field.

And to my grandmother's right sits her eldest daughter, my mother, Helen. Her body slightly leans towards my grandmother's, but it's not a lean of deference or due to lazy posture. Rather, it's a lean more reminiscent of a cool that comes from being deep in your twenties, where you have a strong idea of who you are but you're still young enough to believe any change is possible. Her hair is styled in a short crop Afro, head held high, she's the only unsmiling face in the frame. She is, what we would call today, smizing. She sits in what looks to be a metal folding chair. It's a furniture hodge-podge made elegant by the slants of each woman's body, the poise of their hands, the cross of their feet. This would be the daughter who had to become her mother's eyes, ears, and mouth at twelve years-old when her father left and the family had to go on welfare. Lillie Mae couldn't read or write very well and so under the cover of acting as though she had poor vision, Helen would read and fill out the welfare applications. One of Dazelle's daughters taught Helen how to do this.

In spite of, or perhaps, because of this history, three Black women—a mother with her sister and daughter—partied at a cabaret and posed for a photograph, both to mark the occasion and to participate in an activity of Black social life that included planning to go to the club, getting dressed for it, securing rides to it, vibing to the music, imbibing, dancing, smoking cigarettes, paying $2-$4 for a photographer to take the picture, and possibly afterward, going to a photo center to have the photograph, a 3x5in frame, enlarged, framed, and displayed on a mantle in their homes. And in the middle of the photograph, aesthetically framing the heads of all three women is the rattan wicker chair in which my grandmother sits. Colloquially, it's known as the "peacock" chair, so named because its wide-spanning back matches the wings of the bird that, unable to fly, remains the most majestic of land animals. Despite its majestic bearings, this chair, often brown or white, is a quotidian piece of furniture that appears in so many Black photographs of joy and nightlife.

This essay examines a photograph of Black social nightlife, privileging Black mothers as the subjects. I focus on this particular photograph to think more critically about similar images taken at cabaret parties and after-hour joints throughout Cleveland, Ohio during the 1970s and 1980s. The location of these sites is as important as the subjects in the pictures. The cabarets the Black women frequented in this essay are different from the conventional cabarets portrayed on Broadway or depicted on art deco-designed posters. Conventional cabarets have set performers, engaged in musical and/or theatrical entertainment, taking place in non-theater spaces, such as bars or nightclubs. Burlesque and drag shows are two types of cabarets. The cabaret parties that are part of the social repertoire of the Black women in this essay are empty halls that individuals or groups rent for events with other services, such as liquor, food, and security, being a la carte.

After-hour joints, on the other hand, are unofficial gatherings/house parties that continue the celebratory mood once clubs and bars officially close according to local and state mandates. Run by particular individuals (usually the person or persons who own or rent the home), the "after" of after-hour speaks to going outside of the bureaucratic system that doles out permits dictating admissible practices. For clubs and bars, these include age and capacity limits, volume of music, beverages and food served, and yes, the hours of operation. "Nightclubs, afterhours spaces, and illicit speakeasies," Shane Vogel asserts, "provided places of public sociality for sexually deviant figures such as the 'fairies,' 'pansies,' 'sheiks,' 'bull dikes,' and 'wolves'." And they also enabled "the possibilities of intimacy, sexuality, and libidinal exchange [that] was not limited to the teleological direction of same-sex object choice," "allow[ing] for a range of sexual subjectivities, arrangements of masculinity and femininity, libidinal possibilities, and identificatory relationships" (Vogel: 2009, 20–21). After-hour spaces and cabarets were also tied to other types of extra-legal activities, such as drug-use and distribution, physical violence, and gambling. Consequently, these spaces represented threats against the supposed safety and knowability that comes with surveilling and maintaining the heteropatriarchal home, and thus local politicians and police exercised authority and legal power by marking these spaces of Black nightlife as havens of crime and routinely raided them. The journalistic trail of after-hour spots in Cleveland supports this perspective crafted by those in power.

The specter and reality of violence and perceived criminality were part of the intimate structure of Black nightlife and joy. Thus, my attempt here is to read poor and working-class Black mothers within complex visions that include pleasure and repose *within* spaces of precarity that arose from struggling to support families in a declining rust belt city. In this way, my emphasis on Black mothers reorients the illicit spaces of Black nightlife (illicit simply in their extralegal existence) into larger social structures that are both within and outside of systems of racism to understand some of the ways they achieved reprieve. Doing so reveals other relations, webs of labor, work, pleasure, joy, process, and rituals that Black mothers existed within.

Although I pay special attention to one photograph in this essay, I am also referencing the myriad images in my family's photo albums that chronicle nightlife during the 1970s and 1980s where the main subjects are my grandmothers, mother, and aunts while they danced, looked sexy, and had a good time. Importantly, these photos showcase families, extended communities, and Black folks during particular generations that get enlivened when we consider the experience of looking at these photos and the memories and conversations they evoke. This is about the "personal" and how it is a method to get a fuller picture from a still image. It privileges the relationship between the archive and the repertoire that Diana Taylor (2003) explains as always co-existing and in fact, co-constitutive. My engagement with photographs of Black mothers in after-hour spots and cabarets (from my personal family history) builds on this in order to think about the stories that these images evoke that are as important as the image. It secures the document with liveness, the being with, or what D. Soyini Madison (2007) calls "co-performative witnessing". The photographs I reference are a blend of studio portraits that are heightened and special, and repositories of mundane action, exemplifying an aesthetic practice that Nicole Fleetwood calls "non-iconicity," one that "exposes the limitations of its framing and the temporality and specificity of the moment documented." As an image that "resists singularity and completeness in a narrative," the non-iconic sharply contrasts that of the "iconic" images that have come to stand in for entire movements, ideologies, time periods, and even populations (2011: 64). Fleetwood's use of non-iconicity to read for mundane actions in the image shows that having a personal connection to the subjects photographed is not required to do such analyses. However, the personal, like sole archival digging, can unearth certain possibilities, pleasures, and systems of relation evoked from photos that are both quotidian non-events and special events. I use these reading practices for Black mothers who are often overdetermined by their real conditions of precarity to help show the otherwise that existed alongside and because of various levels of precarity.

Taking "liveness" seriously as a mode to (re)(un)cover the quotidian requires a return to the common usages of "quotidian" that, upon first glance, may seem interchangeable. The first definition of quotidian: "of everyday character; commonplace; mundane, ordinary" (Fleetwood 2011: 64) refers to the ubiquity of an element in a particular place that may cause us to regard it as nothing special. Often, it may become an identifying marker of a place that its presence is noticed only in its absence. Example: I live in St. Louis where summers are hot, long, and humid. This is due to the city's geological location and the fact that it is nestled by three rivers. Because of this, mosquitoes are quotidian in the summer. They're everywhere and while they are deeply annoying (and for those allergic to their bites, possibly debilitating), the amount of mosquitoes in St. Louis during the summer is commonplace, as natural to the city as what the Arch has become. Despite being a nuisance, if a summer were to arise and there were no mosquitoes, their *absence* would signal something amiss. Mosquitoes, in their numbers, faithful seasonal appearance, and universal location, may spark frustration, but importantly, they mark the natural development of seasons, that being of spring and summer. This definition and example highlight a function of quotidian as that which both stands out while marking the expected.

This meaning of quotidian underscores the ubiquity of the peacock wicker chair on which my grandmother sits, and whose woven rattan back frames the heads of my mother and great-aunt. This type of chair seemed to be everywhere during the 1970s and 1980s, appearing in photographs such as the one I described, and on the album covers that played the hits to which the people in those photographs danced and had to speak over. In a seven-minute video published in 2019, Vox describes the history of the chair.[2] Coming into popularity at the turn of the 20th century, the rise of wicker furniture coincided with the architectural popularity of large porches and verandahs on middle- and upper-class homes. Lauded for its "breeziness" and lightness, wicker furniture represented the extended domestic sphere of outside space that predated the invention and domestic accessibility of air-conditioning. The style and make of wicker furniture also made it popular in portraiture, offsetting the hot, bright studio lighting that subjects had to sit under for long periods to achieve an unblurred image. The furniture's use on porches and in early portraiture illustrate its racialized history that aligns with white middle- and upper-classes."[3] According to the video, the popularity of the chair among Black Americans skyrocketed with the iconic 1967 image of Black Panther Party co-founder Huey Newton seated in a peacock chair with a rifle in one hand and a spear in the other. Admittedly, the turn to Newton piqued my personal interest in the chair's ubiquity in photographs of Black nightlife because while I am well-aware of the photo of Newton, I was surprised how its position as a historical artifact impacted Black youths' relationship to the chair. Pictures of my parents—youthful, dewy-skinned, and head full of black hair—sitting in these chairs have always lined our walls. Pictures of my uncles, aunts, and other family friends sitting in these chairs fill out photo albums. And they never mentioned the Black Power Movements or any other social movement that has been historically catalogued.

This highlights an oversight that can arise when we treat objects as the basis for content analysis where we follow the mere frequency of its presence without reading its presence within a lifeworld. This leads to a second definition of quotidian, "of or occurring every day; daily."[4] Similar to the first definition, this meaning of quotidian emphasizes a temporal regularity. Yet it is important not to collapse frequency with the inability to be notable. This distinction stands out when we home in on the verb "occurring," a repetitive *action* that may or may not happen in a particular place. Example: the way to create a fire may be the same, but the look and dance of the flame is always unique. This points to the fact that objects are part of embodied rituals but with all performance, nothing is ever exactly done twice.

Not just visual artifact, these photographs offer a snapshot to the larger ritual that made nightlife possible for Black mothers.[5] What led up to the photograph of my mother, grandmother, and great-aunt probably happened something like this: My grandmother either dialing my great-aunt's phone number on a touch-tone phone or fitting her finger in holes to swing the numbers of a rotary phone. Her house was always brimming with children, teenagers, and young adults, so possibly, my grandmother fussed at one of the kids for running in the house, probably mumbled her slight annoyance under her breath about them, as she listened to the line ring and ring until her sister picked up.[6] "Hey, gal, what you doin'?" Her sister Dazelle worked nights cleaning rooms in an office building, so my grandmother would know the hours to call that her sister hadn't designated for daytime sleeping. Most likely after more small talk about kids and neighborhood gossip, my grandmother would ask Dazelle if she had to work that night. My great-aunt would answer no, but "my right hand been itching me all day, so I *must* be comin' into some money!" Dazelle diligently plays the numbers. Some way between the inhalations of a cigarette that Dazelle periodically brings to her lips throughout the conversation, they would decide they would go out that night. Neither of them drive.

After they hang up, my grandmother now dials my mother's number. After some small talk, my grandmother would ask her daughter what she was doing that night. "I don't know yet. Why?" My grandmother would see if her daughter wanted to go out with her and Dazelle. Someone she knows is throwing a cabaret party. My mother would weigh up her options, but only briefly, because she enjoyed going out with her mother, a woman she knew always had her back in case anything wild happened—and at cabaret parties and after-hour joints, the likelihood was there. Helen would say, "ok," and tell my grandmother what time she was going to drop off her only child at the time. This would signal to my grandmother that there would be a switch-off between her and my eldest sister, who is my grandmother's first grandchild, since Helen would drop my sister off at her mother's to be watched by one of her younger sisters. This was a family home. There was always someone in the house. The time my mother stated would also let my grandmother know the approximate time she should be prepared to leave the house. Goodbyes on my mother's side of the family are always a multi-step process. Ending a phone conversation quickly comes across as rude.

"Alright, then, Mama, let me get going."
"Ok, then, bay."
"Alright."
"Bye."
"Bye."

They would both proceed with getting dressed for the night, deliberating over things they may have worn in the too recent past, and the fickleness of Cleveland weather.

My engagement with the photograph, in which I imagine the possible words spoken, minor gestures done, and strategic planning for availability, transportation, childcare and sartorial choices, in other words, all of the small rituals that emerged in preparing for going out, is one that I learned over years of knowing these women and hearing the memories spurred from witnessing their engagement with these photos. In this view, wicker chairs and the ways Black women dressed and posed in them mark an archive of performance and an archive of being. Often, these archives are vocalized in the recitation of the place upon seeing the photograph, eliciting memories that sometimes begin with: "Aww, remember when we went here?" "Wasn't that the night so-and-so got mad and left us? So we had to call so-and-so and she picked us up (laughter)" "This was so-and-so after hours spot. She always had the place laid out!" "Aww, that's where I met so-and-so. I wonder whatever ever happened to him..." "Oooo, I was slim, trim, conti-NEN-tal back then! That was before I had my second baby." "We always went there after such-and-such spot closed." Or, "that was the last time me and so-and-so went out before she died…"

These recitations remind us that these photographs are part of archival performances that reveal the repertoires of our lives. These layers of communication, sparked by memories from nightlife images allow others to glean small details of our mothers' past lives that they may have not mentioned deliberately, or simply slipped their minds because of the smallness of gestures. These informal photographs snapped in moments of pleasure at after-hour joints and semi-formal photographs, taken by photographers who created makeshift photo shoots at cabarets, create what bell hooks (1994: 51) calls "pictorial genealogies" that were "the means by which one could ensure against the losses of the past". The losses can be momentous, such as that of death or losing touch with one's community for various reasons, and minute, such as forgetting your favorite fragrance, or that indoor smoking was allowed nearly everywhere. Or to be reminded of the fullness of your mother, grandmother, and great-aunt outside of the roles they enacted in front of you because you were unable to see them as anything else.

The image of my mother, grandmother, and great-aunt at a cabaret party bespeaks another mode of existence that pushes against narratives of loss for women once they become mothers, and especially for poor and working-class Black mothers who are deeply entrenched in narratives of loss and decline. This thought is prompted by my grandmother's smile, daring in its fullness. It captured me. The smile reappeared in so many other pictures of my grandmother, the majority of which were taken in cabarets and after-hour spots. She's in her forties and fifties in these photographs. She has birthed all eight of her children and by the time the majority of the pictures have been taken, she has already buried one of them. She's also a grandmother with two of her daughters, my mother being one of them, having their first child as teenagers. But in these photographs, taken in what looks to be basements remade into after-hour spots and makeshift studio spaces in cabaret parties, her wide smile is ubiquitous. After coming across a few photos shot in the scene of Cleveland Black nightlife, my grandmother's smile comes to mark the occasion. Mark the space. At this point, it's not about the furniture anymore, the style of clothing, or whether the photo is taken in front of wood paneling or velvet. It's about her smile, with gleaming teeth shown at full stop. It's quotidian.

Wide-open smiles that are so leaned into they create permanent eye creases also don't fit the common image of poor and working-class Black mothers. They're often believed to be too down-trodden to smile. In his essay "A Sunday Portrait," novelist Edward P. Jones meditates on a portrait of his mother—beautifully young, "complacently smiling," and smartly dressed. The photograph is undated, but from the looks of her style of dress it was taken before Jones' birth in 1950; it must have been taken sometime in the 1940s in Washington D.C., the location marked by a cardboard backdrop of the Capitol. The background was typical of photos taken at the time, according to Jones. Referencing a short story in which the narrator dreams of his parents' first date and attempts to issue a warning of their doomed courtship, Jones shares that if he had the power of time travel, he would have forsaken his own birth to tell his mother: "Save yourself." Instead of marrying Jones' father who would leave after their third child; instead of being an illiterate single Black mother in Washington, D.C. whose best way to survive would be as a domestic; instead of working hard and having little affection to outwardly show her children; instead of losing the gleam of fearlessness in her eyes in that Sunday portrait, Jones would have told his future mother to "go off and see as much of the world as she could, come back, and then go off and see it all over again. See so much of the world that you come to learn the hearts of men-people and what kind of heart will best be a companion for yours, for my father's heart would not be, my heart will not be, and the hearts of the men who come after him will not be either" (Jones 1994: 38). This photograph of his mother, taken on the precipice of marriage, motherhood, and the limits both further imposed upon an illiterate Black woman, haunts Jones because it freezes her at a point where her straight back, crossed legs, daintily placed hands, and her face "on the verge of a smile," suggested she believed "only good and wonderful things will come her way" (35). But Jones knows otherwise. That her dreams of freedom, however she imagined them, would exist only in that verge of a smile. That her excitement would quickly fade. That the monotony of misery would last long.

The same could be said of my grandmother and perhaps of my own mother. My grandmother is illiterate, and the pressures of raising eight children on her own with no formal education and little work history constrained her choices. And my mother, achieving a GED, had the pressures of being the eldest daughter who had to take on adult-like responsibilities early; who would be cast as the ride-or-die woman from being in a relationship with my father who took many years to be centered in peace. But here's my grandmother, smiling *in the thick* of being a mother. And her eldest daughter beside her with a proud, daring stare. The overdetermined iconicity of Black mothers being too stressed and overburdened to signal anything but toil makes seeing the joy, wide-open smiles, and daring flirtation *within* the space of motherhood marked by poverty and racism deeply significant.

Through the thickness of daily life in the midst of a city in economic and environmental decline, these Black mothers found reprieve at cabaret parties and at after-hour joints, the latter of which were viewed as civic scourge. They were denizens of gambling, prostitution, violence by knives that graduated to violence by guns, and illegal alcohol sales. Or at least, Cleveland officials would have you think so. Police officers and local councilmen tracked these joints with a fury. One article included the addresses of private homes that, allegedly, operated as after-hour joints.[7] I recognize many of these streets, dotted throughout the east side of the city, although my imagination of the area surely doesn't match what it looked like then. By the time I came of age in the 1990s and early 2000s, many of these homes were the few remaining on the block. My upbringing came when Cleveland had declined. But in the 1940s-1970s, Cleveland had more structures and less empty lots. Then, it was a city *in the process of* decline. Cleveland itself was a scourge fighting its destiny. In a photo essay on the city, published in 2015, journalist John Petkovic describes 1970s Cleveland as "gritty." Petkovic opens with a staggering statistic that in one decade, the city had lost 23.6 percent of its population, making it "the first major American city since the Great Depression to default on its loans." The photos he chose depict the look of devastation from deep loss in little time. Thick billows of smoke from factory stacks make the city's skyline appear like smudged charcoal. What goes up must come down. And those pollutants did, falling into Lake Erie so that one of the largest freshwater lakes in the world was "dying" and flowing into the Cuyahoga River, which the Environmental Protection Agency (EPA) had marked as "dead." The EPA placed a sign on a fence that said, "WARNING: This water is polluted. It is not safe for wading…"[8] These are the iconic meanings attached to Cleveland in the 1970s, beset with decline, polluted water and air, and pocked with architectural carcasses from buildings destroyed during the Hough and Glenville riots that "sent" white businesses running to the suburbs from the mid- to late 1960s. In the middle of all of this, Black mothers maintained their communities of joy and repose.

In Zora Neale Hurston's day, after-hour joints were called "jook houses." In a mostly tongue-in-cheek essay published in 1934, Hurston outlines the "Characteristics of Negro Expression" to describe Black people's predilection for dramatic acts and linguistic flourish in all social settings. "Action. Everything illustrated. So we can say the white man thinks in a written language and the Negro thinks in hieroglyphics" (50). The importance of action is that it always happens in a setting and according to Hurston, one of the most crucial settings for Black cultural production is the "Jook," "the word for a Negro pleasure house. It may mean a bawdy house. It may mean the house set apart on public works where the men and women dance, drink, and gamble. Often it is a combination of all these" (62). Hurston credits the Jook for the creation and dissemination of the blues, the "slow and sensuous" Black social dances where the main goal of dancing is "to gain sensation, and not so much for exercise," and where the women "gambling, fighting, and drinking" at the Jook became the basis for Black theater (63). Violence is always alongside the pleasure, and that pleasure is deeply tied to both acute and diffuse sensation. Hurston's account of the Jook speaks against the archival records of these spaces as plagues on the community. Rather, they are its raucous life source.

Similarly, the photos of Black mothers in Cleveland nightlife document another type of process that occurred alongside, because of, and in spite of the large-scale failures and destruction that supported the city's unflattering tagline: "The mistake by the lake." The makeshift nature of cabaret parties and after-hour spots speak to larger overlaps of Blackness, geographic precarity, and challenges to archival capture if pursued traditionally. Photographs of Black mothers convening around and getting to the places of joy, reprieve, and pleasure are less about a process of attrition and more about making space to get by and to do so with sensuality.

The iconicity of poor and working-class Black mothers doubles with the iconic meanings of Cleveland in the 1970s and 1980s. And yet, like a city you can appreciate only if you're *from* there, the common meanings attached to the city and/or subject explode once a close look by the right person makes them start with a statement like, "Oooo, ain't that so-and-so?!" or "Oooo, we was fine as day wine!" The photograph of my mother, grandmother, and great-aunt is, in many ways, a family photo. And of both my grandmothers who were in their 40s and 50s, the majority of pictures that I've come across have been of them in nightlife settings. From my understanding, my maternal grandmother was far from a party animal. She was not in clubs multiple times per week or even every weekend. My paternal grandmother, on the other hand, "loved to ball" and partied every weekend. But in the age before point-and-shoot, then disposable, then part of one's cellular device, cameras were not readily possessed by everyone. Rather, in families and among friends' circles, there was most often a self-designated picture person, and it was gendered. It was often a picture-man, and in nightlife, he made it into a hustle, charging a few dollars for staged pictures, or was just around to informally take them. In all honesty, most of the pictures I've encountered of both of my grandmothers were taken in the midst of revelry. And for both grandmothers, there are many pictures in which they are posing with their eldest daughter. Was this a rite of passage between Black mother and eldest girl? What opens up about the processes of rituals between mothers and daughters when we journey into the club space of cabaret parties, bars, and after-hour spots? Were they each other's bits of freedom after all?

Notes

1   Commodores. "Brickhouse," *Commodores*, Motown, 1977.
2   Caswell, E. "How This Chair Became a Pop Culture Icon," October 4, 2019, https://www.youtube.com/watch?v=_V10kWLh71U&t=390s, accessed December 13, 2019
3   The video also reveals the chair's imperialist underpinnings in being manufactured in South Asia, particularly the Philippines.
4   Oxford English Dictionary
5   Freeing black women from the spectacle that has come to define and make legible their bodies aligns with Saidiya Hartman's turn to critical fabulation that enables her to use fiction and imagination to free black people from archival meanings, "Venus in Two Acts."
6   Even the language of "pick up" the phone showcases a ritualized embodiment as landline phones were attached to a weighty handle that could only be picked up and brought to the ear, unlike the options we have today with picking up phones, such as flicking our wrist in a particular way to alert our apple watch to answer the call, blue tooth technology or pressing a button to enable speaker phone.
7   "Informant Blows Whistle on 'After Hours Joints'," *Call and Post*, 6 March 1976, 4A.
8   Petkovic, J. (1973) *Cleveland Plain Dealer*, National Archives, https://www.cleveland.com/entertainment/2015/03/cleveland_in_the_1970s_a_gritt.html. Accessed 15 December 2019

Works Cited

Caswell, E. (2019). "How This Chair Became a Pop Culture Icon." last modified October 4, 2019, https://www.youtube.com/watch?v=_V10kWLh71U&t=390s.
Commodores, "Brickhouse," recorded 1976-1977, track 2 on *Commodores*, Motown, vinyl LP.
Fleetwood, N. (2011). *Troubling Vision: Performance, Visuality, and Blackness.* Chicago: University of Chicago Press.
Hartman, S. (2008). "Venus in Two Acts." *Small Axe* 12.2 (June): 1–14.
_____ *Scenes of Subjection: Terror, Slavery, and Self-Making in Nineteenth Century America.* New York: Oxford University Press, 1997.

hooks, bell (1994). "In Our Glory: Photography and Black Life." In *Picturing Us: African American Identity in Photography*, edited by Deborah Willis, 42–53. New York: W.W. Norton.

Hurston, Z. N. (2000). "Characteristics of Negro Expression." In *African American Literary Theory: A Reader*, edited by Winston Napier, 49–68. New York: New York University Press.

"Informant Blows Whistle on 'After Hours Joints'." *Call and Post*, 6 March 1976, p. 4A.

Jones, E. P. (1994). "A Sunday Portrait." in *Picturing Us: African American Identity in Photography*, edited by Deborah Willis, 34–40. New York: W.W. Norton.

Petkovic, J. (1973). *Cleveland Plain Dealer*, National Archives, https://www.cleveland.com/entertainment/2015/03/cleveland_in_the_1970s_a_gritt.html.

Soyini Madison, D. (2007). "Co-Performative Witnessing." *Cultural Studies* 21.6: 826–831.

Taylor, D. (2003). *The Archive and the Repertoire: Performing Cultural Memory in the Americas*. Durham: Duke University Press.

Vogel, S. (2009). *The Scene of the Harlem Cabaret: Race, Sexuality, Performance*. Chicago: University of Chicago Press.

PART FOUR

"IN SEARCH OF MY MOTHER'S GARDEN, I FOUND MY OWN":* BLACK FEMALE PHOTOGRAPHERS AND THE MATRILINEAL SPACE

---

* Walker, A. (1984). *In search of our mothers' gardens: womanist prose*. San Diego: Harcourt Brace Jovanovich.

13 LETTER IV: WHERE ARE THEY?
– M/OTHERING R/EVOLUTIONS

Renée Mussai _____

Dear Muholi

A year has passed, and then another: we have not seen each other in too long. I miss you, my friend. And I hope that you are feeling well, safe, loved, cared for, held—I believe, hope, that you are.

This is not really a letter, but rather a collection of fragmentary notes, re/ memories, ideas, quotations, to frame—hold—your words and images, here. I have not felt much like writing, lately. Words have not been forthcoming, nor flowing freely, these past two years; thoughts, yes—ruminations, circulating and morphing endlessly—but not written words, somehow. Today however is important ... as you know, of course.

In lieu of writing, I have been walking on my own, for hours and hours, appreci- ating the time for reflection that these solitary excursions offer despite the pre- carity we face each time we walk alone ... but I digress. Where was I? Walking, yes, and today. As I write, an anniversary beckons. On this day in 1956—9 August— something extraordinary happened: the Women's March on Pretoria.

My thoughts circle back to 2016, when you first told me about this important event in your ancestral (his)tory, 60 years on, while we discussed a new com- mission to be unveiled at our future exhibition [at Autograph]: a new chapter in your growing, living, breathing visual memoir and archive-of-the-self that is *Somnyama Ngonyama*.

We spoke about commemorating—in our present—a constituency of coura- geous women from the past: brave, determined, revolutionary women who refused the apartheid regime's intimidations, limitations, and violations. Thousands of women—black, white, brown, queer, straight, lesbian, bi, trans,

cis, non-binary—coming together to march for their—our—freedom(s) …
for you, for us, for them; for their daughters, mothers, sisters.

And we talked about prescription and inscription—in art, in life—to ensure
that no one is left behind, forgotten or 'lost to history'[1], but all are accounted—
and advocated—for. When we revolt and protest against myriads of permeating
injustices, from racism to classism, homophobia to misogyny, and many other
discriminatory ideologies, we do so, of course, to birth revolutions from a
space that is resolutely 'for'—for freedom, for love, for equality, for visibility,
for justice … for different, possible futures: to imagine and pursue this
generative 'otherwise'—the remedial for—explored in my last letter to you, if
you remember.

Today, as I revisit the three images you created in response to this significant
moment in time – *Bayephi I, II* and *III*[2]—I see both a potent visual meditation of
loss—the loss of lives, the loss of freedoms, the loss of selves—all so pertinent
now, in this pandemic time of perpetual turmoil, contagion and viral dis/ease,
as well as a commemoration of tremendous courage, care and commitment to
change, of prescience and, importantly, hope. Are not all revolutions—personal
and universal, collective and individ-
ual—birthed from, in and with hope?

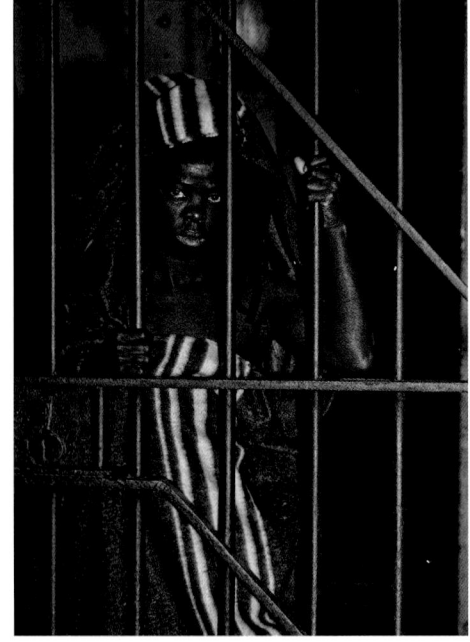

In *Bayephi III*—in tandem with this sense
of acute/resolute aspiration—I see resilience, too, imbued within the image's
dissonant chromatic zones of being and
becoming—a futurity, if you will. The
cracks on the wall symbolise an opening, or rather multiple openings, plural,
and multiplicities: new ways of seeing,
feeling, sensing, doing, and looking

Zanele Muholi, *Bayephi I*, Constitution Hill,
Johannesburg, 2017. Commissioned by and
courtesy of Autograph, London. © Zanele Muholi

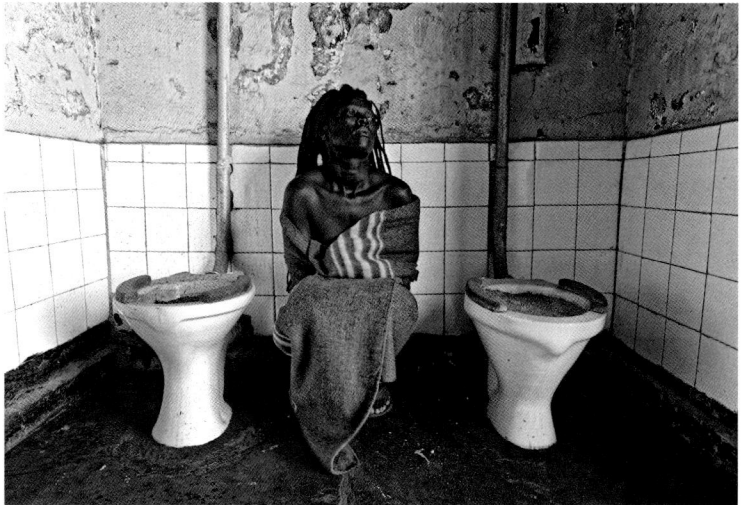

Zanele Muholi, *Bayephi II*, Constitution Hill, Johannesburg, 2017. Commissioned by and courtesy of Autograph, London. © Zanele Muholi

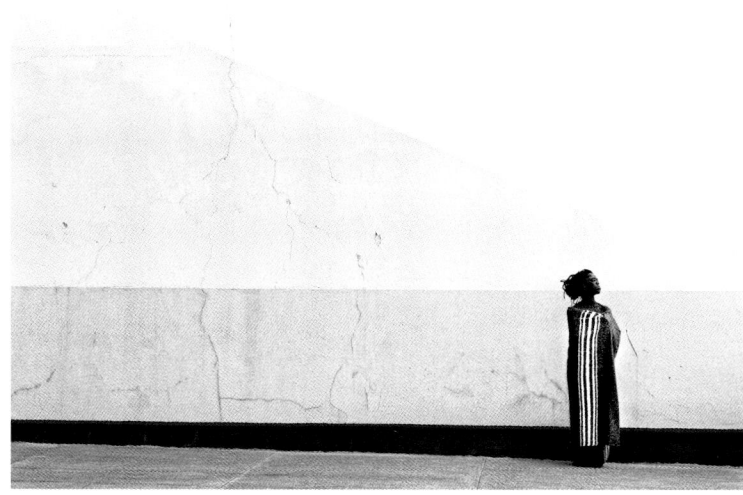

Zanele Muholi, *Bayephi III*, Constitution Hill, Johannesburg, 2017. Commissioned by and courtesy of Autograph, London. © Zanele Muholi

that fill me with hope, and with an ambience of resolution and tenacity, in these times of precarity.

I am deeply grateful for these images, for the healing, remedial currency—visual, textual and otherwise—they hold. How relevant they are today, as analeptic, as tonic: a remedy and a reminder of the courage we require to face—and keep facing—the daily challenges and injustices so deeply ingrained in our systems, institutions, laws, and societies, exposed so very violently and openly in the wake of the pandemic with its devastating impact on communities of colour, especially in the global south.

I remember the day you went to Constitution Hill, armed with your camera and blanket, to create these portraits: conjuring, commemorating, calling those who dared to walk—to 'reclaim these streets'[3]—60 years ago. I recall asking you about the meaning of *Bayephi* in your mother tongue— the conscious naming itself an act of indigenous reclamation, revelation, re/creation and liberation. I remember you telling me that *Bayephi* constitutes both a question and a proposition: 'where are they? / they are here', which reminds me of something poignant I reread recently, about photography and its enduring presences, and how those portrayed are always 'still here'[4]. And this is what you told me, then:

> '*The 1956 protest was based on women saying "enough is enough": enough with these passbooks, enough with restricting our liberty to move freely, enough with violating our rights—as human beings, as mothers, workers, sisters, daughters, lovers. These portraits are about the women's struggle in South Africa during apartheid—they are about solidarity—but they can be read as a metaphor for women and queer people's ongoing struggle elsewhere, too. They connect* Somnyama Ngonyama *directly with black lives and black bodies in incarceration. The former women's jail, where the photographs were taken, was built in close proximity to the Old Fort: a space of confinement, a place of brutality, where precious lives were lost, taken ... a space where countless polit- ical prisoners were held during apartheid, awaiting trial for violating pass laws and other discriminatory regulations, for being in the wrong place at the wrong time. The three images speak to each other: the prison cell, the toilets, and the courtyard—the setting for* Bayephi III. *The open-air atrium was the spot where prisoners could find relief and breathe, momentarily. Inside, the space is dark and cold, haunted: it has the air of a history that leaves you feeling otherwise.*'[5]

Otherwise: here it is again, this word—sentiment, idea, premise—which has been with me, intimately, tenaciously, ever since our conversation that day, back in 2016, with all its promise, percipience, and potential. To allow oneself to feel—and imagine—otherwise, is a prerequisite for the birthing of r/evo- lutions: to practise, cultivate, visualise, manifest and imagine freedom every day. *Somnyama Ngonyama* represents both a commemoration and a refusal of the here and now, fuelled by a desire to infuse/suffuse the here and now with

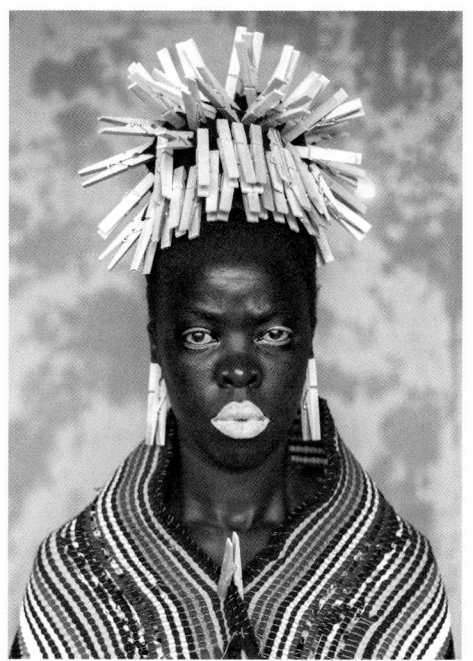

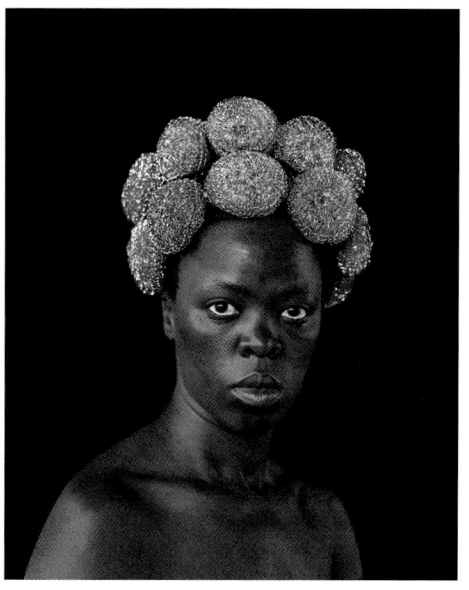

Zanele Muholi, *Bester I*, Mayotte, 2015. Courtesy of Stevenson, Cape Town/Johannesburg/Amsterdam and Yancey Richardson, New York. © Zanele Muholi

Zanele Muholi, *Bester V*, Mayotte, 2015. Courtesy of Stevenson, Cape Town/Johannesburg/Amsterdam and Yancey Richardson, New York. © Zanele Muholi

illuminating darkness, with beauty and breath and face and flesh: to embody and inhabit the here and now, to claim the here and now, in all its tenses—for the past, the present and the future.

And speaking of commemoration, don't all r/evolutions also, existentially, fundamentally, begin with our mothers and acts of m/othering? We can think of these as (non-gendered) deliverance, as birthing, caring and nurturing, especially considering that, at the core of *Somnyama Ngonyama* is your late mother, the breathing, beating heart of the series, whom you commemorate so profoundly, so beautifully, so powerfully in each portrait: simultaneously defined, and refined, by the tools of her labour, her—your—head crowned with scouring pads and laundry pegs; her—your—body wrapped in softly textiled armour, at times enveloped wholly by my pleated garments at our home in London, cocooned in a collaborative, remedial, recuperative embrace. It is such an honour, and a privilege, my friend, to be invited, again and again, into this visual commemoration.

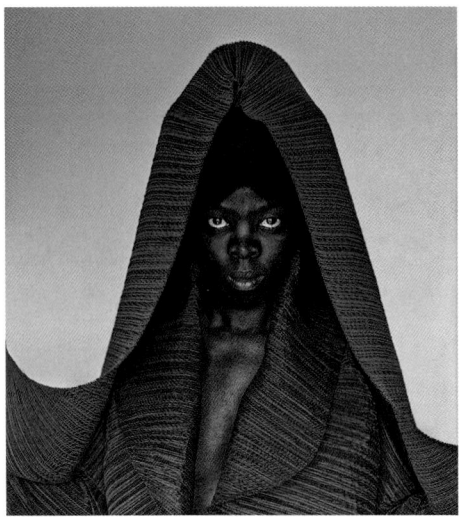

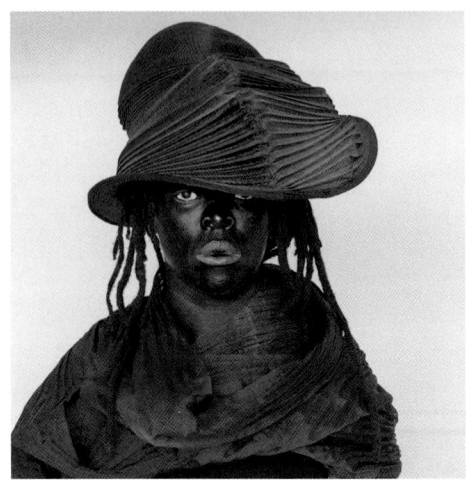

Zanele Muholi, *Thembeka II*, London, 2014. Courtesy of Stevenson, Cape Town/Johannesburg/Amsterdam and Yancey Richardson, New York. © Zanele Muholi

Zanele Muholi, *MuMu XIX*, London, 2019. Courtesy of Stevenson, Cape Town/Johannesburg/Amsterdam and Yancey Richardson, New York. © Zanele Muholi

In your own words:

'In *Thembeka II, Bester VI, VII and IX, and MuMu XIX, I use your Issey Miyake pleated dresses, to create a connection—to speak about intimacy, trust, and friendship. And to destabilize notions of elegance and access. How do we learn to look at ourselves, consume ourselves? Reclaim how we want to be seen, or looked at by the other?*

Somnyama Ngonyama began as a tribute to my mother, Bester Muholi (1936–2009), who was a maid. She was a beautiful Zulu woman who never made it onto the cover of a magazine. Her prison was someone's kitchen ... so these portraits ask us to bear in mind that Bester herself was locked into 42 years of servitude. They are a statement of reclamation, and the staging of beauty: to release her from a fixed position of servitude. I thought of domestic workers whose beauty had never been celebrated, whose life stories were never contextualised: who deserve to be recognized, like the great heroines of our times ...

My practice as a visual activist looks at black resistance—existence as well as insistence. This is what keeps me awake at night ... Thus Somnyama is not only about creating beautiful photographs as such, but also about bringing forth political statements, and historical incidents, while giving affirmation to those who doubt, whenever they speak to themselves, whenever they look

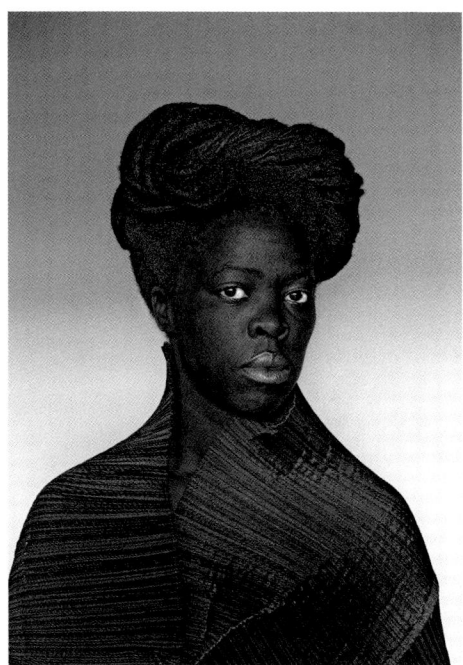

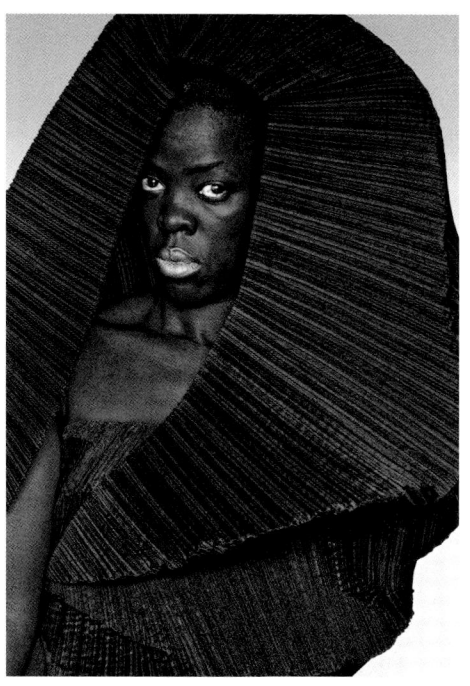

Zanele Muholi, *Bester VI*, London, 2017. Courtesy of Stevenson, Cape Town/Johannesburg/Amsterdam and Yancey Richardson, New York. © Zanele Muholi

Zanele Muholi, *Bester VII*, London, 2017. Courtesy of Stevenson, Cape Town/Johannesburg/Amsterdam and Yancey Richardson, New York. © Zanele Muholi

in the mirror, to say to them, and to myself: "You are worthy, you are beautiful, you count, nobody has the right to undermine you: because of your being, because of your race, because of your gender expression, because of your sexuality, because of the colour of your skin, because of all that you are."

I was thinking about resistance photography, the many images that have simply never been captured, and how this lack of access informs our history. Hence, I am producing this photographic document to encourage individuals in my community to be brave enough to occupy spaces, brave enough to create without fear of being vilified, brave enough to take on that visual text, those visual narratives … to re-think what history is all about, to re-claim it for ourselves: to encourage people to use artistic tools such as cameras as weapons to fight back.'[6]

When you manifest Bester, and the many others—mothers and sisters and daughters—repeatedly, continually transforming our collective labour(s) into generative visuality, you remind us to not only 'imagine otherwise'[7] and 'shape change',[8] but occasionally *to be still*, too—for your mother knowingly named you Zanele—meaning, as you once told me, 'enough' | 'they are enough' in isiZulu.

And so, I picture you, again, at Constitution Hill, conjuring all the women who said 'enough', who 'dared to be powerful', practising refusal,[9] reclaiming these streets—ours, yours, mine, theirs—birthing r/evolutions, m/othering Blackness, 'transforming silences into actions'[10], and images, in their moment of radical protest. Feeling your presence palpably, I see the many r/evolutions you have birthed, and keep birthing, visual and otherwise.

Feel embraced.

Yours, always
Renée

Notes

1   Benjamin, W. (1940) *On the Concept of History/Theses on Philosophy* ('lost to history').
2   *Bayphephi I, II, III* were commissioned by Autograph, London.
3   In-text references include: https://reclaimthesestreets.com ('reclaim these streets')
4   Azoulay, A. (2008) *The Civil Contract of Photography*. New York: Zone Books. ('still here').
5   Quotations by Zanele Muholi are re-edited / re-assembled excerpts from a series of interviews originally conducted for, and adapted from, 'Archive of the Self: Zanele Muholi in conversation with Renée Mussai', first published in Zanele Muholi, *Somnyama Ngonyama, Hail the Dark Lioness* (London: Autograph, 2017/New York: Aperture, 2018).
6   See Renée Mussai, R. (2020) 'Letter III: The Archive Other/Wise', in Sarah Allen and Yasufumi Nakamori (eds), *Zanele Muholi*. London: Tate Publishing.
7   Sharpe, C. (2016) *In The Wake: On Blackness and Being* (Durham, NC and London: Duke University Press ('to imagine otherwise').
8   Butler, O. (1993) *Parable of the Sower*. London: Headline Publishing Group, 2019. ('shaping change').
9   Campt, T. (2017) *Listening to Images* (Durham, NC and London: Duke University Press. ('to practice refusal').
10 Lorde, A. (1984) *'The Transformation of Silence into Language and Action*, in When I Dare To Be Powerful (London: Penguin/Random Books, 2007).

All images are reproduced with kind permission by the artist, and their galleries.

14 EVERY DAY IS MOTHER'S DAY IN MY BOOK

Black Motherhood in the Work of Nona Faustine Simmons

JONATHAN MICHAEL SQUARE ──────────────────────

In her ongoing series *Mitochondria*, the African American visual artist Nona Faustine photographs herself, her mother, her sister, and her daughter in their shared home in Brooklyn's Flatbush neighborhood. We see her daughter, Queen, reclined on a plush, eggplant-colored sofa, costumed as a princess for Halloween.

We see Faustine's mother staring pensively at the camera in their living room in crisp natural light. We see Faustine herself fording waves at Coney Island—one of her favorite places in the world, and a site of another of her photographic series, *From My Beach Chair*—with Queen straddling her back. We see Queen holding out a slice of red velvet cake on her sixth birthday.

The series, began in 2008, reveals the intimacy of their familial relationship and the tenacity of their attachment to each other. Its title refers to the

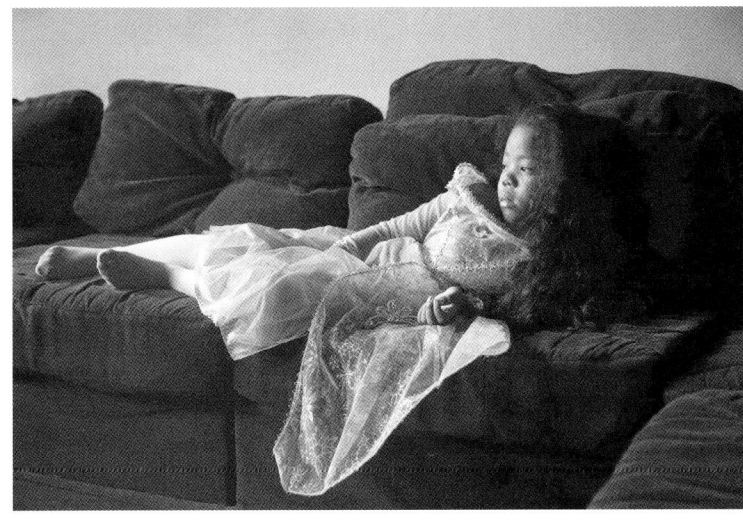

Nona Faustine Simmons, *Blue Queen*, 2015. Courtesy of the artist. © Nona Faustine Simmons

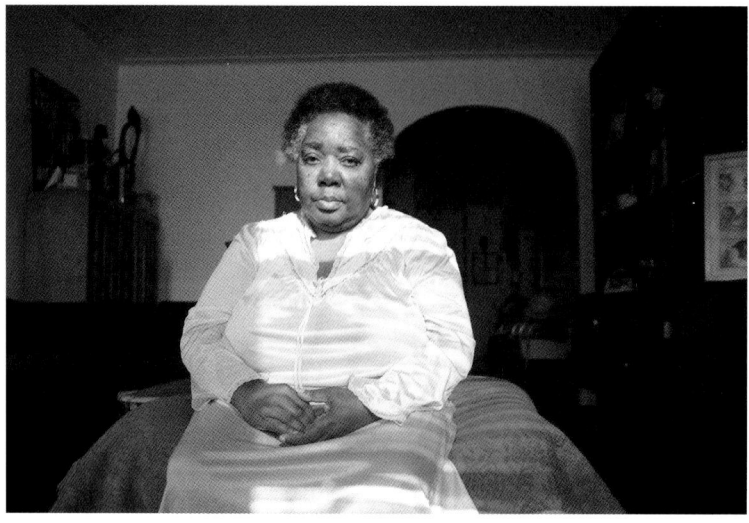

mitochondrial DNA encoded in human genes, which is inherited from mothers. By tracing maternal lineages through mitochondrial DNA, scientists have identified the Mitochondrial Eve (also known as mt-Eve, mt-MRCA, or the "Eve Gene") as the most recent common ancestor of all living human beings. This means we can trace the lineage of all mothers, grandmothers, great-grandmothers, and so on, to a gene from one woman, estimated to have lived 150,000 to 200,000 years ago.

Although it is difficult to pinpoint the exact location in which the Eve Gene originated, due to geographical changes over time, scientists suggest that the earliest humans derived from the Makgadikgadi Pan, the modern-day Kalahari Desert in Botswana. Thus, the discovery of Mitochondrial Eve highlights the power and importance of women of African descent. From her mitochondria arose humanity's phenotypical diversity. In other words, without the genes from this African woman, modern humans would not exist.

Faustine's own maternal lineage, unearthed in a genealogical quest, originated in precolonial Africa and culminates in the present with her daughter, Queen. Through AfricanAncestry.com, Faustine discovered that she descends from the Bubi, Hausa, Fulani, and Tikar peoples of West Africa. She also learned the name of her oldest maternal ancestor: Dido. Born enslaved, Dido worked as a domestic on a plantation in New Hanover County, North Carolina, for most of her life. She may not have engaged in agricultural work, but the coastal plains of North Carolina were constructed on the unpaid labor of enslaved people who worked the region's hundreds of plantations. From Dido, future generations emerged, living with dignity and regality, as befits the

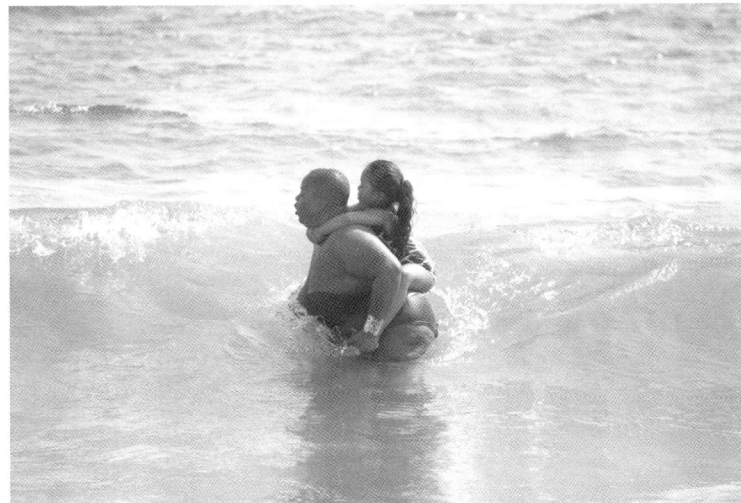

Nona Faustine Simmons, *Rough Waters*, 2012. Courtesy of the artist. © Nona Faustine Simmons

descendants of a woman named for the legendary queen of Carthage; indeed, Faustine's mother, like Faustine's daughter, was named Queen. In the last wave of the Great Migration, Faustine's parents moved from North Carolina to a pre-gentrified Brooklyn. Faustine can trace a maternal line encompassing her daughter, herself, her mother, her grandmother Maggie, her great-grandmother Martha, her great-great-grandmother Dido, and countless unknown foremothers. It is this maternal lineage that she documents in *Mitochondria*.

Faustine's creative practice is grounded in unearthing the stories of women—free and enslaved, past and present—who shaped her life. Trained at the International Center of Photography, she received her MFA in 2013 from Bard College, and she has since gained widespread acclaim for her photographic work examining the relationship between place, the Black female body, and the memory of slavery. In her photographs, she reclaims spaces for herself, her family, and other Black women within the Western artistic canon, and reflects on the centrality of Black women to the founding and maintaining of longstanding Black communities.

Reclaiming Motherhood

The *Mitochondria* series serves as a corrective to poisoned images of Black women characterized by extremes and stereotypes: the desexualized and masculinized Mammy, the hypersexualized and exploitable Jezebel, the sharp-tongued neck-rolling Sapphire. Far from occupying stereotypical roles assigned to Black women, Faustine, her mother, her sister, and her daughter embody their own identities. In this series, they are complex, graceful, and beautiful—adjectives infrequently associated with Black motherhood and femininity.

Writer and historian Sarah Knott notes that "mother" is a verb; rather than a static state of being, it emerges out of active caring and nurturing.[1] Yet enslaved mothers were not allowed to mother. "The idea of a black woman being a mother could not be embraced," says Faustine.[2] It was not unusual for enslaved mothers to be separated from their children—nor, in a perverse twist of irony, to be asked to care for their enslavers' children. Moreover, in the British colonies, and subsequently the United States, the legal doctrine *partus sequitur ventrem*—meaning "that which is born follows the womb"—rendered the children of enslaved women slaves themselves. Thus, enslaved women were not only laborers but also potential reproducers of more enslaved laborers. In the United States, one of the first nations—along with Britain—to abolish the slave trade, reproduction was a means of amassing a future labor force throughout most of the nineteenth century.

Toni Morrison's Pulitzer Prize-winning novel *Beloved* was inspired by the story of Margaret Garner, a formerly enslaved woman, who escaped with her family across the frozen Ohio River to Cincinnati in January 1856. Apprehended by U.S. marshals acting under the Fugitive Slave Act of 1850, and unwilling to have her daughter raised in the yoke of slavery, Garner committed infanticide. Against the backdrop of tragic histories like Garner's, Black mothers caring for their children—as Faustine documents in *Mitochondria*—becomes an act of resistance.

Reclaiming Place

Africa—the motherland—is the site at which the umbilical cord was severed in the Middle Passage, and it figures prominently in Faustine's imagination and lived experience. Sociologist Orlando Patterson famously argued that Diasporic Blacks suffered from a form of natal alienation, which he termed "social death."[3] Many scholars have rejected this notion, arguing that Black communities were able to maintain institutions from the African continent and construct new meaning in the New World context. Saidiya Hartman, for example, embraces the trauma and kinlessness of the transatlantic slave trade in her seminal work, *Lose Your Mother: A Journey along the Atlantic Slave Route*. Hartman explores the public memory of slavery and how, amid the brutality

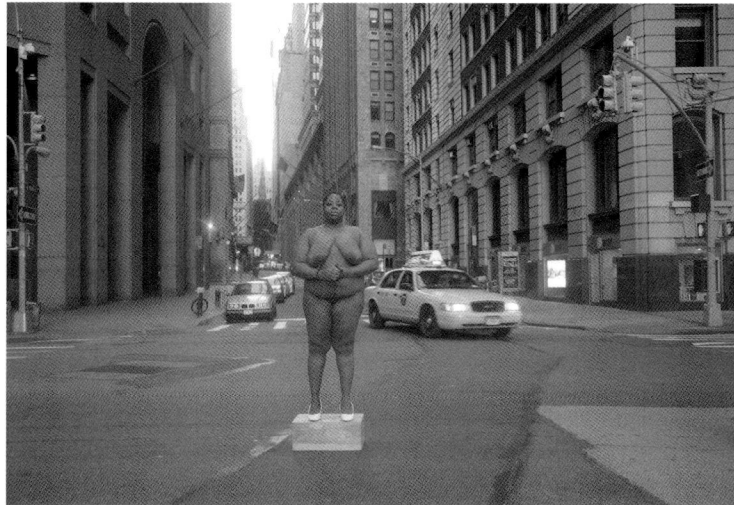

Nona Faustine Simmons,
*From Her Body Sprang
Their Greatest Wealth*, 2013.
Courtesy of the artist. © Nona
Faustine Simmons

of the Middle Passage and the daily ordeal of slavery, enslaved people and their descendants managed to survive and build a sense of community that endures to the present day, injecting her personal narrative along the way.[4]

With her photographs, Faustine is, in essence, doing the work of nurturing community and creating meaning. Like her, many African Americans have spent time in Africa to help suture the wounds of separation that many Diasporic Blacks feel, bridge the fissure between Old and New World Blacks, and learn about their maternal roots. Faustine highlights the preservation of African cultural elements in American society, using her own presence and the presence of her mother, sister, and daughter as proof of the strength and survival of Black people even in the most harrowing circumstances.

While working on *Mitochondria*, Faustine began *White Shoes*, a series exploring the history of slavery in New York City. In all the photographs, she wears a pair of white pumps that represents the effects of whiteness on the Black body. Among other locations, she wears them on Wall Street, in a lot bounded by Water and Pearl Streets that is widely accepted to have been the site of an eighteenth-century slave market.[5] In posing nude on this Wall Street block, she stands in for her enslaved descendants who might have been bought and sold on this parcel of land. Moreover, by choosing a location on Wall Street, which has become a symbol of American capitalism and a major tourist destination, Faustine is representing Black women who continue to be subjected to misogyny, racism, and coercive labor conditions. One of the motivations behind the series was Faustine's desire to document Black women's presence in Brooklyn so that future residents will know that enslaved women and

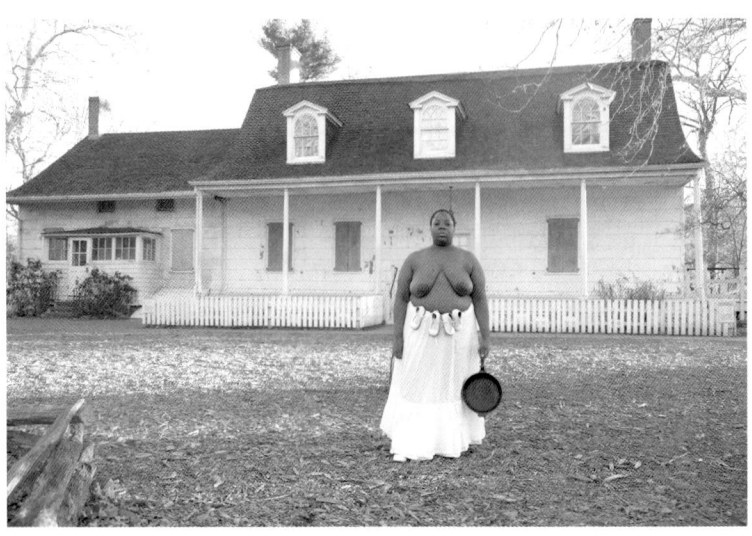

their descendants helped found the borough and lived there before they were pushed out by gentrification and other forces of structural racism. In this way, her work is a reflection on the past, present, and even the future, refracted through a radical Black feminist lens.

In *White Shoes*, Faustine uses herself as a metonym for the presence of enslaved women in the city throughout history. As a Black woman and descendant of enslaved people, she turns the lens on herself, photographing herself nude in sites of slavery around New York, uniting her personal history and African Americans' collective testimony of enslavement. In so doing, she reclaims sites in New York City where the history of slavery has been forgotten and summons those narratives into our present day, connecting herself to a lineage that extends from the African continent to contemporary Brooklyn. She uses self-portraiture—whether in her artistic series or in selfies that she posts on social media—as a radical affirmation of her beauty and subjectivity as a Black woman and mother who descends from enslaved people.

One work in the series, *Not Gone with the Wind*, speaks to the blurring of past and present, and the permanence and perseverance of Black women. For the photo, Faustine posed partially nude in front of the Lefferts Historic House, the former home of the prominent Lefferts family, in what is now Prospect Park, Brooklyn. The Lefferts were wealthy property owners who engaged in the trade, sale, and purchase of enslaved people until emancipation was enacted in New York State in 1827. Faustine places herself in solidarity with those enslaved people, bare-chested and solemnly positioned in front of the homestead. Sites such as the Lefferts House, often seen as benign landmarks or tourist attractions, have histories steeped in enslavement. Faustine demands recognition of this history and reminds viewers that Black women's bodies are integral to understanding these sites.

Reclaiming the Body

Nudity is a key component of Faustine's creative practice. Undress was an important mechanism of control in slave societies: It facilitated the inspection of bodies for disease and the removal of potential implements of suicide and prevented the hiding of weapons. Coercive disrobing not only severed enslaved individuals' principal material link to their families, communities, and native cultures, it also magnified their powerlessness, marking their entry into captivity.

While enslaved women were forced to expose their bodies for scrutiny and capitalist exploitation, Faustine undresses in full self-possession. "I didn't see women like me in art. A body like mine. With complexions like mine. I wanted to place myself as a full-figured, dark-skinned woman within the canon," says Faustine.[6] Black women are stigmatized for having bodies that are too this or too that. Too thin. Too fat. Too masculine. Too voluptuous. Too muscular. Too flabby. Too ugly. Too sexy. By contrast, Faustine's state of undress is a statement of self-love and body positivity. She is full-figured and unapologetically bares her curves, including her breasts, in these photos. "It was about growth. It was about acceptance. Becoming a mother was a part of that change. When I became a mother, there was a part of me that wanted to celebrate my body," says Faustine.[7] With her keen historical awareness, she takes ownership over her body and reproductive capabilities, giving herself the agency that her enslaved foremothers were denied.

As a descendant of enslaved peoples and a lifelong resident of Brooklyn, Faustine uses her body as an archive into which she and her ancestors' experiences are recorded. In *Of My Body I Will Make Monuments In Your Honor*, she placed life-size cutouts of her nude body as a stand-in for the headstones of lost graves of enslaved women located somewhere in the Dutch Reformed Church Cemetery. Faustine reveals the forgotten history of these women by embodying their presence in the cemetery. As American society continues to reckon with its racist past and monuments of enslavers are toppled or removed, Faustine's memorialization of slavery becomes even more apt. Black people have historically been forced to put their bodies on the line, sometimes

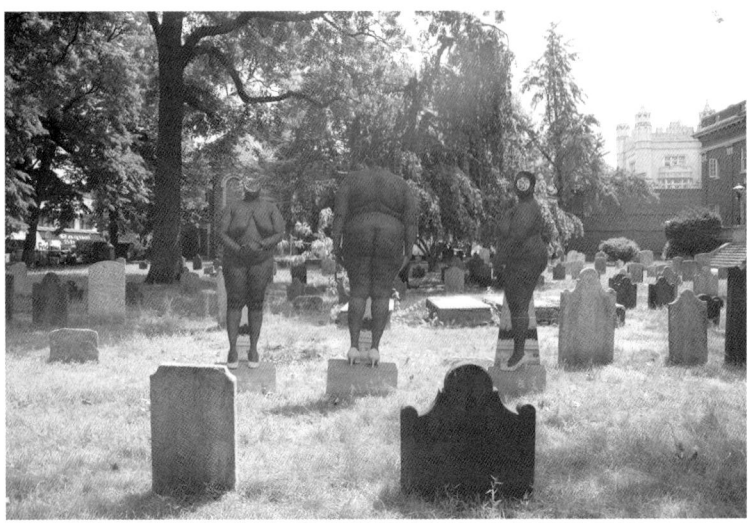

with deadly consequences. Faustine uses her nude or semi-nude body as a counter-monument to Confederate iconography and as a testament to the legacy of slavery that is literally enshrined in her physical person.

Conclusion: Celebrating Black Motherhood

Faustine's assertion of her naked body in *White Shoes* and focus on familial intimacy in *Mitochondria* can be seen as answers to the legacy of violence and abuse that is foundational to the development of modern medicine. The field of gynecology originated in a series of operations performed, without anesthesia, by Dr. J. Marion Sims on enslaved women. Sims's legacy endures, and the vestiges of abuse against Black femme bodies still plague the American medical system. Studies have shown that today, a troubling number of medical professionals believe Black people have higher pain tolerances, resulting in disparities in treatment and pain management.

Slavery's legacy lives on through the subpar medical treatment to which Black mothers are subjected.[8] For example, the world-famous athlete Serena Williams, who suffers from pulmonary embolisms, was not properly attended to during and after the birth of her daughter. If Williams, a multimillionaire Wimbledon-winning tennis star, faced such disparities, imagine the medical treatment experienced by less affluent and notable Black people. According to the Centers for Disease Control and Prevention, pregnancy mortality rates are three to four times higher among Black women than among white women.[9]

The reasons for such disparity are multifaceted: poverty, the prevalence of chronic diseases, the stress of racism, lack of access to hospitals, inadequate prenatal and postnatal care, and the weight of historical oppression.

Faustine's oeuvre, a celebration of the grace and beauty of Black femininity and motherhood, is a brave riposte to the continual and blatant undervaluing of Black women present in the medical profession and leveled, for example, in the infamous 1965 Moynihan Report, which explored the deep roots of Black poverty in the United States. The report controversially concluded that the high proportion of families headed by single mothers greatly hinders the progress of Blacks toward economic and political equality. *Mitochondria* and *White Shoes* serve as forms of visual activism and counternarratives to stereotypes outlined in the report. In this reframing, Black women, far from being the source of African Americans' plight, are a wellspring of creative inspiration and life.

Faustine's career as an artist did not flourish until she became a mother. She says, "I've heard some mothers say that they lost something after the birth of their children. My daughter helped me rekindle my interest in photography. Through her, I found my calling and my craft." Caring for and protecting her daughter are fundamental to her creative process, and motherhood is a central theme that runs throughout all of her series and her photographic practice. By reflecting on Black motherhood historically, drawing inspiration from her mother and foremothers, and becoming a mother herself, Faustine honed her skills and sharpened her sensibilities as a photographer. In documenting her family and examining Black motherhood, she attests to her own assertion that "every day is Mother's Day in my book."[10]

Notes

1   Knott, S. (2019) *Mother Is a Verb: An Unconventional History*. New York: Farrar, Straus and Giroux.
2   "In Conversation: Corinne Botz, Nona Faustine and Rachel Zucker, Moderated by Michi Jigarjian," Camera Club of New York, May 4, 2019, YouTube video, https://youtu.be/u9zNQbIL04A.
3   Patterson, O. (1982) *Slavery and Social Death: A Comparative Study*. Cambridge: Harvard University Press.
4   Like Faustine's recovery of Dido's story, Hartman's point of departure for the exploration of the legacy of slavery was the discovery of the testimony of her enslaved maternal great-great-grandmother Polly in a Yale library. See Hartman, S. (2008) *Lose Your Mother: A Journey along the Atlantic Slave Route*. New York: Farrar, Straus and Giroux.
5   "Slave Market," Mapping the African American Past, Columbia University, accessed on July 3, 2020, https://maap.columbia.edu/place/22.html.

6   Nona Faustine, interview by the author, January 15, 2018.

7   Faustine, interview.

8   Sabin, J. A. and A. G. Greenwald (2012) "The Influence of Implicit Bias on Treatment Recommendations for 4 Common Pediatric Conditions: Pain, Urinary Tract Infection, Attention Deficit Hyperactivity Disorder, and Asthma," *American Journal of Public Health* 102, no. 5 (May): 988–95; Kelly M. Hoffman et al., (2016) "Racial Bias in Pain Assessment and Treatment Recommendations, and False Beliefs about Biological Differences between Blacks and Whites," *Proceedings of the National Academy of Sciences of the United States of America* 113, no. 16 (April): 4296–301.

9   "Pregnancy Mortality Surveillance System," Centers for Disease Control and Prevention, updated November 25, 2020, https://www.cdc.gov/reproductivehealth/maternal-mortality/pregnancy-mortality-surveillance-system.htm?CDC_AA_refVal=https%3A%2F%2Fwww.cdc.gov%2Freproductivehealth%2Fmaternalinfant-health%2Fpregnancy-mortality-surveillance-system.htm; Tucker, M. J. et al. (2007), "The Black-White Disparity in Pregnancy-Related Mortality from 5 Conditions: Differences in Prevalence and Case-Fatality Rates," *American Journal of Public Health* 97, no. 2: 247–51.

10   "In Conversation," May 4, 2019.

15 THE MOTHERLAND BETWEEN US

Grace Aneiza Ali ⎯⎯⎯⎯⎯⎯⎯⎯⎯⎯⎯⎯⎯⎯⎯⎯⎯

> What is separation's geography?
> The mother's body is the country
> of our earliest memory, the soil
> from which we are formed.
> Our lives are an arc of flight:
> *away, toward, away.*
> — Shara McCallum, "From the Book of Mothers"[1]

I am a daughter who grieves a motherland. I am a daughter of a mother who also grieves a motherland. Twenty-five years ago, my mother Ingrid and I departed the land of our birth, Guyana. My mother is my strongest connection to Guyana, stronger than the land itself. It is a remarkable thing I am often in awe of—that in our mothers, grandmothers, great grandmothers, and oldest mothers are our deepest and most tangible connection to our ancestral lands. For those of us who leave one place for another, fueled by choice or by trauma,

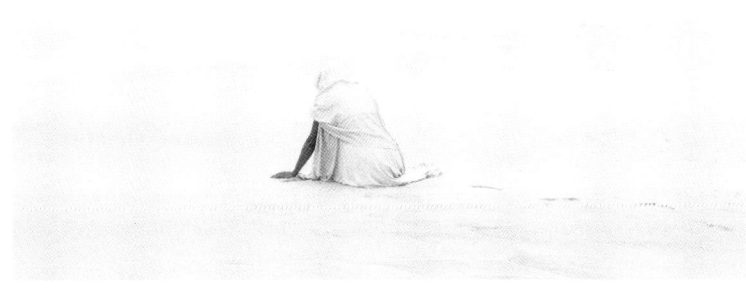

Keisha Scarville, Untitled #1, from the series, Mama's Clothes, 2015, archival digital inkjet print. © Keisha Scarville. Courtesy of the artist.

finding language to reconcile that loss, that rupture and severing, can be at once beautiful and fraught. For beauty, I often turn to the Guyanese-born poet Grace Nichols, whose words emerge from the page as both balm and praise song. When language fails or is simply absent, I find solace in the immensely moving and tender portraiture series, *Mama's Clothes*, by the first-generation American photographer Keisha Scarville. She too is a daughter of a Guyanese-born mother, Alma, who migrated to the United States. Her photographs, paired with Nichols' poem, "Praise Song for My Mother" are meditations on the ways in which motherland, migration, death, and loss are inextricably linked.

Motherlands and Other-lands

To talk about mothers is to talk about daughters. As daughters of Guyanese mothers—myself, Nichols and Scarville—we are bonded in the loss of and separation from mothers and motherlands. In her essay, "Motherlands and Other Lands: Home and Exile in Jamaica Kincaid's 'Lucy' and Paule Marshall's 'Praisesong for the Widow'", literary scholar Kattian Barnwell deconstructs the twin ideas of "motherlands" and "other-lands." She writes, "Motherland may be variously defined as a place of birth, "land" or home of the mother, the site of the self. Conversely, other-land refers to the site where each character experiences alienation and "othering," the place of exile."[2]

In *Mama's Clothes*, Scarville captures these intertwined experiences of motherhood and daughterhood, motherland and other-land, belonging and exile. Writing about the curiosity for her mother's migration story in the essay "Surrogate Skin: Portrait of Mother (Land)," Scarville reflects:

> I became curious as to how my mother's presence within this American landscape influenced her sense of belonging. How had the process of becoming an American citizen affected her? What was the impact of her shifting relationship to Guyana? Even now, I find myself left with more questions than answers.[3]

The questions Scarville takes on in *Mama's Clothes* are at once literal and allusive. I am reminded of how rare this dual quality—for a work of art to be equally literal as it is allusive or abstract—is when I recall the words of the British-Ghanaian figurative painter Lynette Yiadom-Boakye who underscores her character studies of imaginary Black men and women with the most splendid literary titles (for example, "Mercy Over Matter," "Sister to a Solstice, "A Whistle in A Wish," or "Ever the Women Watchful") as perhaps a poet would. "My writing parallels my painting, but I don't paint about the writing or write about the painting… I write about the things I can't paint and paint the things I can't write about."[4]

Throughout Scarville's ongoing portraiture series *Mama's Clothes*, the artist drapes, layers and wraps her body in her mother's clothes. "I allowed the assemblage of clothes to drip off my body as though it were a residual, surrogate skin," she notes.[5] In some of the evocative portraits, we also see the artist fashion out of her mother's clothes headwraps and sculptural crowns that adorn her head; in others we see her create masks and veils that cover, shield and hide her face, which is always obscured from the viewer. The lush, organic landscapes and seascapes of the images in *Mama's Clothes* shift between Guyana and the United States. They hold emotional and geographical significance for both the artist and her mother. In merging her body with her mother's clothes on dual soils, Scarville marries both time and space—two generations, two lands—motherland and other-land—and the complexities in between.

At the heart of *Mama's Clothes* is an homage to Scarville's Guyanese-born mother, Alma, who migrated to New York in 1967. She was the eldest of five siblings and the first in her family to leave Guyana, "driven by a promise of opportunity and a new narrative to be unearthed within foreign landscapes."[6] In the 1960s, a politically volatile decade that saw Guyana gain its independence from the British, Scarville's mother found her way to New York where she took on new roles: an immigrant in the United States, a young Black woman witnessing America's civil rights era, a wife and mother. She nevertheless maintained a connection to Guyana, returning often and taking a young Scarville back with her. However, as time passed, those visits became less frequent and Guyana lived mostly as a mythical motherland for the artist. Of her mother's migratory dance between transient spaces, Scarville shares, "She maintained a connection to the land of her birth, firmly planting one foot under a tamarind tree in Buxton[7] and the other, rooted on the rooftop of an apartment building in Flatbush."[8][9] In 2016, grappling with "a sense of displacement and an internal fracturing"[10] after her mother's passing just a year earlier, Scarville returned to her mother's land of birth. She carried back to Guyana with her a suitcase of her mother's clothes—dresses, skirts, scarves, shawls—all marked by her signature style of bright colors, strong prints, and long flowing fabrics. It was Scarville's first time returning to Guyana without her mother. She explains her intention to photograph herself in her mother's clothes, in her mother's homeland, on the Buxton soil her mother planted her feet. "I wanted to peel back the ancestral layers and examine my own sense of belonging. I brought a suitcase of my mother's clothes and returned to Buxton … a first-generation American-daughter searching for home."[11]

The Things We Carry

It is quite telling that in *Camera Lucida: Reflections on Photography*, noted French literary theorist Roland Barthes came to shape and define the provocative idea of a photograph's *punctum*—the Latin word meaning "to sting, prick, or cut"—through a close reading of an image of his mother when she was a child. *Punctum*—the elusive sensory, intensely subjective effect of a photograph is "that accident which pricks me (but also bruises me, is poignant to me)," wrote Barthes.[12] He describes how a small detail or even an unnamable emotion in a photograph can "rise from the scene, shoot out … like an arrow, and pierce" the viewer.[13] For Barthes, this particular image which he called "Winter Garden," was like no other photograph of his mother; in it he saw a kindness of spirit and temperament she had about her even as a child. What many have found remarkable about Barthes' *Camera Lucida* is that while he delves deeply into describing with great care and meticulous detail the physical characteristics of the photograph and of his mother, framing it as the heart and soul of the book, the image is, and has never been, seen. As a reader, you find yourself touched and moved by a beloved mother you can't see.

The suitcase she filled with her mother's clothes is never seen in Scarville's *Mama's Clothes*. Yet, whenever I return to this series, I think about that suitcase—its absent presence, the symbolic weight of all it carries. Scarville writes of the intangible things her mother and her belongings embody: "On August 13, 2015, my mother passed away, taking with her a treasure chest of stories and deep knowing. Like how to properly clap a roti skin, or how to speak the vegetal language of soil and plant life, or how to clean and prepare your house so that good luck will come in the new year."[14] I think of that suitcase, of its precious contents, of its journey across the Atlantic, of its return to a motherland, and of the daughter accountable for it. Scarville, like Barthes, searches for her mother's presence as she notes, "I am interested in how the absent body lives in the photograph and the materiality of absence. I am seeking invocation, something celebratory that rethinks absence as a threshold."[15] For me, the absent suitcase is the *punctum* of *Mama's Clothes*, inviting into the work daughters who carry our mother's things across borders to return them to their motherlands.

At fourteen years old, I nervously boarded my first airplane in 1995—a one-way flight from Guyana's Timehri International Airport bound for New York's John F. Kennedy Airport. I had long resented planes as the violent machines that fragmented families. Before my mother, Ingrid, boarded that same flight at thirty-nine years old with three children in tow, she had in the years prior, witnessed her brothers and sisters, one by one, all board similar planes to leave Guyana. By nineteen years old, a cycle of poverty and the final straw, the loss of both her father and then her mother within a few short years of each other, ushered in for my mother a series of constant departures. Beginning in the 1970s, my mother's six siblings joined the mass exodus of Guyanese leaving Guyana.[16] "The injection into the Caribbean immigration literature of the biblical diasporan term "exodus" in effect implied that, relative to its size, Caribbean people had become the most mobile people in the postwar world," writes Carol Boyce Davies.[17] My aunts and uncles first left for neighboring Caribbean islands then later Canada and the United States, through student visas, work visas, marriage visas—whatever it took.

During the ten years that my mother spent waiting for our family's visas and immigration papers to be vetted by two governments, Guyana and the United States, she watched the ones she loved the most leave her country and leave her, multiple times over. For this reason, I often find myself caught in a liminal space between those who leave a place and those who (must) remain—because for many years it was my story, and for many years before that, it was my mother's story. My mother was no stranger to bearing witness to the ritual of her beloveds packing up a life in one land to start anew in another. During my childhood in Guyana, neither was I. When in 1995 the papers finally 'came through' as we say in Guyana, and it was our turn to be the ones doing the leaving, we followed the blueprint that my mother's family had mapped in their prior departures from Guyana. We made our way to North America to join her siblings whose migration path was now split between the United States and Canada. She was the last in her family to leave Guyana.

On the eve of our 6:30 a.m. flight bound for JFK, we had gleaned our Georgetown house of its remaining furniture, knick-knacks, linens, and kitchen wares—all the things we could not carry. The state of my mother's bedroom—ground zero for where our family had been packing five large suitcases for the past month—was relatively calm, considering this was the eve of our departure from our motherland. My mother was thankful that it wasn't one of the scheduled blackout nights in our part of Georgetown. At least there was electricity as she finished packing. Our suitcases were almost ready. The jars of wiri wiri pepper sauce and mango achars, sealed in their thick masking tape, still needed to be wrapped and wedged into the nooks between our clothing. My mom had one major problem to solve. The large cast-iron *karahi* bulged under the layers of clothes she had carefully swaddled it in. There was no minimizing its presence in the suitcase. She knew with it the luggage would be over the weight limit. She also knew that to take the pot, she had to leave something behind.

The *karahi* is a thick, circular, and deep cooking pot that originated in the Indian subcontinent. It was first introduced in Guyana by the Indian indentured servants who were brought by the British, beginning in 1838 and throughout the early 1900s, to work the sugar plantations and rice farms in then British Guiana. The *karahi* has transformed into an unmistakable staple in every Guyanese kitchen. Our *karahi*—aged, scratched, chipped, nicked, scraped and blackened—had hit its sweet spot. For two decades, it had absorbed into its pores the perfect medley of oils and spices, which it now infused into whatever meats, vegetables, and sauces were poured into it. My mother had grown up as a young girl watching her mother cook for her family in the same *karahi*. Daily, it produced curries or stews or an occasional chow-mein or fried rice for my mother and her six siblings and then later my siblings as the *karahi* was passed down to her. In her suitcase bound for America, there was no prized jewelry, no priceless antiques, no precious silk saris. Wrapped in my mother's signature style of bright colors, strong prints, and long flowing fabrics, very much like the clothing of Scarville's mother, there was only the *karahi*—the sole valuable possession she had after her mother died. It was not going to be left behind. It was coming to America with us.

On April 8, 1995, my mother departed Guyana and took her entire family with her. She had spent a decade of her life in limbo between present and future, between living in one land and making plans for an unknown one. As she prepared for that early April morning flight, ten years of waiting, of not knowing when the time would come to leave, of preparing for the unknown, had come to an end. Despite all of these things, or perhaps because of them, it was non-negotiable for my mother that the *karahi* come with us to America. It embodied within its pores all of her stories and her mother's stories. Twenty-five years after that departure, it survives. It is the object that bridges my mother's past with her present, her motherland with her other-land. My mother still cooks her curries and stews in that *karahi* in her American home. Oceans and lands apart from its origin, that *karahi* sustains and nourishes my family. It is now over 40 years old. I hope to one day inherit it from my mother as she inherited it from hers.

The Geography of Separation

Each day, more and more women, mothers and daughters, from all over the world, do whatever they need to, they get on planes and boats and ships and make-shift rafts, while many simply walk, to cross both real and imaginary borders, fences and walls. Instead of narratives that allow us a window into the humanity of these women, their stories of migration have instead been hijacked by politics and politicians, policy, sensational headlines, and data.[18] Where do we find their real stories? Where is the poetry of their lives? Can we turn to art, to language, to poetry, to the image to find their voices? How can the photograph map the emotional terrain of separation from a motherland?

When my mother got on that plane with her three children and left for the unknown, what did she feel about leaving her homeland? Was she fleeing? Or, was she clear-eyed that she was now free to move about the world? Did she think of her act, and the acts of what so many Guyanese women had done before, as an act of activism, as brave or remarkable? Did she understand at the time how mythical the 'American Dream' was, and decided to go after it? Was she prepared for the inevitable disappointment?

In her poem, "From the Book of Mothers," Jamaican-American poet Shara McCallum invites us to ponder a mother, and symbolically a motherland, that is distant, silent, or absent, when she asks: "What is separation's geography?"[19] In tandem, Scarville attempts to answer this question in *Mama's Clothes* by bridging two geographic spaces and setting her self-portraits in Buxton and Brooklyn, the dual soils from which her mother was shaped and formed, to borrow McCallum's words. Scarville reflects on how the loss of her mother co-mingled with separation from home and motherland:

> I wanted to ease the anxiety of separation by conjuring her presence within the photographic realm... In the months leading up to her passing, we often talked about the idea of home. I wondered whether she would ever return to Guyana. Or, like so many immigrants who moved to the States, let time and distance alter her relationship to the land. Did she now consider America her permanent home? In recounting her experiences when she arrived in the United States, she often discussed the first sensation of real cold, the strange taste of American chicken, and overcoming the embedded alienation of this place.[20]

The alienation Scarville speaks of is an all too familiar refrain of the migrant. At thirty-nine years old, on the cusp of her second act, my mother too started over in a foreign land. She left a homeland where the tragedies often eclipsed the joys. She left a country she saw violently transition from a colonized territory to an independent republic. She left a country on whose soil she buried her mother while still mourning her father. She transitioned from an orphaned daughter, to a bride, to a wife, to a young mother of three. She tried to survive in a place where, like her mother before her, she struggled to keep her children from the deep abyss of poverty. Despite these constant companions of death and departure, she forged a family of her own.

Praise Song for My Mother

I envision particular photographs of the *Mama's Clothes* series as a beautiful pairing with the language of another daughter of Guyana, the indomitable Grace Nichols, whose poetry collections such as *I Is A Long Memoried Woman* have been instrumental in centering the voices of Guyanese women—mothers and daughters—in the Caribbean literary canon.[21] Nichols' oeuvre, over the last forty years, is steeped in a robust history of Caribbean women's literature on mother-daughter relationships. As Susheila Nasta notes in *Motherlands: Black Women's Writing from Africa, the Caribbean, and South Asia*, "Motherhood and maternity feature prominently in Caribbean women's writing out of a need to rediscover, recreate, and give birth to the genesis of new forms and new languages of expression."[22]

In 1977, Nichols, a young mother herself with a four-year-old daughter at the time, left Guyana for England. Her story of departure, rooted in absence and defined by what did not exist, is a familiar refrain for the many Guyanese families who were leaving Guyana. For those ambitious dreamers—artists, writers, poets—who found their way to England, it was necessary that they imagine a world beyond Guyana as a desire for professional and economic advancement inevitably meant emigration. Nichols, who has lived in England now for over forty years, is part of a community of Guyanese-born women who have lived in our other-lands lands longer than we have lived in our motherlands. It's a remarkable threshold we've crossed. We who have left our old-world selves to fashion, in Nichols' words, our "new-world selves." Nichols' oeuvre often explores an inner landscape, informed by the poet's migration from Guyana to England. In the quote below, we see Nichols, much like Scarville, pondering how her work examines the *geography of separation*. She writes:

> A sense of place has always been important to me as a writer. Coming from Guyana with its Atlantic coastline, its deep interior spirit of rivers, waterfalls and vast rainforests, have all made me into the kind of writer I am, one that keeps an eye on landscape and likes the elements to move in my work. But how do you deal with living in another landscape when the older native one is so imprinted in your mind?[23]

The sense of place and land that Nichols outlines, of coastlines and of bodies of water, is certainly visible throughout Scarville's *Mama's Clothes*. Even more so, these portraits of Scarville draped in a selection of her mother's garments that are light, muted, neutral colors, where the artist embeds herself in a white-washed seascape and faces a calm body of water conjure the opening lines from Nichols's poetic homage to her mother, "Praise Song for My Mother."[24]

> You were
> water to me
> deep and bold and fathoming

"You were," continues Nichols, "water," and "moon's eye" and "sunrise to me."[25] Using the traditional African poetic form of a praise song, Nichols unfurls the essence of her beloved mother in metaphors of land, sea, and sky, further bridging the ideas of motherland and other-land and Shara McCallum's line, "The mother's body is the country."

We are also meant to surmise, through Nichols' repetition of the past tense "You were" that the mother in "Praise Song for My Mother," as in *Mama's Clothes*, is departed or distant. However, what drives me to think of Scarville's photographs and Nichols' poem as works in conversation with each other, lies most profoundly in the use of the word "mantling" in the second stanza.

> You were
> moon's eye to me
> pull and grained and mantling[26]

Here, "mantling"—as a singular phrase—is the *punctum* of the poem. The verb "to mantle" comes from the Latin *mantellum*, which means "cloak." In her use of "mantling," Nichols invokes Scarville's gestures of cloaking herself in her mother's clothes—gestures that convey a sense of a daughter shrouded, protected, armored, secured, warmed, clothed, bathed, wrapped, embodied— all at once.

Through several great migrations that crisscrossed three countries, Guyana, the United States, and the United Kingdom, Scarville and Nichols have known great loss within their maternal histories. Both *Mama's Clothes* and "Praise Song for My Mother" are poignant works of art that engage the tensions between motherland and other-land. To create these visual and literary works, Scarville and Nichols have generously mined their mother-daughter relationships, allowing us to see their relationship with their mothers as both extension and metaphor for their relationship with Guyana, a space frequently wrestled with as a mythical motherland. While their work features a daughter's gaze on her mother, that gaze is full of compassion and tenderness. Collectively, they leave us to ponder the question: Even when we commit to preserving a motherland's memories, rites and traditions, how do we navigate the inevitable loss that pervades? How do we make peace with absence and erasure? In the midst of grappling with loss, absence, and grief, the photography of Keisha Scarville and poetry of Grace Nichols are thoughtful examples of how, as daughters of Guyana, we constantly reach to our mothers as collaborators in our lives as well as in our art.

Notes

1   McCallum, S. (2011) "From the Book of Mothers," in *This Strange Land*, Farmington, ME: Alice James Books, pg. 60.
2   Barnwell, K. (1994) "Motherlands and Other Lands: Home and Exile in Jamaica Kincaid's 'Lucy' and Paule Marshall's 'Praisesong for the Widow'," Caribbean Studies, Vol. 27, No. 3/4, Extended Boundaries: 13th Conference on West Indian Literature (July-December 1994), pg. 452.
3   Scarville, K. (2021) "Surrogate Skin: Portrait of Mother (Land)," *Liminal Spaces: Between Arrivals and Departures* by Grace Aneiza Ali (Editor), Cambridge, UK: Open Book Publishers, pg. 27.
4   Laster, P. (2017) "Lynette Yiadom-Boakye Talks About Creating Fictional Characters Through Portraiture," *Time Out*, May 2.
5   Scarville.
6   Scarville.

7 Buxton is located in the Demerara-Mahaica Region of Guyana. It was founded in 1840 by a group of freed former slaves after emancipation was enacted in 1838.

8 There are about 150,000 Guyanese immigrants living in New York City, making them the fifth-largest immigrant community in the city. Over the last fifty years, many Afro-Guyanese immigrants have settled among other Afro-Caribbean immigrants in places like Flatbush in Brooklyn.

9 Scarville.

10 Scarville.

11 Scarville.

12 Barthes, R. (1981) *Camera Lucida: Reflections on Photography*. New York: Hill and Wang.

13 Ibid.

14 Scarville.

15 Keisha Scarville. "Artist Statement," for the Lightwork exhibition, *Keisha Scarville: Alma* on view November 1 – December 13, 2018 at the Kathleen O. Ellis Gallery, Syracuse, New York.

16 An estimated 2 million Guyanese citizens are living around the globe while the country itself has a population of around 760,000.

17 Davies. C. B. (2008) Encyclopedia of the African Diaspora: Origins, Experiences, and Culture, Volume 3. Santa Barbara, CA: ABC-CLIO.

18 Khalid Koser. '10 migration trends to look out for in 2016'. World Economic Forum 18 Dec. 2015. ‹https://www. weforum.org/agenda/2015/12/10-migration-trends-to-look-out-for-in-2016/›.

19 McCallum, S. (2011) "From the Book of Mothers," in *This Strange Land*, Farmington, ME: Alice James Books, pg. 60.

20 Scarville.

21 Nichols, G. (1983) *I Is A Long Memoried Woman*, Karnak House Publishers.

22 Nasta,S. (1992) *Motherlands: Black Women's Writing from Africa, the Caribbean, and South Asia*, Rutgers University Press, pg. xix.

23 Nichols, G (2021) "Surrogate Skin: Portrait of Mother (Land)," *Liminal Spaces: Between Arrivals and Departures* by Grace Aneiza Ali (Editor), Cambridge, UK: Open Book Publishers, pg. 129.

24 Nichols, G. (1984) "Praise Song for My Mother," in *The Fat Black Woman's Poems*. London: Virago.

25 Ibid.

26 Ibid.

16 THE IMPOSSIBILITY OF BREATHING WHEN THE SUN COVERS YOUR FACE

MARCIA MICHAEL ────────────────────────────────

> I was going to run away.
> Surrounded by water, I did not care, I had been here before, surrounded
> by water, my birth, all births, remember. I was set free, then, again and
> again.
> Why should this one be any different?
> —Marcia Michael, *I go away* taken from *My History is in Her(e)*, 2020

It is only breath that enables us to be, to see and to feel; without it many believe that life does not continue (that is, if we do not breathe), we are dead. Yet many of our ancestors knew better, my mother knew better, I know better. Somehow, we decided that she would show me how to breathe forever. In asking many questions about her past, I was instructed to communicate with her body and hear her voice, the camera was my choice to enhance this learning. She then taught me how to read my own body and memories, allowing me to gaze upon my ancestors, recognizing them in me. This challenging and controversial dialogue (controversial because most of the time our bodies were naked) became an act of Black matrilineage that only my mother and I as her daughter could participate in. In be-coming her, I reclaim a fragment of my ancestral narratives and share this with you.

At the end where everything is told as if it were a story, I open my heart and speak the histories that I have reclaimed. We seem to remember better and longer if the information we want to keep and hold and share is retold to us in a story, therefore, stories matter.

If some stories cannot be told, where do we go? How do we find them?

I had to ask my mother.

In revealing to me how our ancestors' stories survived in her body with the need for them to be transplanted into mine, she uncovers a language I do not know. She thinks because I was pulled out of her stomach too young, too weak, that the contractions of this new birth that would have secreted onto me as I passed through the birth canal, remained inside her. Meaning that for their journey to become mine, she had to find a way to teach me her voice. I wanted to know the stories of my ancestors. I wanted to find them and honour them, I also wanted to honour my mother.

Turning always to mummy when things got tough, I told her that I could not locate any information about her mother in the Jamaican archives. To find out about my mother's grandmother, and so on and so forth, this information was crucial to me: when was my grandmother born? How else was I to begin the search for the mother of all mothers, *my* African Queen? As the years went by and still no information surfaced, my mother drew me into an act which I had only ever experienced through reading the novels of Toni Morrison's *Beloved* (1987), Gayl Jones's, *Correigdora* (1975), and Alice Walker's *The Color Purple* (1982). This was an act that between mother and daughter, somehow, some way, recovered histories: this act was Black matrilineage. I never knew what it was at the time, I never knew at the time what it was, but years after it began, I now understand everything. For with it I was taught so many things, for with it I was shown and heard so many things. Turning to Morrison to find an attachment, I became familiar with "another way of knowing" (Morrison 1984). This is because there simply was no other way. My mother opened her archived body to me and through this, my mother guided me through my search, in the ritual art of conjuring.

I understand what conjuring is. Introduced through Pryse's (1985) essay, Zora Neale Hurston, Alice Walker and the Ancient Power of Black Women (Pryse and Spillers 1985), I began to see who these other women could be. Describing conjuring as a folk art similar to quilt-makers, fine cooks, gardeners, seamstresses (also mentioned by Walker in *In Search of Our Mothers Garden* (1983) as the places were creativity was kept), which is passed on by mother to daughter, it's acknowledgment as spiritual and magical "provides an alternative, unofficial basis of cultural authority…[and becomes the] medium of temporal wholeness and continuity, countering the daughter's traumatic experience of historical dislocation" (Dubey 1995: 254–255). A conjure woman is one who is able to "blend the acceptance of the supernatural and a profound rootedness in the real world at the same time with neither taking precedence over the other" (Morrison 1984: 342), conjuring, to remind you, is "another way of knowing things" (Morrison 1984). Our mothers had always been con-juring—as resistance.

As literary matrilineage is that which uncovers the slave mother through the mother and daughter relationship, not only is conjuring an embodiment but for Pryse, "Zora Neale Hurston took conjuring as a great leap forward and with it, transposed the terms of literary authority for women writers" (Pryse and Spillers 1985: 10).

Looking back now, I understand the connection between Hurston and Walker, who are held to be the mother and daughter of Black matrilineage (Sadoff 1985). And how through them, what I was to re-experience, as a tradi-tion, was a ritual. My mother's voice and me with my camera, would become the tools of tradition that would begin and hopefully affirm my place in the tradition of conjuring, but also as a storyteller.

Drawn to Hurston's and Walker's respective literature and how they both used photography and photographic imagery in their work, there were aspects in their writings that pronounced themselves to me more than others. The first was that Hurston, as part of her observations as an anthropologist, took photographs and video footage of the people and experiences she was researching. For her book, *Tell My Horse*, published in 1935, Hurston went to Jamaica (my mother's place of birth) and other countries to research Voudoun. Whilst there, witnessing the ceremony for a female priestess, Hurston gained an understanding of the sovereignty of women. In answering the question of truth, the priestess in this ceremony, revealing her genitalia, it is under-stood that here, with men kissing her organs, they "come face to face with the truth" (Hurston 1990: 114). In highlighting the female aspect of the deity in *Tell my Horse*, it is clear in her description of Erzulie (a Goddess) as "the perfect female" (121) that this image of the female struck a chord with Hurston. This chord may have been what Maya Deren described Erzulie as, a woman who owns "the capacity to conceive beyond reality, to desire beyond adequacy, to create beyond need" (Deren 1983, 138). Nonetheless, the image of the woman figure that Hurston was captivated by, became rooted in her writing.

Hurston as a mother figure, according to Pryse "served as a kind of bridge for an imaginative matrilineage extending from the tradition of conjure to the lit-erary genius of Black women writers in the last two decades" (Dutton 1993: 148).

The second was Walker's literal call for Zora whilst searching for her grave in *Looking for Zora*. This shows that when we cannot find what we are searching for, we will call for those that we need, "Zora ... are you out here?... I'm here, are you? (Walker 1983: 403), and come they will. Walker's (1989) *The Temple of My Familiar* is also a significant source. Creating a woman who remembers living many life-times including experiencing the full horrors of slavery, is Lissie. All her previous lives are re-remembered and re-seen through photographs taken of her current self: "The selves I had thought gone forever, existed only in my memory, were still there! photographable" (Walker 1989: 92). Lissie remembers women teaching their traditions to their daughters. Lissie's consciousness is Black. Lissie's rein-carnations of the female persona as Goddess, is Hurston's Erzulie. Hurston trans-mutes Erzulie through the literary tradition developing between mother and daughters, which begets a concoction for Walker's, "womanist: 3. Loves music. Loves dance. Loves the moon. Loves the Spirit. Loves love and food and round-ness. Loves struggle. Loves the Folk. Loves herself. Regardless" (Walker 2006: 19).

This is one of the abilities of photography, transferable, transportable, exchangeable. Such power that these images have to actually see the past, but to stay true: it's up to you to see it, if you can, if you dare. Lissie's life story, written in invisible ink disappears when it has been read, so be quick, or learn another way?

I am a woman who conjures.
I can offer a vision of that which cannot be seen.
Like Douglass's revenant, a return from a social death, (Wexler 2012: 33), a task which the photograph performs, wilfully, now through me, created by a Black mother behind the camera.
I aid them to return.
I am a conjuring woman.

I now become a daughter who is poised to shatter the illusion that patriarchal white bodies created to soothe their troubled minds. As a photographer, I am poised to consider the past they wanted me to see. In showing me her past, my mother inducted me into the tradition of our family to be able to see the future. Most importantly, she reminded me that I knew how to travel through time and the camera was my transportation and preferred method of travel. Hers was her voice, she had the ability to poly-vocalise her soul, allowing the strands to stretch to and fro to the time they remembered, catapulting her there. My maternal grandmother's method of transfiguration was her names, shifting between them, to shift between worlds. My great-great maternal grandmother could simply walk to her chosen destination.

In continuing this story, I have to tell you how it started, knowing that the dream future becomes a utopian vision of Black life. I did not know how to get there. My mother taught me all of the histories that she had heard. Her body transmuted the information and like a child I gazed mesmerized at it, trying to discern what it actually was. As a reminder of my own history, being born in Britain to a mother who was born in Jamaica, I had to translate my mother's coded Black language. As I have said already, I was mesmerized by gazing on this Blackness that was more than beautiful and thereafter transfixed as I was, it became the object of my gaze.

Are you ready for the story?

We invent, reclaim, and appropriate those aspects used previously against our Black bodies, winning our survival by signifyin(g). Those words and phrases used once, twice, too many times to determine our Black bodies: you remember them, right? Partus Sequitur Ventrem, Matriarch, Jezebel, Mammy. In a sign of strength and love for who we are and have always been, we use the same terminology and apparatus you thought would destroy us.

The story

My mother's body and my own are presented to be read openly, publicly, and examined as if re-enacting the bodies transacted at a slave market. I am hoping that this image will allow you to remember. Here is where we declare our sovereignty and present our stories to be read, remembered and understood. With our bodies glistening and enjoying the feel of the diamonds that emerge from our skin as the sun shines, I hope you are listening and not looking at the value of our bodies. Remember the past but know that there are new ones waiting to be your past. We present your story, for we are here to provide you with another way of remembering and recovering: your history/ourselves.

I ask you to imagine that these bodies you see are not for sale but are vessels that elucidate a scene beyond memory, filling *your* space with information you needed to know. These bodies have a worth that devalues the labour of the historicized Black body, simply because these bodies appear and exist in a place where they are wanted. Having only travelled to places where the condition of their historicized Black bodies is not recognized—these bodies appear different, unaffected; imagine that! Conscribing to this body a showering of attention, admiration and awe, this magnificent vessel of a being, a Black woman, becomes time without time. She comprehends time and transforms time. In finding within herself an ability to navigate time, to hold and make visible on her body, her family: her body becomes more than a depository of memories. Her body archived you. It is a beautiful detailed treasured atlas, which glistens like a star-filled universe immersed and bathed in auroral moonlight. These memories of people and places past resurface after being bade and they wait: emerging then projecting themselves over and over on this body, shapeshifting, time-travelling, click, click, click. Capturing what they offer, what they need to tell, their bodies are a language they know you will soon learn to understand. The watcher who is not a witness, recreates and repeats all that it has seen and heard, mesmerized by the object of my gaze: a story is retold.

I have been repeating all along and I will keep on repeating my ancestors' echoes—gather them if you can, treasure them if you can. Having travelled to present themselves to you, you are offered a story; there within this poly-vocality you are told the story. All that my mother has remembered is revealed. She sings, she shows, and she hands you objects to know the passageway that was created to pass this information on. The vessel that reforms itself as a physical reckoning of being, you called for and this you named: a photo-graphic image.

It is this entity filled with reflections of dreams, words heard and steadied, floating where they were said, yet touching each other, reacting. In love they come together when not being gazed upon, hurrying when they feel the warmth of their image in your hands. Changing forms as quickly as dreams are made and lost in their own worlds that you create. Other beings enter, bringing colours to share and hide: they ask permission to create a story of what is, what was and what could never be again. This entity placed in this object is weighty, and through its scent, comes in contact with the skin that absorbs it, supports it. The t of t-------------i----------------m------------e------------ bends its head and curves its tail: tightening, reaching, merging, and in its place a scene emerges, right before your eyes—magic! Leaving in its wake, I, and Me.

This photograph is what could be kept when the vessels departed, continuing their journey: they left a passageway. The vessels continue their journey and must depart. The photographic image given to us is, in our present day, a glimpse of the past it has seen and ones you wanted to know. Piecing together the fragments, remembering their history and your own, the wall you placed the pictures on, the book you read them from tells a story. Each, changing sequence, configuring narratives of you and them replenishing your understanding of this body and your family. Each sequence changing as the narrative deepens and resurfaces, revealing something you had not remembered before, and not known until you tell their story through you. This is the story you tell yourself; this is the story you tell everyone else. This is the story my mother told me. This is the story I will tell my children, the possibility of breathing when the sun covers your face...will you follow my lead?

The Photographs

Photographs can be a performative link between the past and present, between ancestors and descendants. These photographs are able to conjure memories: produce a story already imagined and perhaps already told. This performative link is the important part to remember because depending on how YOU tell a story and how you construct your world, [it becomes] "culturally inscribed at a very profound level (Poignant, 1996: 10), but not forever, but for – ever for it all begins again.

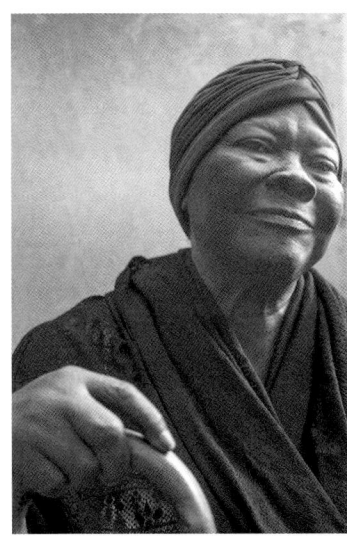

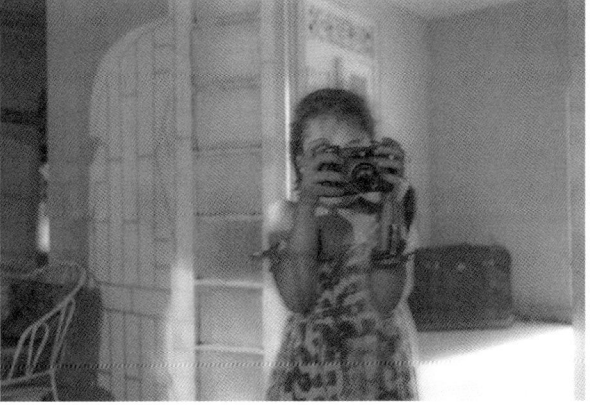

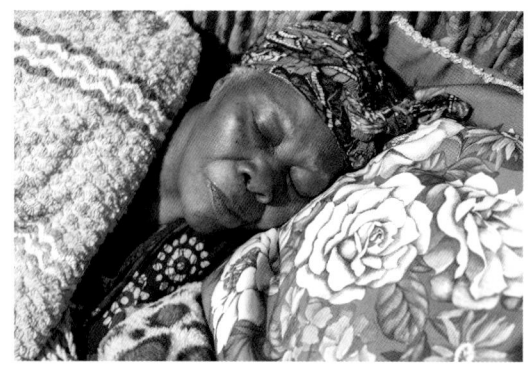

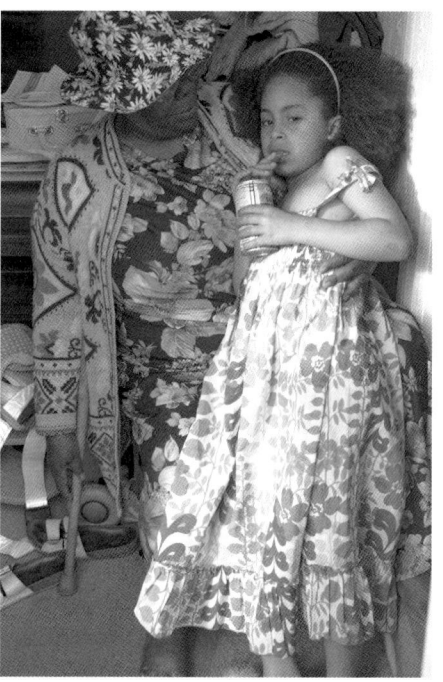

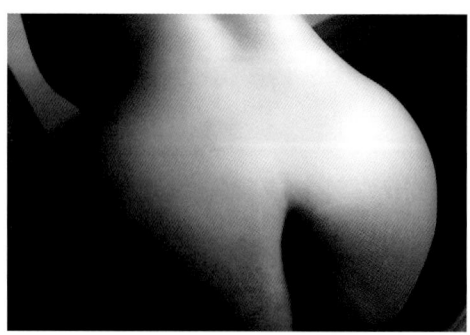

THE IMPOSSIBILITY OF BREATHING WHEN THE SUN COVERS YOUR FACE

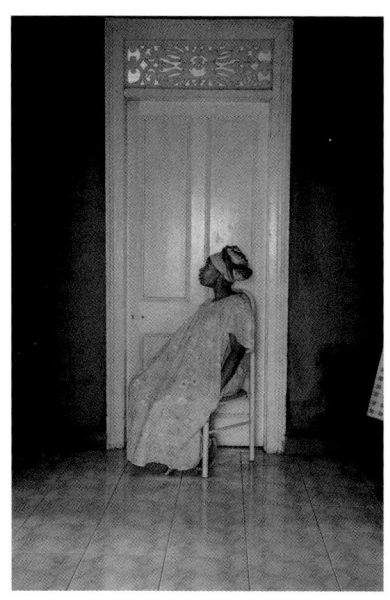

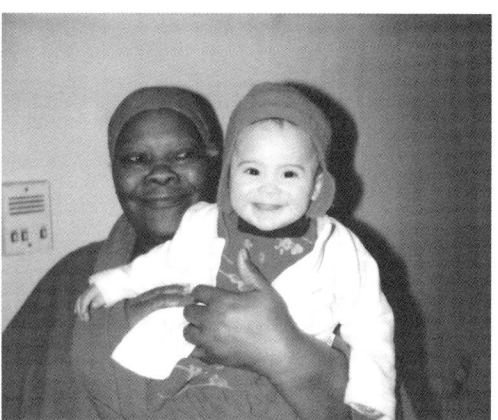

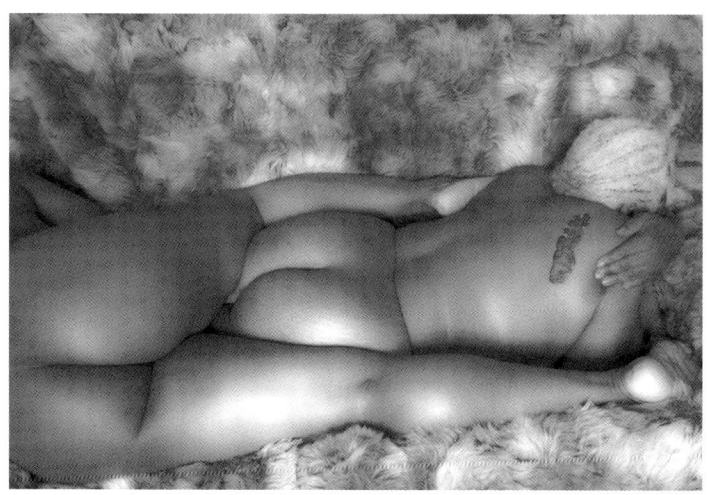

Always remember the one that sees first enough—the child, the photographer—to hold on to it for you—mothers. "I didn't want these pictures to go to just anybody. They're special and I wanted to give them only to someone who understands" (Walker 1989: 89).

You.

Works cited

Dubey, M. (1995). "Gayl Jones and the Matrilineal Metaphor of Tradition." Signs, *Journal of Women in Culture and Society*, 20, (2): 245–267.

Jones, G. (1975). *Corregidora*. New York: Random.

Gallop, J. (1992). *Around 1981: Academic Feminist Literary Theory*. New York: Routledge.

Hurston, Z, N. (1990). *Tell my horse: Voodoo and Life in Haiti and Jamaica*. New York: Perennial Library.

Michael, M. (2020). [forthcoming] *My History is in Her(e)*. London

Morrison, T. (1984). "Rootedness: The Ancestor as Foundation." In *Black Women writers (1950-1980): A Critical Evaluation*, edited by M. Evans. Garden City, NY: Anchor Press/ Doubleday.

—— (1987). *Beloved*. New York: Albert A. Knopf.

Poignant, R. (1996). *Encounter at Nagalarramba*. Canberra: National Library of Australia.

Pryse, M. and H. Spillers (1985). *Conjuring*. Bloomington, Ind.: Indiana University.

Walker, A. (1983). *In Search of Our Mothers Gardens*. USA: Harcourt Brace Jovanovich.

—— (1983). "Womanist." In *The Womanist Reader* (2006), edited by L. Phillips. Taylor and Francis New York, NY.

—— (1989). *The Temple of My Familiar*. Harcourt Brace Jovanovich.

Wexler, L. (2012). "A More Perfect Likeness: Fredrick Douglas and the image of the nation." In *Picture and Progress: Early Photography and the Making of African American*, edited by Wallace, M, O. and Smith, S, M., 18–40. Durham, NC: Duke University Press.

PART FIVE

"THE ASSERTION OF THE LIFEFORCE"*: A SELECTION OF WORKS CURATED BY WOMEN PICTURING REVOLUTION

Nydia Blas, Samantha Box, Andrea Chung, Nona Faustine,
Adama Delphine Fawundu, vanessa german, Ayana V. Jackson,
Lebohang Kganye, Deana Lawson, Qiana Mestrich, Marcia Michael,
Wangechi Mutu, Keisha Scarville, Mickalene Thomas, Mary Sibande

* Lorde, Audre. *Uses of the Erotic: the Erotic as Power*. Freedom, Calif.: Crossing Press, 1978.

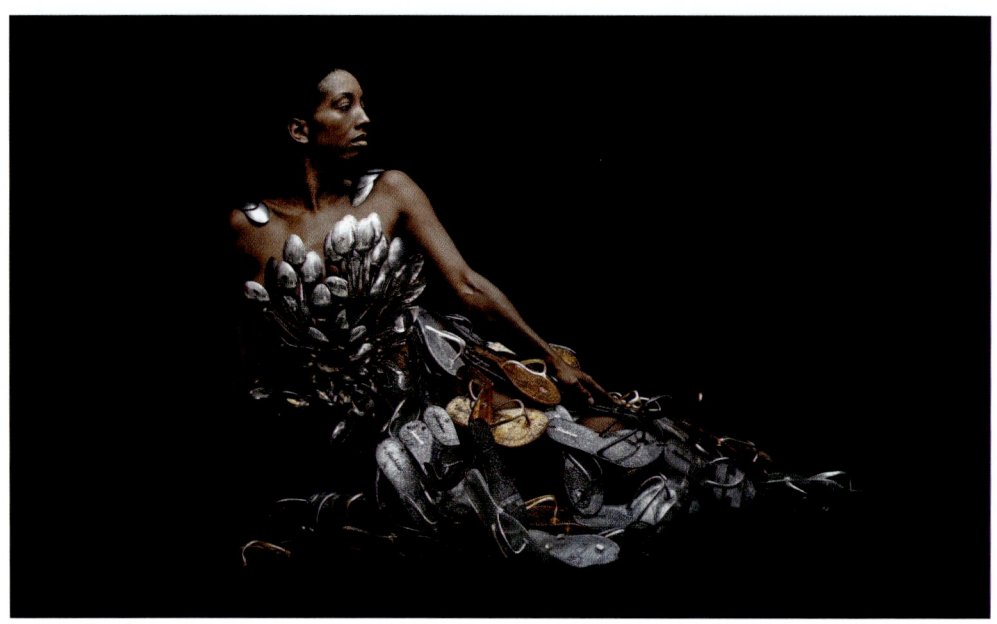

Ayana V. Jackson, *The Rupture Was Her Story*, 2019

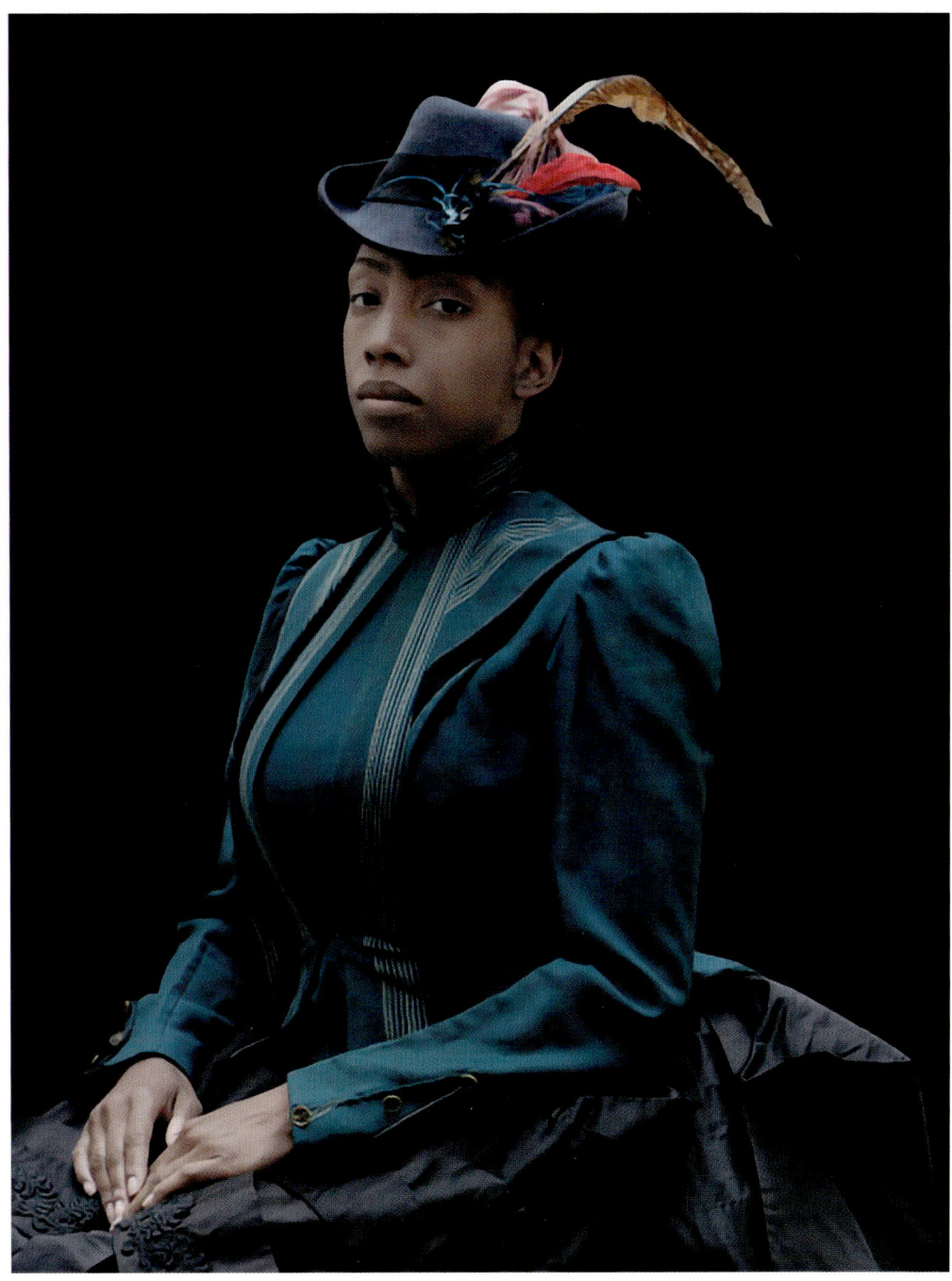

Ayana V. Jackson, *Godo*, 2016

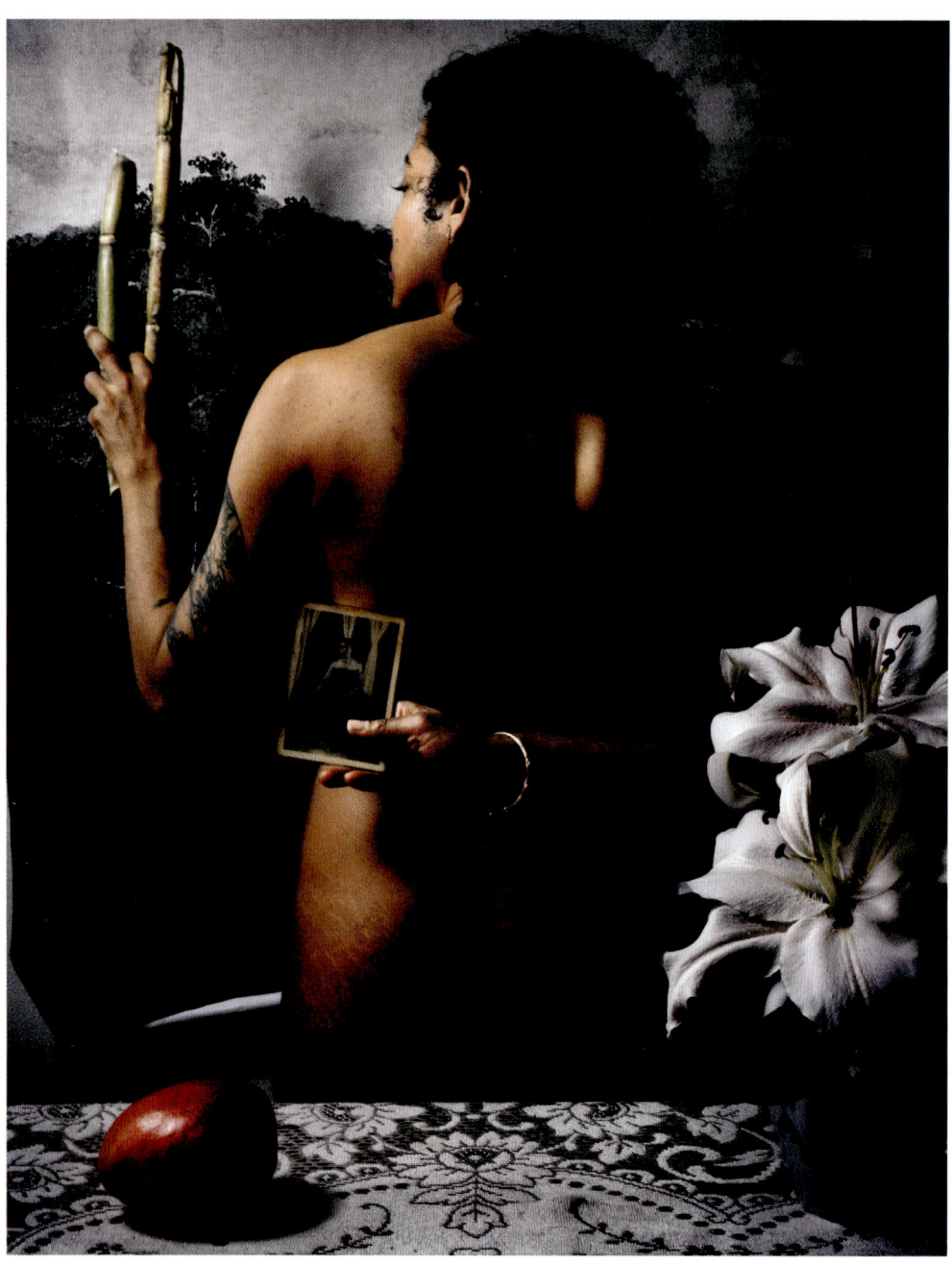

Samantha Box, *Caribbean Dreams,* 2019

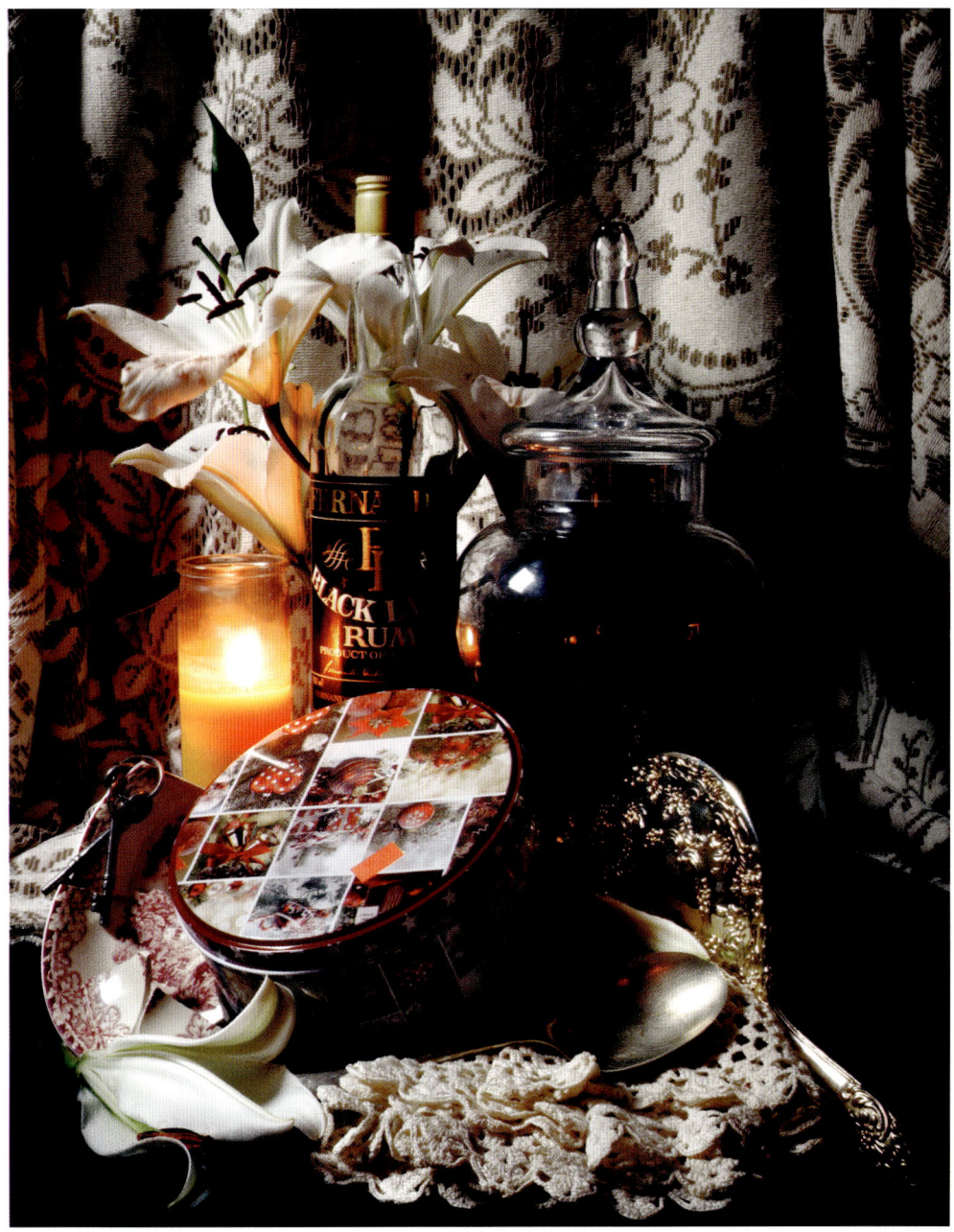

Samantha Box, *Caribbean Dreams*, 2019

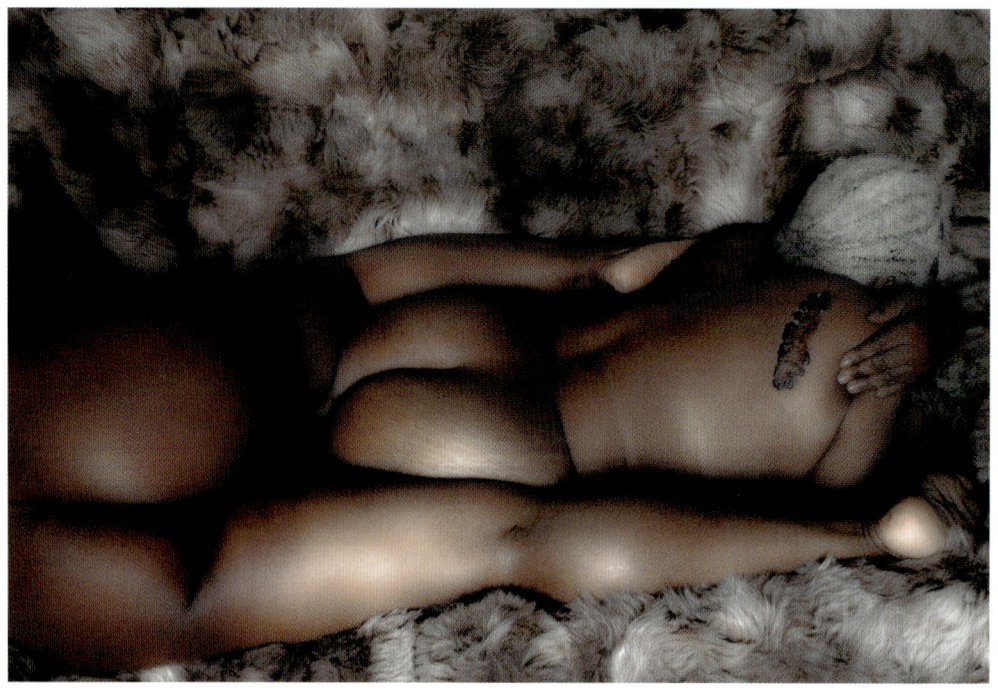

Marcia Michael, *Partus Sequitur Ventrem* from the series The Object of My Gaze (2015-ongoing)

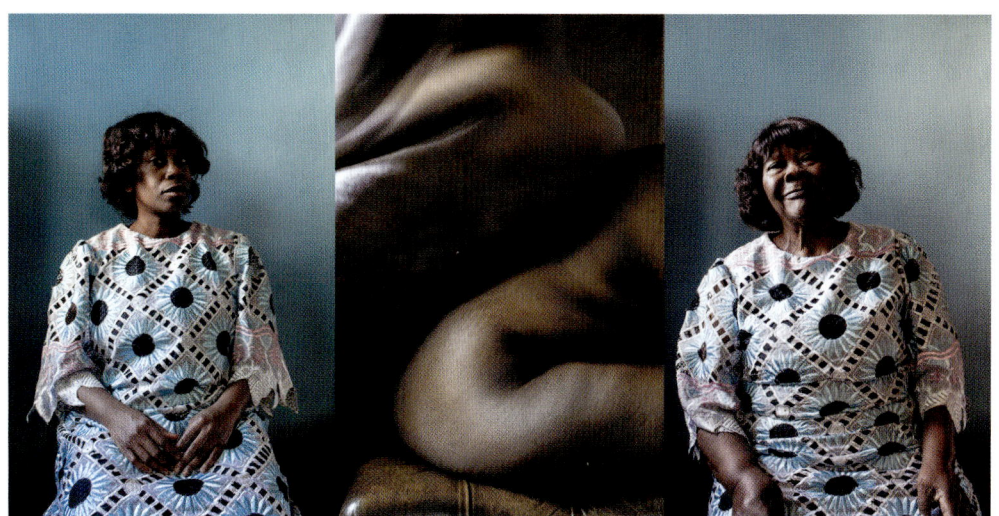

Marcia Michael, *Partus Sequitur Ventrem* from the series The Object of My Gaze (2015-ongoing)

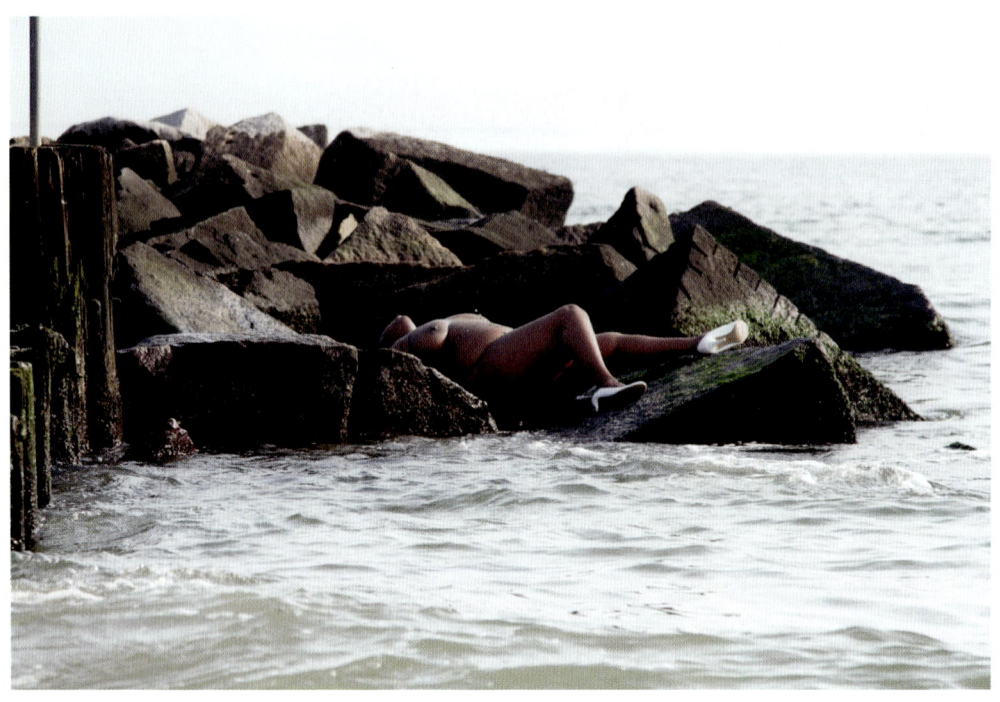

Nona Faustine, *Like a Pregnant Corse the Ship Expelled Her Into the Patriarchy*, Atlantic Coast Brooklyn, 2012

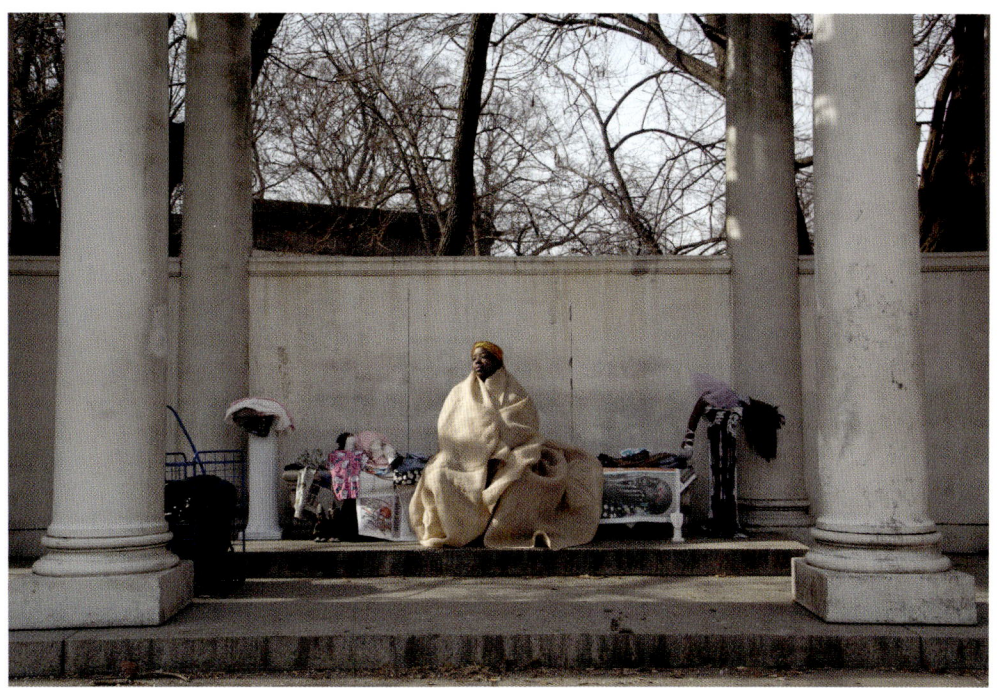

Nona Faustine, *Demeter's Morning*, 2019

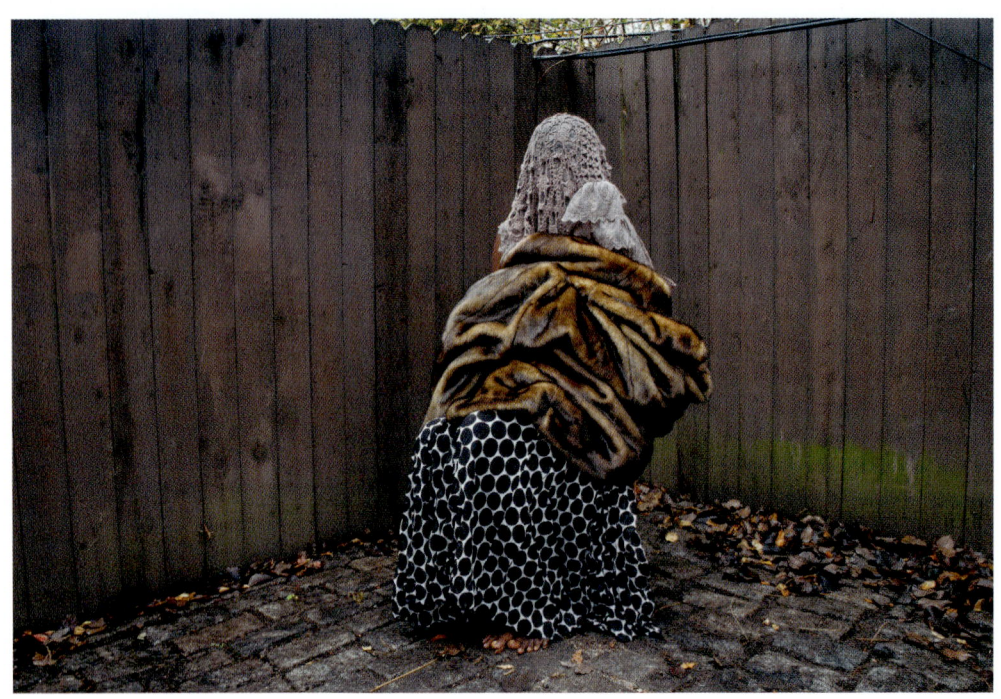

Keisha Scarville, *Mama's Clothes*, 2020

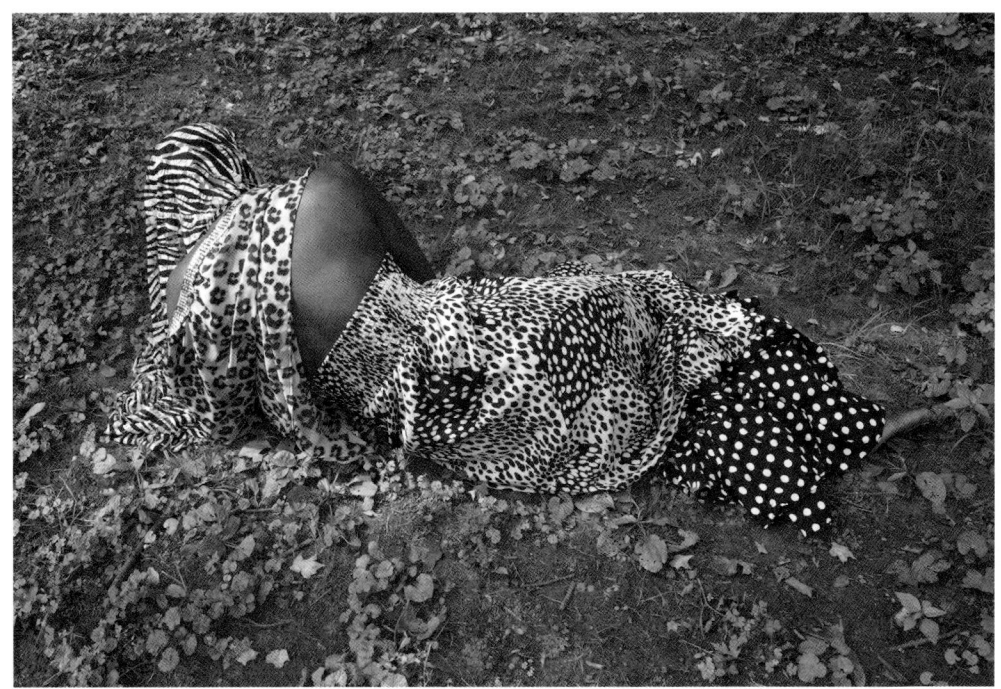

Keisha Scarville, *Mama's Clothes*, 2020

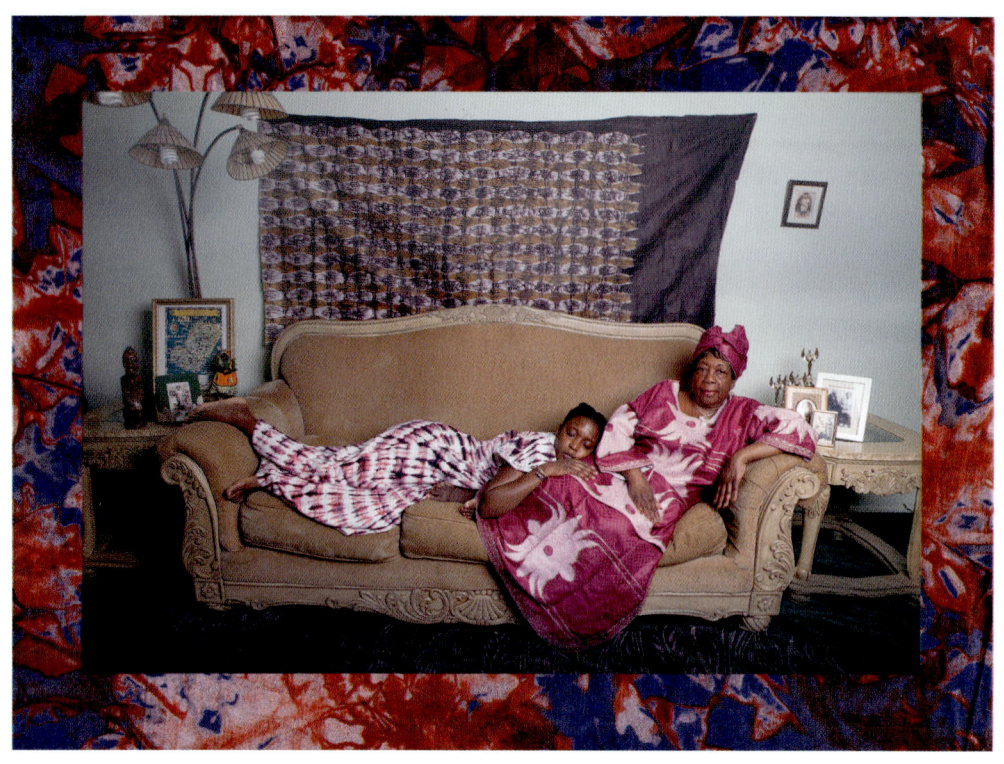

Adama Delphine Fawundu, *Passageways #2, Secrets, Traditions, Spoken and Unspoken Truths or Not*, 2017

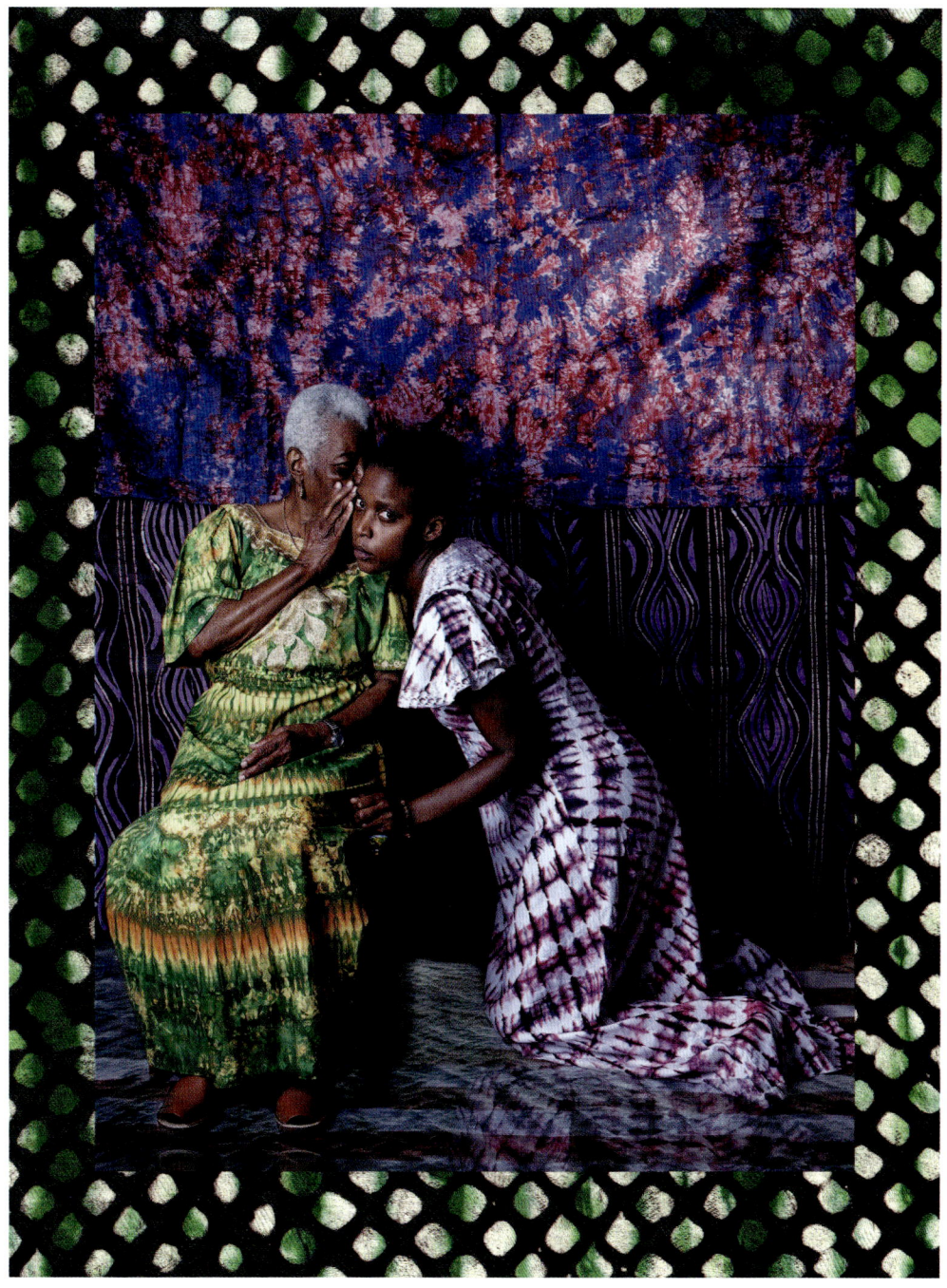

Adama Delphine Fawundu, *Passageways #1, Secrets, Traditions, Spoken and Unspoken Truths or Not*, 2017

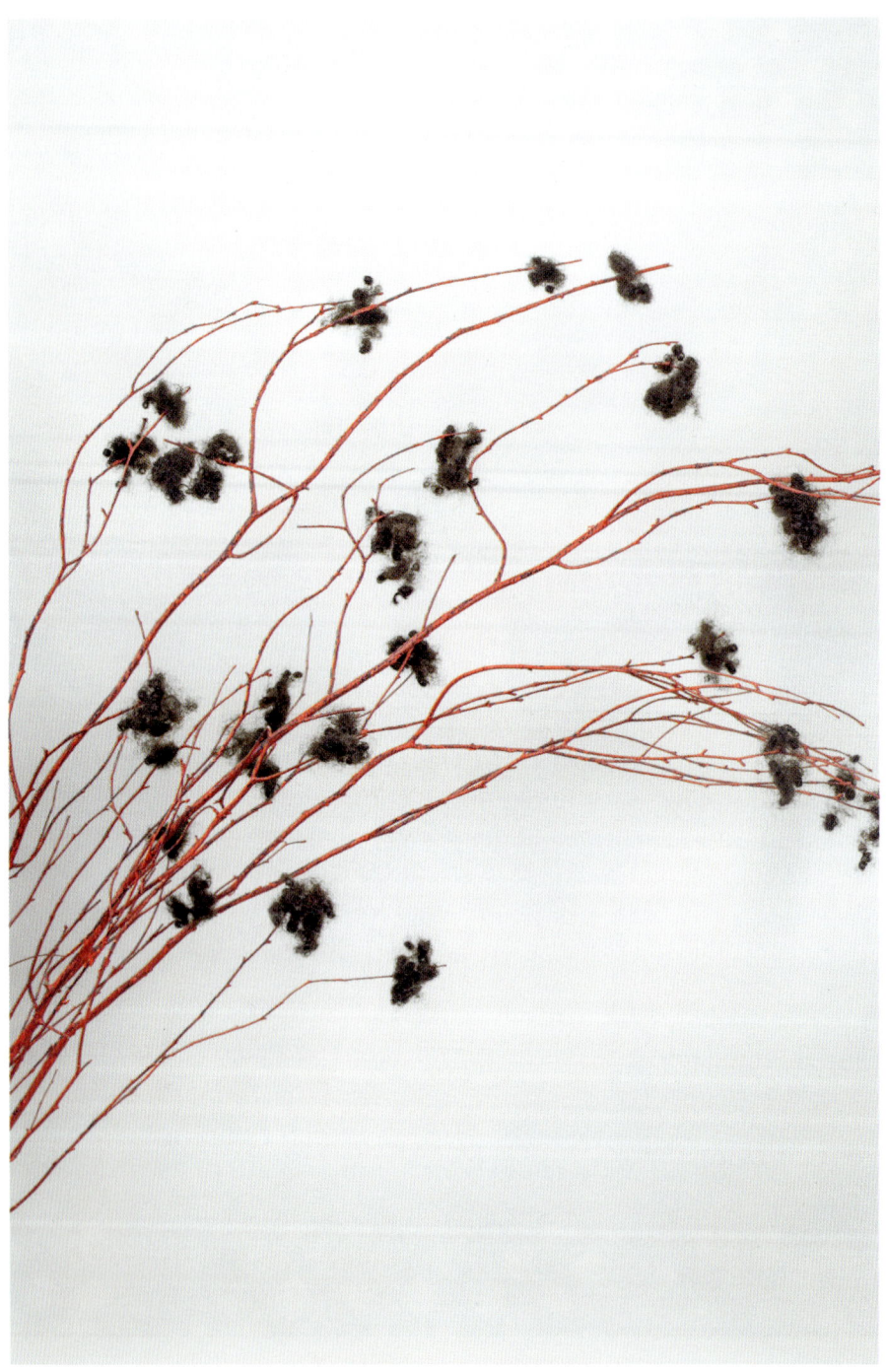

Qiana Mestrich, *Strange Bush,* from the *Thrall* series (2017-2020)

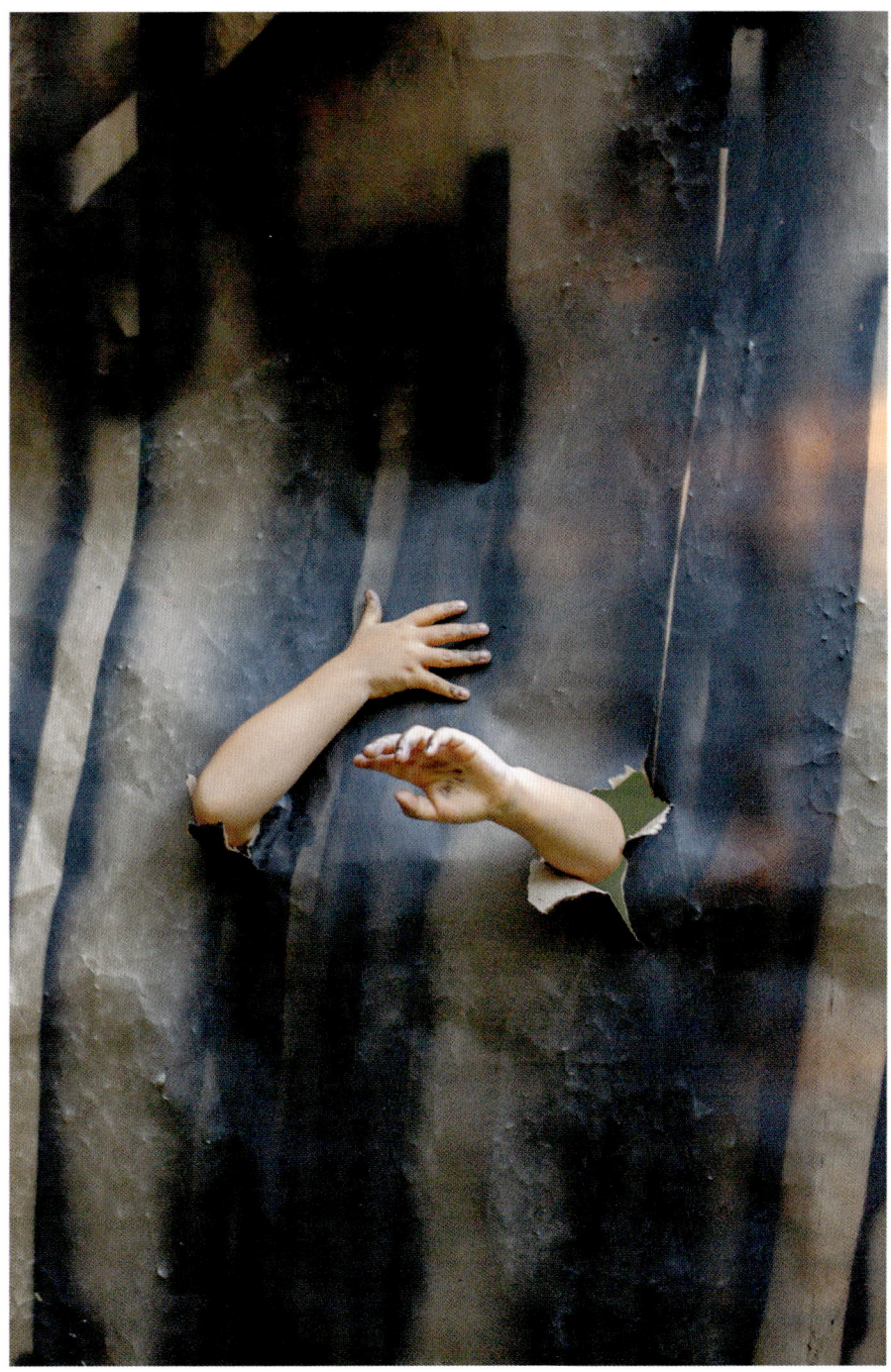

Qiana Mestrich, *The Embrace* from the *Thrall* series (2017-2020)

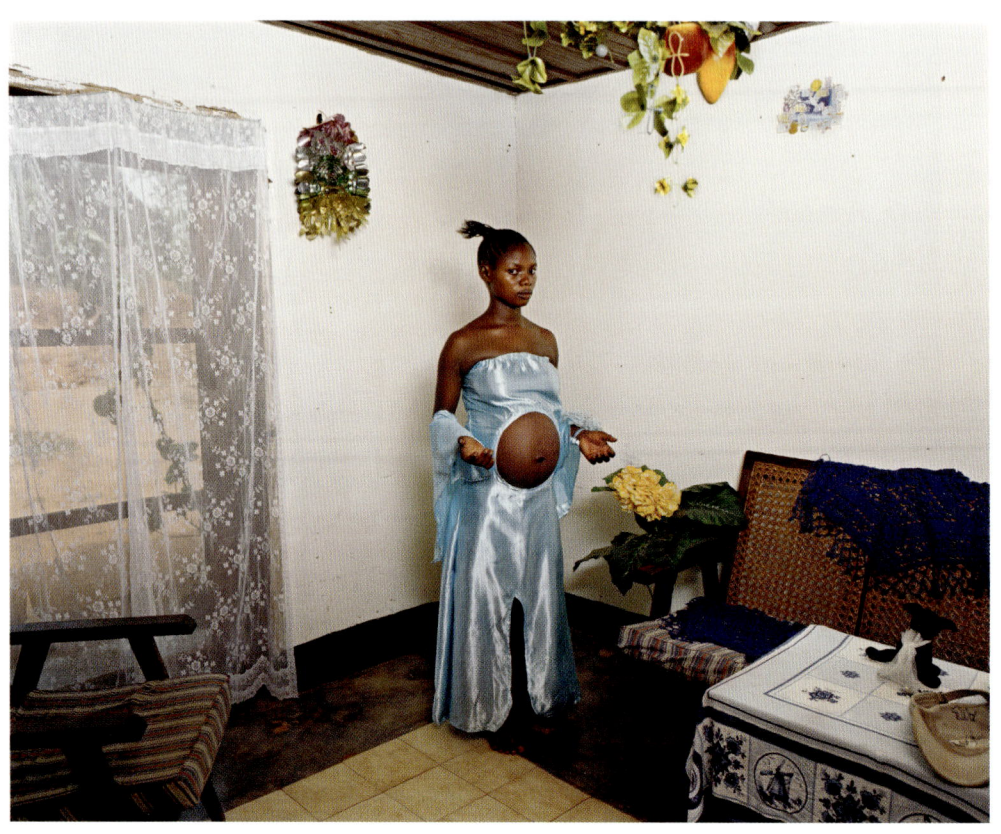

Deana Lawson, *Mama Goma, Gemena, DR Congo,* 2014

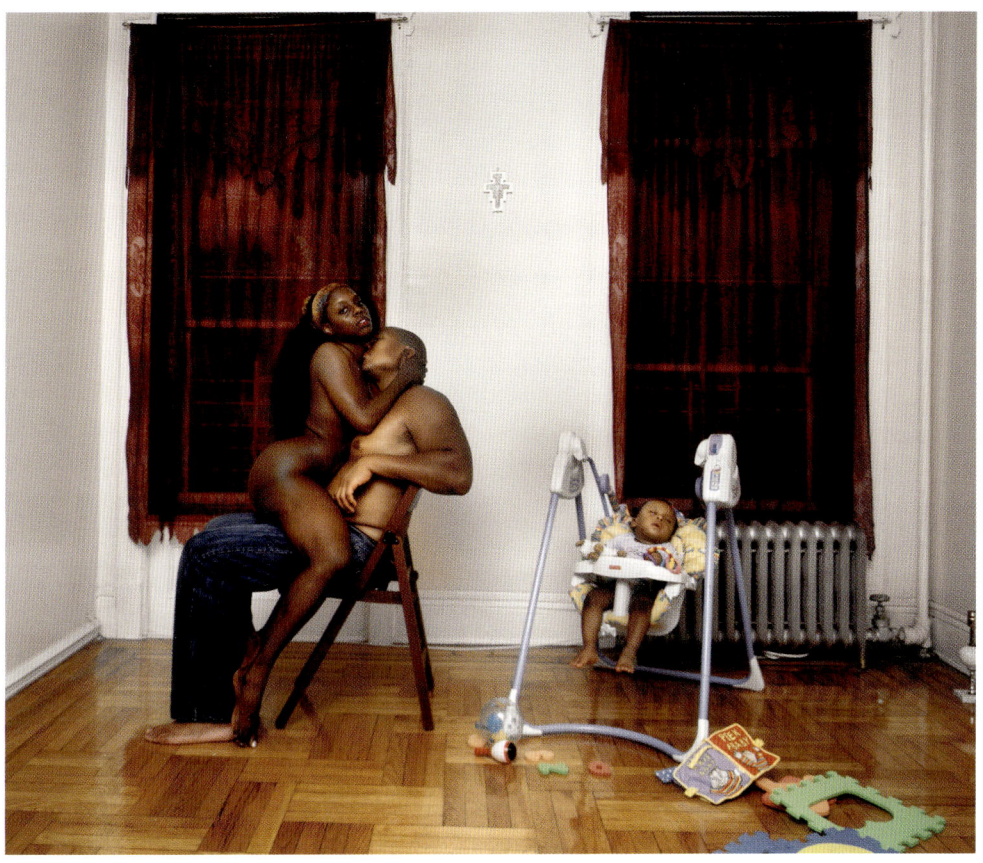

Deana Lawson, *Baby Sleep*, 2009

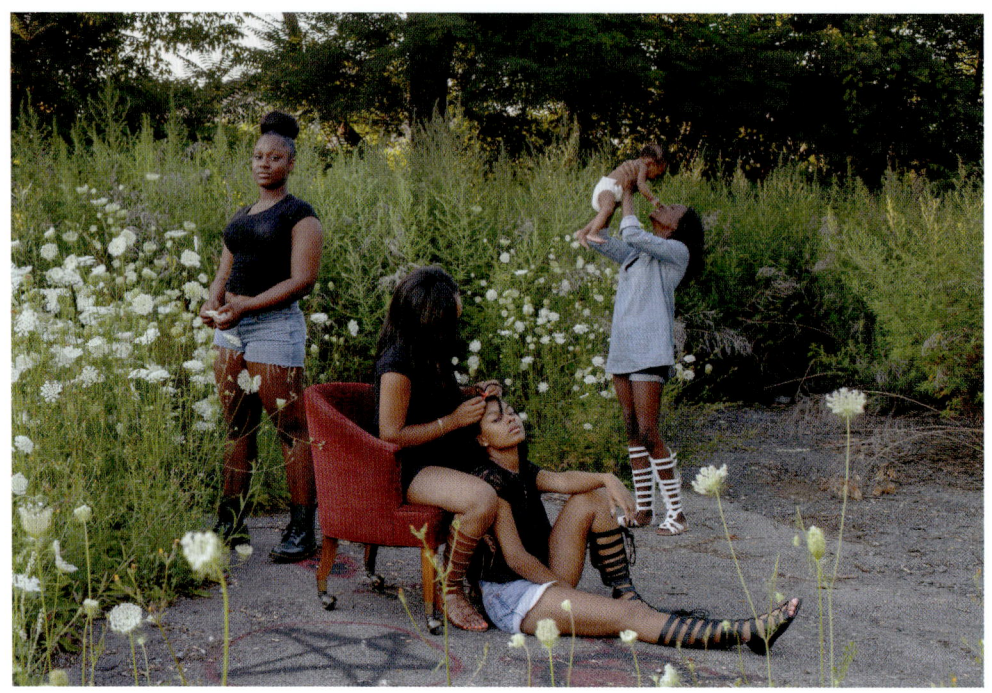

Nydia Blas, from *The Girls Who Spun Gold*, 2016

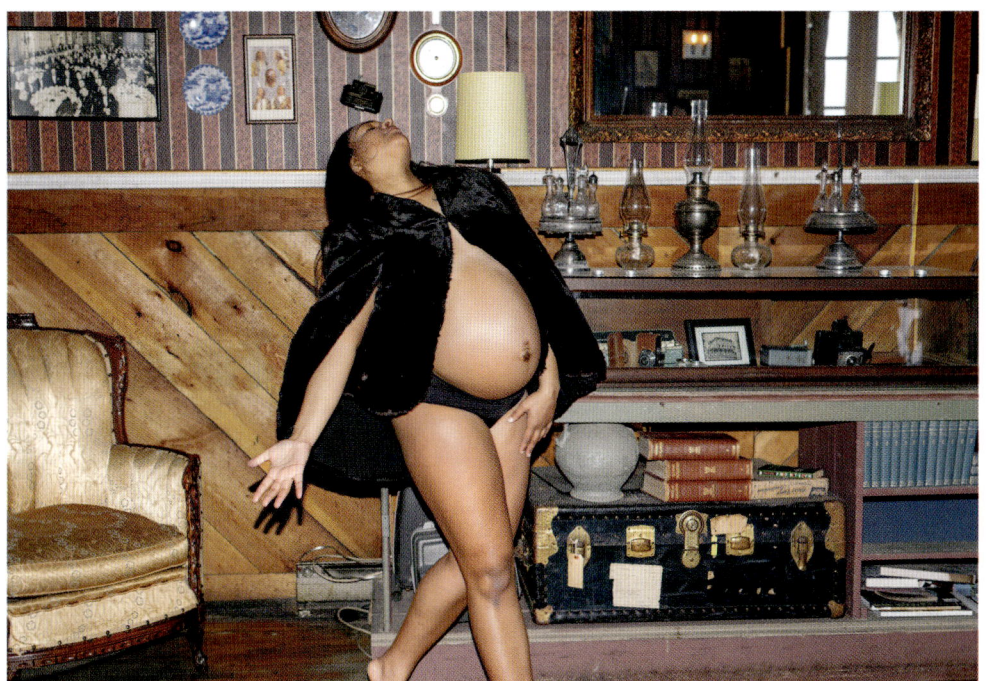

Nydia Blas, *Untitled, Revival*, 2019

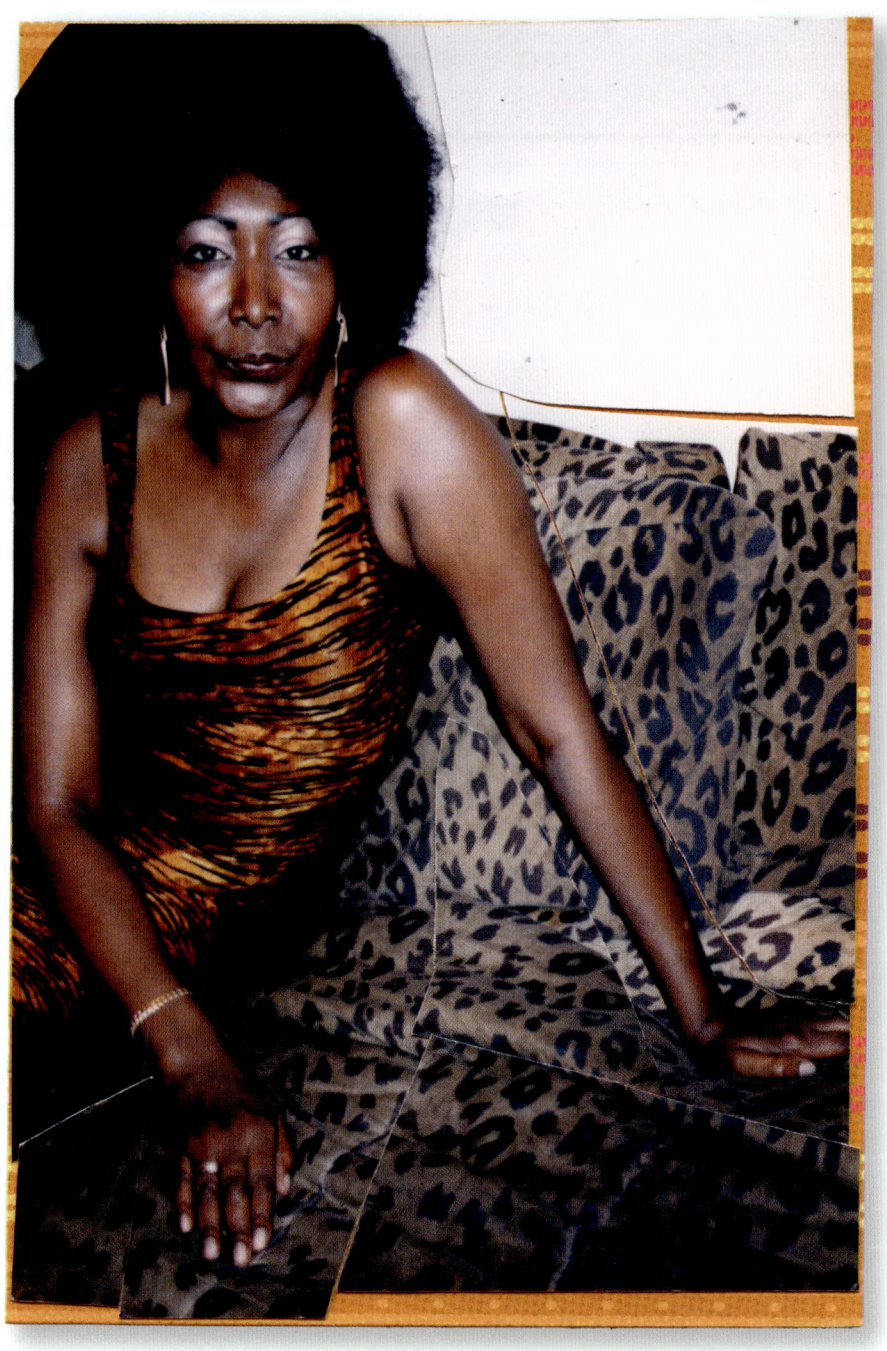

Mickalene Thomas, *Mama Bush: I'm Waiting Baby*, 2010

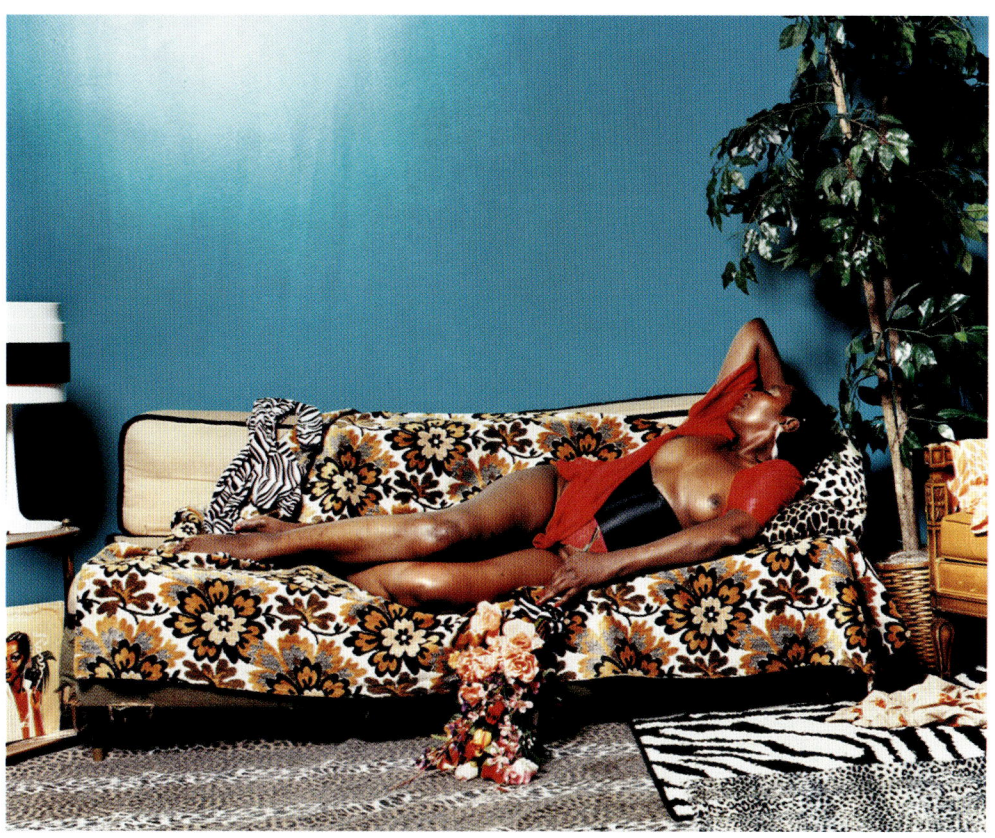

Mickalene Thomas, *Madame Mama Bush*, 2006

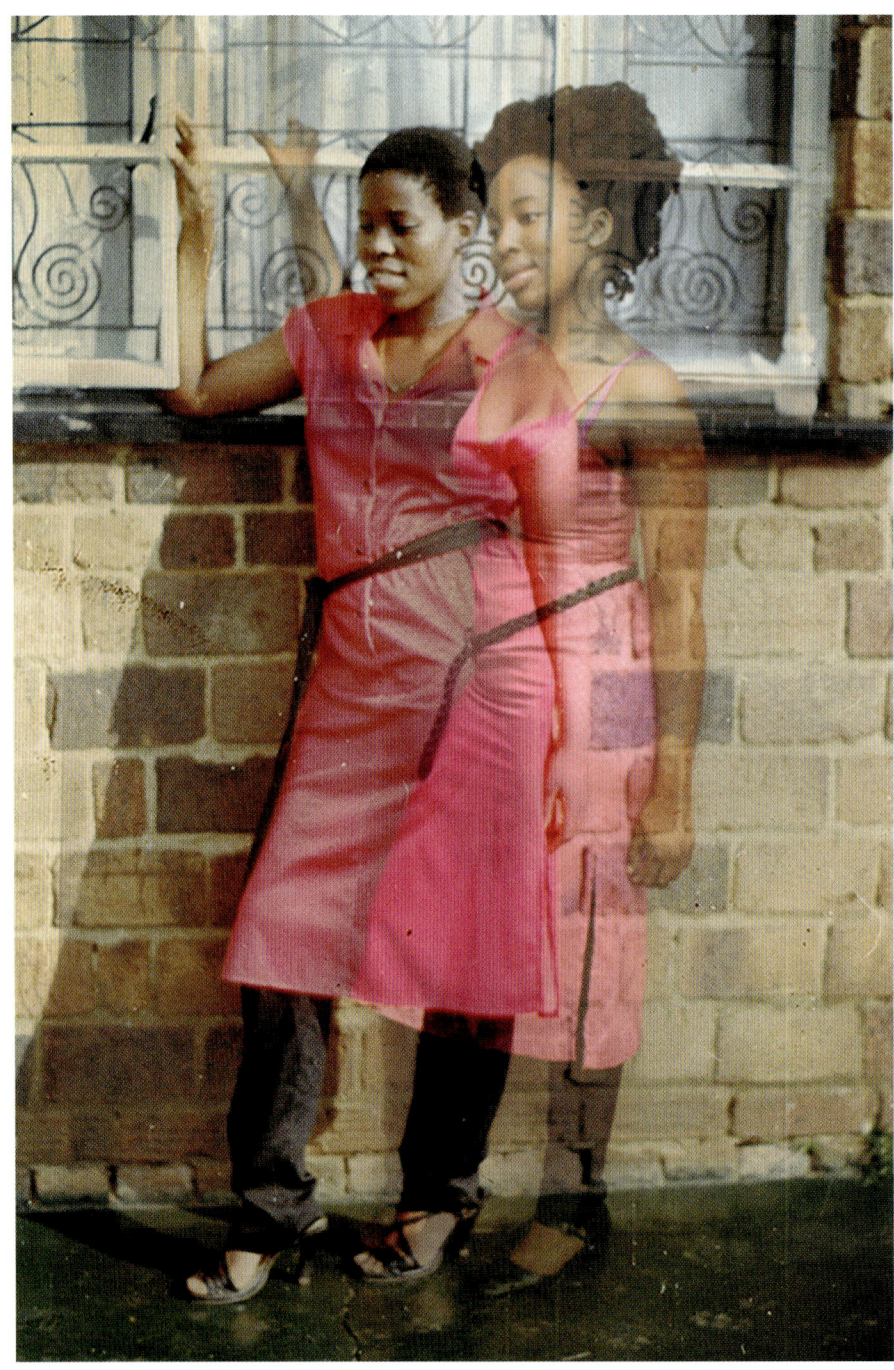

Lebohang Kganye, *Setupung sa kwana hae I,* 2013

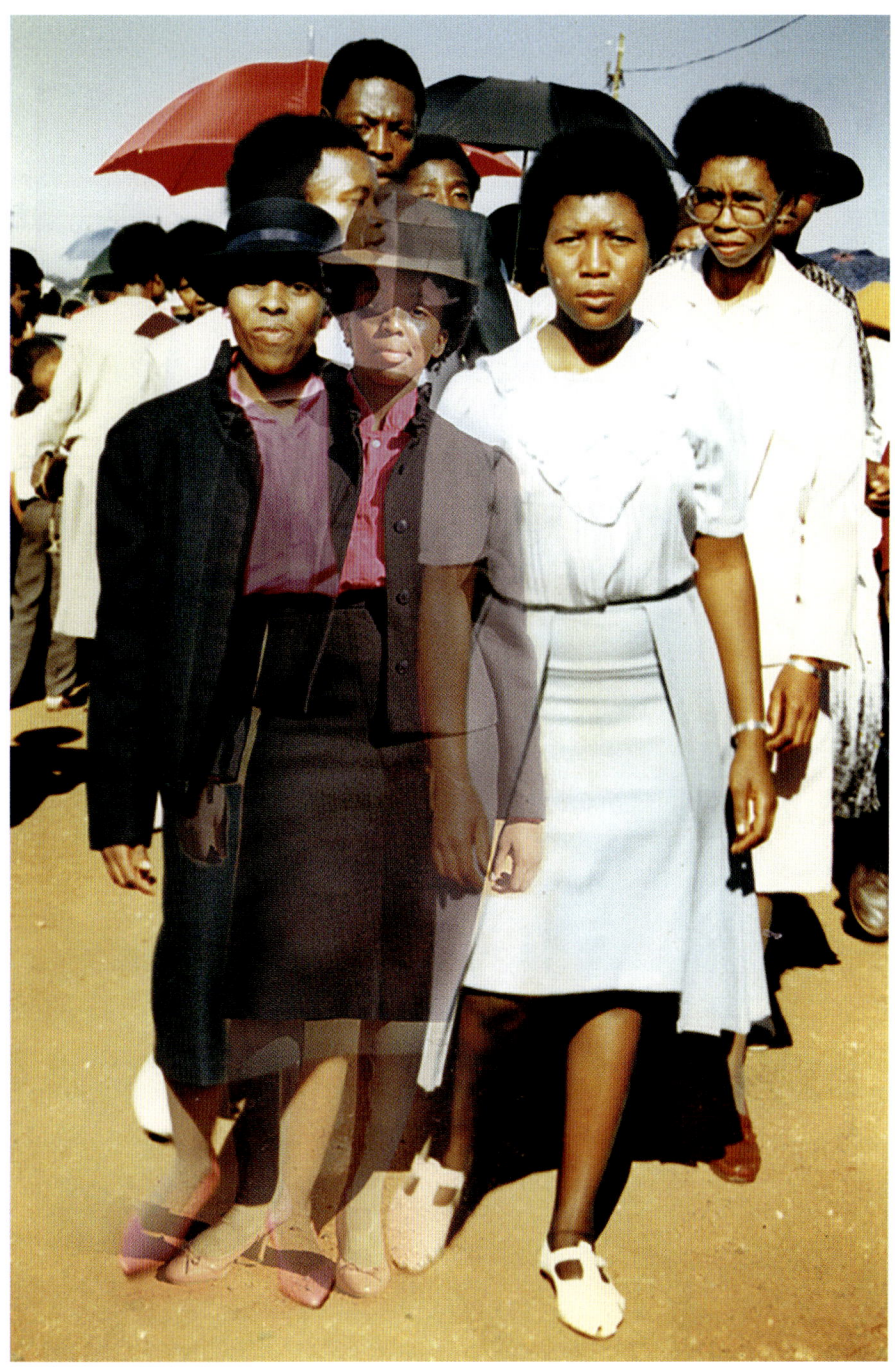

Lebohang Kganye, *Re Shapa Setepe sa Lenyalo II*, 2013

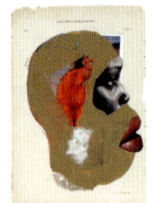 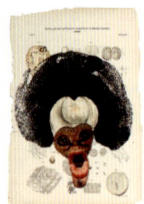 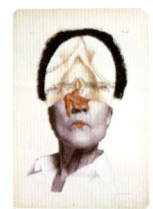 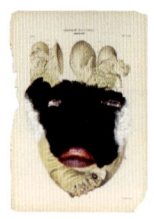 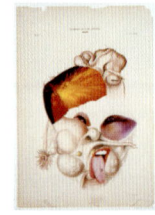 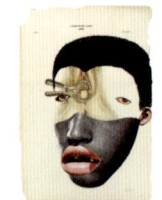

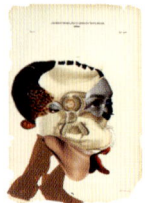 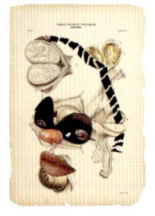 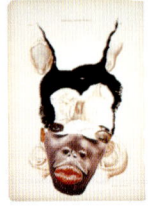 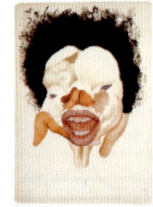 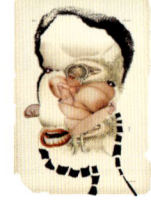 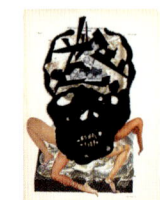

Wangechi Mutu, *Histology of the Different Classes of Uterine Tumors*, 2006

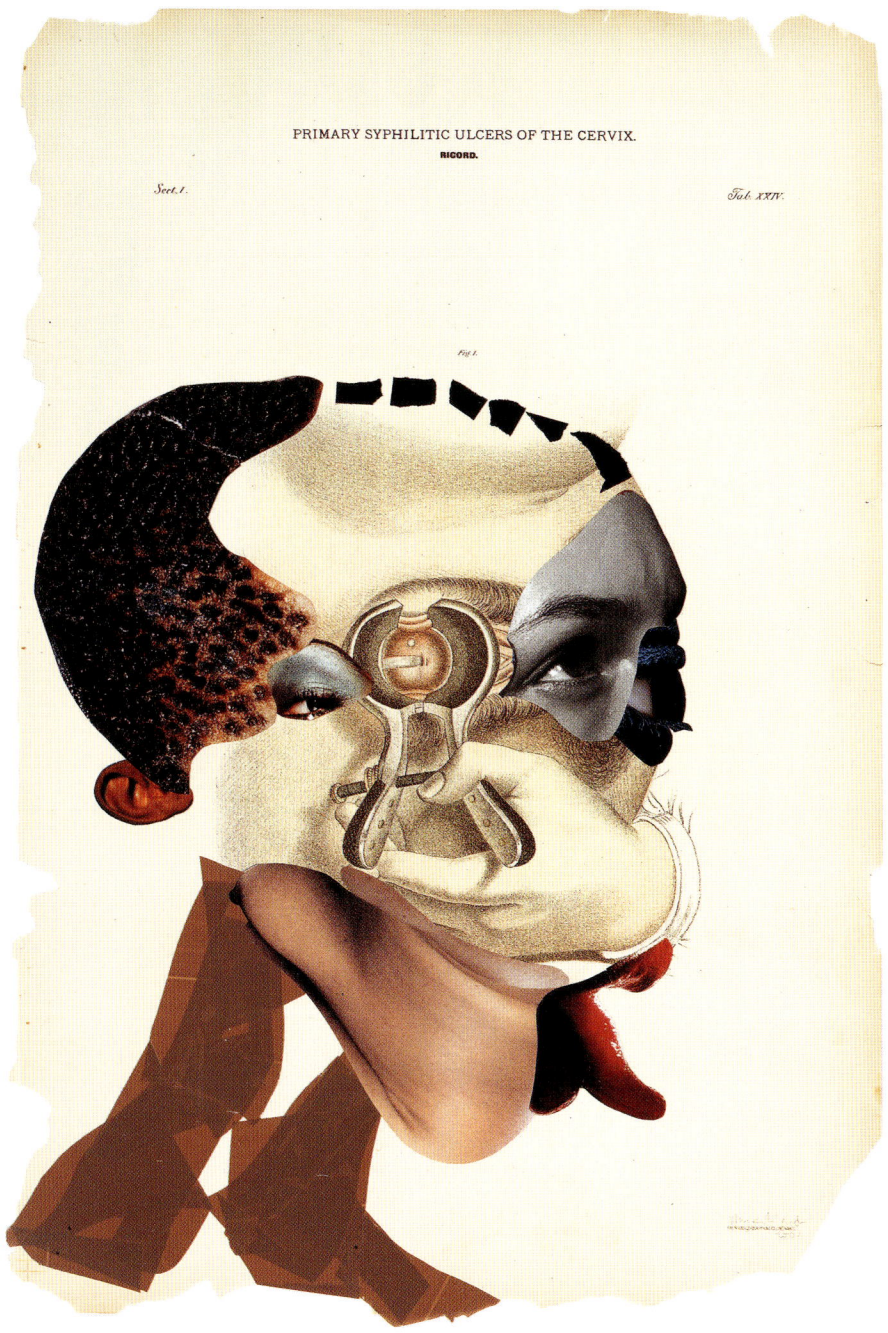

Wangechi Mutu, *Histology of the Different Classes of Uterine Tumors*, 2006, (detail)

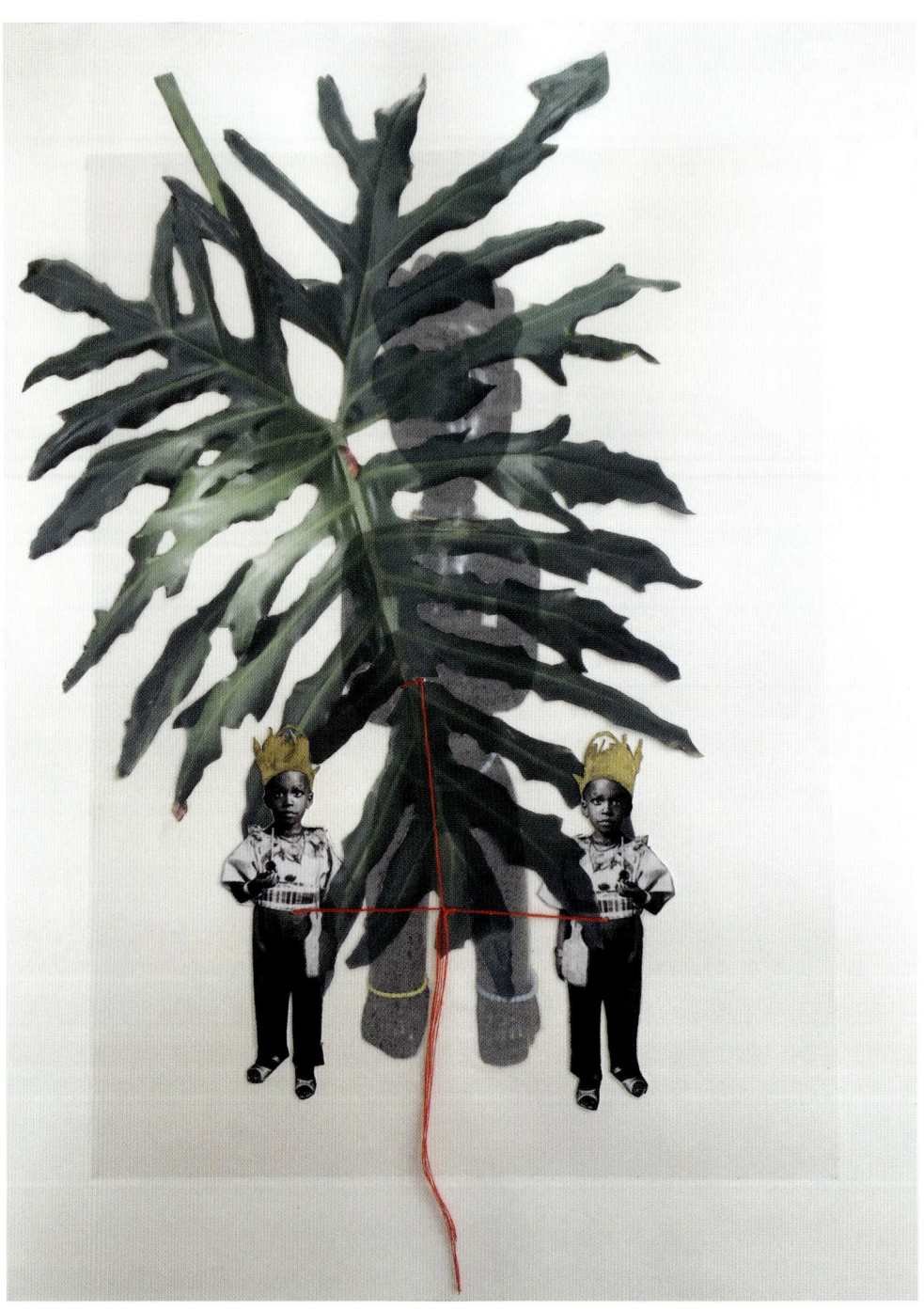

Andrea Chung, *Midwives II*, 2017

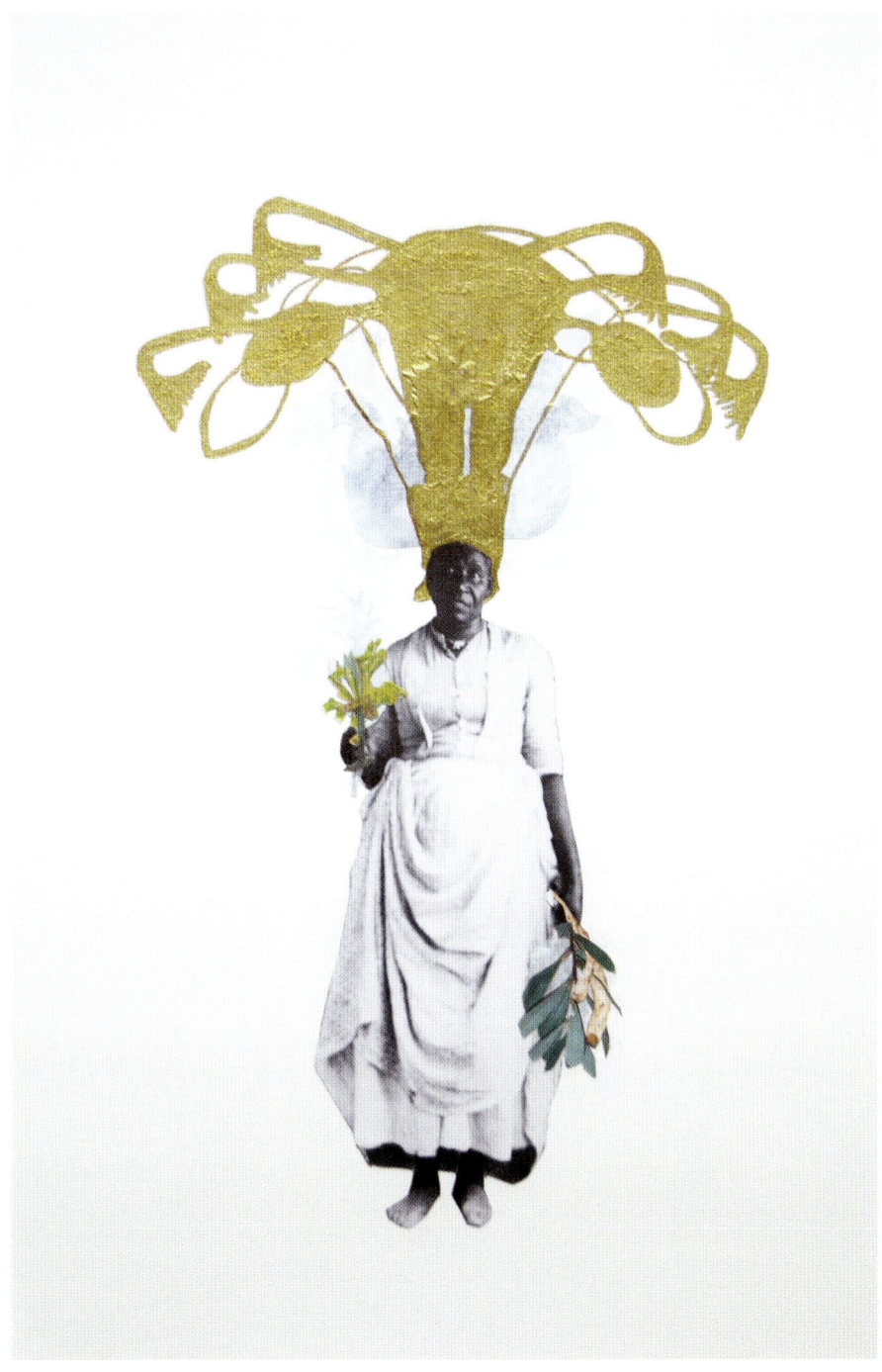

Andrea Chung, *Crowning I*, 2014

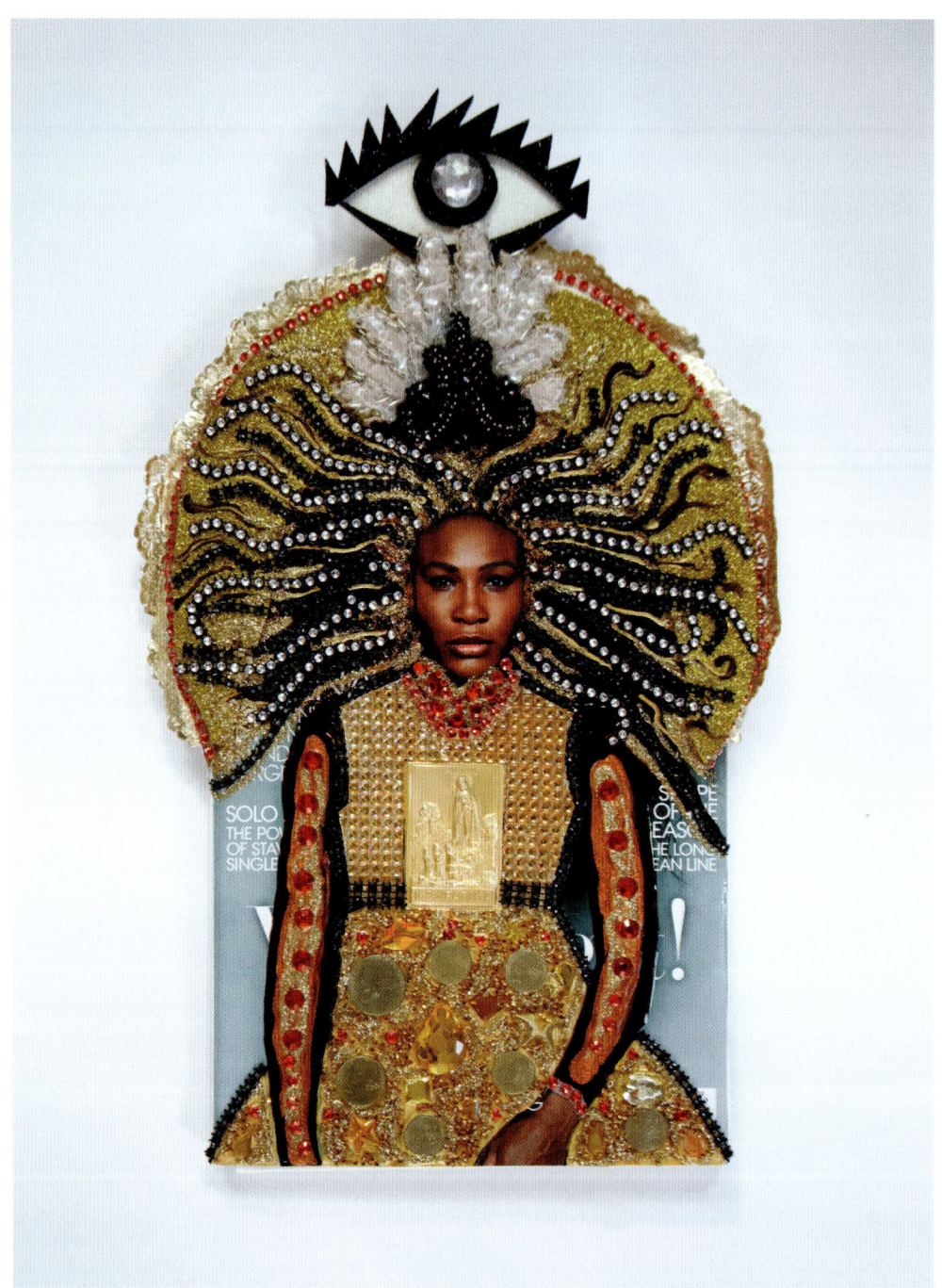

vanessa german, *Serena as Black Madonna #2*, 2015

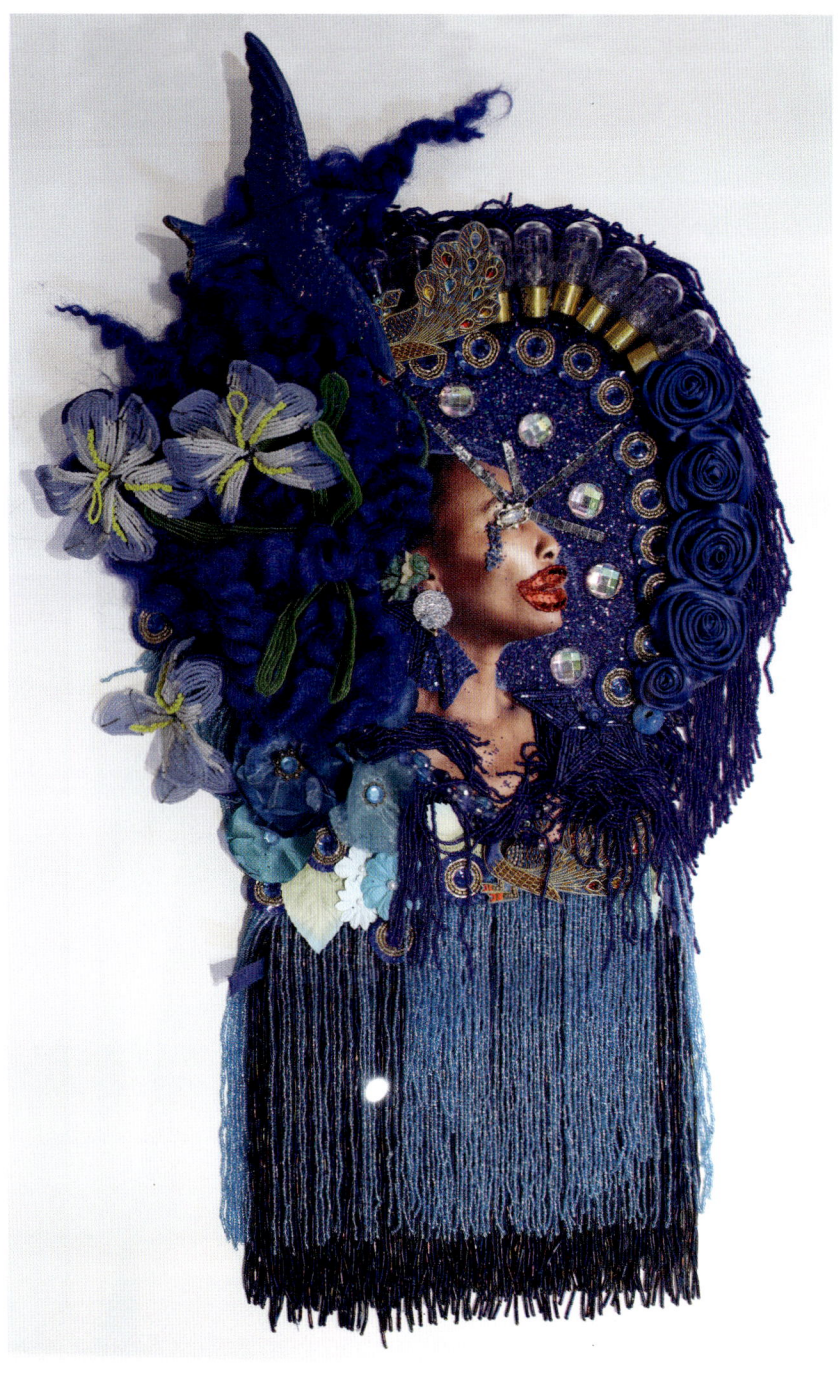

vanessa german, *(That the Healing come complete; That we no longer have to drag the trauma from body to body.)*, 2019

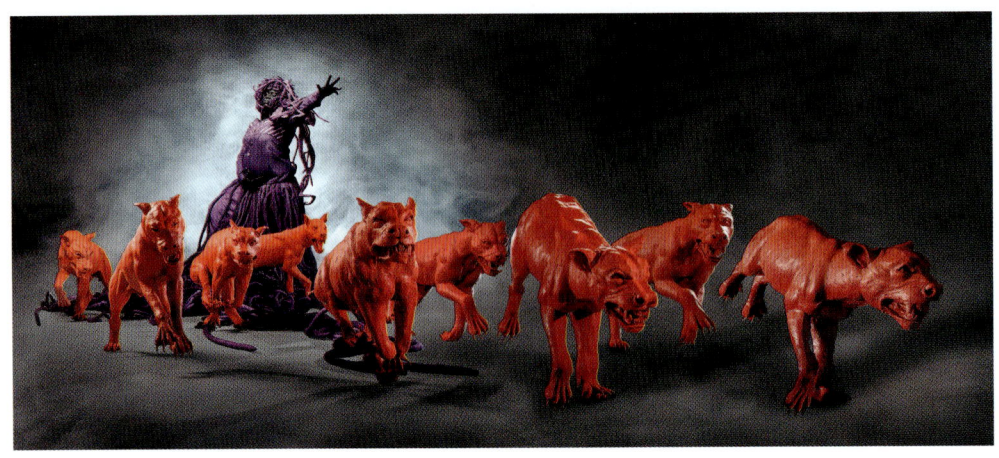

Mary Sibande, *The Purple Shall Govern,* 2013

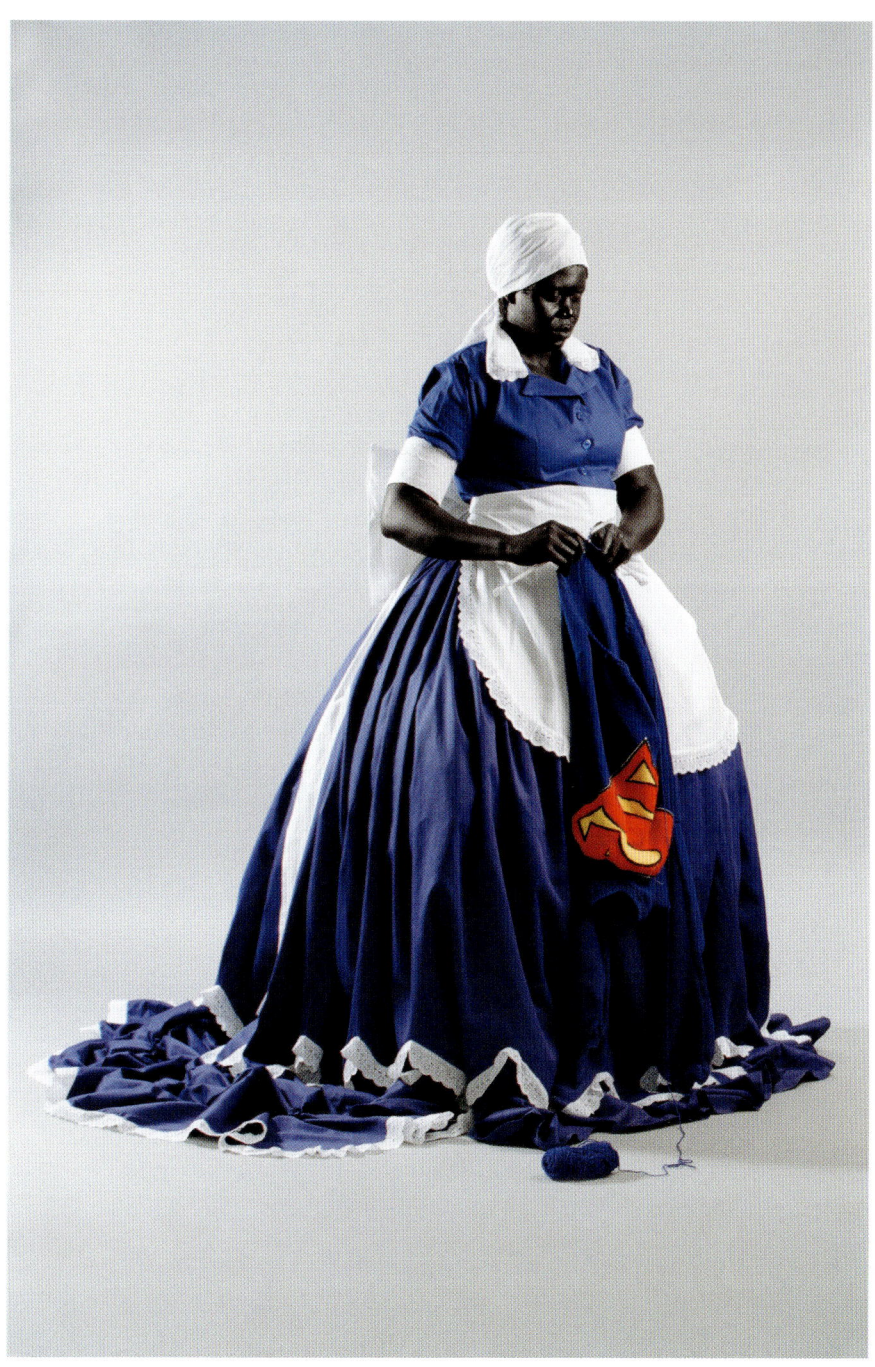

Mary Sibande, *They Don't Make Them Like They Used To*, 2008

IMAGE LIST

Fig 1. Ayana V. Jackson, *The Rupture Was Her Story*, 2019, archival pigment print on German etching paper, 25 5/8 x 42 7/8 in, 65 x 109 cm, edition of 8 plus 3 artist's proofs, courtesy of the artist and Mariane Ibrahim

Fig 2. Ayana V. Jackson, *Gede*, 2016, 51 1/8 x 39 3/8 in, 130 x 100 cm, edition of 8 plus 3 artist's proofs, courtesy of the artist and Mariane Ibrahim

Fig 3. Samantha Box, *Caribbean Dreams,* 2020, 11x14 inches, courtesy of the artist, archival inkjet print, courtesy of the artist

Fig. 4. Samantha Box, *Caribbean Dreams,* 2020, 32x40 inches, archival inkjet print, courtesy of the artist

Fig. 5. Marcia Michael, *Partus Sequitur Ventrem* from the series The Object of My Gaze (2015-ongoing), courtesy of the artist

Fig. 6. Marcia Michael, *Partus Sequitur Ventrem* from the series The Object of My Gaze (2015-ongoing), courtesy of the artist

Fig. 7 Nona Faustine, *Like a Pregnant Corse the Ship Expelled Her Into the Patriarchy*, Atlantic Coast Brooklyn, 2012, courtesy of the artist

Fig. 8 Nona Faustine, *Demeter's Morning*, 2019, courtesy of the artist

Fig 9. Keisha Scarville, *Mama's Clothes*, 2020, courtesy of the artist

Fig 10. Keisha Scarville, *Mama's Clothes*, 2020, courtesy of the artist

Fig. 11. Adama Delphine Fawundu, *Passageways #2, Secrets, Traditions, Spoken and Unspoken Truths or Not*, 2017, courtesy of the artist

Fig 12. Adama Delphine Fawundu, *Passageways #1, Secrets, Traditions, Spoken and Unspoken Truths Not,* 2017, courtesy of the artist

Fig. 13. Qiana Mestrich, *Strange Bush,* from the *THRALL* series (2017 -2020), courtesy of the artist

Fig. 14. Qiana Mestrich, *Not Coming Back Whole* from the *THRALL* series (2017 -2020), courtesy of the artist

Fig 15. Deana Lawson, *Mama Goma*, Artwork © Deana Lawson, courtesy of Sikkema Jenkins & Co., New York

Fig. 16. Deana Lawson, *Baby Sleep*, 2009, Artwork © Deana Lawson, courtesy of Sikkema Jenkins & Co., New York

Fig. 17. Nydia Blas, from *The Girls Who Spun Gold*, 2016, courtesy of the artist

Fig. 18. Nydia Blas, *Untitled, Revival*, 2019, courtesy of the artist

Fig. 19. Mickalene Thomas, *Mama Bush: I'm Waiting Baby*, 2010, Color photograph and paper collage on archival board, 6 x 4 inches, all images are © Mickalene Thomas

Fig. 20. Mickalene Thomas, *Madame Mama Bush*, 2006, Chromogenic Print, 16 x 20 inches, all images are © Mickalene Thomas

Fig. 21. Lebohang Kganye, *Setupung sa kwana hae I*, 2012, 2013, 17.91 x 12.09 cm, photographic inkjet print on cotton rag paper, courtesy of the artist

Fig. 22. Lebohang Kganye, *Re Shapa Setepe sa Lenyalo II*, 2013, 28.07 x 18.92 cm, photographic inkjet print on cotton rag paper, courtesy of the artist

Fig. 23. Wangechi Mutu, *Histology of the Different Classes of Uterine Tumors*, 2006, digital prints and mixed media collage, 23 x 17 in. each, portfolio of 12, courtesy of the artist and Gladstone Gallery, New York and Brussels

Fig. 24. Wangechi Mutu, *Histology of the Different Classes of Uterine Tumors,* 2006, (detail), digital prints and mixed media collage, 23 x 17 in. each, portfolio of 12, courtesy of the artist and Gladstone Gallery, New York and Brussels

Fig. 25. Andrea Chung, *Midwives II*, 2017, Collage, vellum, string and watercolor pencils, 15 x 11 in (38.1 x 27.9 cm), courtesy of the artist

Fig. 26. Andrea Chung, *Crowning I*, 2014, Collage, ink and color pencil, 14 x 11 inches (35.6 x 27.9 cm), courtesy of the artist

Fig. 27. vanessa german, *Serena as Black Madonna #2,* 2015, Mixed-media collage on Vogue magazine, 16 x 10 1/4 x 1 1/5 inches, courtesy of the artist and Pavel Zoubok Fine Art, NY, photographer Fort Gansevoort, NY and vanessa german

Fig. 28. vanessa german, *(That the Healing come complete; That we no longer have to drag the trauma from body to body.)*, 2019, Mixed-media collage on New York Times magazine, 29 x 16 x 5 inches, courtesy of the artist and Pavel Zoubok Fine Art, NY, photographer Fort Gansevoort, NY

Fig. 29. Mary Sibande, *Right Now!,* 2013, digital pigment print on textured archival rag with non-fugitive ink, (edition of 10 + 3AP), 101.2 x 235.6cm, photographer, Jurie Potgieter, image courtesy of the artist

Fig 30. Mary Sibande, *They Don't Make Them Like They Used T*o, 2008, Digital pigment print on textured archival rag with non-fugitive ink, (edition of 10 + 3AP), 90 x 60cm + 104.5 x 69.5cm, photographer, Carla Liesching, image courtesy of the artist

Images pp. 269-271

Marcia Michael, Images were taken from *The Family Album* (2009) and *The Object of My Gaze* (2015-ongoing), courtesy of the artist.

AFTERWORD

Black Matrilineage, Photography, and Representation:
Another Way of Knowing

Régine Michelle Jean-Charles ─────────────────

What does it mean to see a Black mother? What does it mean to see *as a Black mother*? How do we see Black mothers in ways that extend beyond looking? How can Black mothers be seen for the multitudes we contain, in our glorious heterogeneity? These are the questions that *Black Matrilineage: Photography and Representation* invites us to meditate upon. By calling the viewer into another way of knowing, *Black Matrilineage* acknowledges that Black motherhood deserves to be looked at differently. First, it must be looked at through the lens of matrilineage. A word that means to trace our heritage through the maternal line, to privilege the perspective of mothers above all, in the context of a patriarchal culture, matrilineage is defiantly resistant. It resists patriarchy, resists phallocentricity, and resists centering masculinity. The idea of the line invokes generations, a line from one woman to the next traced through mothers, grandmothers, and daughters. A line that resists and invites. Indeed, the images in this book resist, invite, embrace, and encompass. These images draw lines that at times we have not seen or looked for. *Black Matrilineage* brings Black mothering into the public realm showing us its politics and in so doing invites us to do more than look at Black mothers and Black mothering. It invites us to see.

In a world where Black motherhood has been spectacularly over-defined by the high rates of maternal death and stoically rendered by the mothers of the Black Lives Matter generation—women whose lives now exist in response and in relation to the deaths of their Black children killed by police—narrow definitions of Black mothers abound. As Jennifer Nash argues in *Birthing Black Mothers*, the figure of the Black mother occupies a fraught position and her image is often deployed in service of agendas that are far removed from her flourishing. By offering an alternative set of images posits a new way of knowing that imagines and enacts maternal freedom as an act of flourishing.

This maternal freedom is necessary because too often, our visions of Black mothers are held captive by even our own blind spots. These images and invitations to see teach us that knowing a Black mother does not always mean that we see her. It also reminds me of my own Black mother and how difficult it can be for me to see her. The only photograph of my mother as a girl that I have ever seen emblematizes how possible it is to look at a Black mother without seeing or knowing. This image[1] is a black and white photograph of my mother taken when she was less than one year old; she is probably about eight or nine months. She sits with her precious baby feet touching and soft thighs forming a butterfly position. Dressed in a smooth white outfit with delicate bows at the top and a scalloped neck, she had almost no hair but somehow, they (my grandmother? my aunt who raised her?) managed to situate a generous bow on top of her head. A long necklace with what can only be a pendant of a Catholic saint dangles from her neck. She has two tiny, precious, little teeth.

The image stands out in my mind because it marks the first time I realized that my mother was once a girl. As I child I could not fathom that she had been so small. That my mother was once a baby girl never occurred to me until I saw this photograph, which for me was a marvel. To me she was and would always (only) be a mother. I had no other way of knowing her. I could not possibly see her as otherwise. Now a mother myself, I laugh at my inability to see my mother beyond the role that she played in my life. I look at my children and wonder if they too are unable to see me as anything more than their mother. Their Black mother.

The poem "Speaking of Unspeakable Things Unspoken" by Sasha Turner takes us through a series of words famously strewn together by bell hooks. Turner takes apart and disassembles hooks' infamous "white supremacist capitalist patriarchy" phrase. The act of speaking what was unspoken is exactly the work that *Black Matrilineage* performs as it demonstrates that these *are* stories to pass on. Like the mother whispering to a girl (daughter? Granddaughter?) in Adama Delphine Fawondu's *Passageways #1, Secrets, Traditions, Spoken and Unspoken Truths Not, 2017, Black Matrilineage* tells the story of one generation passing stories onto the next. This visual exploration of Black motherhood passes these stories on—which is to say that it refuses the silences and challenges dominant tropes. *Black Matrilineage* is a work of recovery, repair, and redress that Black mothers need and deserve. With its emphasis on alternative ways of knowing this collection initiates its viewers into a practice of seeing Black mothers and looking at us in multiple ways.

The photography that makes up this collection is wonderfully alive in the sense that Kevin Quashie describes in *Black Aliveness, or, A Black Poetics of Being*. In that book Quashie writes, "We are not the idea of us, not even the idea that we hold of us. We are us, multiple and varied, becoming. The heterogeneity of us. Blackness in a Black world is everything, which means that it gets to be freed from being any one thing. We are ordinary beauty, Black people, and beauty must be allowed to do its beautiful work." Now that Black Matrilineage is in the world, let the ordinary and extraordinary beauty of these Black mothers do its beautiful work. And may it be so.

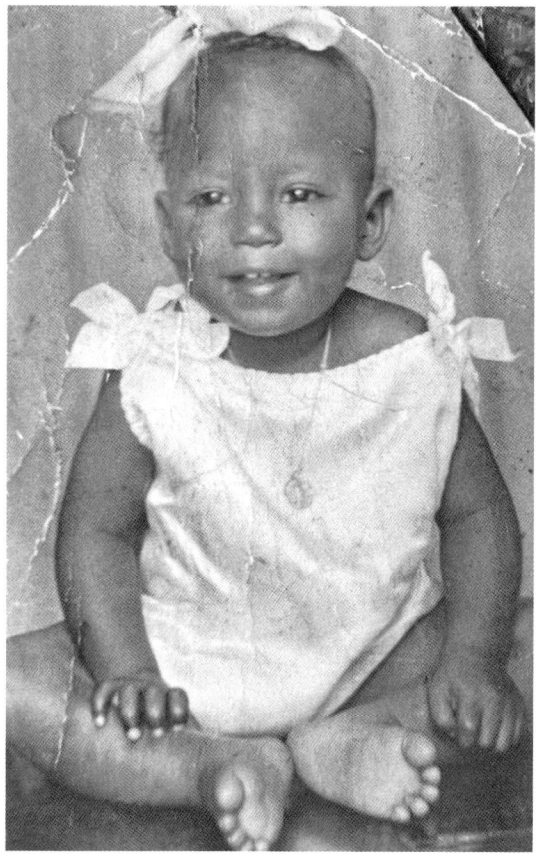

From the personal collection of Régine Michelle Jean-Charles. Mother of the author, circa February 1946, Cape Haitien, Haiti

CONTRIBUTORS

TOMI AKITUNDE is the founder and editor-in-chief of *mater mea*, a platform that answers Black mothers' biggest questions about motherhood, life, and career through content and community (she's come to think of it as Black Mom Google). Raised in Kansas City, Missouri on a healthy diet of books and magazines, her decision to be a journalist was inevitable. After graduating from the University of Chicago and Northwestern's Medill School of Journalism, Tomi moved to New York City to further her journalism career, freelancing for *The New York Times*, *Fast Company*, Fortune.com, and *The Root* to name a few. Always bothered by the lack of diversity in her favorite magazines—she even wrote letters to *Ebony* and *Essence* when she was 12, proposing they create a teenaged version of their publications and make her editor-in-chief—Tomi was especially struck by the dearth in mainstream media of professional women of color. *mater mea* became the answer to that gap in the media, and a safe space for so many mothers trying to find themselves in a media landscape that equates motherhood with whiteness.

GRACE ANEIZA ALI is a Curator and an Assistant Professor in the Departments of Art and Art History at Florida State University in Tallahassee, Florida. She also serves as Curator-at-Large for the Caribbean Cultural Center African Diaspora Institute in New York City. Her curatorial, research, and teaching practices center on curatorial activism, art and social justice, art and migration, global contemporary art, and art of the Caribbean Diaspora with a focus on her homeland Guyana. She is an Andy Warhol Foundation for the Visual Arts Curatorial Fellow and Fulbright Scholar. Her essays on contemporary art have been published in Asian Diasporic Visual Cultures and the Americas, Wasafiri, Harvard's Transition Magazine, Small Axe, and Nueva Luz Photographic Journal, among others. Her recent book, *Liminal Spaces: Migration and Women of the Guyanese Diaspora*, explores the art and migration narratives of women of Guyanese heritage. Ali was born in Guyana and migrated to the USA when she was fourteen years old.

EMILY BRADY earned her PhD in American Studies from the University of Nottingham. Her PhD thesis, *"I Didn't Know She Took Pictures": African American Women Photographers in the Long Civil Rights Movement* explores how African American photographers cultivated and reclaimed space through their photography. Their work—which frequently emphasises the role of African American women's grassroots activism—poses a challenge to the dominant canon of Civil Rights photography. Brady has presented her work at national (British Association of American Studies Annual Conference, University of Sussex, 2019; Historians of Twentieth Century United States, University of Liverpool, 2019) and international conferences (College Arts Association, Chicago, 2020; North-Eastern Modern Language Association, Boston 2020). For her research and contribution to the postgraduate community, Brady was awarded the Heymann Research Scholarship, University Tri Campus Postgraduate Prize in March 2020. Since September 2021, Brady has been working as a Teaching Fellow in American History at the University of Leeds.

LESLY DESCHLER CANOSSI (she/her) is a photographer, photography educator, and cultural producer. She holds an MFA from the Maryland Institute College of Art, where she focused on the museological object's role in constructing culture. She is a faculty member at the International Center of Photography (ICP) and has taught at Columbia University, the Metropolitan Museum of Art, the Lamar Dodd School of Art in Cortona, Italy and has lectured at Tate Modern, ICP, among others. In 2016, she and Zoraida Lopez-Diago co-created Women Picturing Revolution, an organization dedicated to woman photographers who have documented conflicts, crises, and revolutions in private realms and public spaces. Along with Lopez-Diago, she edited *Black Matrilineage, Photography, and Representation: Another Way of Knowing*, Leuven University Press. Her ongoing personal photographic practice and teaching projects *Domestic Negotiations* (2012-present) and *Into the Fold: Artist / Mother Identity* (2019-present) explore autonomy, loss and the role of the mother as artist.

NICOLE J. CARUTH is a Black queer writer, educator, and certified holistic health coach. As a curator, her work examines the intersections of place, race, food, and health. Her writing has been published widely in print and online. In 2019, she was a recipient of the Arts Writers grant from the Andy Warhol Foundation and Creative Capital.

HAILE ESHE COLE received her PhD in Anthropology from the University of Texas at Austin with a concentration in African Diaspora Studies and a portfolio in Women's and Gender Studies. Her scholarly interests include Black feminisms, community-engaged/social justice research methodology, Black motherhood, health, and more recently visual media. Over the years, she has conducted research on women's mass incarceration and Black women's maternal and infant health disparities in Texas. Her most recent research project considered how rates of maternal and infant mortality are impacted by on-going processes of racism and structural inequality. Haile is currently an Assistant Professor at the University of Connecticut but has devoted many years to community and social justice activism centered on the needs of poor and working-class mothers and women of color. She is passionate about reproductive justice work. Most important, she is the mother of two beautiful children and in her free time enjoys spending time with family, listening to music, yoga, creating art, and photography.

ATALIE GERHARD (she/her) is a doctoral researcher in the International Research Training Group "Diversity: Mediations of Difference in Transcultural Spaces" at Saarland University. The working title of her project is "Diversity and Resistance in North American Women's Containment Narratives from the 21st Century". In addition, she is an engaged member of the Emerging Scholars' Forum of the Association for Canadian Studies in German-speaking Countries. Thereby, her research interests include Black and Indigenous cultural resistance against colonialism and self-representations of women with ethnic backgrounds in North American art and literature. She holds a Master of Arts degree in North American Studies as well as a Bachelor of Arts degree in English and American Studies and French Studies from the Friedrich-Alexander-University of Erlangen-Nuremberg, where she had also worked as a student research assistant and interim secretary. The Bavarian State Ministry of Work and Social Affairs, Family, and Integration awarded her a certificate for civil commitment for providing integrational services as a volunteer in a refugee shelter with the local press reporting on her work. She speaks German, English, French, Spanish, Italian, and Romanian at various levels and enjoys learning Arabic in her spare time.

KELLIE CARTER JACKSON is an Associate Professor in the Department of Africana Studies at Wellesley College. She is the author of the award-winning book, *Force & Freedom: Black Abolitionists and the Politics of Violence* which won the James H. Broussard Best First Book Prize, was a finalist for the Frederick Douglass Book Prize, a finalist for the Museum of African American History Stone Book Prize and listed among 13 books to read on African American History by the *Washington Post*. Carter Jackson is also co-editor of *Reconsidering Roots: Race, Politics, & Memory*. Currently, she is completing her latest book, *The Remedy: Black Response to White Violence* (Basic Books). Her essays have been featured in *The New York Times, Washington Post, The Atlantic, The Guardian, The Los Angeles Times, NPR*, and other outlets. She has also been interviewed for her expertise on *CBS Mornings*, MSNBC, PBS, Vox, 1A, the BBC, Al Jerzeera, Slate and a host of documentaries. Carter Jackson is also a Historian-in-Residence for the Museum of African American History in Boston. She is the co-host of the podcast, "This Day in Esoteric Political History" and the Executive Producer and Host of "Oprahdemics: The Study of the Queen of Talk." You can follow her on Twitter @kcarterjackson.

RÉGINE MICHELLE JEAN-CHARLES is the Dean's Professor of Culture and Social Justice, Director of Africana Studies, and Professor of Women, Gender and Sexuality Studies at Northeastern University. A Black feminist scholar who works at the intersections of race, gender and justice from a global perspective, her scholarship and teaching include subjects and areas such as rape culture, Black France, African diasporic literatures, Caribbean Studies, Haiti and the Haitian diaspora. She is the author of *Looking for Other Worlds: Black Feminism and Haitian Fiction* (2022), *The Trumpet of Conscience Today* (2021) and *Conflict Bodies: The Politics of Rape Representation in the Francophone Imaginary* (2014). She has written numerous publications that have appeared in books, edited volumes, and peer-reviewed journals. She is also a regular contributor to media outlets like Ms. Magazine, *The Boston Globe*, WGBH, and Cognoscenti, where she has weighed in on topics such as #metoo, Black girlhood, and issues affecting the Haitian diaspora.

RACHEL LOBO is a PhD Candidate and Sessional Lecturer with the Faculty of Environmental and Urban Change at York University, supported by the Social Sciences and Humanities Research Council of Canada. Her research explores how archival practices can sustain people's histories of resistance and create historical agency. Rachel received her Masters in Photographic Preservation and Collections Management from Ryerson University. She has held curatorial and archival internships at both the Royal Ontario Museum and the Ryerson Image Centre, where she investigated the role that photographs played in documenting Britain's colonial activities in India, and catalogued press photographs of the Civil Rights Movement, respectively. Her work has been published in *Archivaria: The Journal for the Association of Canadian Archivists*, and the *International Journal of Canadian Studies*.

ZORAIDA LOPEZ-DIAGO stands at the intersection of visual, social and environmental justice; she is a photographer, curator, activist and co-founder of Women Picturing Revolution (WPR) with Lesly Deschler Canossi. Her photographs focuses on themes of gender, race, incarceration, and migration and have been exhibited at institutions throughout the US and Latin America. She has lectured at Harvard University, the Tate Modern, and La Universidad de Antioquia (Colombia), among others. Zoraida is currently writing an essay, paired with images, on the intersection of photography, the Black body and nature. She co curated "Picturing Black Girlhood," an exhibition from February to August 2022, as part of the conference "Black Portraiture[s] VII: Play and Performance" at Rutgers University-Newark and with Deschler Canossi, co-edited *Black Matrilineage, Photography and Representation: Another Way of Knowing*, published by Leuven University Press, distributed by Cornell University Press in North America.

BRIE MCLEMORE is a PhD student in the Jurisprudence and Social Policy Program at the University of California, Berkeley. Brie has a Master of Public Policy/Master of Arts in Women's, Gender, and Sexuality Studies from Brandeis University and a Bachelor of Arts in Anthropology and Gender Studies from the New College of Florida. Her work has been published in the *Virginia Law Review*, the *Iowa Journal of Cultural Studies*, and *Truthout*. Brie is a proud Florida native who enjoys fencing, caring for her plants, and watching reality television with her dog Pickles.

RENÉE MUSSAI is a London-based curator, writer, and scholar with a special interest in Black feminist, queer and afro-diasporic lens-based visual arts practices. She is Senior Curator and Head of Curatorial & Collection at Autograph, London, a charitable arts organisation working internationally in photography and film. Mussai has organised numerous exhibitions in Europe, America and Africa, co-commissioned a diverse constituency of artists, and developed a range of research-led artistic programmes—including the critically-acclaimed 'Black Chronicles—The Missing Chapter' (2014–present; publication forthcoming 2022/23). Her recent editorial and curatorial projects include

'Care, Contagion, Community – Self & Other' (2021), 'Lina Iris Viktor: Some Are Born to Endless Night—Dark Matter' (2019/20) and 'Dark Testament' (2020); 'Zanele Muholi: Somnyama Ngonyama—Hail the Dark Lioness' (2017–2021); 'Phoebe Boswell: The Space Between Things' (2018/19)'; 'Black Chronicles IV' (2018), and the audio-visual installation 'The African Choir 1891 Re-Imagined' (2016–18). In 2018, she co-curated the collaborative 'Women's Mobile Museum' for the Philadelphia Photo Arts Center, initiated by Zanele Muholi. Mussai lectures internationally on photography, visual culture, and curatorial activism; her writing has appeared in numerous artist monographs and anthologies by Aperture, Phaidon, Tate, and *Nka: Journal of Contemporary African Art*, amongst others. In 2019, she co-guest edited Issue 6: Volume 33 of *Critical Arts* entitled 'Ecologies of Care: Speculative Photographies, Curatorial Re-Positionings' (Taylor and Francis, 2020). Previous edited volumes include 'James Barnor: Ever Young' (2015) and 'Glyphs: Acts of Inscription' (2013). Mussai is also Research Associate at the Visual Identities in Art and Design Research Centre, University of Johannesburg, and Associate Lecturer at University of the Arts London. Since 2009, she has been a regular guest curator and former non-resident fellow at the Hutchins Centre for African & African American Research at Harvard University.

MARLY PIERRE-LOUIS is a copywriter, editor and creative strategist living in Amsterdam. She is the co-founder of Amsterdam Black Women collective—a community of diasporic Black women chasing their dreams through Europe and co/editor for Versal Editions; a small press dedicated to community-centered publishing and curation. Marly sits at the feet of Toni Morrison, James Baldwin, and Hip-Hop. She is a first-generation Haitian-American, a big sister, a mother, and an introverted Taurus (Leo moon) through and through. When she's not working, she can usually be found practicing tarot, listening to emo music, reading speculative fiction, and overwatering her plants.

JONATHAN MICHAEL SQUARE is an Assistant Professor of Black Visual Culture at Parsons School of Design. He has a PhD in history from New York University, a master's degree from the University of Texas at Austin, and a B.A. from Cornell University. He has written for *British Art Studies*, *Fashionista*, *Fashion Studies Journal*, *Hyperallergic*, *International Journal of Fashion Studies*, *Refinery29*, *Small Axe*, and *Vestoj*. He has also curated *Slavery in the Hands of Harvard*, *Odalisque Atlas: White History as Told through Art*, and *Freedom from Truth: Self-Portraits of Nell Painter*. A proponent in the power of social media as a platform for radical pedagogy and the democratization of higher education, he founded and runs the digital humanities project *Fashioning the Self in Slavery and Freedom*, which explores the intersection of fashion and slavery.

SUSAN THOMPSON is curator and writer based in Brooklyn. Since 2020, she has served as project manager for *Simone Leigh: Sovereignty* presented at the U.S. Pavilion as part of the 59th Venice Biennale. From 2009-2020, she worked as a curator at the Solomon R. Guggenheim Museum, New York, where she organized numerous exhibitions, including the two-part project *Implicit Tensions: Mapplethorpe Now* (2019-20), *Simone Leigh: Loophole of Retreat* (2019), *Anicka Yi: Life is Cheap* (2017), and *Paul Chan: Nonprojections for New Lovers* (2015). She also provided curatorial support for solo exhibitions of artists Carrie Mae Weems (2014), Rineke Dijkstra (2012), and Francesca Woodman (2012), as well as the thematic group exhibition *Photo-Poetics: An Anthology* (2015–16). Her writing has appeared in various volumes, including *Ghada Amer: Painting in Revolt* (Skira, 2022), *Mernet Larsen* (Kerbler-Verlag, 2021), *Danh Vo: Take My Breath Away* (Guggenheim Museum, 2018), and *Adam Pendleton: The Black Dada Reader* (Walther König Books, 2017), among others. Thompson holds an MA in modern art from Columbia University and a BA in art history and political science from the University of North Carolina at Chapel Hill.

SALAMISHAH TILLET is a Pulitzer Prize winning writer, scholar, and activist who is the Henry Rutgers Professor of African American and African Studies and Creative Writing at Rutgers University, Newark. She is a contributing critic-at-large at the New York Times, author of "Sites of Slavery: Citizenship and Racial Democracy in the Post-Civil Rights Imagination" and "In Search of the Color Purple: A Story of an American Masterpiece." She is currently working on a biography on the civil rights icon, Nina Simone, for which she received the Whiting Foundation Creative Non-Fiction Grant in 2020. In 2021, she became the director of Express Newark, a center for socially engaged art and design at Rutgers University, Newark as well as co-hosted and produced the podcast "Because of Anita" with Cindi Leive on the 30th anniversary of Anita Hill's testimony before the Senate Judiciary Committee. She was also named a 2021 Carnegie Fellow by the Carnegie Corporation of New York for her next project, "In Lieu of the Law: A Cultural History of the #Me Too Movement."

SCHEHERAZADE TILLET is a photo-based artist, curator, and feminist activist who explores the themes of Blackness, pleasure, play, and trauma, and healing. Blending social documentary, staged portraits, and social practice, Tillet intimately photographs the inner lives and public performances of Black girlhood throughout the United States and the Caribbean, while also centering the gaze of and actively collaborating with her Black girl subjects. Born in Boston, growing up in Port-of-Spain, Trinidad and Newark, NJ, and now working in Chicago, Tillet received her B.A. in Child Development from Tufts University with a minor in Fine Arts from the School of the Museum of Fine Arts in Boston, and her Masters of Art in Art Therapy from the School of the Art Institute in Chicago. Her work has been exhibited at Columbia University, Rutgers University, Newark, and the Museum of Contemporary Art in Chicago. In 2021, she was an artist-in-residence at the Weinberg/Newton Gallery in Chicago, and selected by the Four Corners Public Arts project to exhibit her photo mural, "Will You Be My Monument" in downtown Newark, NJ. She is currently the Executive Director of A Long Walk Home, a nonprofit that she founded with her sister, Salamishah, in 2003, that uses art to empower young people to end violence against girls and women.

JENNIFER TURNER is Assistant Professor of Sociology at Hollins University in Roanoke, Virginia. Her research focuses on the intersection of race, class, and gender in the context of families. Currently, her research focuses on how the intersection of race, class, and gender shapes the lives and experiences of low-income African American single mothers. Her work can be found in the journals *Sociology of Race and Ethnicity* and *Social Currents*.

SASHA TURNER is Associate Professor of History at Johns Hopkins University. She is the author of Contested Bodies: Pregnancy, Childrearing, and Slavery in Jamaica, winner of the Julia Cherry Spruill Book Prize from the Southern Association of Women Historians, the Berkshire Conference of Women Historians Book Prize, earning an Honorable Mention from the Murdo J. McLeod Book Prize in the Latin American and Caribbean Section, Southern Historical Association. She is currently working on a new book on slavery and emotions. A recent article from this book, "The Nameless and the Forgotten: Maternal Grief Sacred Protection, and the Archive of Slavery" published in Slavery and Abolition has also won awards from the African American Intellectual History Society; the Association of Black Women Historians; Southern Association of Women Historians; the North American Conference on British Studies; and the Latin American & Caribbean Section of the Southern Historical Association. She also serves as co-President of the Coordinating Council for Women in History.

RHAISA KAMEELA WILLIAMS is Assistant Professor of Theater at Princeton University. Williams' research uses mixed-archive methods—spanning across literature, family history, archives, and public policy—to focus on the intersections of Blackness, motherhood, affect, and disquieting modes of freedom. Currently, she is writing her manuscript, *Mama, Don't You Weep: Motherhood, Blackness, and Performances of Grief*, that traces the intimate relationship between grief and Black motherhood from the civil rights movement to the present. Offering discontinuous readings of grief, the book asserts that Black women, no matter their personal relationship to offspring or othermothering, have specifically mobilized grief inherent to Black motherhood as a tactic to perform, remake, and critique forms of citizenship. Williams earned her Ph.D and M.A. in Performance Studies at Northwestern University and a B.A. in Africana Studies from the University of Pennsylvania. Her work has been supported by the New England Regional Fellowship Consortium, and the Mellon, Woodrow Wilson, and Ford foundations; and has appeared or is forthcoming in *College Literature, Transforming Anthropology, Callaloo*, and *Biography: An Interdisciplinary Quarterly*.

ARTISTS

NYDIA BLAS is a visual artist who grew up in Ithaca, New York, and currently resides in Atlanta, Georgia. She holds a B.S. from Ithaca College, and received her M.F.A. from Syracuse University in the College of Visual and Performing Arts. She is an Assistant Professor in the Department of Art and Visual Culture at Spelman College in Atlanta, Georgia. Nydia uses photography, collage, video, and books to address matters of sexuality, intimacy, and her lived experience as a girl, woman, and mother. She delicately weaves stories concerning circumstance, value, and power and uses her work to create a physical and allegorical space presented through a Black feminine lens. The result is an environment that is dependent upon the belief that in order to maintain resiliency, a magical outlook is necessary. She has completed artist residencies at Constance Saltonstall Foundation for the Arts and The Center for Photography at Woodstock. Her work has been featured in the book *MFON: A Journal of Women Photographers of the African Diaspora*, The New York Times, New York Magazine, The Huffington Post, Topic, Dazed and Confused Magazine, Strange Fire Collective, Lenscult, Yogurt Magazine, PDN, Fotografia Magazine, and more.

SAMANTHA BOX is a Jamaican-born, Bronx-based photographer. In her studio-based practice, she uses self-portraiture, sound, and installation to explore her intersecting diasporic Caribbean histories and identities. This work has been exhibited at the Houston Center of Photography (2019) and the Andrew Freedman House (2020). In 2021, Box joined the Bronx Museum of the Arts' AIM Fellowship program, and was in residence at the Center of Photography at Woodstock. Her previous documentary work focused on New York City's community of LGBTQ youth of color and was widely recognized, notably with a NYFA Fellowship (2010), and shown, most prominently, as part of the ICP Museum's Perpetual Revolution (2017) exhibition. This work is part of the permanent collections of the Open Society Foundation, EN FOCO, and Light Work, where she was in residence in 2015. Box holds a certificate in Photojournalism and Documentary Studies from the International Center of Photography (2006). She also holds an MFA in Advanced Photographic Studies from the International Center of Photography/Bard College (2019).

ANDREA CHUNG (b. 1978, Newark, NJ) lives and works in San Diego, California. She received a BFA from Parsons School of Design, New York, and an MFA from Maryland Institute College of Art, Baltimore. Her recent biennale and museum exhibitions include Prospect 4, New Orleans, and the Jamaican Biennale, Kingston, Jamaica, as well as the Chinese American Museum and California African American Museum in Los Angeles, and the San Diego Art Institute. In 2017, her first solo museum exhibition took place at the Museum of Contemporary Art San Diego, *You broke the ocean in half to be here*. She has participated in national and international residencies including the Vermont Studio Center, McColl Center for Visual Arts, Headlands Center for the Arts, and Skowhegan School of Painting and Sculpture. Her work has been written about in the Artfile Magazine, New Orleans Times, Picayune, Artnet, The Los Angeles Times, and International Review of African-American Art among others.

RENEE COX is one of the most controversial African-American artists working today using her own body, both nude and clothed, to celebrate Black womanhood and criticize a society she often views as racist and sexist. She was born on October 16, 1960, in Colgate, Jamaica, into an upper middle-class family, who later settled in Scarsdale, New York. Cox's first ambition was to become a filmmaker. "I was always interested in the visual" she said in one interview, "But I had a baby boomer reaction and was into the immediate gratification of photography as opposed to film, which is a more laborious project." From the very beginning, her work showed a deep concern for social issues and employed disturbing religious imagery. In *It Shall be Named* (1994), a Black man's distorted body made up of eleven separate photographs hangs from a cross, as much resembling a lynched man as the crucified Christ. In her first one-woman show at a New York gallery in 1998, Cox made herself the center of attention. Dressed in the colorful garb of a Black superhero named Raje, Cox appeared in a series of large, color photographs. In one picture she towered over a cab in Times Square. In another, she broke steel chains before an erupting volcano. In the most pointed picture, entitled *The Liberation of UB and Lady J*, Cox's Raje rescued the Black stereotyped advertising figures of Uncle Ben and Aunt Jemima from their products, labels. The photograph was featured on the cover of the French newspaper Le Monde. Cox continues to push the envelope with her work by using new technologies that the digital medium of photography has to offer. By working from her archives and shooting new subjects, Cox seeks to push the limits of her older work and create new consciousnesses of the body. Cox's new work aims to "unleash the potential of the ordinary and bring it into a new realm of possibilities". "It's about time that we re-imagine our own constitutions," states Cox.

NONA FAUSTINE is a native New Yorker and award winning photographer. Her work focuses on history, identity, representation, evoking a critical and emotional understanding of the past and proposes a deeper examination of contemporary racial and gender stereotypes. Faustine's images have been published in a variety of national and international media outlets such as Artforum, The New York Times, The Huffington Post, Hyperallergic, The Guardian, New Yorker Magazine and the LA Times, among others. Faustine's work has been exhibited at Smithsonian National Portrait Gallery, Harvard University, Rutgers University, Maryland State University, Studio Museum of Harlem, Brooklyn Museum, Schomburg Center for Black Research in Harlem, the International Center of Photography, Saint John's Divine Cathedral, Tomie Ohtake Institute in Brazil and many others. Her work is in the collection of the David C. Driskell Center at Maryland State University, Studio Museum of Harlem, Brooklyn Museum and the Carnegie Museum. Her work was recently acquired by the North Dakota Museum and the Frederick R. Weisman Art Museum in Minnesota, Baltimore Museum, Milwaukee Art Museum, Lumber Museum in Oregon, Herbert F Johnson Museum Cornell University, The Center for Creative Photography in Arizona, Rose Art Museum, Brandeis University, MA. Her book *White Shoes* published by Mack Books debuted in 2021.

ADAMA DELPHINE FAWUNDU is a photographer and visual artist born in Brooklyn of Sierra Leonean descent. Fawundu co-founded the collective MFON while co-editing and publishing the book *MFON: Women Photographers of the African Diaspora*. Fawundu's works are in the collections at the Brooklyn Museum of Art, Princeton University Museum, Norton Museum of Art, The David C. Driskell Art Collection amongst other museums and collections. She is an Assistant Professor and the Visual Arts Director of Graduate Studies at Columbia University.

VANESSA GERMAN is a citizen artist creating sculpture, performance, immersive installation and photography, that center the earthling's experience with loving, connection, intimacy, vulnerability and creative power, as definitive Human Technologies. German's work centers the insistence of heart, Soul, and, loving, as critical engines of shape-shifting and future-making in the dynamic ecosystems of body and community. She is the founder of Love Front Porch and the ARThouse, a community arts initiative for the children of Homewood. German's work has been exhibited widely, most recently at the Figge Art Museum, The Union for Contemporary Art, The Fralin Museum of Art at the University of Virginia, Flint Institute of Arts, Mattress Factory, Everson Museum of Art, Spelman College Museum of Fine Art, Wadsworth Atheneum Museum of Art, Studio Museum, Ringling Museum of Art and Crystal Bridges Museum of American Art. Her work has been featured on *CBS Sunday Morning*, NPR's *All Things Considered* and in The Huffington Post, O Magazine and Essence Magazine. She is the recipient of the 2015 Louis Comfort Tiffany Foundation Grant, the 2017 Jacob Lawrence Award from the American Academy of Arts and Letters, the 2018 United States Artist Grant and most recently the 2018 Don Tyson Prize from Crystal Bridges Museum of American Art.

AYANA V. JACKSON (b. 1977 East Orange, NJ; based in Brooklyn, NY) uses archival impulses to assess the impact of the colonial gaze on the history of photography and its relationship to the human body. By using her lense to deconstruct 19th and early 20th century portraiture, Jackson questions photography's authenticity and role in perpetuating socially relevant and stratified identities. Her practice maps the ethical considerations and relationships between the photographer, subject and viewer, in turn exploring themes around race, gender and reproduction. Her work examines myths of the Black Diaspora and re-stages colonial archival images as a means to liberate the Black body. Her work is collected by major local and international institutions including The Studio Museum in Harlem, The Newark Museum, The JP Chase Morgan collection, Princeton University Art Museum, the National Gallery of Victoria, Melbourne, The Museum of Contemporary Photography and the Bill and Melinda Gates Foundation. Jackson was a 2014 New York Foundation for the Arts Fellow for Photography, and the recipient of the 2018 Smithsonian Fellowship.

DEANA LAWSON is a photo-based artist whose work examines the body's ability to channel personal and social histories, addressing themes of familial legacy, community, romance, and religious spiritual aesthetics. Lawson is visually inspired by the materiality of Black culture and its expression as seen through the body and in domestic environments. She meets her subjects in everyday walks of life: grocery stores, subway trains, busy avenues in

Bed-Stuy, Brooklyn, and road trips taken to the deep south. Born in Rochester, New York in 1979, Lawson received a BFA from Penn State in 2001 and an MFA in Photography from RISD in 2004. Her work was the subject of a survey show co-organized by the ICA Boston and MoMA PS1 in 2021. Other recent solo exhibitions include Kunsthalle Basel (2020), Huis Marseilles, Amsterdam (2019); The Underground Museum, Los Angeles (2018); and the Contemporary Art Museum St. Louis (2017). She is the recipient of the Guggenheim Fellowship, Art Matters Grant, John Gutmann Photography Fellowship, Rema Hort Mann Foundation Grant, Aaron Siskind Fellowship Grant, and an NYFA Grant in 2006. Lawson is currently a professor, teaching photography at Princeton University.

Qiana Mestrich is a photography-focused, interdisciplinary artist based in New York. Born to parents from Panama and Croatia, Mestrich's work often references Black, mixed-race experiences from her perspective as a first-generation American. She has been exhibited worldwide including Frankfurt's RAY Triennial in 2021, the BRIC Biennial Volume III in 2019 and London Art Fair's Photo50 in 2018. Mestrich's work is held in the Peggy Cooper Cafritz collection of contemporary art and private collections in the United States. In 2007 she founded *Dodge & Burn: Decolonizing Photography History* (est. 2007), an arts initiative that aims to diversify the medium's history by advocating for photographers of color. Mestrich has written essays on photography for exhibition catalogs and published other critical writing in art journals such as Light Work's *Contact Sheet* and En Foco's *Nueva Luz*. She is also co-editor of the book *How We Do Both: Art and Motherhood* (Secretary Press), a diverse collection of honest responses from contemporary artists who dare to engage in the creative endeavors of motherhood and making art. A graduate of the ICP-Bard College MFA in Advanced Photographic Practice, Mestrich is represented in New York by sepiaEYE gallery.

Marcia Michael, a multidisciplinary artist of Afrodescent, reconstructs and critiques an archive of Black British life through the auspices of a Black family album. Her previous series *The Study of Kin* (2009), referenced the image of the 'Black family' as seen through the perspective of 19th-century photography. Challenging the image made against the colonial archive, Michael began a recovery of Black life influenced by both British and Caribbean cultural discourses that have been absent from the family album discourse in the UK. In extending her photographic search for her matrilineal ancestry, Michael turned to her mother's body as her archive and thus began a quest to reignite a tradition passed on from mother to daughter of Black matrilineage as a way to recover her histories. Michael's works have been awarded, exhibited and mentioned in publications internationally, such as Autograph ABP in the UK; Mae Petra/Black Mother Sao Paulo, Brazil; Encontros da Imagem, Portugal, Femmes Feroces: New Orleans, USA and The Taylor Wessing Photographic Prize. Awards from, IPA, Womxn Of Colour and selected as a Royal Photographic Society Hundred Heroine. Michael Lives and works in London, UK.

SIR ZANELE MUHOLI is a visual activist, humanitarian and photographer from Umlazi, Durban. They currently live and work in Umbumbulu. Muholi is invested in educational activism, community outreach and youth development. In 2009 they founded Inkanyiso (www.inkanyiso.org), a forum for queer and visual (activist) media and in 2002 co-founded the Forum for Empowerment of Women (FEW). They facilitate access to art spaces for youth practitioners through projects such as Ikhono LaseNatali and continue to provide photography workshops for young women and in the townships through PhotoXP. Muholi studied Advanced Photography at the Market Photo Workshop in Newtown, Johannesburg, and in 2009 completed an MFA in Documentary Media at Ryerson University, Toronto. In 2013, they became an Honorary Professor at the University of the Arts/Hochschule für Künste Bremen. Recent awards and accolades received include the Spectrum International Prize for Photography (2020); Lucie Award for Humanitarian Photography (2019); the Rees Visionary Award by Amref Health Africa (2019); a fellowship from the Royal Photographic Society, UK (2018); and France's Chevalier de l'Ordre des Arts et des Lettres (2017). In 2019, Muholi won 'Best Photography Book Award' by the Kraszna-Krausz Foundation for *Somnyama Ngonyama: Hail, The Dark Lioness (Aperture)*, and in 2015 was shortlisted for the Deutsche Börse Photography Prize for the publication *Faces and Phases 2006–14* (Steidl/The Walther Collection). Other publications include *Zanele Muholi: African Women Photographers #1* (Casa Africa and La Fábrica, 2011), *Faces and Phases* (Prestel, 2010) and *Only Half the Picture* (Stevenson, 2006). A survey exhibition of Muholi's work took place at Tate Modern, London, UK (2020–21), travelling to Gropius Bau, Berlin and Bildmuseet, Umeå in 2021/22. Previous solo presentations have taken place at institutions including the Sprengel Museum, Hannover, Germany (2021); Cummer Museum, Florida, USA (2021); Norval Foundation, Cape Town, South Africa (2020); Ethelbert Cooper Gallery of African and African American Art at Harvard University,

USA (2020); Seattle Art Museum, USA (2019); Colby Museum, Maine, USA (2019); Spelman College Museum of Fine Art, Georgia, USA (2018); New Art Exchange, Nottingham, UK (2018); Museo de Arte Moderno de Buenos Aires, Argentina (2018); LUMA Westbau, Zurich, Switzerland (2018); Fotografiska, Stockholm, Sweden (2018); Durban Art Gallery, Kwazulu Natal, South Africa (2017); Market Photo Workshop, Johannesburg, South Africa (2017); Stedelijk Museum, Amsterdam, the Netherlands (2017); and Autograph ABP, London, UK (2017). They exhibited in *May You Live in Interesting Times*, the 58th Venice Biennale (2019), produced a city-wide project titled *Masihambisane – on Visual Activism* for Performa 17, New York, USA (2017), and featured in the inaugural exhibition at the Zeitz Museum of Contemporary Art Africa, Cape Town, South Africa.

WANGECHI MUTU has worked with figures—using and representing the body—most often African women, to express what it means to exist, to behave, to interact and live as human. Using a variety of media including painting, collage, sculpture, performance, installation and video, Mutu re-imagines versions of herself, of how gender, race and cultural trauma shape us and how this and our inhumanity have led to environmental destruction. With her characteristic morphing, hybrid, and organic forms, she portrays shared alienation and mythologization. In Mutu's work she portrays identity as performative, using her characters to rewrite and reimagine oneself and to break certain restrictive codes of the man-made that are at odds with nature. Mutu has been the subject of major solo exhibitions at institutions worldwide. Most recently she was included in the 2019 Whitney Biennial and was in The Metropolitan Museum of Art's "The Façade Commission: Wangechi Mutu, The NewOnes, will free Us". Mutu works in New York and Nairobi, Kenya.

SHEILA PREE BRIGHT is an acclaimed international photographic artist who portrays large-scale works that combine a wide-range of knowledge of contemporary culture. She is known for her series, #1960Now, Young Americans, Plastic Bodies, and Suburbia. Bright is the author of '*#1960Now: Photographs of Civil Rights Activists and Black Lives Matter Protest*' published by Chronicle Books. The work is a feature in the New York Times and she has appeared in the 2016 feature-length documentary film *Election Day: Lens Across America*. Her series has been exhibited at the High Museum of Art, Atlanta; Smithsonian National Museum of African American Museum, Washington, DC; The Museum of Contemporary Art, Cleveland; The Art Gallery of

Hamilton, Ontario, Canada and the Leica Gallery in New York. Bright is the recipient of several nominations and awards; recently, she has been awarded the commission 'Picturing the South' by the High Museum of Art, Atlanta. Her work is included in numerous private and public collections, to name a few: Smithsonian National Museum of African American History and Culture, Washington, DC; The Library of Congress, Washington, DC; National Center for Civil and Human Rights, Atlanta, GA; Oppenheimer Collection: Nerman Museum of Contemporary Art, Overland, KS; Pyramid Peak Foundation, Memphis, TN; de Saisset Museum, Santa Clara University, Santa Clara, CA; David C. Driskell Center, University of Maryland, College Park, MD; The High Museum of Art, Atlanta, GA; Spelman Museum of Fine Art, Atlanta, GA; Saint Louis Museum, Saint Louis, MO; Clark Atlanta University Museum, Atlanta GA; The University of Georgia, Athens, GA; The Museum of Contemporary Art, Cleveland; David C. Driskell Center, University of Maryland, College Park, MD and the Do Good Fund, Columbus, GA.

KEISHA SCARVILLE (b. Brooklyn, NY; lives Brooklyn, NY) weaves together themes dealing with transformation, place, and the unknown. She studied at the Rochester Institute of Technology and Parsons/The New School. Her work has been shown at the Studio Museum of Harlem, The Institute of Contemporary Art Philadelphia, Rush Arts Gallery, BRIC Arts Media House, Lesley Heller Gallery, Contact Gallery in Toronto, Aljira Center for Contemporary Art, Center for Photography at Woodstock, the Caribbean Cultural Center African Diaspora Institute, Museum of Contemporary Diasporan Arts, Baxter St CCNY, Lightwork, and The Brooklyn Museum of Art. Scarville has taken part in residencies at Vermont Studio Center, Skowhegan School of Painting and Sculpture, Lower Manhattan Cultural Council Workspace Program, BRIC Workspace Residency Program, and Light Work Residency Program. Her work has been featured and reviewed in The New York Times, Vice, Transition, Nueva Luz, Small Axe, The Village Voice, and Hyperallgeric. Collections include the Smithsonian Institute in Washington, DC. Currently, Scarville is an adjunct faculty member at the International Center of Photography and Parsons School of Art & Design in New York.

MARY SIBANDE, born in Barberton, South Africa, in 1982, lives and works in Johannesburg. She obtained her Diploma in Fine Arts at the Witwatersrand Technikon in 2004 and an Honours Degree from the University of Johannesburg in 2007. Sibande represented South Africa at the 54th Venice

Biennale in 2011 and her project 'Long Live the Dead Queen' was found on murals all over the city of Johannesburg in 2010. Sibande is the recipient of several awards namely, the 2017 Smithsonian National Museum of African Arts Award, University of Johannesburg's Alumni Dignitas Award in 2014 and the 2013 Standard Bank Young Artist Award for Visual Arts. Her work 'The Purple Shall Govern' toured South Africa, ending in Johannesburg at the Standard Bank Gallery in 2014. She is the 2018-2019 Virginia C. Gildersleeve Professor at Barnard College at Columbia University. In addition, Mary has been the recipient of several residencies and fellowships, including the Smithsonian Fellowship in Washington DC, the Ampersand Foundation Fellowship in New York and the University of Michigan Fellowship.

MICKALENE THOMAS is a New York based distinguished visual artist, filmmaker and curator who works in various mediums. She received her MFA from Yale University and her BFA from Pratt institute. She is a recipient of the Yale School of Art Presidential Fellowship in Fine Arts (2020), Pauli Murray College Associate Fellow at Yale University (2020), Meyerhoff-Becker Biennial Commission at Baltimore Museum of Art (2019), United States Artists Francie Bishop Good & David Horvitz Fellow (2015), and is an alumnus of the Studio Museum in Harlem Artist-in-Residency program (2003) and the Versailles Foundation Munn Artists Program in Giverny (2011). Thomas is a recipient of many awards and grants, among them are the Bronx Museum of the Arts Pathmakers Award (2019), Anonymous Was A Woman Award (2013), Brooklyn Museum Asher B. Durand Award (2012), Timerhi Award for Leadership in the Arts (2010), Joan Mitchell Grant (2009), Pratt Institute Alumni Achievement Award (2009), and the Rema Hort Mann Grant (2007). She has been honored by a number of institutions and organizations including the Aperture Foundation, SFMoMA, MoMA PS1, and the Smithsonian Hirshhorn Museum. She has exhibited at prestigious institutions across North America including the Brooklyn Museum, MoMA PS1, Seattle Art Museum, SFMoMA, National Portrait Gallery, Baltimore Museum of Art, Bass Museum of Art, Art Gallery of Ontario, Toronto, Wexner Center for the Arts, and Aspen Art Museum. Her work is in the permanent collections of the Metropolitan Museum of Art, Brooklyn Museum, Whitney Museum of American Art, Solomon R. Guggenheim Museum, the National Portrait Gallery, Newark Museum of Art, Seattle Art Museum, Hara Museum of Art, Rubell Museum, and Studio Museum in Harlem, among other public and private institutions and collections. She is the co-founder of the Pratt›FORWARD 'Artist in the Market' incubator for post-graduate students, and serves on the Board of the Trustees for the Brooklyn Museum and MoMA PS1.

CARRIE MAE WEEMS (b. 1953 Portland, OR; lives and works in Syracuse, NY) is widely renowned as one of the most influential contemporary American artists living today. Over the course of nearly four decades, Weems has developed a complex body of work employing text, fabric, audio, digital images, installation, and video, but she is most celebrated as a photographer. Activism is central to Weems' practice, which investigates race, family relationships, cultural identity, sexism, class, political systems, and the consequences of power. Over the last 30 years of her prolific career, Weems has been consistently ahead of her time and an ongoing presence in contemporary culture. Her work is organized into cohesive bodies that function like chapters in a perpetually unfolding narrative, demonstrating her gift as a storyteller. *The Kitchen Table Series* (1990), for instance, is one of Weems' most seminal works, and widely considered one of the most important bodies of contemporary photography. The series, for which Weems herself posed as the main subject, is set at a woman's kitchen table—a domestic stage—revealing intimate moments of her life as the story unfolds. The protagonist, though in many ways seemingly commonplace, is a multifaceted woman encompassing a variety of roles such as lover, parent, friend, and breadwinner. Through her work, Weems tackles a number of complex contemporary issues, demanding reconsideration of predominant narratives throughout our history.

DEBORAH WILLIS is an artist, author, and curator whose pioneering research has focused on cultural histories envisioning the Black body, women, and gender. She is a celebrated photographer, acclaimed historian of photography, MacArthur and Guggenheim Fellow, and University Professor and Chair of the Department of Photography & Imaging at the Tisch School of the Arts at New York University. Willis received the NAACP Image Award in 2014 for her co-authored book *Envisioning Emancipation: Black Americans and the End of Slavery* (with Barbara Krauthamer) and in 2015 for the documentary *Through a Lens Darkly*, inspired by her book *Reflections in Black: A History of Black Photographers 1840 to the Present*.

COLOPHON

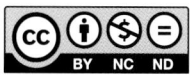 This book emerges from the project Women Picturing Revolution:
http://www.womenpicturingrevolution.com/

The publication of this work was supported by the KU Leuven Fund for Fair Open Access and Knowledge Unlatched

Published in 2022 by Leuven University Press / Presses Universitaires de Louvain / Universitaire Pers Leuven. Minderbroedersstraat 4, B-3000 Leuven (Belgium).
Selection and editorial matter © Lesly Deschler Canossi and Zoraida Lopez-Diago, 2022
Individual chapters © The respective authors, 2022

ISBN 978 94 6270 286 8 (Paperback)
ISBN 978 94 6166 463 1 (ePDF)
ISBN 978 94 6166 473 0 (ePUB)
D/2022/1869/33
NUR: 652
https://doi.org/10.11116/9789461664631
Cover design: Daniel Benneworth-Gray
Cover illustration: Andrea Chung, Sula Never Competed; She Simply Helped Others Define Themselves, VII, 2021. Collage, gold ink, shells, pins, and beads on paper handmade from traditional birthing cloth (Collection of Eric and Renita Woodson, photographer Elon Schoenholz)
Lay-out: Crius Group

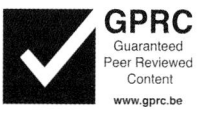